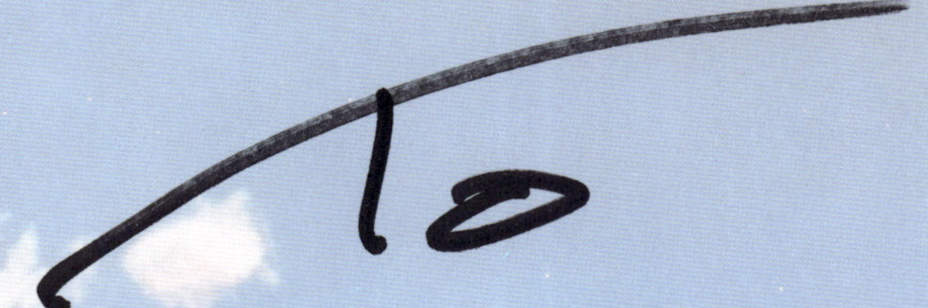

The Life & Work of

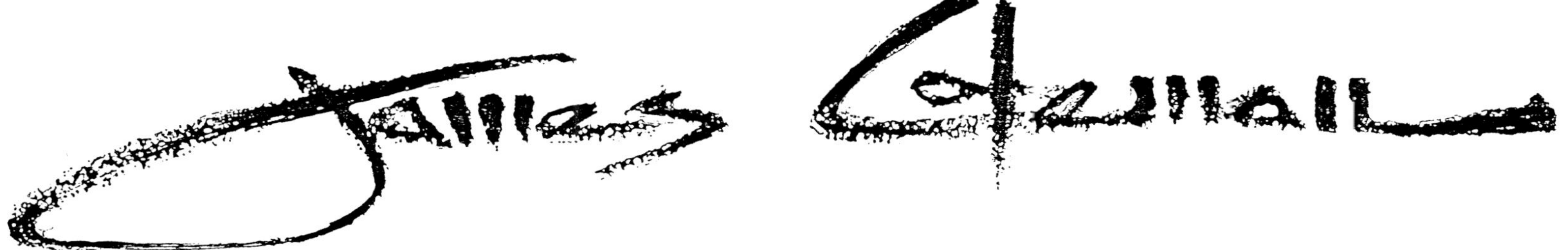

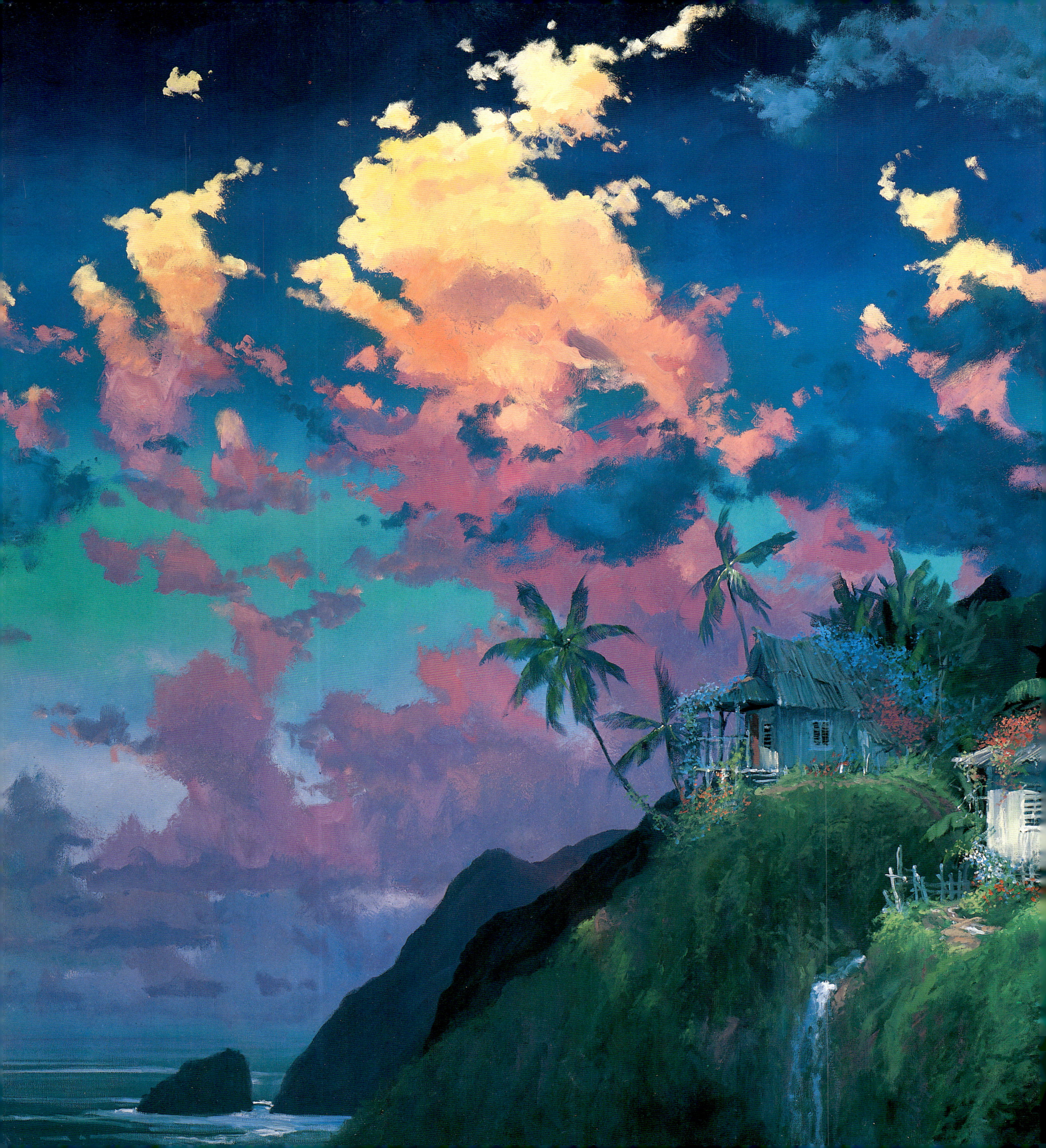

The Life & Work of
JAMES COLEMAN

Introduction by Kenny Loggins

Text by Mark Doyle

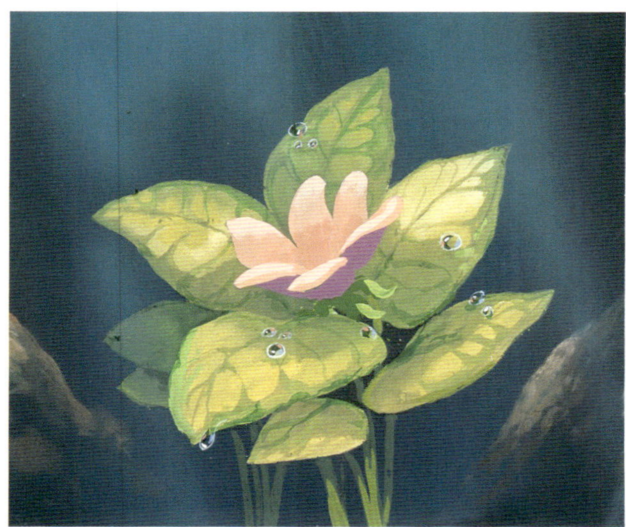

ISBN 0-9646447-0-3

Library of Congress Catalog Card Number: 95-92276

Produced by Coleman Studios, Inc.
31133 Via Colinas, Suite 108
Westlake Village, CA 91362
(818) 889-1949

Managing Editor: Angela Eaton
Art Director: Micky Zondervan
Text: Mark Doyle
Print Director: Richard Lyday
Materials Coordinator: Conni McCarthy

Printed and bound in Hong Kong
by Everbest Printing Co. Inc.

To my mother and father who gave me life and Cathy who gave me the joys of my life – Kim, Scott & Kadie.

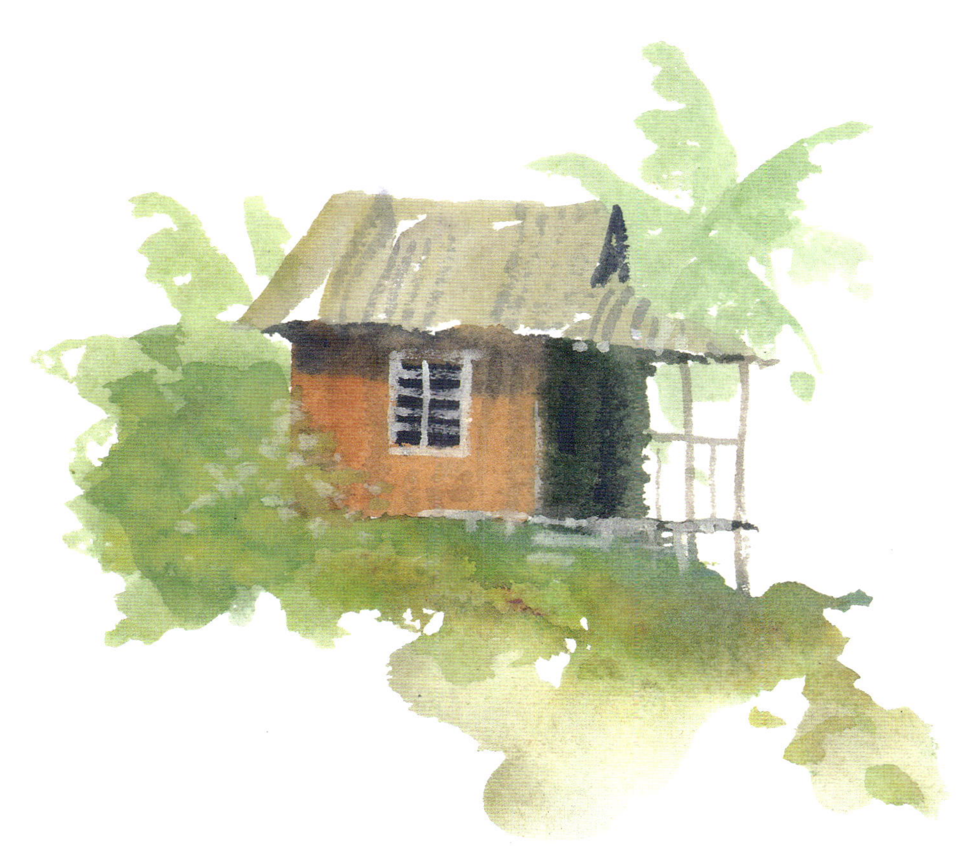

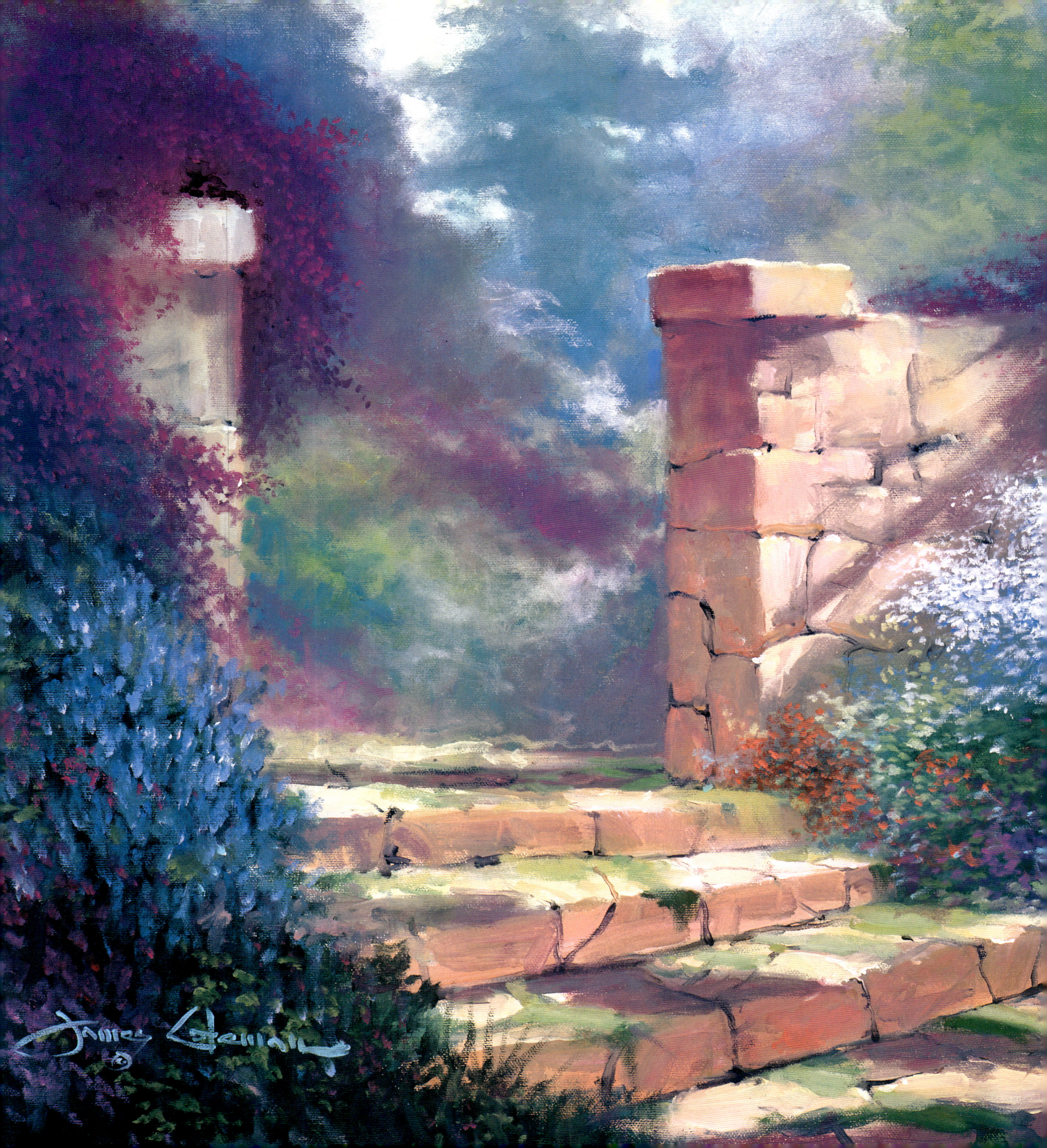

Contents

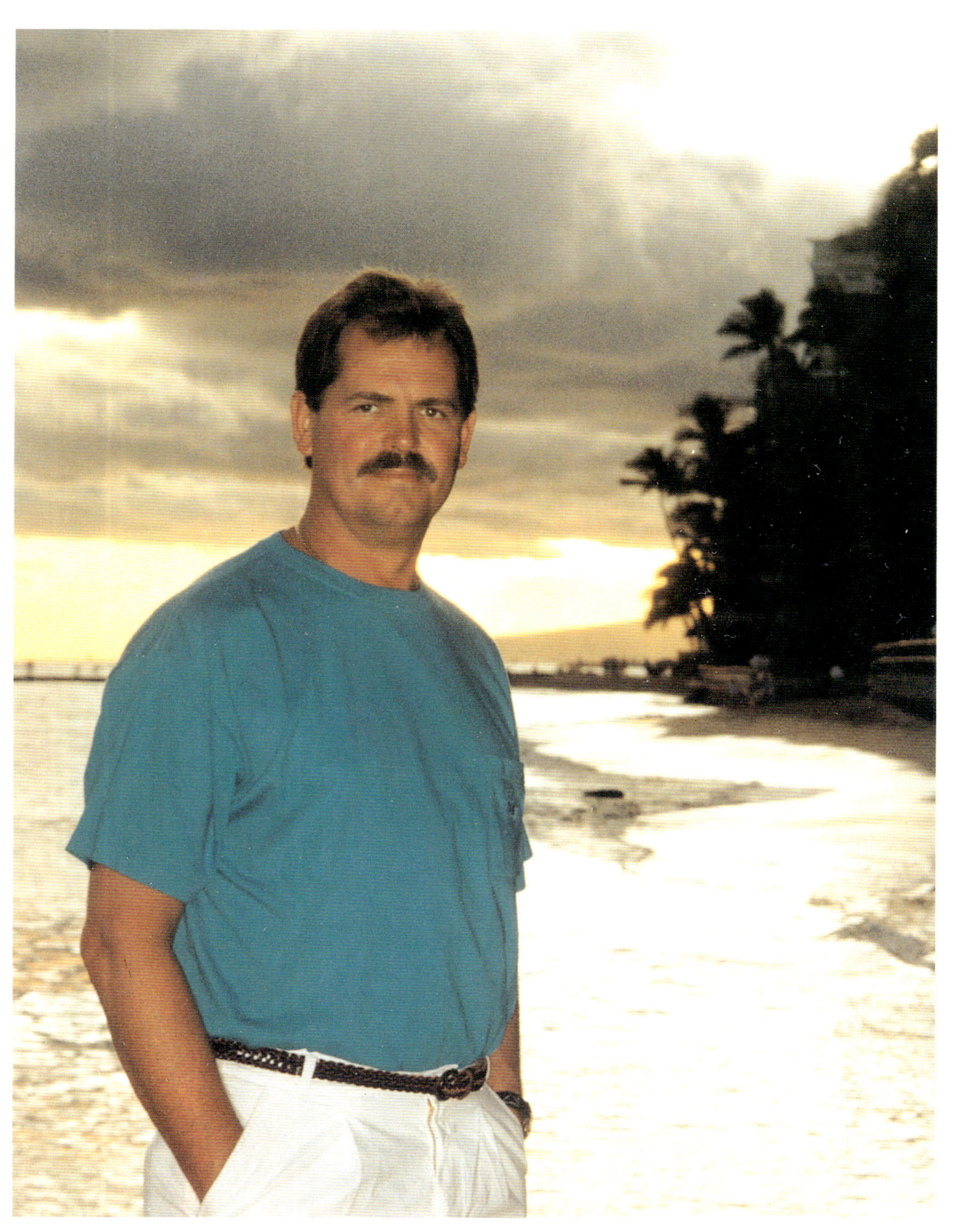

Introduction

By Kenny Loggins

We were supposed to cross the Waiohonu Bridge and stay straight on for five miles or so into Hana, but Love has a mind of her own, and so suddenly, barely realizing it myself, I impetuously decided to turn left up a rutted dirt road hidden within giant Philodendrons, ginger and bamboo.

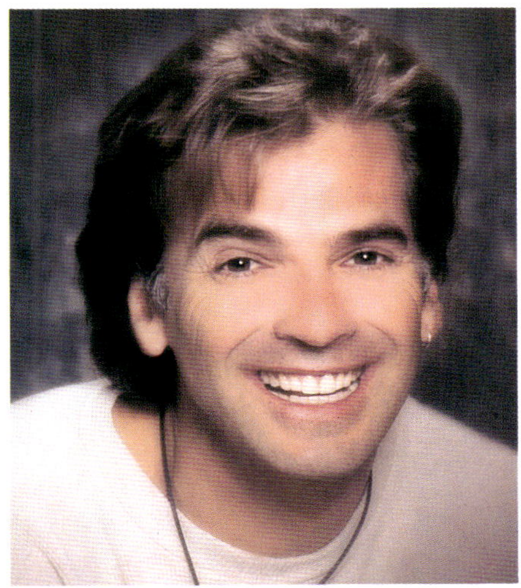

There are moments in our lives where even time is stunned by the beauty of this world and for a split-second it forgets to spin the illusion, then suddenly we come into the truth of it – of *us*.

Where were we? a flower farm or just random jungle? No more then two minutes up from the paved road, yet life-times away, a small farm house, Hawaiian style with a junked pick-up truck in front came into view ahead and off to the right. But without speaking a word I turned intuitively left through more thicket. Twenty feet further the road ended.

It was obvious. This is what had called to us on the highway. The unimaginable life.

I quickly turned off the motor. Silence, the birds, distant surf, a light wind played in the background. Almost imperceptibly, softly we both began to cry as we sat staring at the simple little cottage, corrugated tin roof, wooden front porch with a few hanging pots of red flowers. It was not unlike the many rustic Hawaiian homes we'd seen before. But for us there was only one, this one, and the message it held. We cried because we remembered. And we cried because we knew it would be many years before we could share this vision of life together in this way, just us, simple and free, beside the ocean, in each other's arms. But this life-time we are to be *in* the world. This is our path. And this vision of home was a promise and an omen, a gift of Grace from the Spirit.

Four years later Julia and I were walking together one warm gentle evening in Laguna Beach, California enjoying a moment of peace. Our new baby, Luke, was asleep by now, hopefully, back at the hotel. These quiet times had become too few and far between. I'd been on & off the road incessantly since the release of "Leap Of Faith" and just as we'd seen long ago in Hawaii we were now very much in the world.

Laguna Beach is primarily a tourist town, so when you go for a walk there you only take about twelve steps at a time. You simply throw yourself into a mindless trance and glide Zen-like from shop to shop. Unless you actually *need* a t-shirt, odds are slim you're going to be stunned by a shopping revelation.

So perhaps that essence of just *being together* was what allowed us to be open enough to let James Coleman's work *in* that night. But suddenly there it was, like a reminder from the Spirit, somehow someone had painted our dream, our vision of a home together, our Hawaii. If I couldn't have the dream yet, at least I could have a picture of it to remind me. A sort of souvenir of a life to come, or perhaps a time long ago.

There are places on this earth where Spirit speaks to us more clearly than others if we are ready to listen. Tradition has it that these powerful places choose a few particular artists to speak through, to tell us not only of their aesthetic beauty, but also of the secrets held within us, a memory held in our souls, of a non-ordinary life . . . a distant memory of a quiet halcyon time long ago and yet almost tomorrow . . . the promise of simplicity itself. A life of just home and sea and green and moon; of pure magic; of a woman singing softly to her baby in her arms; of lovers whispering to each other of forever, here in paradise, just the two of us. And is it a memory or a premonition? Perhaps both, but certainly a magic we all have in common within each of us.

James Coleman is one of those gifted souls that these special places speak to. Thankfully, through his work Julia and I see each other there still; our falling in love time, our past and our dreams, our unimaginable life together, someday, simple and free, beside the ocean, under a full moon, in each other's arms.

Kenny Loggins

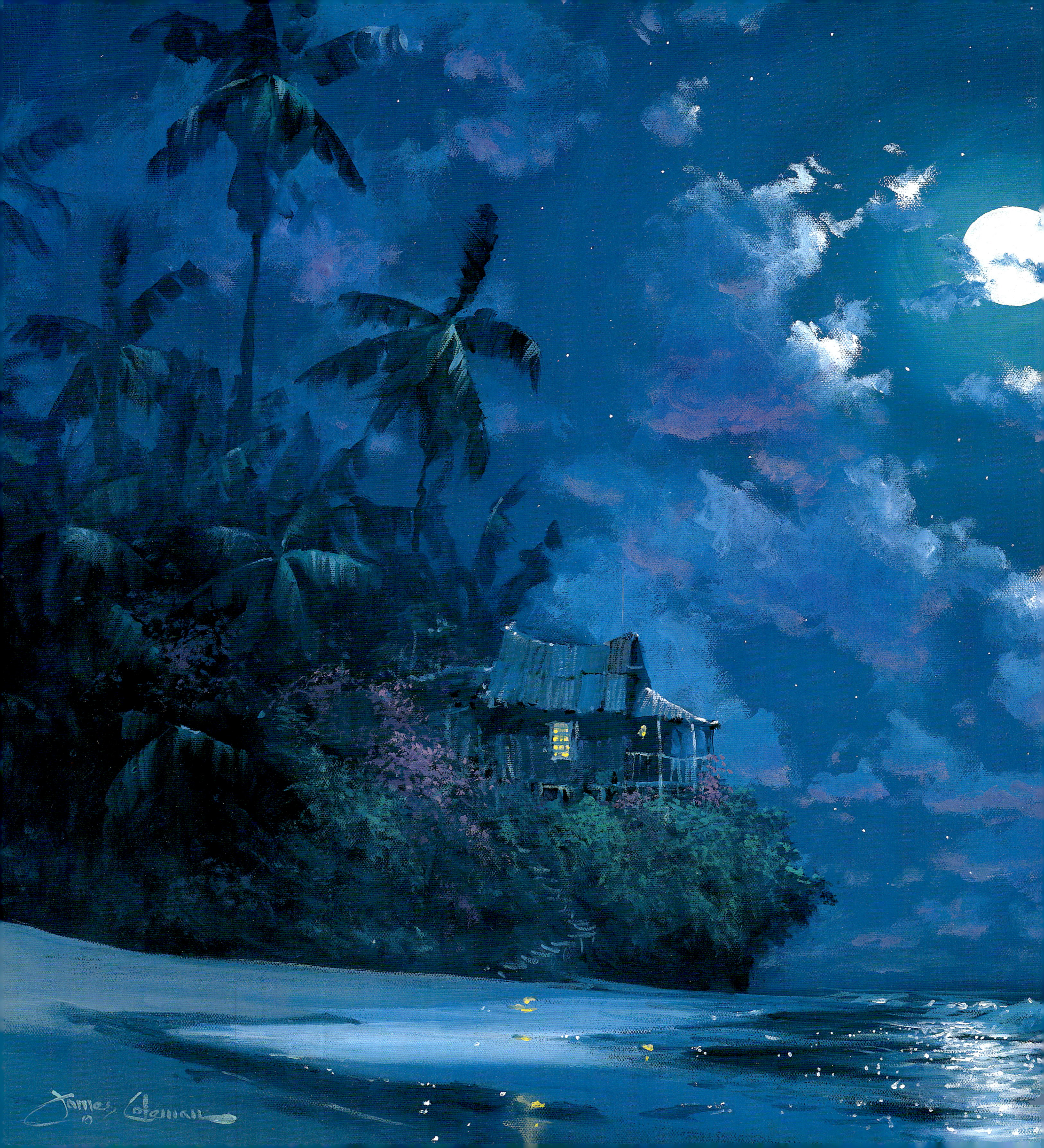
James Coleman

1

Once Upon A Time

A balmy breeze off the Pacific played across Coleman's face, invisible. . . yet everywhere, creating movement in all that lived or breathed along the NaPali Coast. It was well after midnight, and Kauai's afternoon heat had long melted away, allowing the trades to pick up and cool the island until morning.

Tall, curved coco palms swayed in a sweet cadence as their long arms rustled lightly, adding just the right percussion to the sound of a powerful blue ocean lapping against the dark lava rock of the cliffs below. Down the shore, the sea sent forth larger waves, each of which rumbled onto the rocks louder than its predecessor until, with a perfect count, the crescendo reached its peak and crashed in the distance like muted thunder.

The melodies of paradise were music to his ears. But on this night, the artist was more occupied with the appearance of the orchestra. It seemed as if the trees and plants crowding the tiny Princeville home had become, in addition to musicians, shadow dancers. Choreographed by a brilliant full moon, which illuminated the entire surface of the ocean and everything visible on land, the broad leaves of the palms and banana trees staged a ballet of shadows across the freshly cut lawn behind the house.

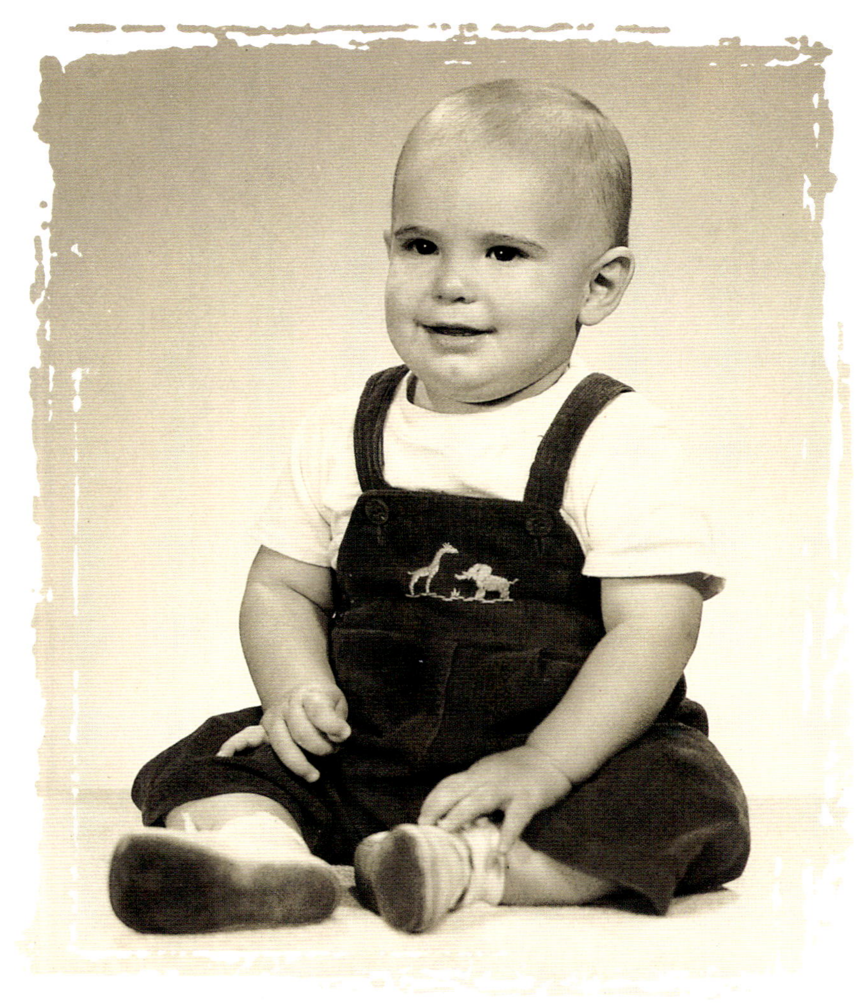

James Coleman at age one, 1950

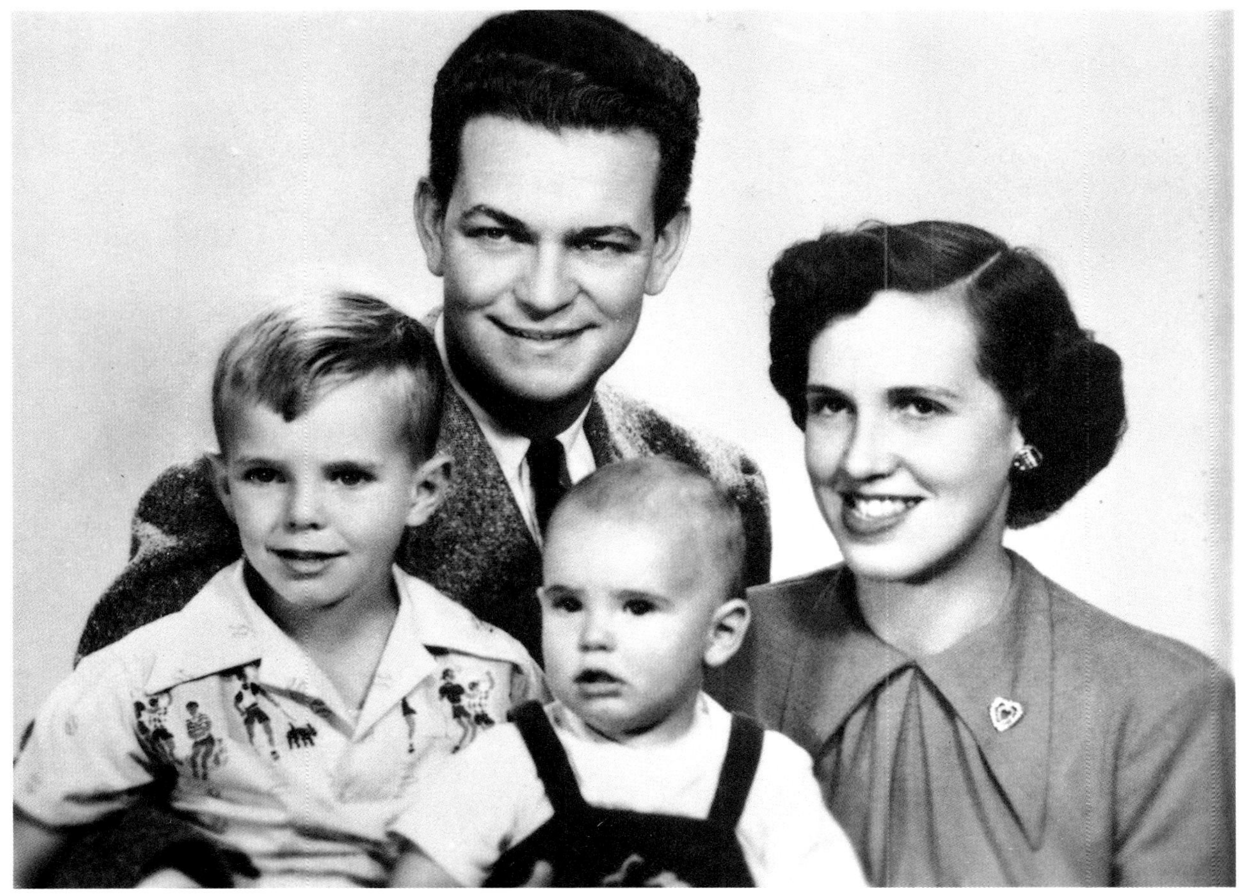

Frank and Beth Coleman with sons Jeff on left and James

One palm in particular swayed delicately up and down as its slender fingers leapt with the wind and pirouetted in circular motions against a white wall.

James Coleman was mesmerized by what was perhaps the most beautiful moon he'd ever seen, a *bella luna*, bathing everything in sight with its cool, glamorous light until one would think the shadow dancers were performing on a state-of-the-art Broadway stage. This, of course, was not the first such night he had spent in Hawaii. He had once again scheduled his entire trip so he would be in the Islands when the moon was full. And once again, he sat alone in the night, drinking in each and every drop of what his mind and heart could see, hear, smell and feel.

"I remember sitting there for four or five hours, just experiencing the night and how the moon affected everything in it," he recalls. "In addition to watching the light itself—how it manipulated the colors, the shapes and the shadows—I wanted to feel the tremendous emotion of it all . . . so I would never forget it."

Astrologists maintain that the moon symbolizes emotion and feeling, sensitivity and receptivity, none of which is lost on Coleman. "You always have to paint moonlight from memory," he explains. "There are just too many things going on that make up the mood of a scene like that. And you have to be able to carry that mood back to your studio. This is what eventually made me decide to paint everything from memory, as opposed to first-hand.

"Basically, I see something, store it in my mind and study it," he continues. "Then, when I get back to the studio, it just comes out. It's like experiences from our childhood. I don't know where they come from or why they're there, but everything we see is imprinted in our brain. And if we're able to connect with those images, we can call them back and use them."

As Coleman talks about making that connection, it becomes obvious his memory is as impressionistic as the artist himself. His recollection of his past, from early childhood on, is somewhat sparse on dates, names and places—but rich in images, moods and feelings.

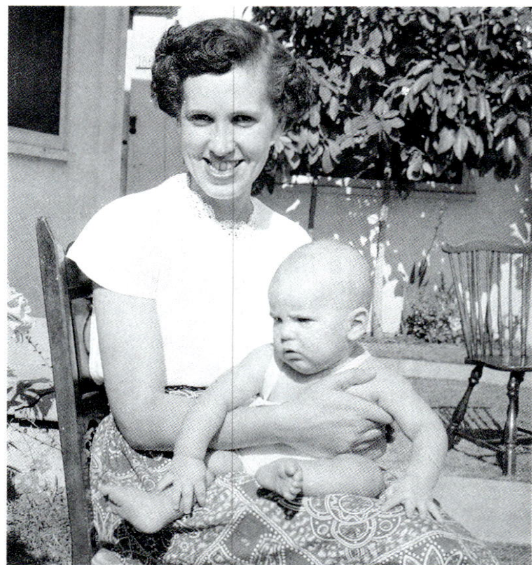

Beth Coleman with 1-year-old James

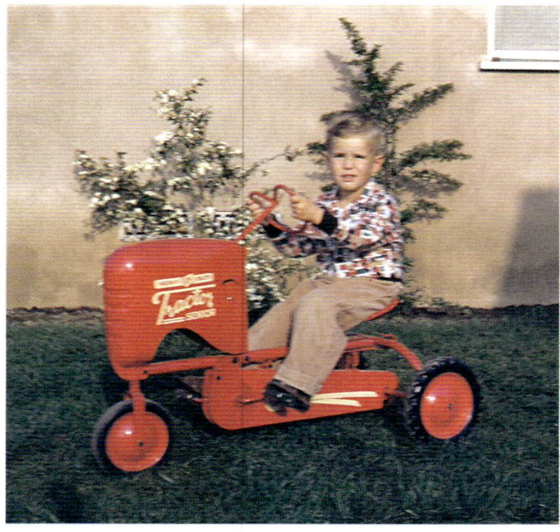

Jim at age 2

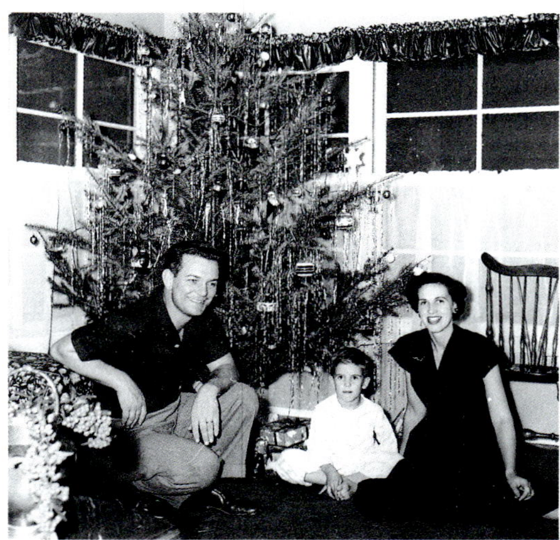

James with his parents, Christmas, 1951

"I was born in Hollywood on March 23, 1949," he states, well aware of the important dates. "But we moved that same year to the San Fernando Valley. I grew up out there. It was a nice place back then, rolling hills and plenty of open areas where kids could get away and play army or baseball. We played and fished in the L.A. River before it was cemented."

Frank Coleman moved to California in 1937 from a farm in McCook, Nebraska, also the hometown of the artist's mother, Beth. She, after graduating from high school at 16, had moved to Los Angeles with her family and coaxed young Frank to come out to the West Coast as well. "We'd liked each other back in Nebraska, but we didn't have a commitment or anything," Frank recollects. "We did write a lot of letters, though, and she kept writing about California and all of the wonderful swing music they were playing out there. Oh, did we ever like to dance to the big bands. So, after I graduated, I hitchhiked the next summer to Los Angeles to find work. Those were Depression years so you had to hitch rides or jump on a freight train."

He initially found employment as a ribbon installer at a typewriter company before trying his hand at a shipyard, then at bookkeeping and, eventually, like so many during the '30s, found himself doing whatever was necessary to make ends meet. Beth got on at a bank and soon became a crack secretary and typist, skills that would later land her a job with a budding filmmaker named Walt Disney.

Meanwhile, as the United States drew closer to entering the war against Hitler, the two decided to get married. The small, intimate wedding was soon overshadowed, however, by the Japanese attack on Pearl Harbor. Frank immediately enlisted in the Army to become a fighter pilot, hoping to face the new enemy over the high seas of the Pacific. The glow of the honeymoon had been interrupted, but the romance burned on. Three years later, just as he was to be shipped to Italy for combat, he remembers Beth telling him: "In case you don't come back. . . I'd like to have your child."

It was a scene right off the silver screen, the same matinee playing to thousands of teary-eyed men and women sitting in movie theaters across the country, watching American heroes kiss their brave wives goodbye—many for the last time. But Frank was lucky. He came back from Europe at the end of the film, embracing his proud wife as she held the first of their three sons in her arms.

Today, their eyes well up with tears, and there are frequent pauses for composure when Frank and Beth talk about their early romance and the war years. The emotion intensifies when they speak of their second son, James.

"He was a shy child," Beth reflects, her watery eyes looking off into the distance for several private moments. "He pretty much kept to himself. Every spare moment he spent drawing or painting. But never, in our wildest dreams, did we think he'd be an artist, especially someone who would be famous."

Their prodigy had friends growing up, Frank adds. And, of course, there were his two brothers, Jeff, the war baby, and John, eight years his junior. But James was one of those kids who had no problem finding ways to entertain himself. He didn't play sports like most of the other boys, but he loved to be outdoors and was always busy making things.

"I didn't participate in organized sports because I wasn't very good at it," he says with a hearty laugh. Those who know Coleman have become accustomed to a good-natured but self-effacing and razor-sharp wit, all of which belies the image of a soulful, withdrawn child searching for an outlet to express himself.

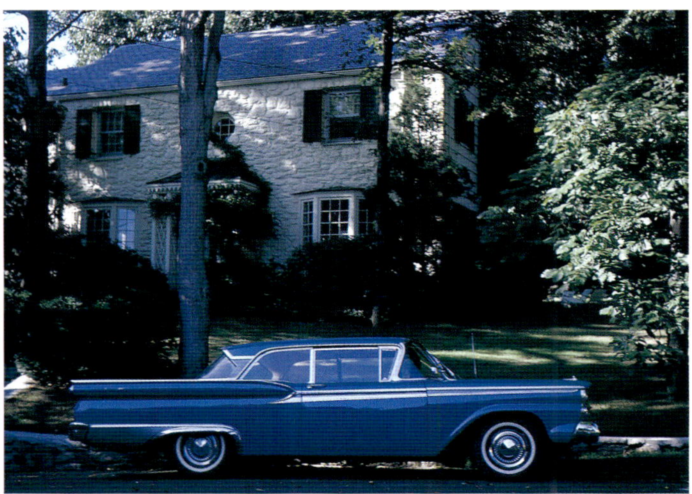

'59 Ford Sedan used on family trips across the country

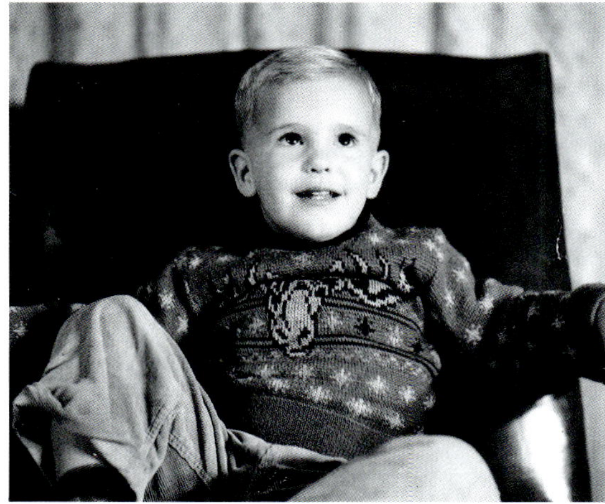

James at age 3

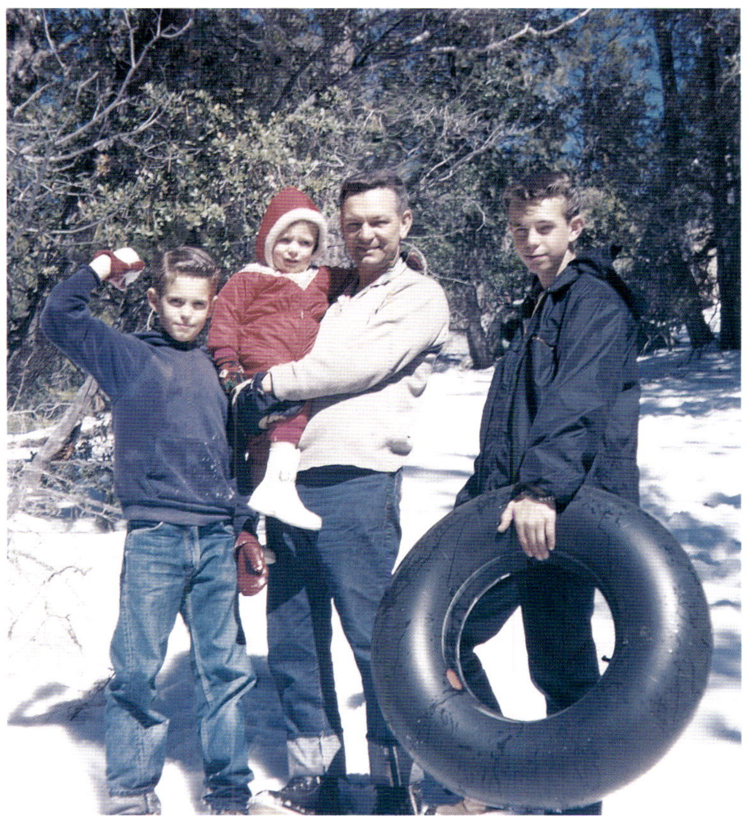

Jim with his father and brothers

"By the time I was interested, I figured everyone else was so far ahead of me that it was just too late," he explains. "I did like to play football in the streets, though, and I'd go to the Little League fields and keep score so I could get free candy."

When he was 12, Coleman took an interest in golf. His uncle, an excellent golfer, gave him an ancient set of clubs, so old that they had metal shafts covered with plastic that resembled wood.

"For my golf bag, I took a long tubular cardboard box and covered it with a towel I'd sewn into a bag," he remembers with a smile. "I had a friend whose father was a pro at a big country club, and this kid had the best clubs and bag money could buy. And there I was, with this thing I'd sewn together."

But his "caddyshack" image didn't bother him. He loved the game and, by the time he was 15, was working at a golf course, washing dishes at the clubhouse and, eventually, running the driving range. From then on, he continued to work after school, on weekends and during the summer, full-time.

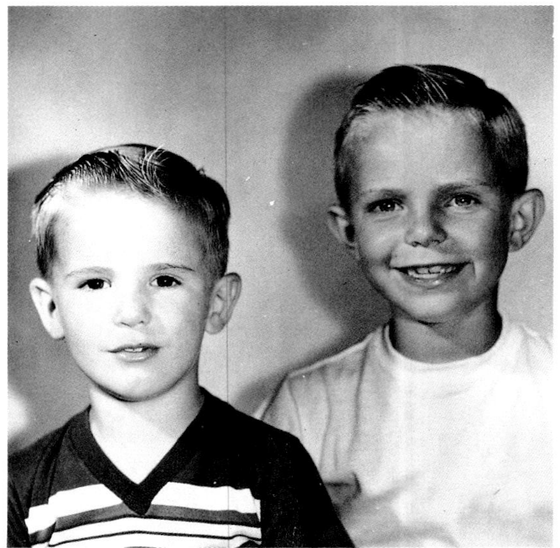

James and his brother Jeff

After the war, Frank Coleman had earned a master's degree and begun teaching elementary school in the San Fernando Valley. His trek as a youth to the West Coast had evidently lit a fire in his belly for travel, a desire that would later expose his impressionable young son to countless images of North America.

"The great thing about my father being a teacher was that he had summers and spring breaks off," Coleman says. "He would hock almost everything we had so we could take trips all around the country."

The family would pile into a '59 Ford sedan and head cross-country with an old, beat-up trailer in tow. "The Ford was dead, but it somehow pulled the trailer all the way to British Columbia," he says, eyebrows raised. "Matter of fact, we drove that car all the way to New York and back. It was the same car I learned to drive when I was 15. We took a lot of trips to the Pacific Northwest, a trip to Canada through Yellowstone and Glacier Park, up to Lake Louise, Jasper, and then through Victoria all the way down the coast."

Coleman often would take something along to sketch with, particularly on camping trips. His parents usually knew that if he was missing, they could find him sitting near a stream or in the woods sketching or drawing. He rarely slept in the trailer or tent, preferring to sleep under the stars in his sleeping bag.

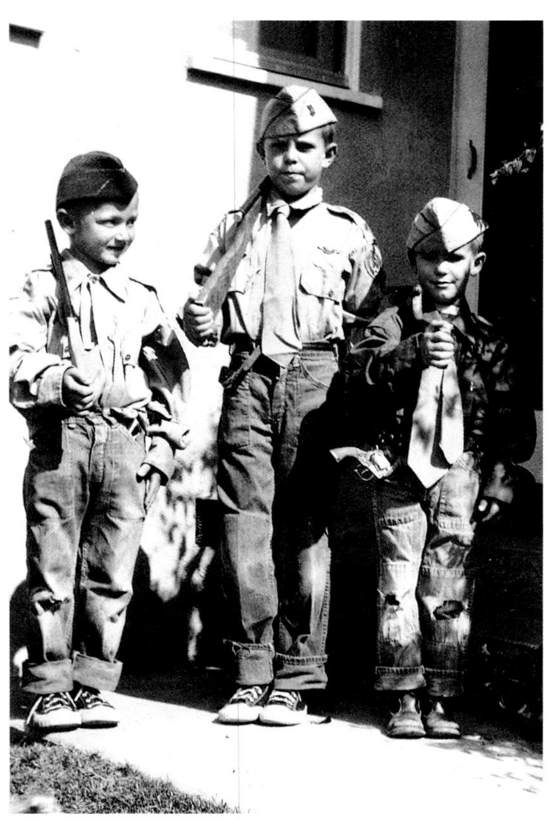

A friend, Jeff and James playing army

"I've always loved the purity of the outdoors," he says. "Growing up, I sketched mostly organic things. If we went on a camping trip, I'd take my colored pencils and pastels along and do a drawing of the campfire or trees and mountains."

Though his parents didn't have the discretionary income at the time to invest in art supplies, his father would save the cardboard that came with his laundered shirts so his son could draw on something resembling a canvas. "I'll never forget how excited I was when I saw a real painting set at the five-and-dime store," Coleman recalls. "It was more or less paint by number, but the tubes were not yet mixed. 'This is exactly what I need to learn how to paint,' I thought to myself. I also knew my folks couldn't afford it, so, after a night of tossing and turning, I went back to the store and . . . stole the set.

"That night at home, my mother asked me where I got the paints. 'Found 'em,' I said, nonchalantly. They never thought, I'm sure, that I'd stolen them. I still feel a tinge of guilt about it, but that little set helped me learn—at an early age— how to mix paint and understand color."

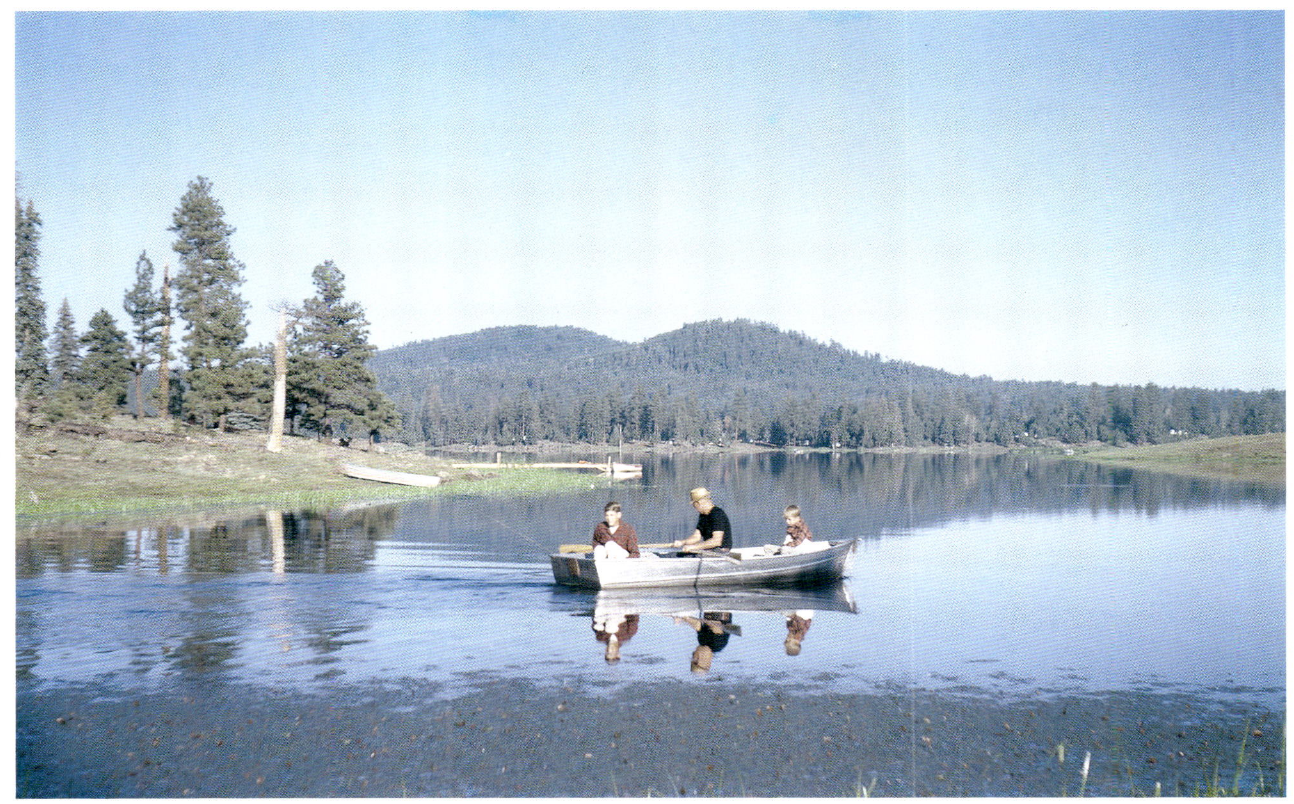

Family vacation at Snake River

Painting was just one of Coleman's early interests. He also was keenly interested in crafts and inventing motorized contraptions. He was especially interested in science and wanted to become a doctor when he grew up. "I enjoyed the creative side of science, rather than the academic side," he's quick to point out. "It was the experimentation I liked. I remember dissecting frogs on my own. I'd buy pickled frogs in the science section of the same five-and-dime where I 'found' my paint set, and then go straight home and dissect them."

The pre-med hopeful loaded up on high school science courses and, again, in his own time, would make up bodies with parts on them so he could operate. In addition, the young Doctor Frankenstein aspired to be a dentist after a friend of the family gave him an old set of dental instruments. But fate took a hand. He was about to receive his first real accolades as an artist.

Coleman had never shown his artwork to anyone outside the family and had not taken an art class until he was a senior in high school. "I was working on an assignment and looking through a 'how-to' book when I saw a French street scene," he remembers. "Then, suddenly, it hit me for the first time that the secret to painting was light. If I could capture the true light of a scene, then I'd really be able to connect with people.

"So, I painted a scene with the sun going down at the end of a street, and everything along that street was reflected in puddles of water. It should have been difficult to do, I found out later. But because I was so naive, I kept it simple and it worked. To my great amazement, the art teacher was beside herself with disbelief, and for days my classmates asked me how I did it."

Soon afterward, Coleman was called in by a career counselor, who told him bluntly that his math skills were so poor that his chances of becoming a doctor or dentist were virtually non-existent. "I just wasn't interested in memorizing numbers and working out mathematical problems," he shrugs. "What I enjoyed was abstract reasoning and why things do this and do that."

The counseling session changed his direction dramatically. Struggling with the basic courses his thoughts immediately turned toward art, and toward the response he'd received for his street scene. His mind drifted back to how he'd begun to draw when he was 6 years old, and how at 8 he created

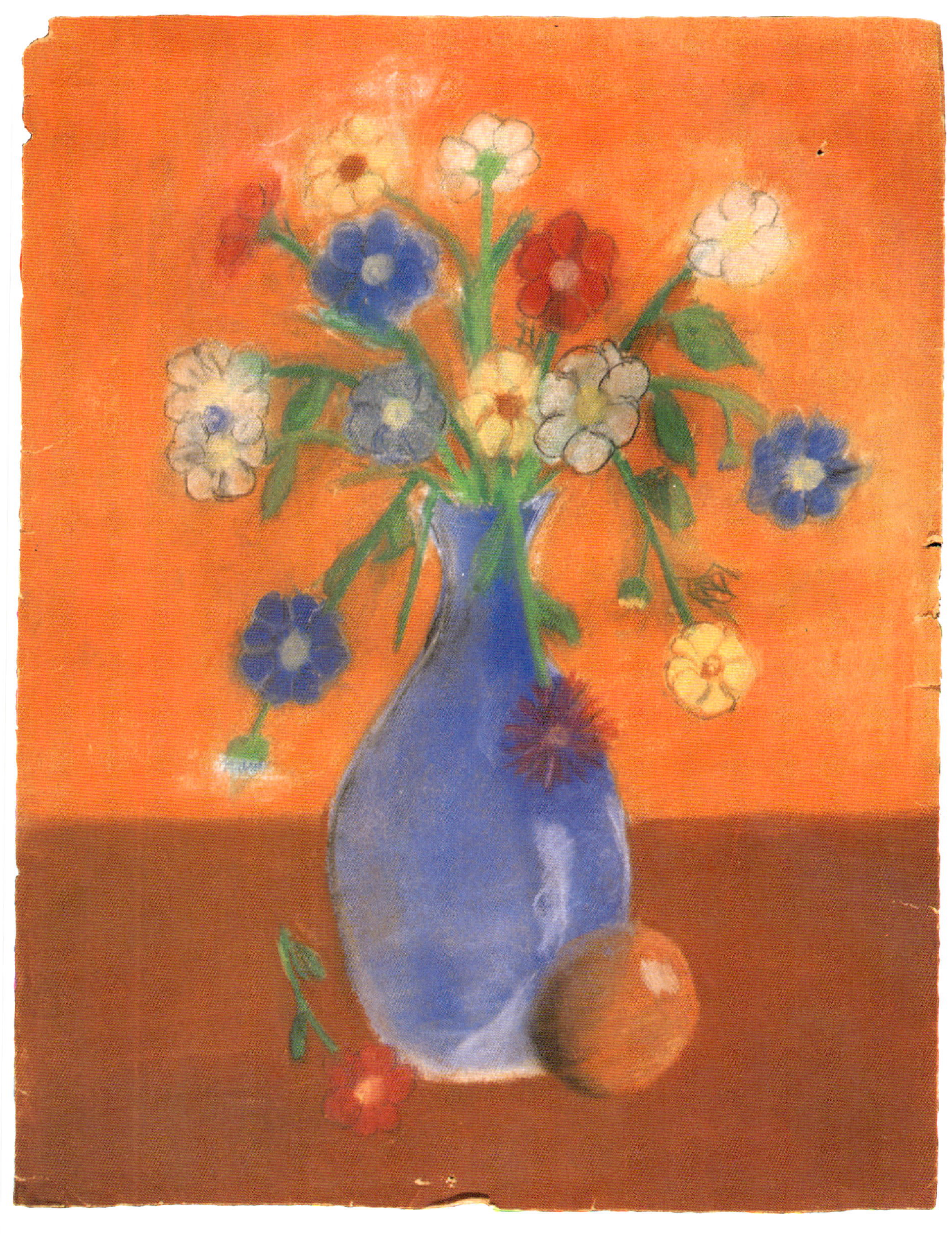

Early painting, 1964

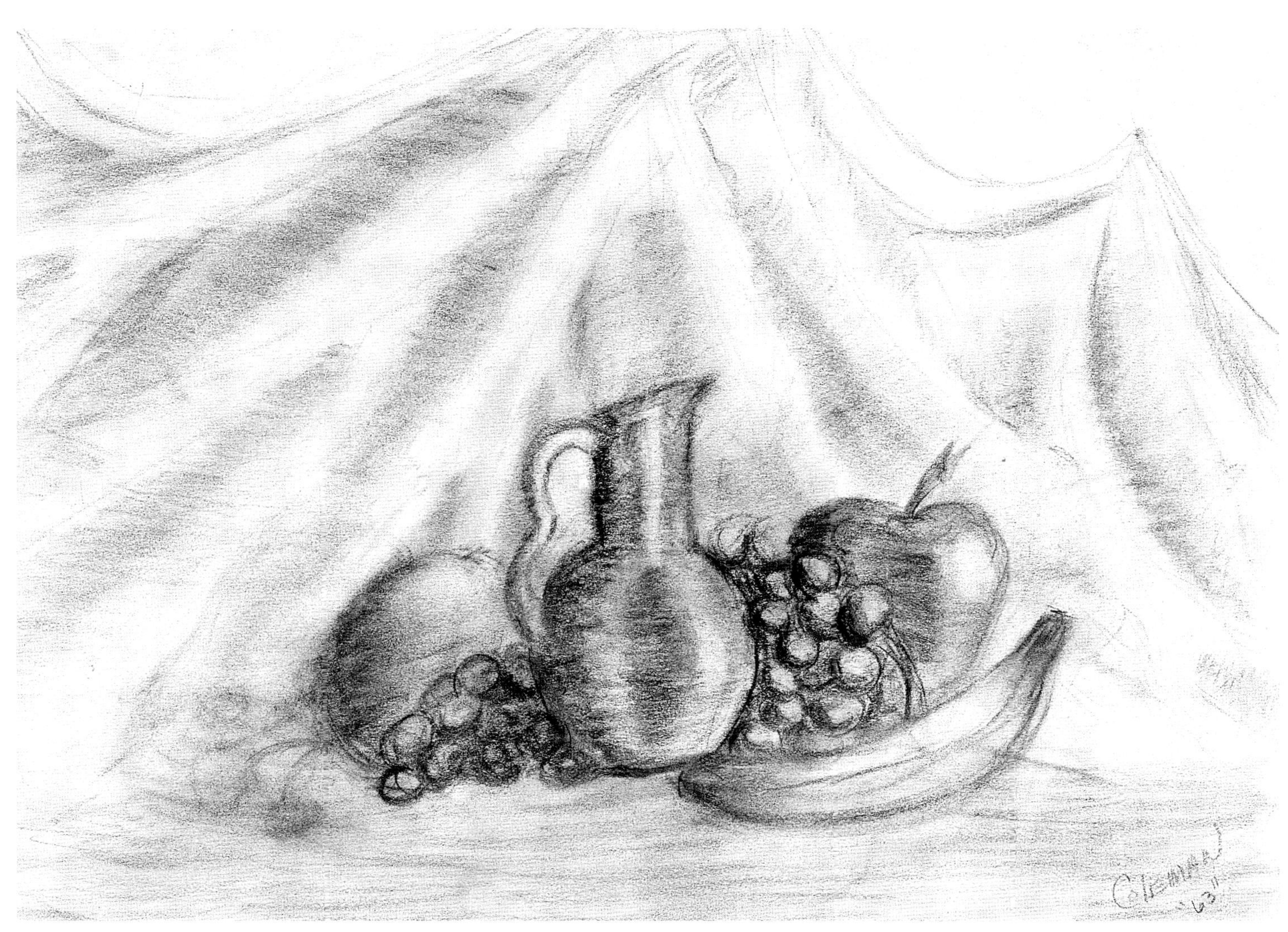

Early pencil drawing, 1963

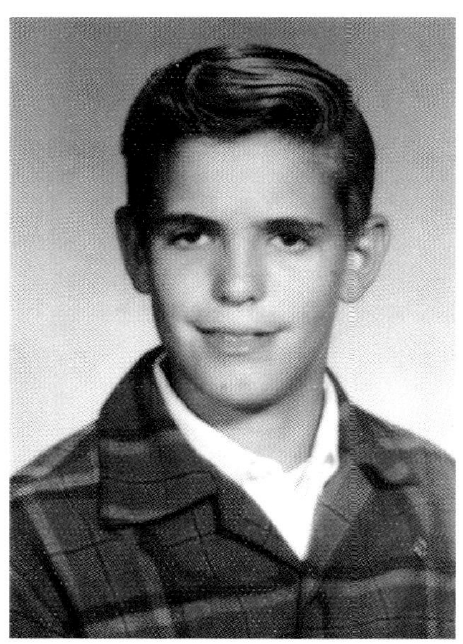

Young James

posters for the plays he and his brother used to stage in their back yard.

"Right then and there, I decided that when I graduated I would go to Pierce Junior College and take art," Coleman says emphatically. There were no artists in the family to encourage this decision. In fact, he didn't know a soul who actually made a living as an artist.

"I would imagine my father would have thought art was sort of a sissy thing, though I don't recall him ever discouraging it," he reflects. "His idea was for me to obtain my teaching credentials first and, then, if I wanted to be an artist—fine."

As planned, he enrolled in junior college to study art, beginning with basic design, painting and drawing courses, where students are traditionally drilled with strict adherence to the sanctity of procedure. His stint at art school was a short one.

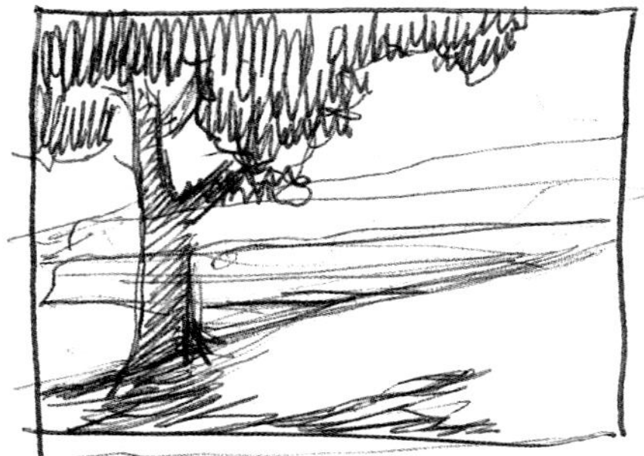

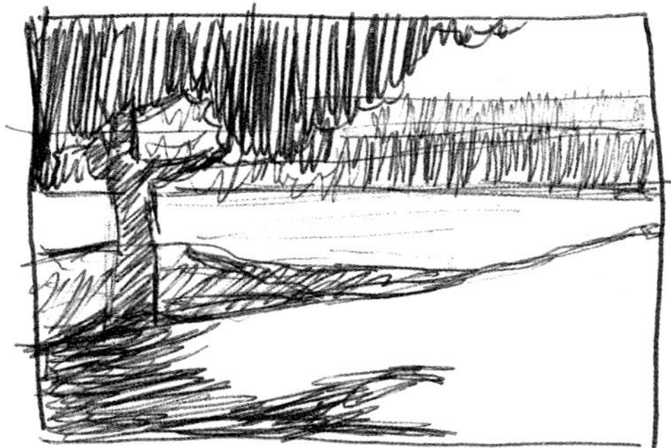

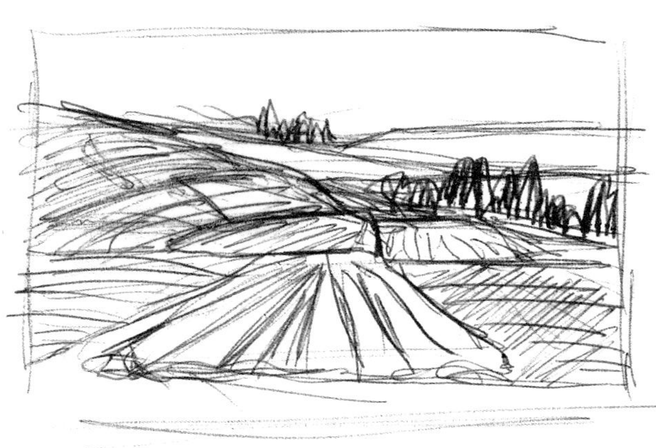

"One of the teachers said he was going to take us into his studio and show us a brush stroke he had worked his whole life to invent," Coleman recalls. "I just looked at this guy and said to myself: 'This is a bunch of nonsense!' I realized he was intellectualizing something that, in my mind, was a spiritual thing. Painting isn't an intellectual study. . . it comes from the heart."

"Theoretically, if you can dream vivid dreams, you should be able to re-create them on canvas or paper," he says. "But it's not that easy—the hardest thing to do in art is to get what's in here (pointing to his chest), and up here (pointing to his head), out through your hand," he explains. "That connection between heart, mind and body has to be working."

Extraneous academia wasn't all that bothered him about art school. The idea of students critiquing the work of other students was, in his view, invalid and unnecessary. "The only way to figure something like that is that if you haven't captured somebody with the art you've created, then you simply haven't captured them. That's about as analytical as it needs to get."

In 1967, the lives of millions of young Americans and their families became entwined with yet another war, this time in a controversial conflict across the globe in Southeast Asia. Coleman, then 18, was prime beef for the American draft. Though he never played high school football, he knew that one of the military branches would soon find a use for a healthy California kid who stood 6 feet 3 inches tall "I didn't want to wait around for them to come get me so I was going to sign for the draft, go to Viet Nam, get it over with and come home," he says, matter-of-factly. "But my father had some strong opinions about that."

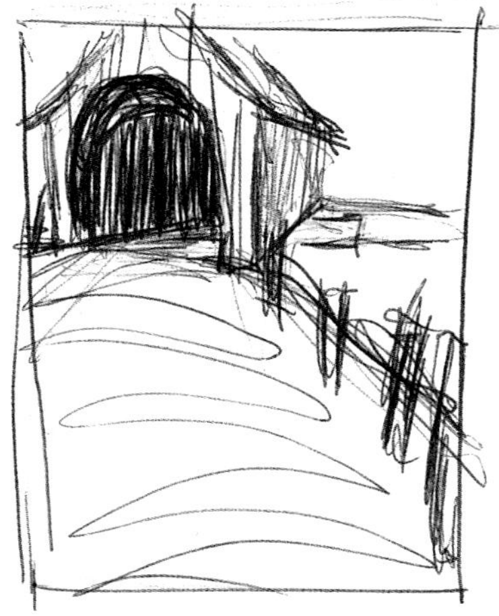

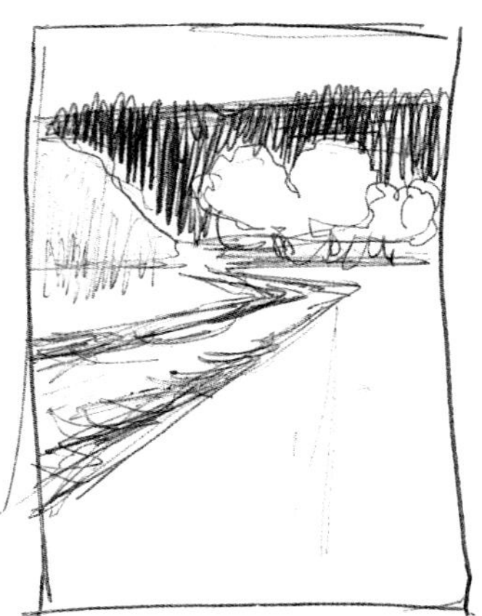

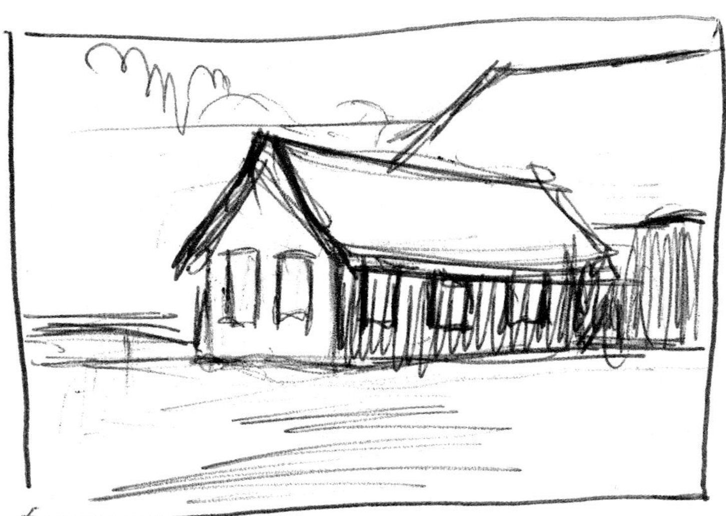

Thumbnail sketches

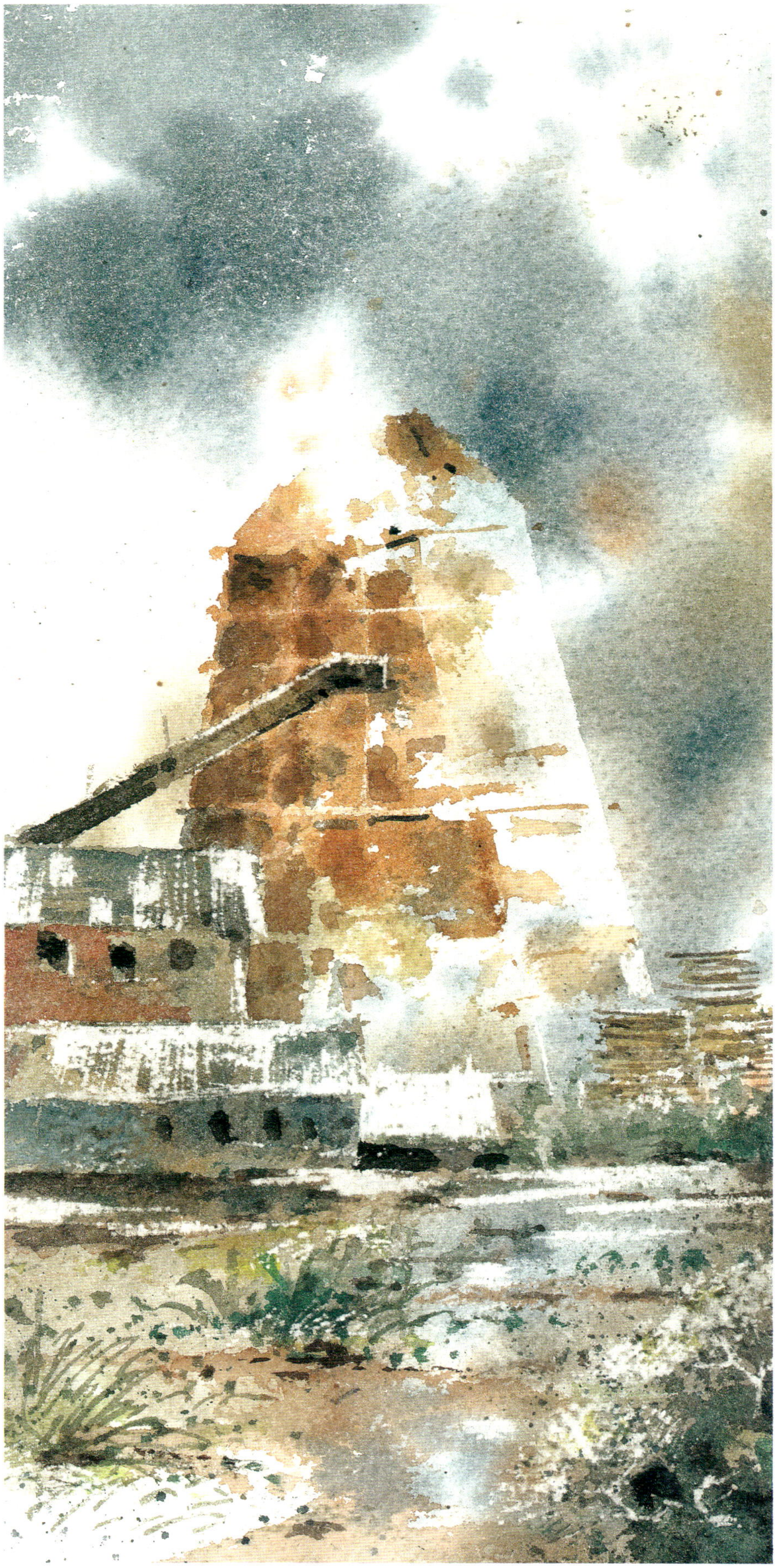

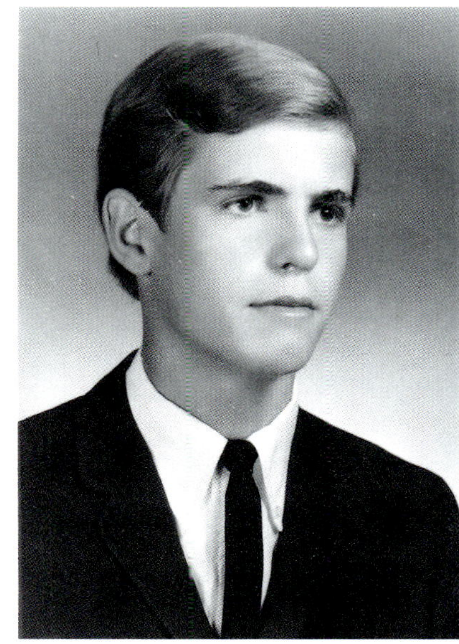

James' high school picture at age 17

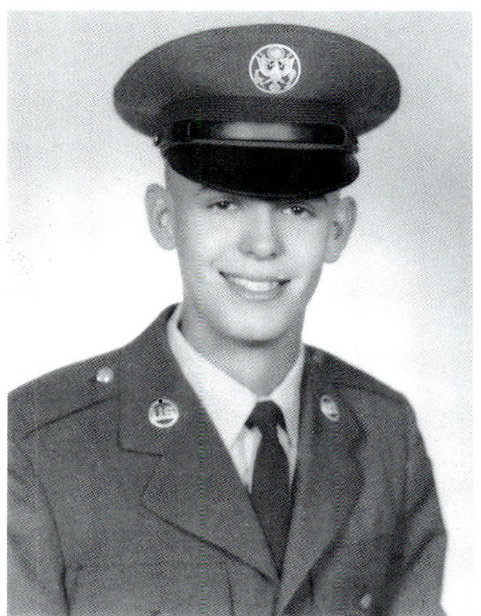

James in the Air National Guard, 1967

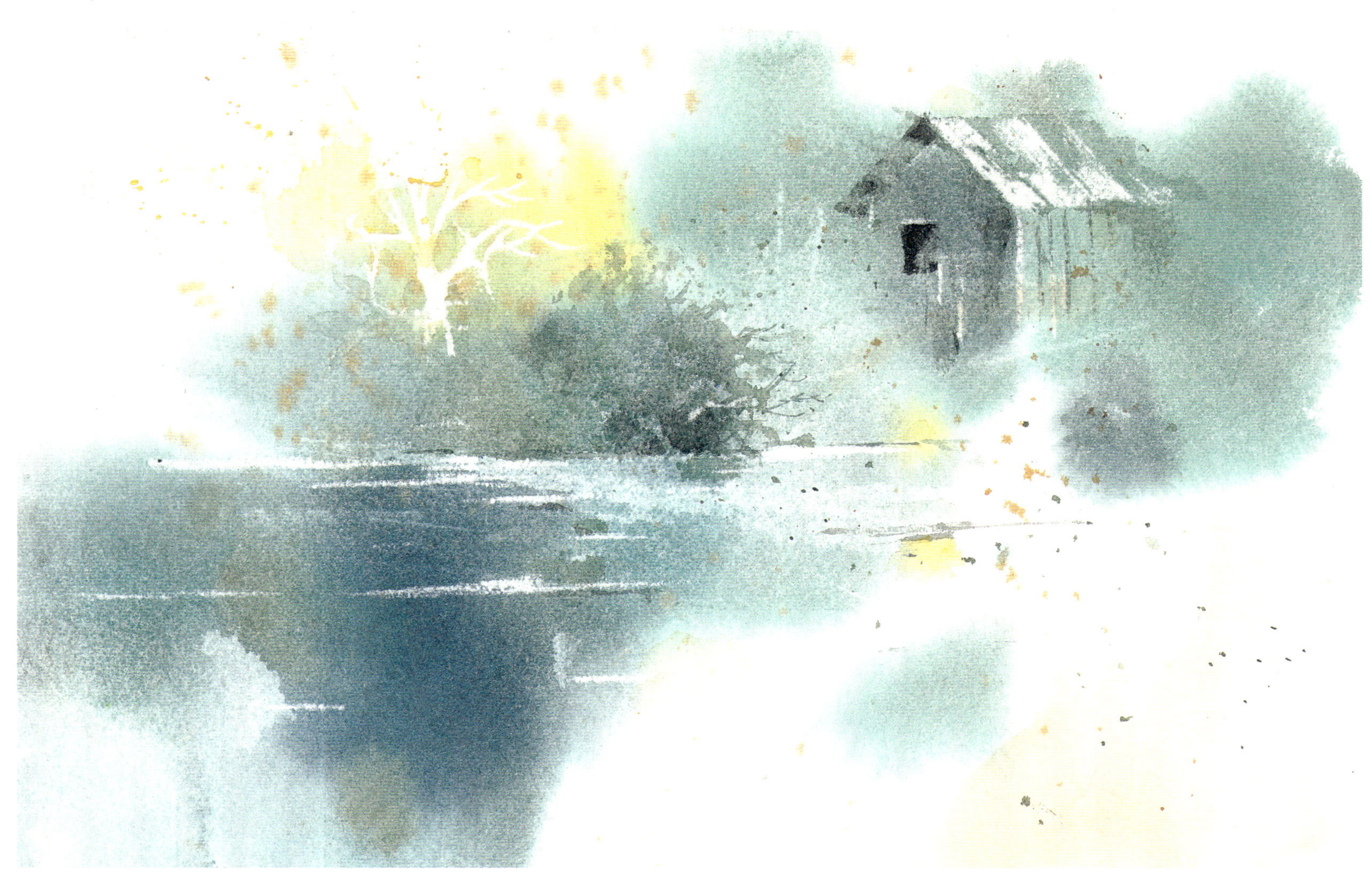

Early watercolor, 1970

"Oh no, you don't, I've been through a war, and you don't want to do that," Frank Coleman assured his son, suggesting instead that James enlist in the Air National Guard so he could stay home and perhaps change his mind about college and continue his education.

Coleman did just that, the Air National Guard part, at least. He had taken a job at Litton Industries for a short while, making circuit boards for the *Mariner*, the space vehicle that took photographs of Mars. He also served in the Guard one weekend a month and two weeks in the summer at an Air Force base in Van Nuys, California. He started out as a mechanic, the result of testing high in abstract reasoning.

"The test was folding and unfolding boxes," he says, following with a belly laugh. "They said I was good at working out mechanical problems, which I suppose had to do with spacial things. Maybe they just needed a mechanic, I don't know."

A few years later, his superiors discovered he was an artist, and he was soon transferred to the base newspaper, where he worked one weekend a month on illustrations and graphic design. Though better-suited to his interests, the new assignment was of little interest to him, however. By then, the shy boy who liked to sketch trees, was well on his way toward an illustrious career at Walt Disney Studios, and then on to become a world-renowned fine artist.

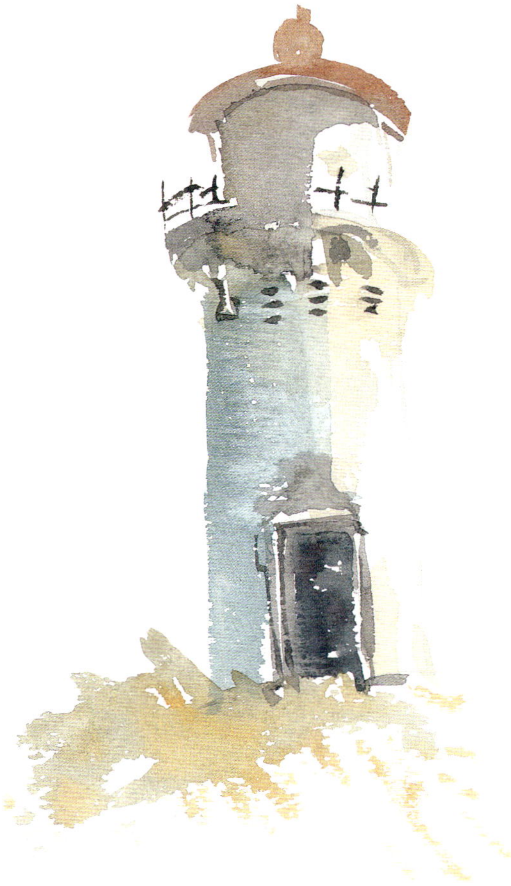

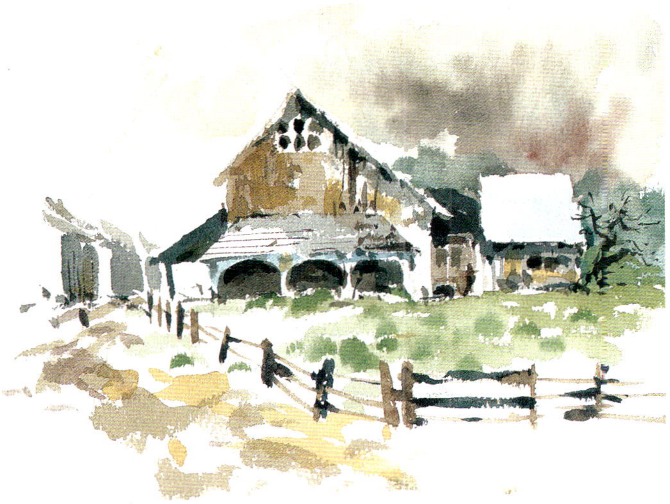

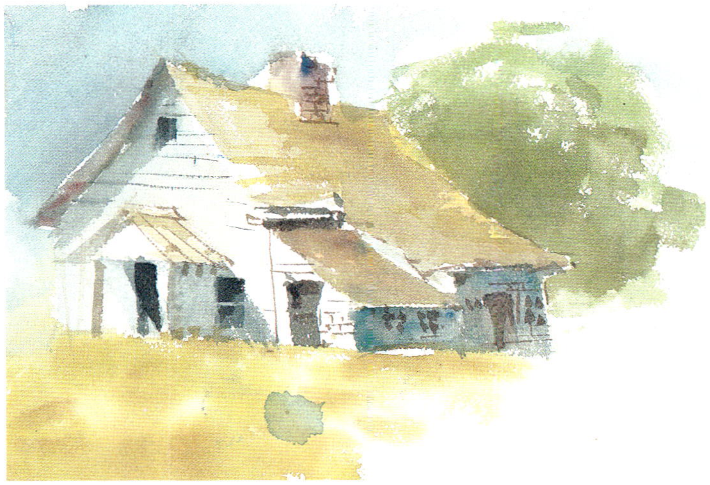

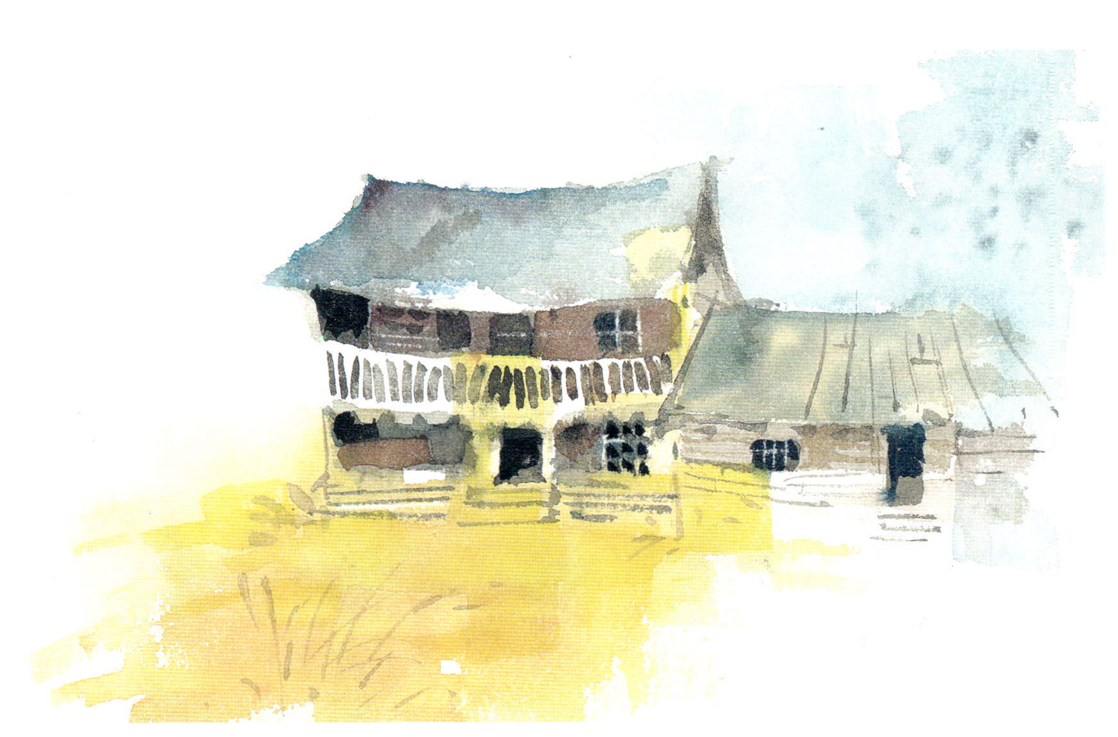

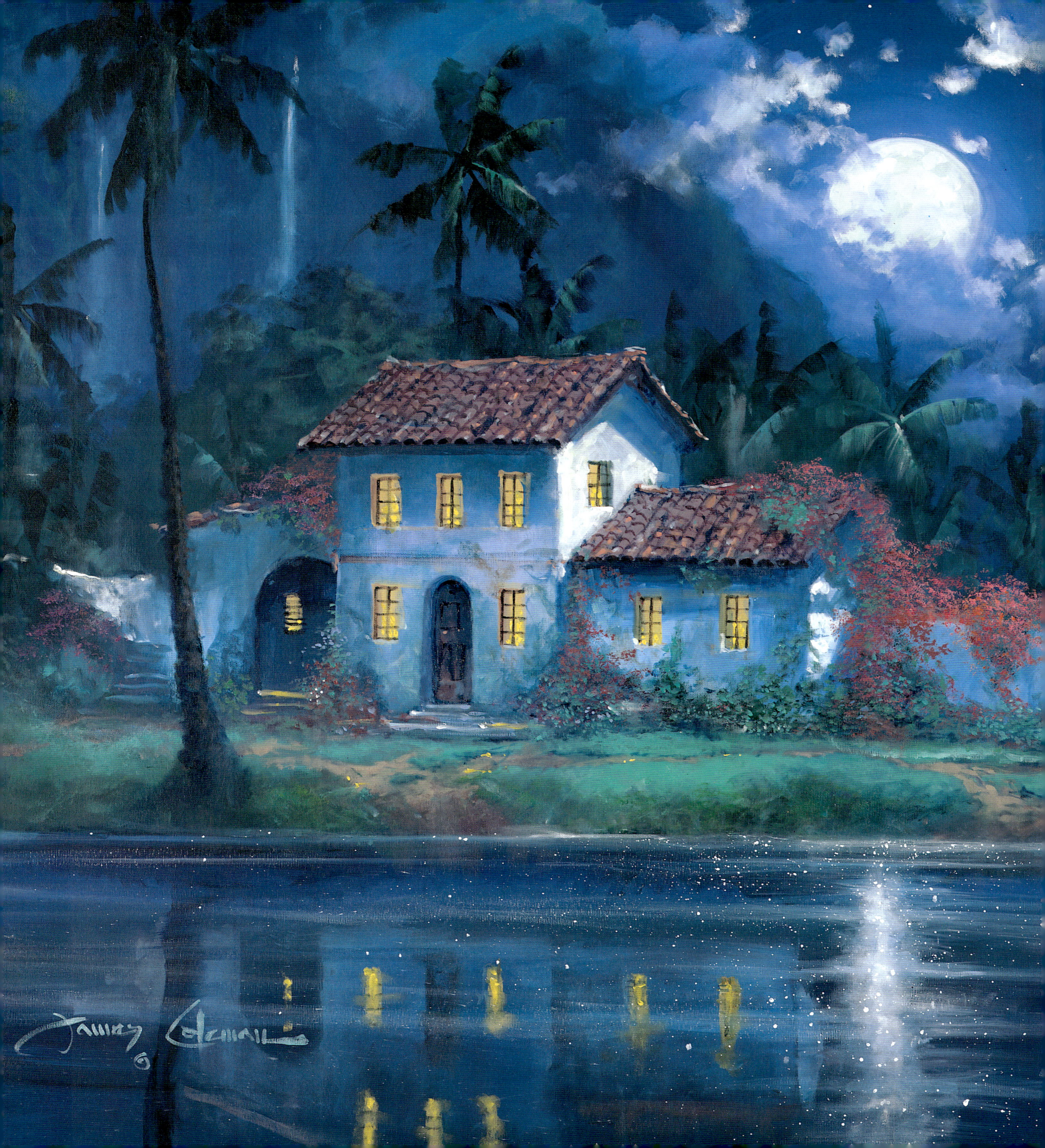
James Coleman ©

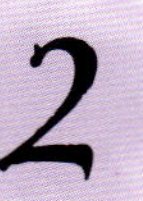

Impressions

Somewhere between the Midwest and the Dakotas, the '59 Ford sedan rambled over miles and miles of hot country asphalt. The beat-up vacation trailer, the car's summer albatross, squeaked and groaned behind, as if to whine: "I'm tired. . . when's the next stop?"

The trailer wasn't alone. Isolated on The Great Plains, every passenger in the car had begun to pester Frank Coleman, family patriarch and summer vacation guide, about the next stop. Everyone, that is, except James. Instead of sleeping, complaining or tormenting his younger brother, the 15-year-old sat forward with his arms folded on the back of the front seat, his eyes transfixed on the horizon ahead.

A storm had darkened the sky in front of them. The bright July sunshine had changed, without their noticing, into a light gray world. The temperature outside the car suddenly dropped. Focused on what lay ahead, Coleman marveled at how the gray gradually deepened from light to dark, and then, where the sky met the land, to black.

"I remember sitting in the back seat of the car and seeing that we were heading toward a storm, or, that a storm was heading toward us," he recalls, as if it were yesterday. "At first, it was miles ahead of us. Then, within a minute or two, everything became dark, and before we knew what was happening, the rain was pelting the car so hard we could barely see out the windshield.

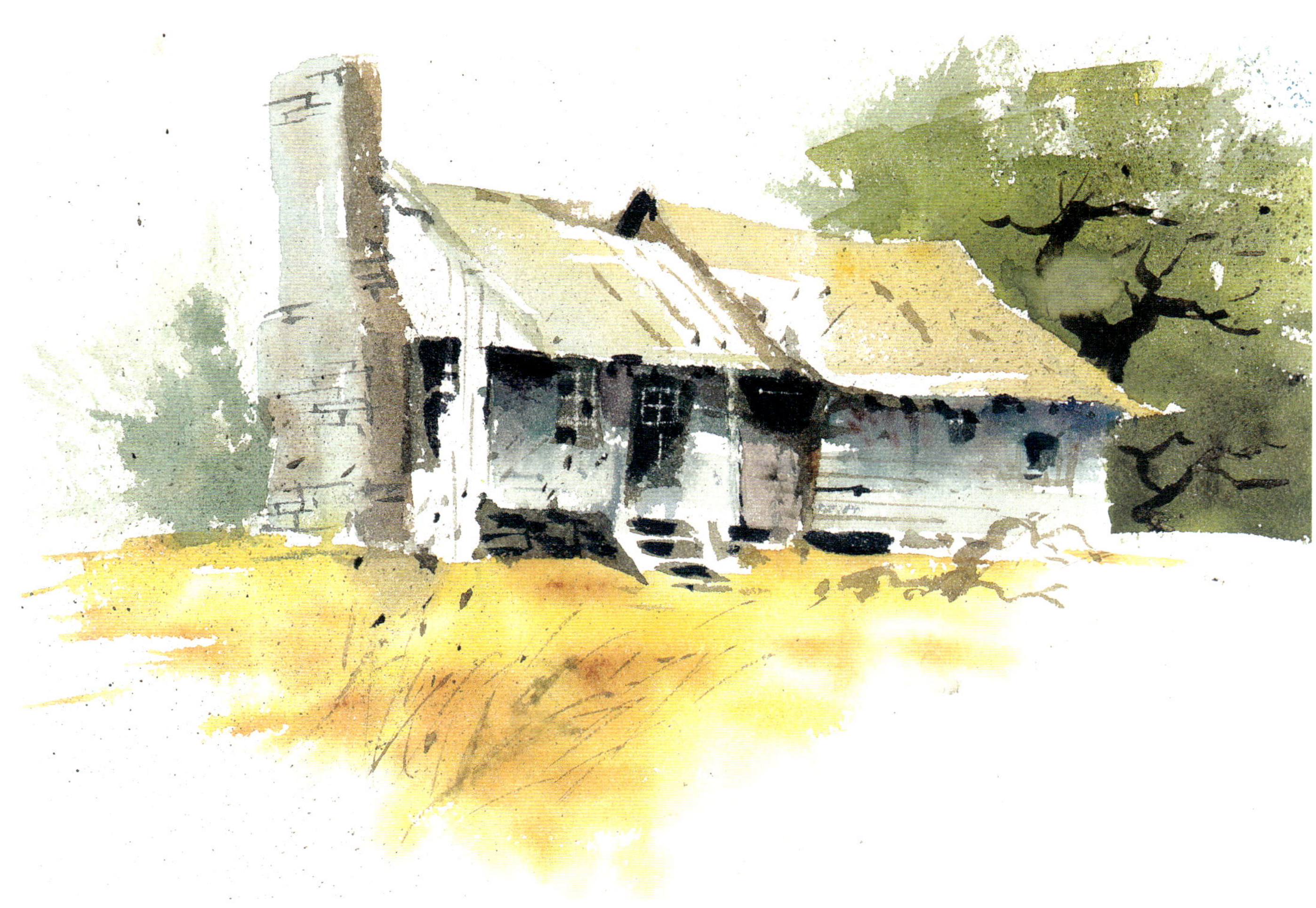

Early watercolor, 1973

"It lasted but a few minutes before it blew right over us, and I turned around and watched it as it kept on going. Everything happened so fast and, yet, I'll never forget how dramatic it was—the way it changed the mood of everything, both inside the car, and outside on the plain."

Five years later, this vivid image would resurface. Coleman landed a job at Walt Disney Studios and had worked in the mail room for only three months when he signed up for a one-man art show in the company's library. The studio would hold these shows once a month, often featuring a group of artists. But on many occasions, including this one, only one artist would have the time to feature his or her work.

Coleman figured he needed 20-30 paintings to stage a respectable show, so he sat down and thought hard about what exactly, it was, he was going to paint. Nature and landscapes had always been his subject, and he would definitely paint the redwoods on the West Coast. But he wanted to come up with some fresh ideas.

"As I thought more about it, memories and images from some of our family vacations just started pouring in," he says. "I thought about the different parts of the country I'd seen, and I couldn't help but remember sitting in the back of the Ford and watching that rainstorm come in off the plains.

"My father grew up in Nebraska, and to him it was nothing special. But it just blew me away. When I sat down to paint it for this show, years later, the impression it had made on me was there like it had happened the day before."

This was the first time the young artist was conscious that everything he had been painting up to that point had been inspired by the impressions and images he had somehow stored in his mind.

"One of the first things I learned at Disney came from one of the older artists there," Coleman says. "He told me I needed to be ready to work around the clock because, as an artist, no matter what I looked at, I'd always be thinking about how the light plays on it and how the shadows fall, and how all of that creates a certain mood.

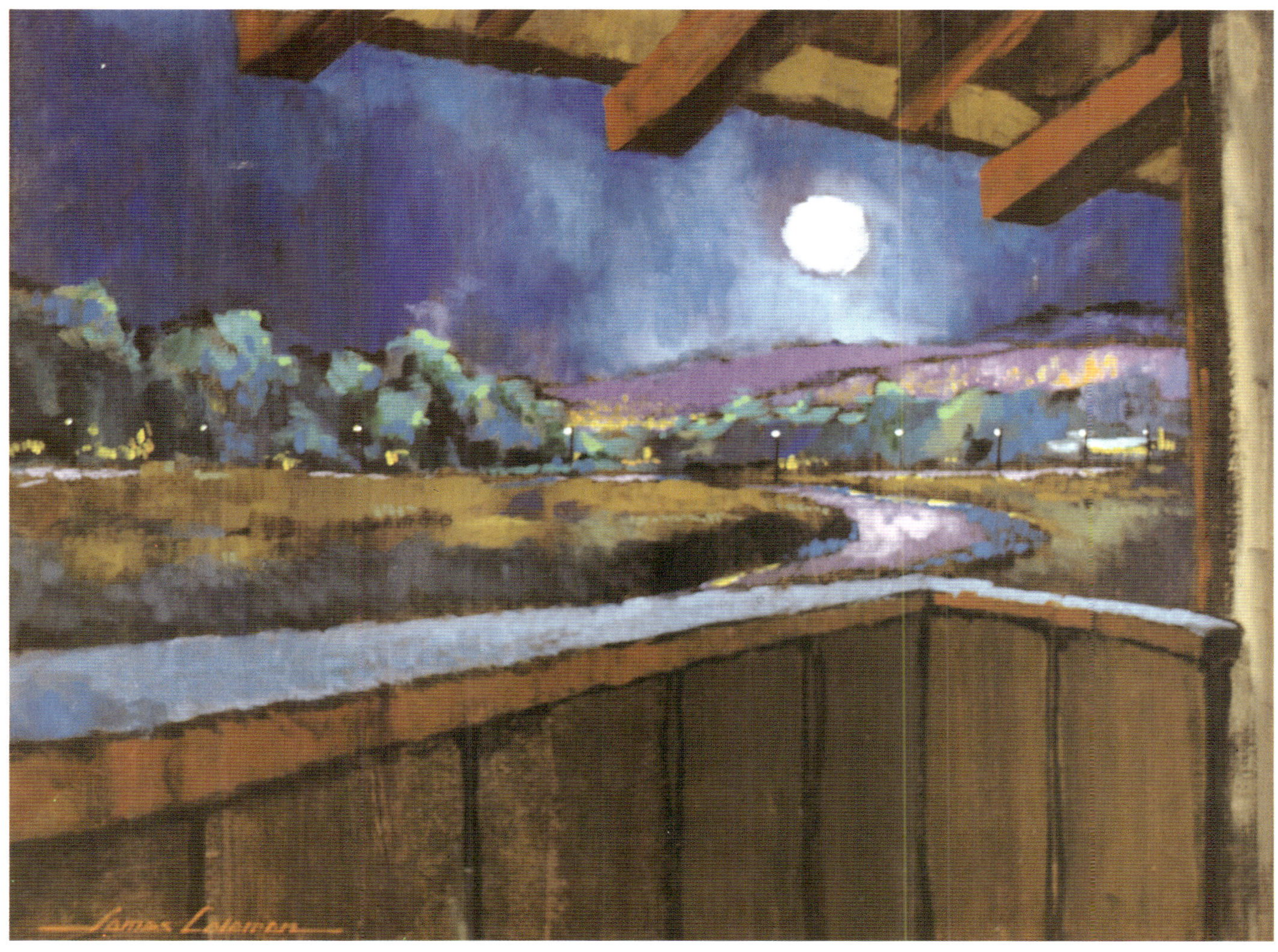

Canoga Park, 1973

"I realized, without even thinking about it, that I'd done that from the time I was a little kid. I'd be out fishing somewhere, and after sitting for a while, I'd become absorbed by the whole area. I'd start looking at the way the shadows fell across the trunk of a tree or across a waterfall. And that would make it almost magical, as opposed to just a bleached-out tree or water pouring over some rocks."

One old bleached-out tree on the Merced River in Yosemite must have been full of magic because Coleman has painted it a number of times. As he describes it, it's actually a thick white stump sitting by the edge of the river and, depending on the time of day you look at it, it takes on a different "spirit."

"In the bright sunlight, it can be warm and inviting," he explains, having planted himself on that same river bank many times over the years. "If it's cloudy or twilight, it can be a little eery because of the roots coming down into the water. In the moonlight, it's almost like a ghost it's so white."

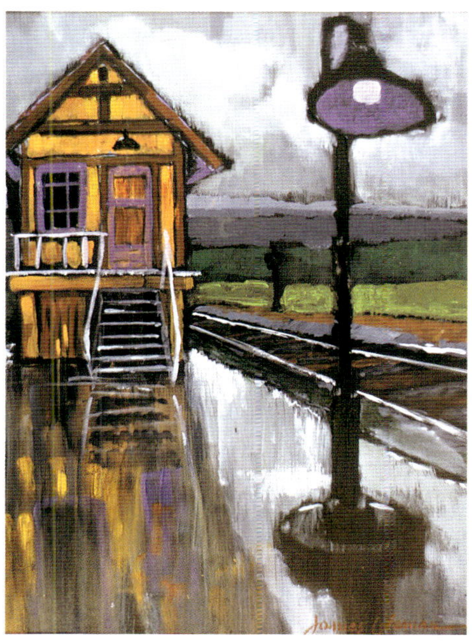

Train Station, 1973

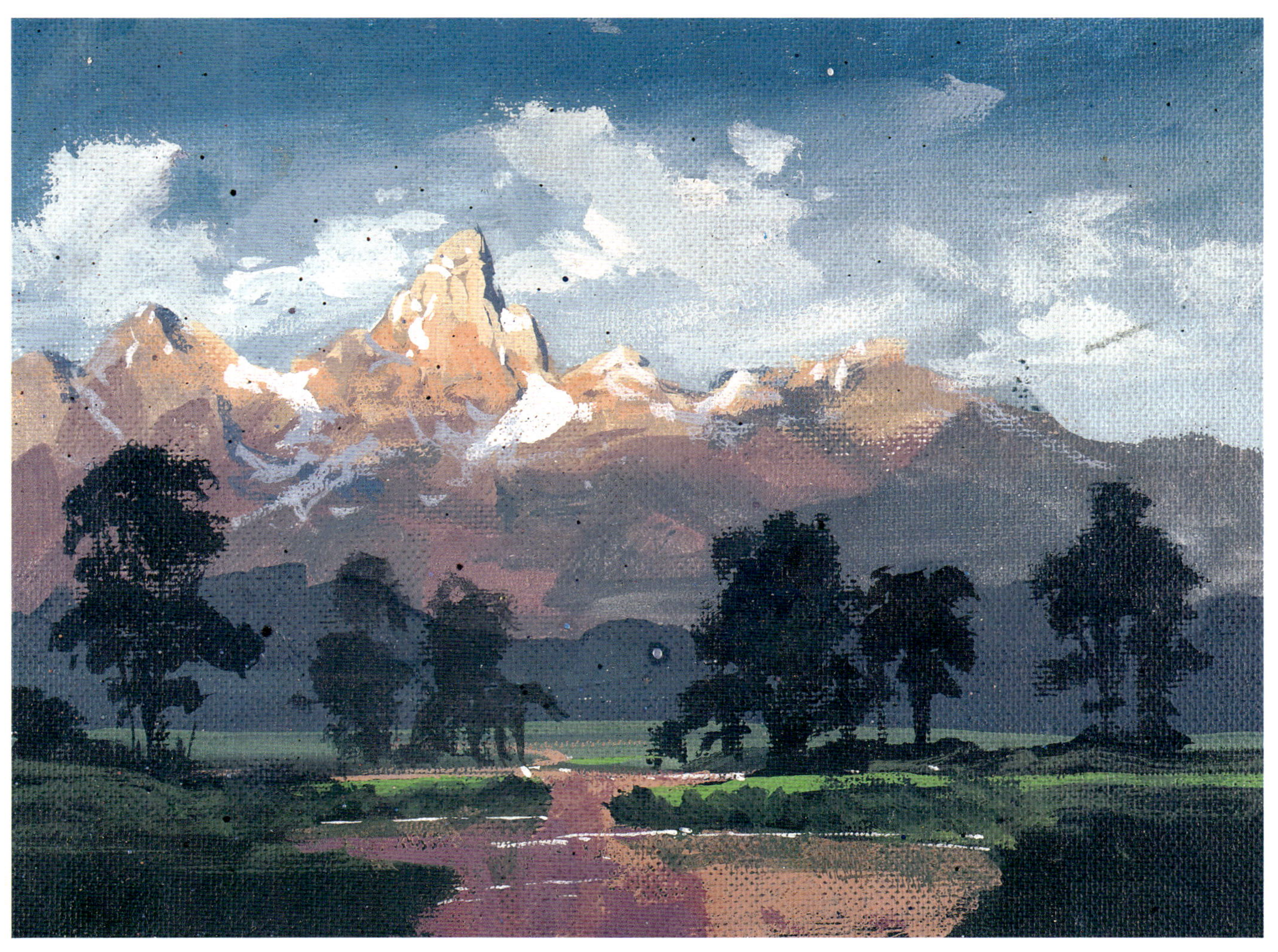

Teton National Park, 1970

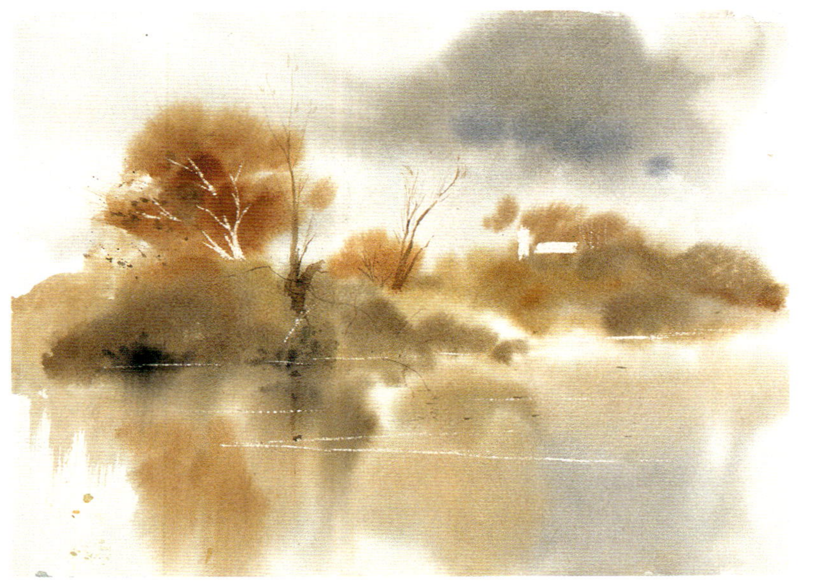

Early watercolors

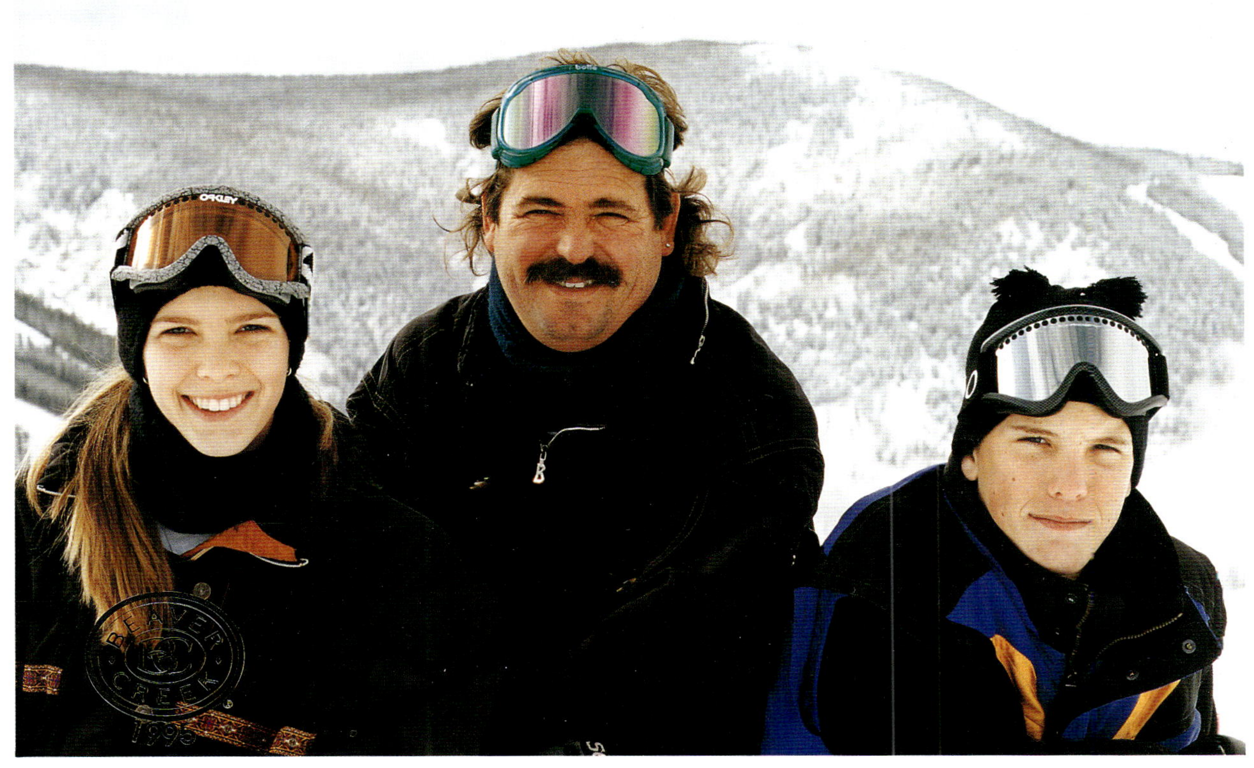

Jim skiing with his children, Kim and Scott

"It's interesting to me because it's simple. If you can translate a plain white tree trunk with different possibilities of light—warm light, cool light, no light, moonlight—it becomes an entirely different thing. It's the same way with waterfalls."

Yosemite has always been a favorite getaway for Coleman. He remembers the great national park as one of the first places his family took him as youth, and the first place he ever witnessed some of America's hidden waterfalls.

"I was so impressed—it was so unbelievably beautiful," he says. "The pools of water, the water crashing in the mist. I've always loved the mountains, and I've always been drawn to water.

"And there I was, watching this spectacular force of nature, which, in a way, was also very calm. It's like the ocean in that it's so powerful, but there's something about it that puts you in a kind of trance as you watch it, something very peaceful."

Coleman's work is full of long, graceful waterfalls cascading down the sides of deep tropical cliffsides or into glassy pools hidden away and protected by thick redwood forests. Nature's power is well represented, but at a safe distance. Coleman manages to paint them as serene elements that blend naturally with their environment.

"Obviously, if you were to go stand under one of the waterfalls in my paintings, it would get you," he allows. "But I paint them in a way that is non-threatening. In fact, that's the way I paint everything. I want people to feel like they could walk right into one of my paintings and feel total peace."

Some of the nation's other national parks burned powerful images into Coleman's memory as well: Yellowstone, Glacier National Park and, of course, the Pacific Northwest, where redwoods and evergreens grow together, and thick forests, veiled by misty fogs, stretch down the mountainsides and into the ocean.

"There's a park in California before you get to Carmel that made such an impression on me that I used to dream about it," he says. "I used to do paintings of the area because the trees were so gnarled and different. We spent a lot of time there when I was a boy, but it wasn't until years later that I went back and found the place. I still can't tell you exactly where it is on the map. But I remember everything about how it made me feel."

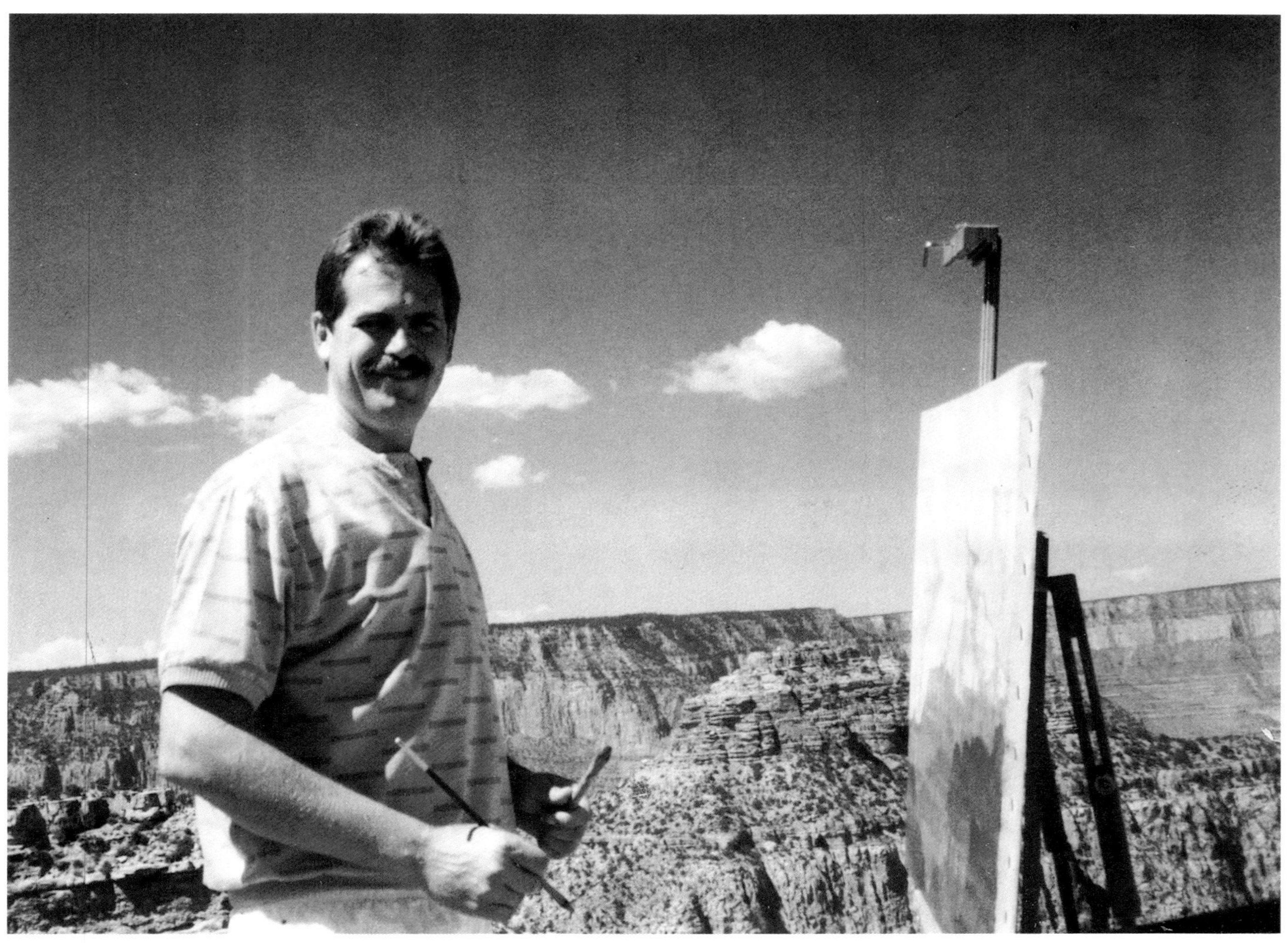

James painting in the Grand Canyon

There was yet another national treasure that had an impact on the young artist, one that is much easier to find on the map. "Seeing the Grand Canyon as a boy exposed me to the classic example of how a tremendous amount of color, which varied all the way from cool to warm colors, could be put together as a result of natural rock formations," marvels Coleman. "They are in such incredible shapes that when the light hits them, you have a tremendous amount of mood."

Though the years, he tried to figure out what it was about some of these places that made them so powerful. What was it that appealed so strongly to people who viewed the Grand Canyon, other than it was so colorful and. . . big?

"I finally figured out that it's the overwhelming spirit of the Canyon that makes it so special," he reveals. "I wanted to capture those emotions and put them in my paintings, and it took me years to get there."

When Coleman talks about the places he visited as a youth, he describes the parks and some of the mysterious treasures that lay hidden in their forests. But he doesn't care to take them out of context. The power and beauty of nature is even more evident, he maintains, on the American plains and in the desert.

"When we were traveling through the Midwest at night, we were surrounded by vast rolling hills of grass and wheat," he recalls. "The moon was so bright you could see everything! I remember my father turning the headlights off just to show us it was bright enough to drive without them.

"Years later, when I started to backpack in the desert, I became aware of the same thing. When the moon came up high in the sky, it was like broad daylight. That was when I realized that it doesn't matter where you are. . . it's all full of emotion."

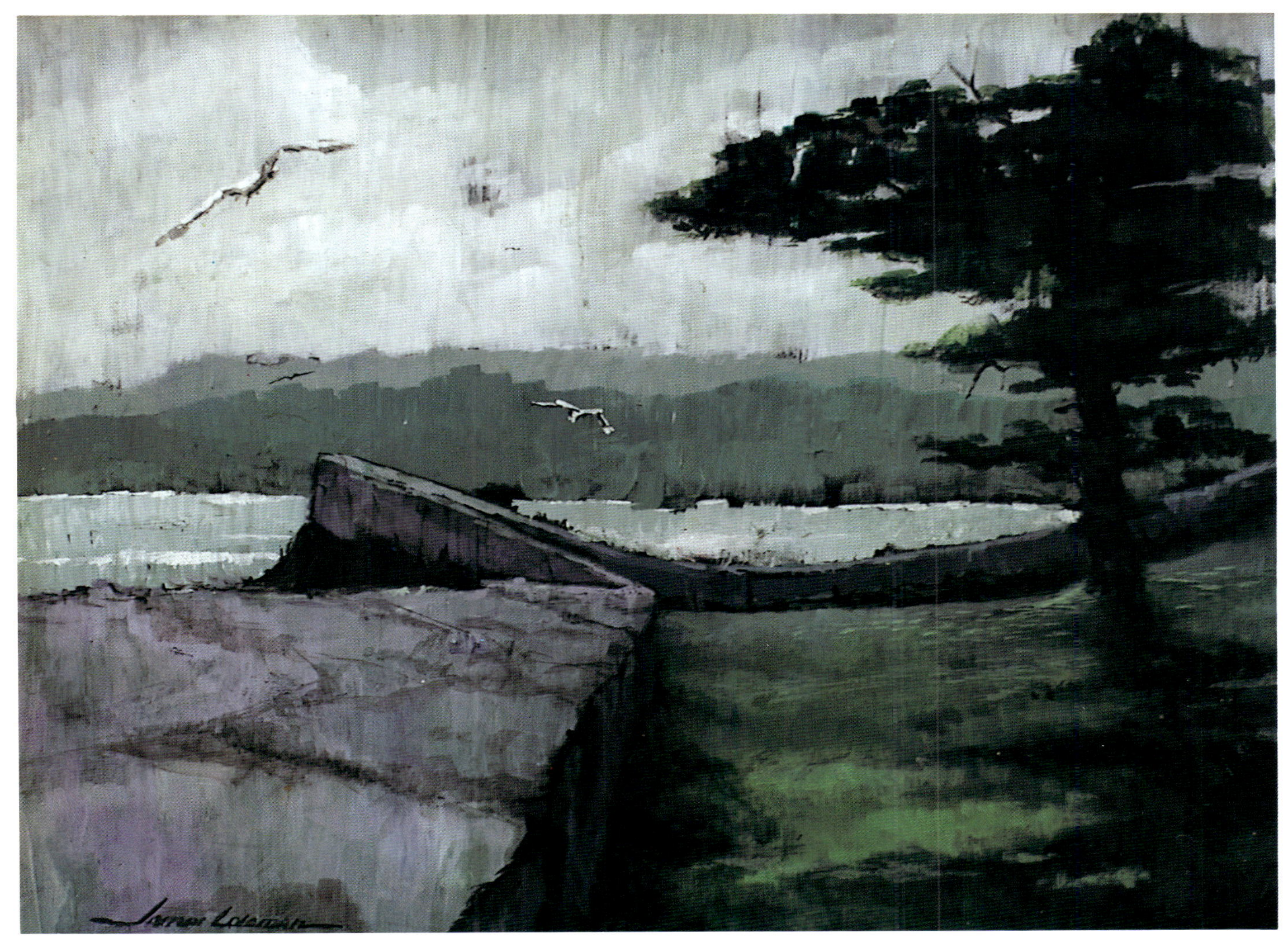

Wednesday Morning

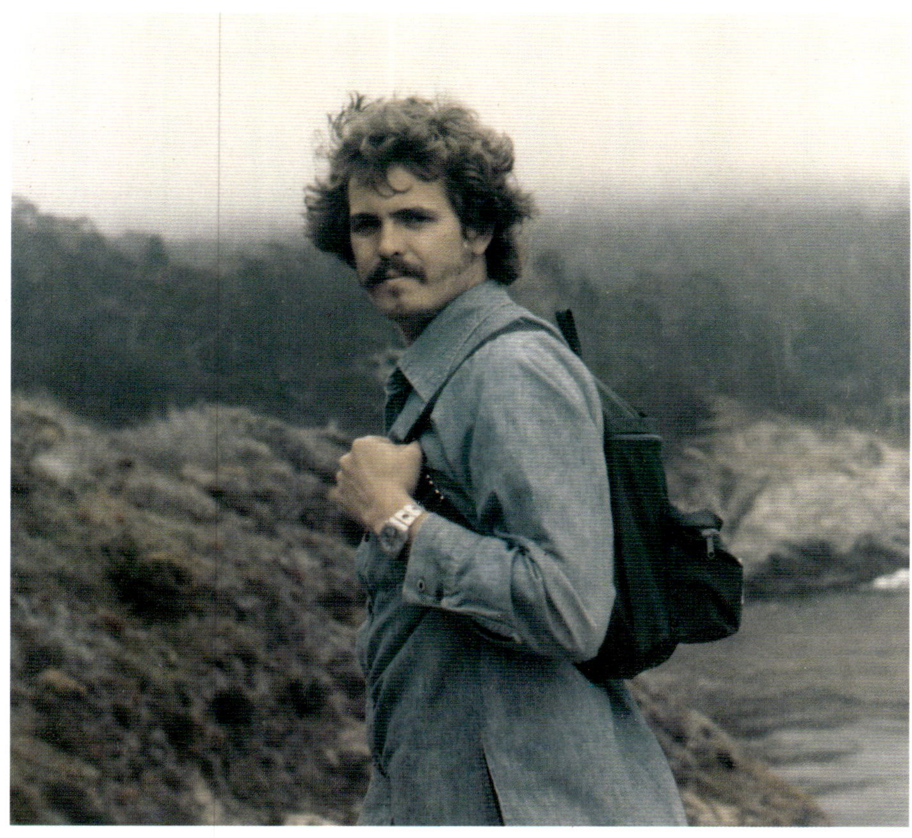

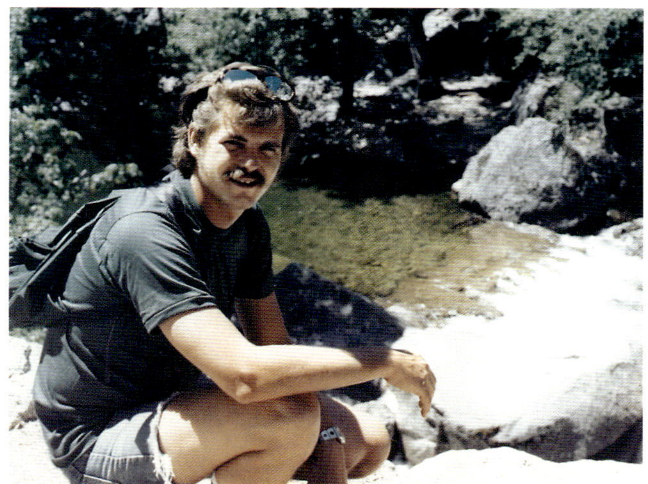

James backpacking in 1975

He also remembers being in New Mexico at the Mesa Verde and seeing the Indian ruins. Much like his experience on the Great Plains, a storm blew in off the desert with a tremendous wind.

"It was just this incredible power!" he exclaims. "When most people look out over the plains or the desert, they say 'So what? It's just a bunch of grass, or a chapparal.' But to me, there was real feeling about it. It was like the ocean. Once you get out beyond the cove, you have the same kind of vastness and cloud formations that are affected by the sun, the moon and the weather."

Though Coleman refuses to "overanalyze" his paintings, one might argue that clouds are a major theme in his work. "It's hard to paint the outdoors and ignore clouds," he points out. "They can change everything in terms of color and mood."

He had plenty of opportunity to study cloud formations growing up. Aside from family vacations, he was raised in California at the edge of the desert. He's also an avid hiker, backpacker and fisherman.

Coleman did a lot of hiking growing up, but he didn't start backpacking until his 30s. Once he got a taste of hiking into the mountains and camping out alone, he was hooked, often disappearing into the Sierras and staying for several days.

"It was a great experience for me because when you back-pack alone, you're really alone!" he says, his eyes growing intense. "It was especially beneficial for me because it built my confidence physically and emotionally knowing that I could be out there and do that, and to know that everything was OK. It made me feel like I was a natural part of it all."

There were things besides nature the young artist wanted to be a part of as well, especially if it was visual. Because his mother had worked at Disney for a number of years, he felt a great affinity for the film industry. When he reached his teens, he was interested in making films of his own and, thanks to an old 8mm camera given to him by his uncle, set his eye on Hollywood.

"I can remember Walt Disney getting the Academy Award for *Mary Poppins* and thinking, 'That's what I want to do someday, be a film director,'" he recalls. "So I experimented

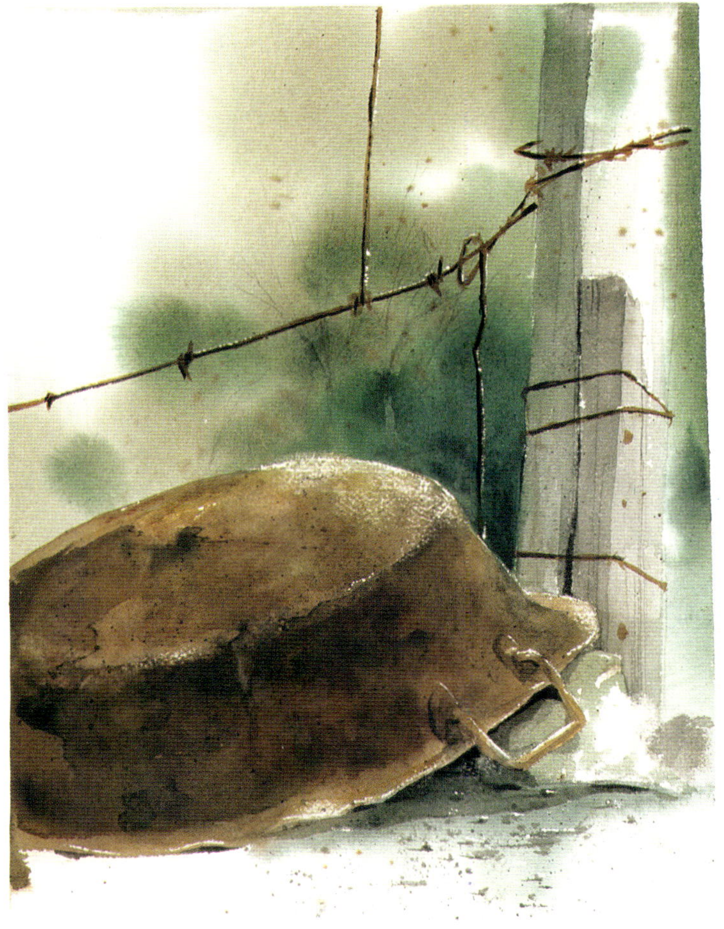

Years Ago, 1973

of creative energy that "had to go somewhere." He likens it to a window that needs to be opened. And once it is, there's a whole new world awaiting.

"The windows can be intimidating because you don't know what's out there," he explains. "But once you step through it, you're faced with this enormous amount of possibility. I never liked looking at windows directly because once I see one, I have to go through it."

Although the window to directing films had been closed before he had a chance to peer through it, Coleman could still buy a ticket to the movies. "The films that really had an impact on me were the ones with music and great visuals like *West Side Story*, which was so artistic and full of emotion, and *The Ten Commandments*, with its gigantic sets and powerful images," he says. "I also liked the Disney true-life adventures about animals, and I saw all of the animated movies.

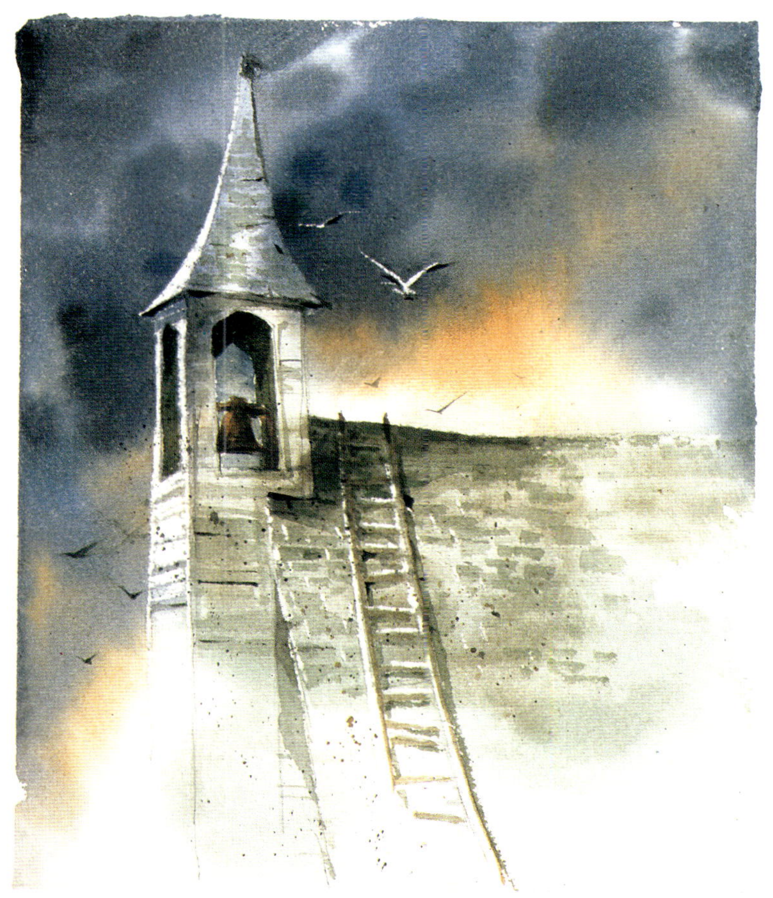

Morning After, 1973

with the camera and made little animated cartoons for a while before I realized I wasn't a cartoonist.

"To be honest, it was all wrapped up into one, which is why I can't recall feeling a special way about painting early on. It was all creative. It was a way of being and a way of thinking about life."

Making films, however, was not to be his livelihood. Like so many young people in Southern California, he was admonished by everything he'd ever heard about breaking into the film industry: "It's a really tough business, kid," or, "Do you realize how many people want to get into the movies?" or, "You're going to have to give up these dreams about making movies, son."

"That, unfortunately, is the worst thing people can do to a young creative person because they stop you before you know if you can make it," he says, shaking his head. "I know I was asked what I thought my chances were, and how I thought I was going to make a living as an artist."

Coleman says he has always had a tremendous amount

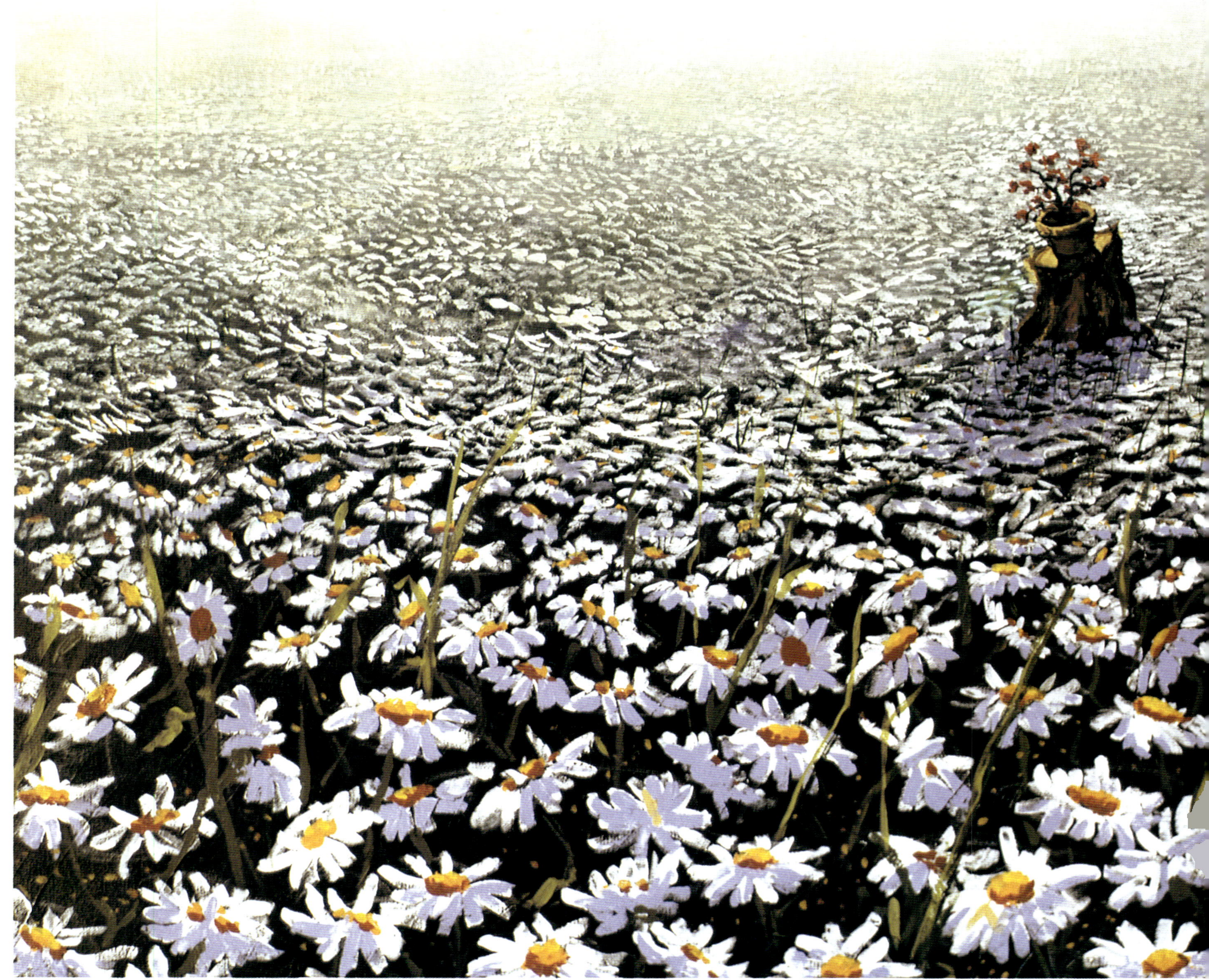

Daisies, 1969

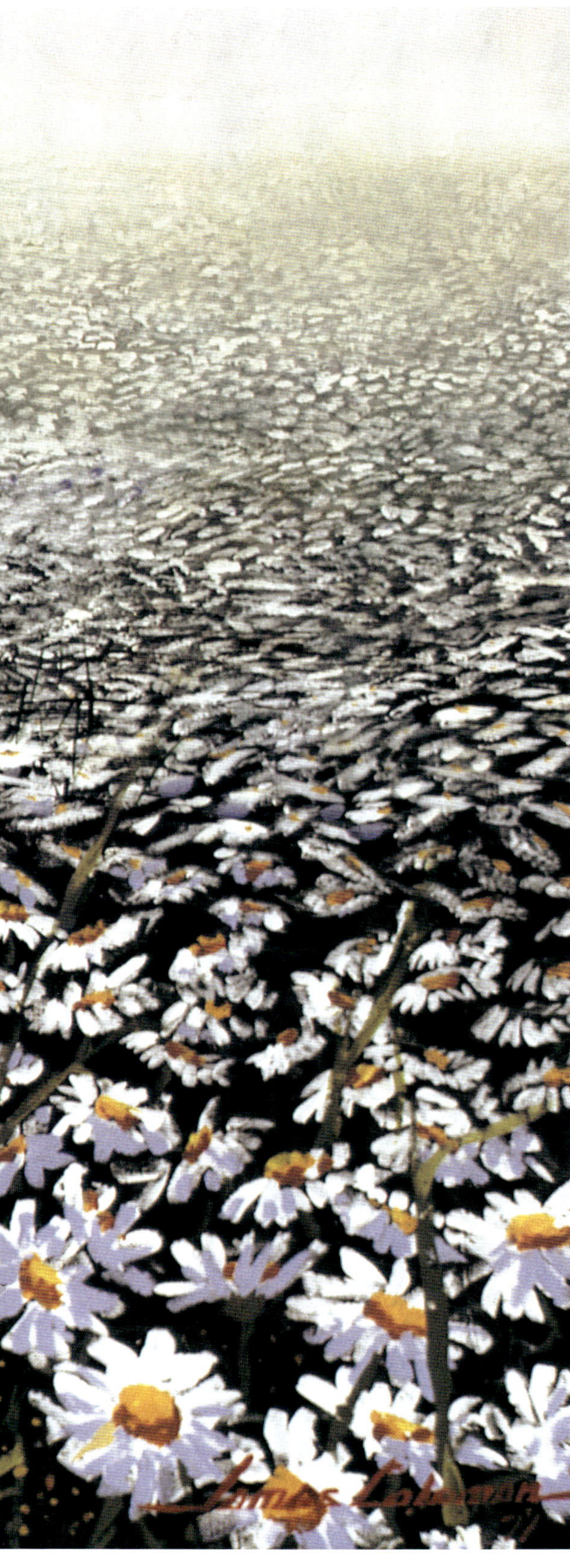

"To this day, I can walk outside with my kids, see a sunset and say, 'Oh my gosh, look at that!' Or, I can be watching a film and it's the same thing: 'Wow! did you see that?'"

It was what he saw outdoors, however, that made the greatest impressions on the young artist. When his parents took him on camping trips, Coleman didn't spend all of his time gazing at the clouds and contemplating how light transformed landscapes. He also loved to fish. As a little boy growing up in the Valley, he fished on the L.A. River, and he always took his tackle and rod and reel when he went camping.

There's nothing, he says, that allows one to settle down and experience the serenity of the outdoors like fishing. It's a pastime in which he has indulged all his life. In fact, in the late '80s, he took up fly-fishing, a sport requiring consummate skill and concentration. Several times each year, he tries to escape from his busy schedule and go fly-fishing for cutthroat trout on the Snake River in Wyoming.

"Fly-fishing has taught me how to immerse myself into nature much more quickly and completely," he explains. "To do it well, you have to be able to really feel the river and its rhythms, and then you have to be able to almost think like the fish.

"It's actually very much like painting. You have to take what you see and feel and then express it through your hand. For me, fly-fishing and painting complement each other very naturally. And they both add balance to my life."

Neither provide him as much balance as his children. Kim, Scott and Kadie create the true light in his world. As busy as he is, he doesn't hesitate to put everything he's doing on hold. "My kids are definitely the priority in my life," he says without hesitation. "Without them, I don't know where I'd be. I love them so much. They'll always be the inspiration for everything I hope to accomplish."

Undoubtedly, nature has been the other major influence in Coleman's life, and in his art. Hiker, backpacker, surfer, fisherman—he has been an outdoorsman all of his life. Yet, he's an extremely gentle man, unafraid to talk about the moods and emotions of what he has seen and how it affects what he paints.

"I believe that on a spiritual level, I'm very connected with nature," he says. "And when I'm feeling that connection, I feel right. Hopefully, that is translated through my work."

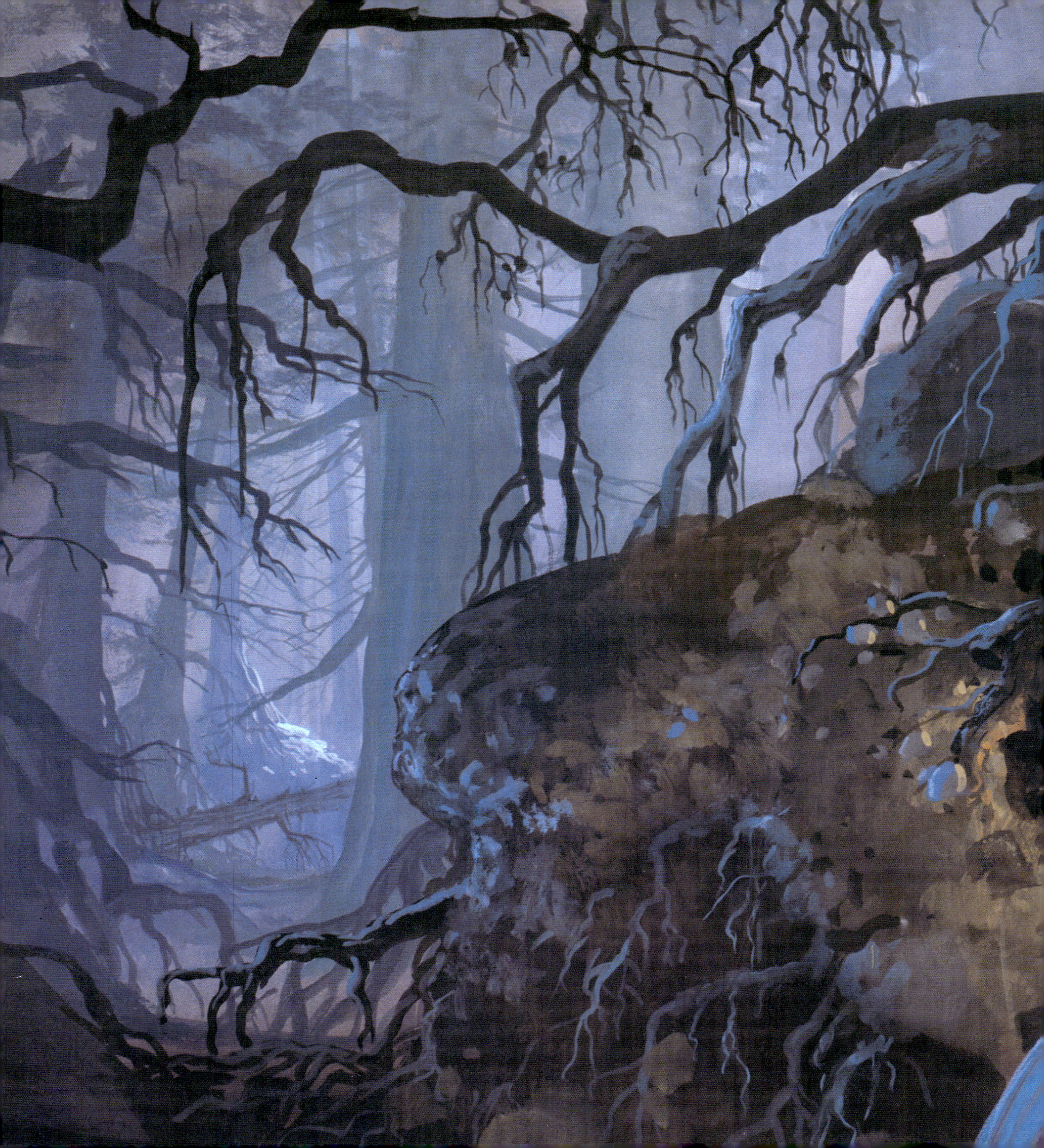

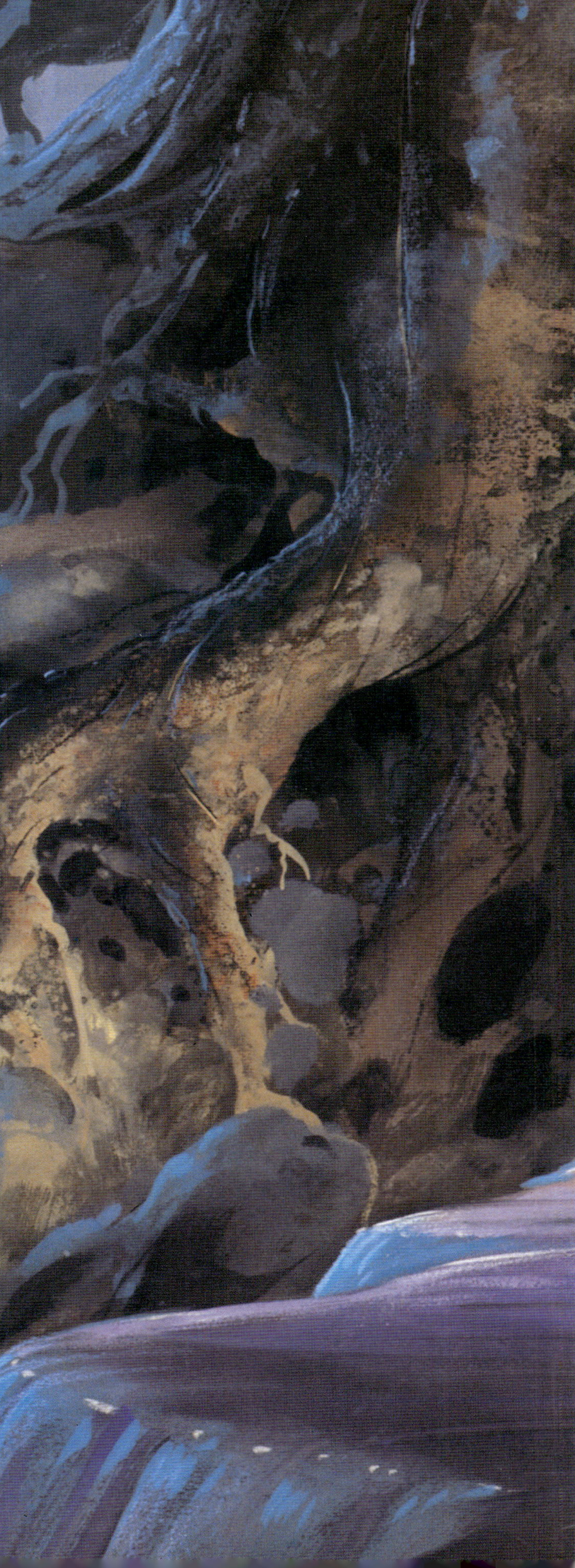

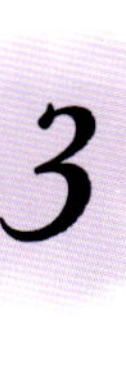

Miracles Do Happen

James Coleman's first glimpse into the "Wonderful World of Disney" promised to be something very special.

His mother had worked as a secretary for Walt Disney since the late '30s. And more than once, the legendary film producer had tousled her little boy's hair when she brought him to the studio. In those days, Walt called everyone who worked for him by their first names, and he never failed to acknowledge their children if he ran into them.

But on this particular occasion, there would be many more children than he would have time to tickle or say hello to. And there would be so many mommies and daddies with them that it would be impossible to remember all of their first names. For this was the big day, the one they'd all been waiting for. It was the opening day for Disneyland!

The 5-year-old Coleman was beside himself. What excitment! What a treat! What would he see at this wonderful place called Disneyland!? His mom and dad and big brother, Jeff, were all dressed in their finest clothes, and for once he didn't mind getting dressed up, either. And why not? This place was supposed to be really neat! His mom sort of worked there, and they were all getting in for free. Plus, he and his brother had seen all of the Walt Disney movies, some more than once, and some before anybody else got to see them. This was shaping up to be the best day of his life!

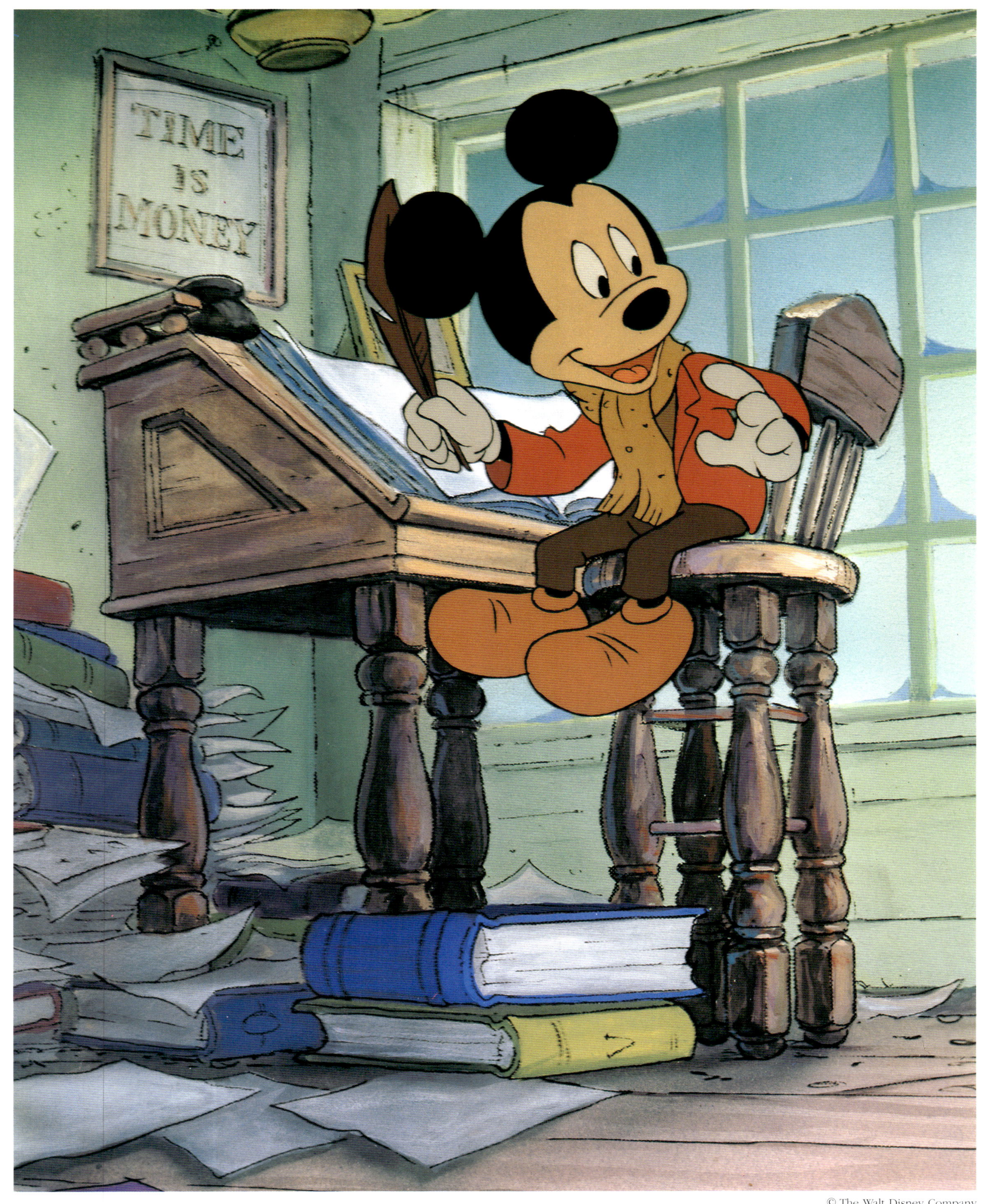

Mickey's Christmas Carol, 1983

"It was 1955, and I'll never forget it, that's for sure," Coleman says. "When we got there, my brother and I could barely contain ourselves we were so excited. But once we got in, it was so crowded with adults all I could see were their rear-ends. I was only 5, and their rear-ends were eye-level. I mean, I couldn't see anything the whole day! It was more like 'Rear-end land.'"

For the next 10 years, of course, Coleman would visit the Magic Kingdom many times, one of the perks from his mom's job. "It was a very visual place," he says. "They created complete environments, and that always intrigued me. You'd go to Tom Sawyer Island, and it was not just some place to go jump on rocks. It was a fantastic little world unto itself that could transport a child in space and time.

"When they built the Matterhorn, it was almost like a painting. Everything there was a caricature of real life, and I liked it because it sparked the imagination. It was much more than another amusement park."

Coleman remembers Walt Disney well from his boyhood. "Oh yeah, he was always just. . . around, and my mother would never miss an opportunity to shove me in front of him," he says, laughing out loud. "Usually when I saw him, he had on a red cardigan sweater. I remember hoping he would choose me for The Mickey Mouse Club."

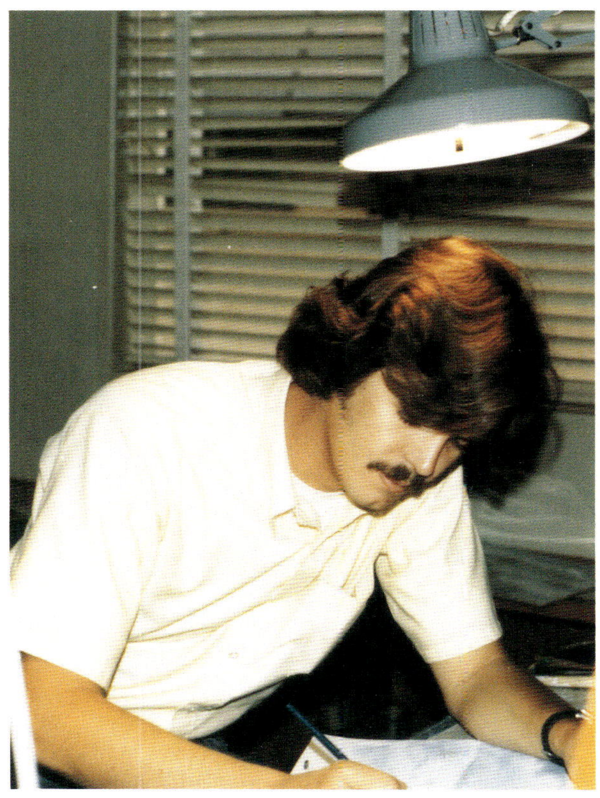

James working at Disney Studios

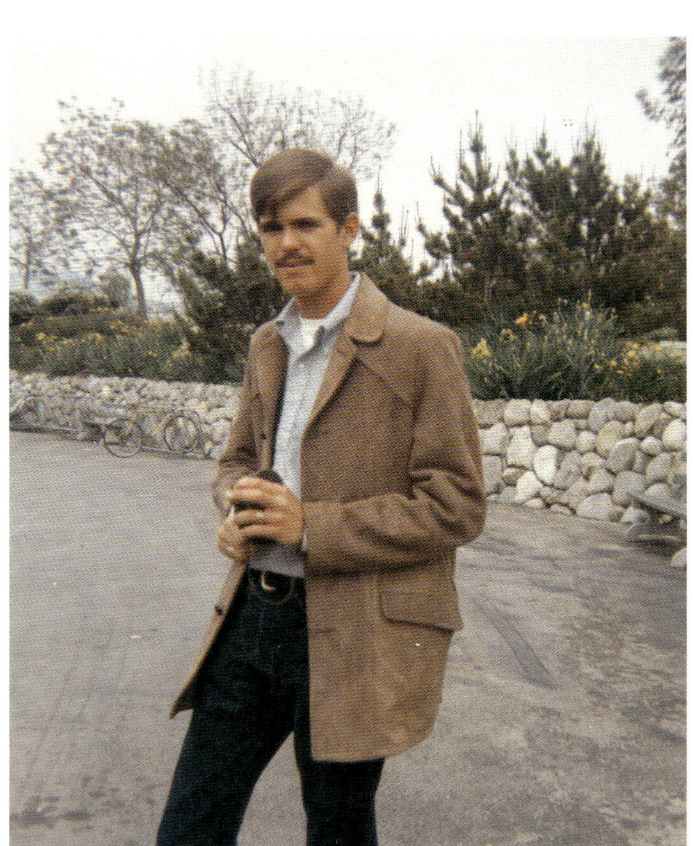

James with first camera

Coleman says Walt was always very nice to him, but whenever he spoke to the boy, he failed to recognize his subliminal theatrical talent as he stood motionless and in awe, clinging to his mother's skirt. Like Pinocchio, who ran off to join the circus with stars in his eyes, he hoped it would be the actor's life for him as well.

Always interested in film, he decided that television might hold the key to his future. His mother told him Disney Studios was looking for mail carriers, and she suggested that he work there for the summer. At least he would be in a related field, and she could introduce him to some people who had connections at NBC.

"I went over to the Disney studio, and they hired me for the mail room," he recalls. "Incidently, they told me I had to shave my moustache off. It was 1969, and they didn't allow moustaches at the company, even though Walt had one."

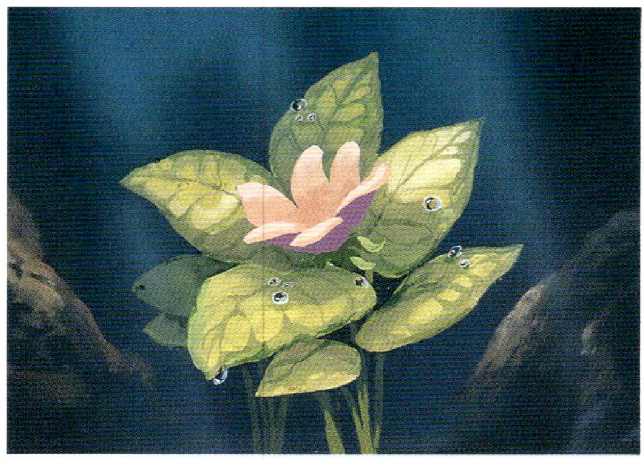

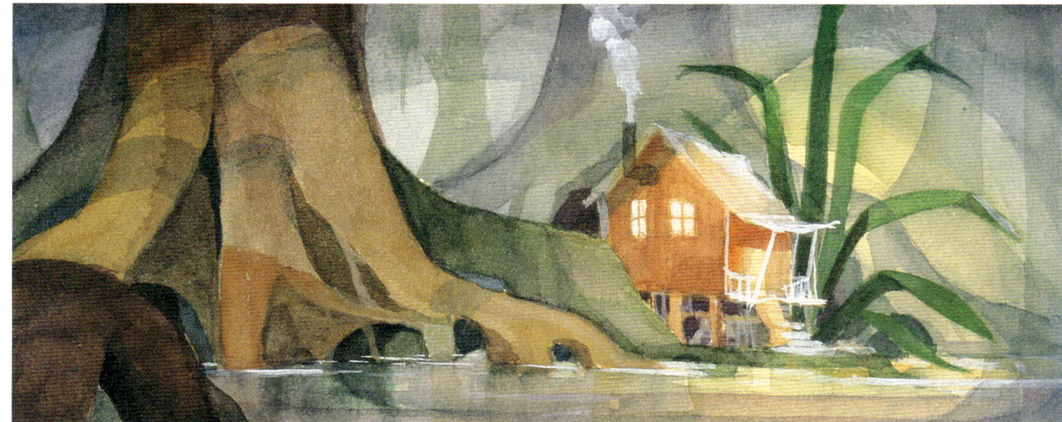

It wasn't long before a friend of his mother's arranged an interview for Coleman at NBC. "I always thought it would be great to be in announcing," he says. "I had the voice for it, and I liked people and had a pretty good sense of humor. In fact, I thought I could be the next Johnny Carson." The interview turned out to be a disaster, however. Trying to compensate for being so nervous, he came off over-confident, and NBC decided they would let Carson keep his job.

It was just as well. Within a few months, someone at Disney who'd heard Coleman liked to paint told him the company was having an art show in the studio library, and that anyone could enter.

"I have to say that Disney, at that time, was very receptive to young people showing initiative, no matter what level," he says. "You could have been the trash man and still been able to show your paintings alongside the work of the top artists in the company. They liked to bring people from the bottom up."

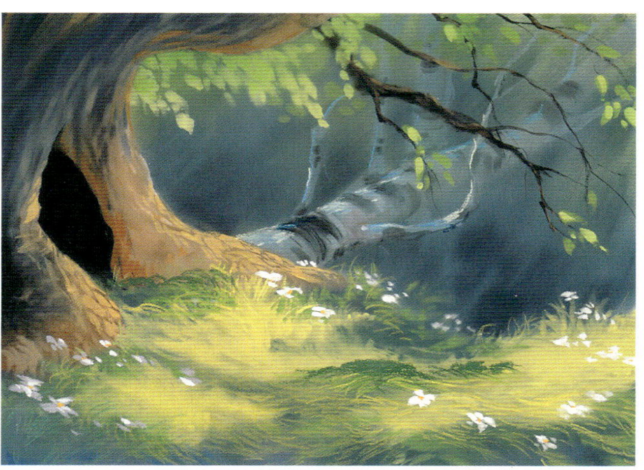

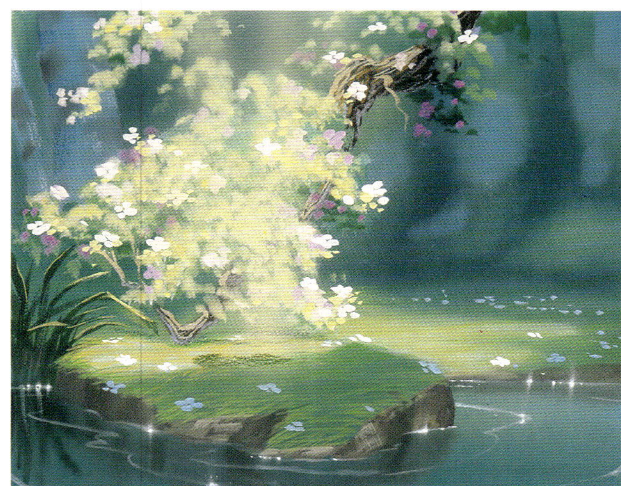

So Coleman entered a painting in the group show. A few days later, he got a call from a man named Ken Anderson, who had been one of the top artists and story men at Disney for years. He had designed the witch for the great Disney classic, *Snow White*, which won a special Academy Award for the first Feature Animated Film. And he did much of the animation sequences for *Mary Poppins*, another big Oscar winner.

"Ken had known my mother for many years, but for me, to be called into his office. . . was just unbelievable," he says with astonishment. "He was a legendary artist. So I went in and he said, 'I saw your painting at the exhibition, and you've got a talent. Some of the other artists here think so, too. Have you ever thought about going further with it and working here as an artist?'"

The opportunity of a lifetime was almost breaking Coleman's door down. But, unbelievably, he politely turned the offer down, explaining that he wanted his art to be his own, and that he really wasn't interested in animation.

"I was slightly idealistic," he admits, rolling his eyes to register his own disbelief. "At the time, I was dating my soon-to-be wife, Cathy, and she said, 'Are you crazy!?' I told her my art was too important to me and that I didn't want it to be part of a company. I wanted it to stand on its own."

Cathy, her feet more firmly planted on the ground, urged him to reconsider. It could be a good way to make a living, and you'll still be an artist, she pleaded. Finally he relented, saying he'd give it some thought.

An interesting side note to the tale was that the painting Coleman had entered in the show was purchased by Disney's head of labor relations. He remembers having a hard time collecting from the executive, but he finally got his money and used it as a downpayment on a wedding ring. It was the first painting he ever sold.

Shortly thereafter, Coleman signed up for a one-man show in the library. He was still working in the mail room, and had just married Cathy, his high school sweetheart. Each night, he went home and painted until early in the morning. By the day of the show, he had 30 paintings ready, and his wife, parents, friends, aunts and uncles came over to the studio to support him.

"This was a major event for me," he acknowledges. "At first, I didn't realize just how major it was. But it literally changed my life. I had no idea what it would lead to."

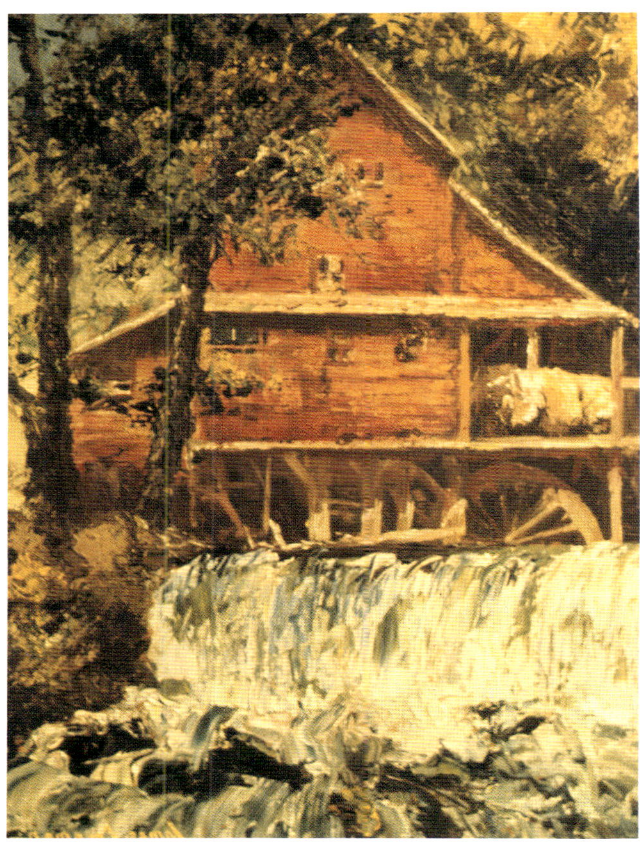

Painting sold to Roy Disney

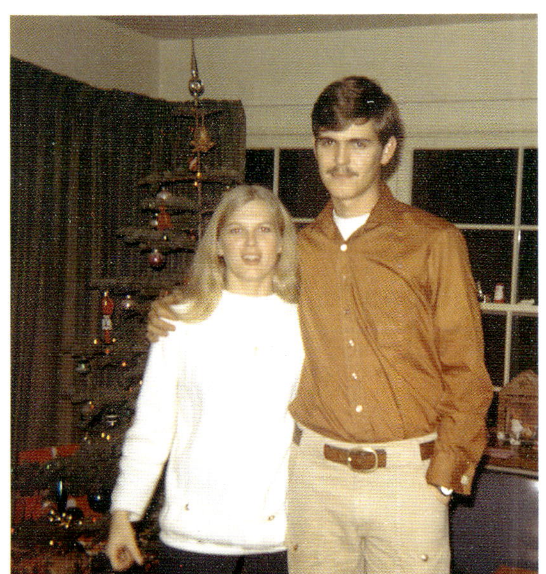

James and his wife Cathy, Christmas 1968

The response to his work was overwhelming. Roy Disney, Walt's brother, bought one of the paintings, shocking Coleman and his friends and relatives alike. "He was really old, and I'd seen him shuffling down the hall a few days before the show," the artist remembers. "I stopped him and said, 'Mr. Disney, I'm having a show in the library, and I'd be honored if you'd come and look at my work, if you have time, sir.' He said, 'It's Roy.' And to my great surprise, he showed up and bought an old mill I'd done for $30. I sold the rest of the paintings to my aunts and uncles."

The real opportunity, though, again came from the Animation department. Ken Anderson and some other artists called him in and asked him if he'd be interested in painting backgrounds for Disney. They told him he had a very unique style and that he used colors they wanted to use in a new film called *The Rescuers*. But, again, Coleman declined, telling them he knew nothing about painting for film.

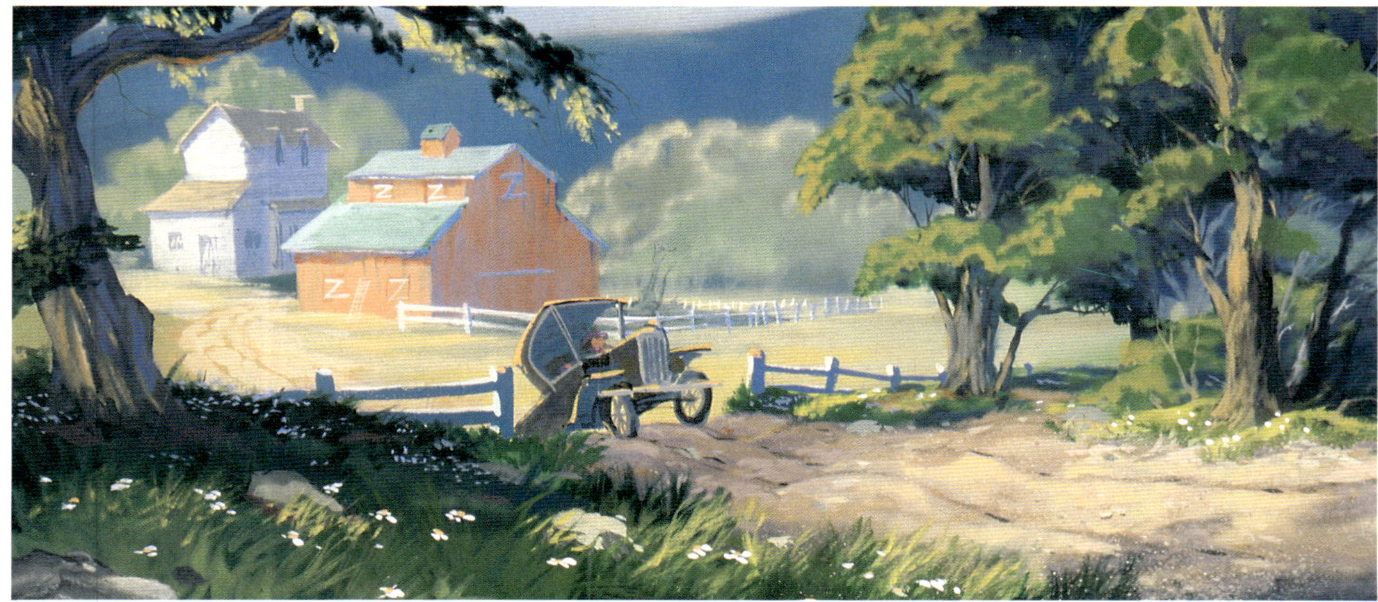

"We don't want anyone who knows anything about this," Anderson responded. "We want someone who's fresh."

Under normal circumstances, Coleman says, they probably wouldn't have taken the time to even view the work, which consisted mostly of landscapes and barns. But, for some reason, they were looking for a different style, a different look for their new film.

He went home after the show and had a long talk with his wife. She pointed out that NBC had never called him back, and she asked him, like so many others had, what he was going to do for a living.

"She had a point, I realized," Coleman admits. "I started thinking about it and figured that this wasn't exactly what I wanted to do, but I would be getting paid while I painted. Plus, I'd probably learn a lot."

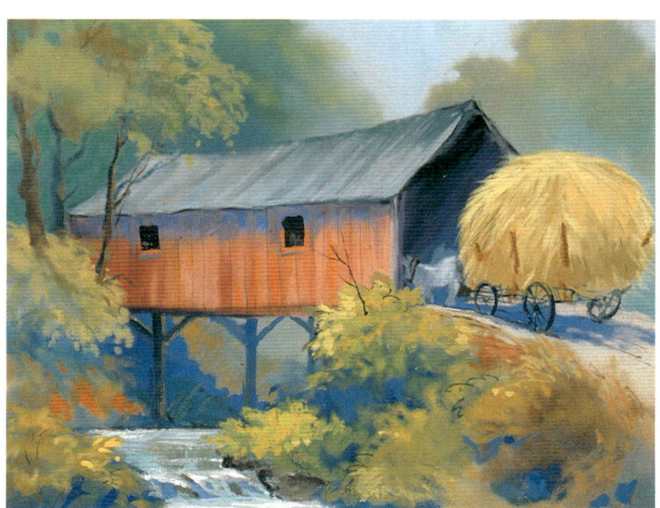

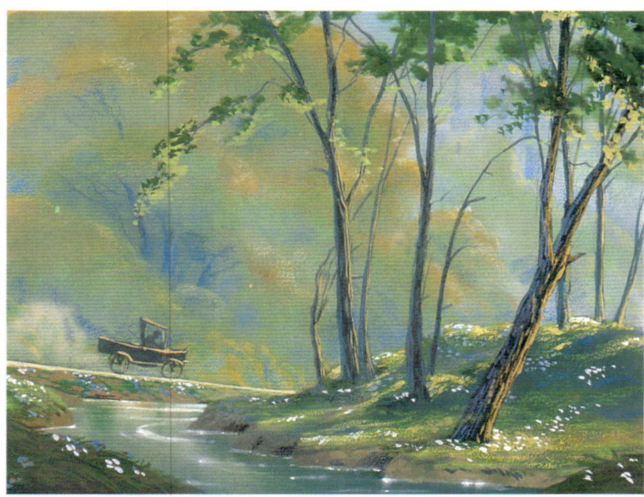

Of course, everyone was astonished at his reluctance. "Are you crazy!?" he heard again and again. "This is Walt Disney Studios offering you a chance!"

So he accepted the offer, which was not exactly a promotion. He was to remain in the mail room and work on backgrounds for *The Rescuers* in his spare time. Anderson took him upstairs and introduced him to the great Al Dempster, the head of the Background department who had been the lead painter and designer for *The Jungle Book*, among many others.

"I also met Ralph Hulett, who was just this incredible artist," Coleman says. "And I don't use the word 'artist' lightly—this guy could paint. He was talented, and he was much more into fine art than the other artists."

Six months after his art show, Coleman was moved to the Art Props department, where he framed, matted and worked in the animation "morgue," which was the storage basement for all of the material from the old films. Meanwhile, he spent every spare moment in Animation talking to the artists and working on storyboards and dry mounts for Anderson.

"Actually, I was working with all of the artists in animation," he says. "One of the biggest influences for me was having a chance to work with Ward Kimball, one of the more innovative talents working there at the time."

The Art Props department often doubled as a support department for Animation, especially on television projects such as the *Wonderful World of Disney*. Coleman, because of his talent and enterprise, soon emerged as a young artist with potential.

"I actually got to work on some art for Ward," he remembers. "He was in charge of a weekly series called '*The Mouse Factory*,' and I remember making these little blow-up men with wing-tip shoes that I had to paint with an airbrush. It was great experience because I knew I was going to have to learn to airbrush if I was going to be in the Background department. And I had an opportunity to work under guys like Ward and John Emerson."

At Walt Disney Studios, Coleman explains, the key word had always been "initiative." While he worked full-time in Art Props and assisted the heavyweights in Animation, he also worked at home on designs for *The Rescuers*. Anderson, the old-timer, loved it.

"That's what it was all about," Coleman adds. "It's how much initiative do you have? That's what gets you there. You have to go that extra mile."

Eventually, he started working on his own on new ideas and designs and showing them to the various artists. In the beginning, they weren't interested. They told him the work was nice but that it wasn't "Disney."

"I thought about it, and a bell went off in my head," he says. "They didn't want anything *that* different. They wanted what Disney had always wanted—beautiful artwork with a slightly different slant on it."

Then it dawned on him that he had the entire animation morgue at his disposal. So he decided he'd go down and look at all of the old films and find out how to duplicate the early artwork. His strategy was to learn the style and then "tweak" it enough to sell it upstairs.

The timing couldn't have been better. Art Props needed more space in the basement and had just assigned him the task of going to the morgue and clearing out some of the old cels.

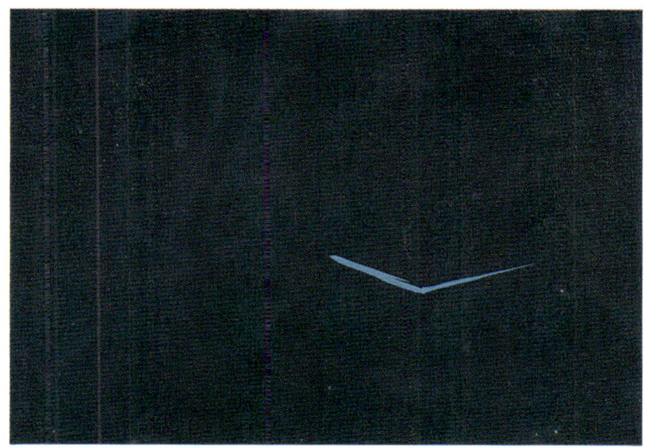

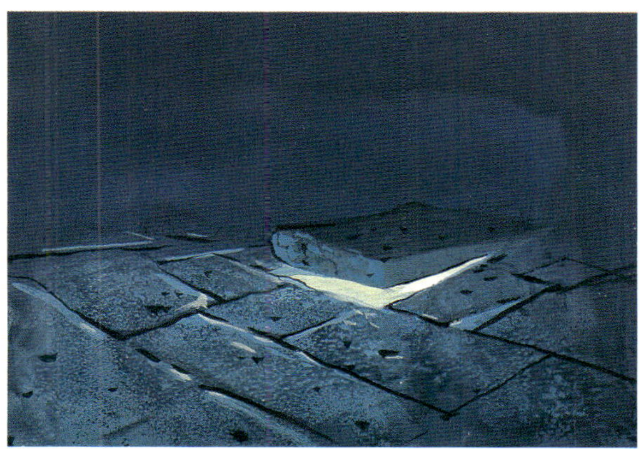

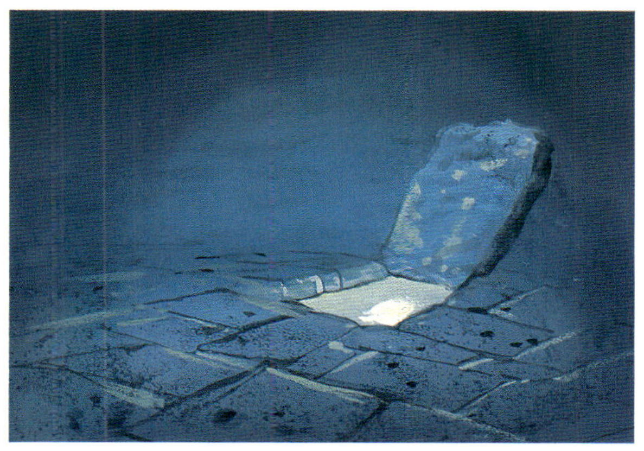

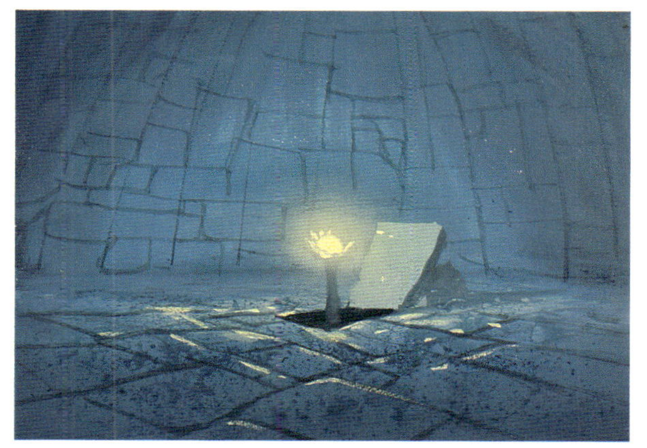

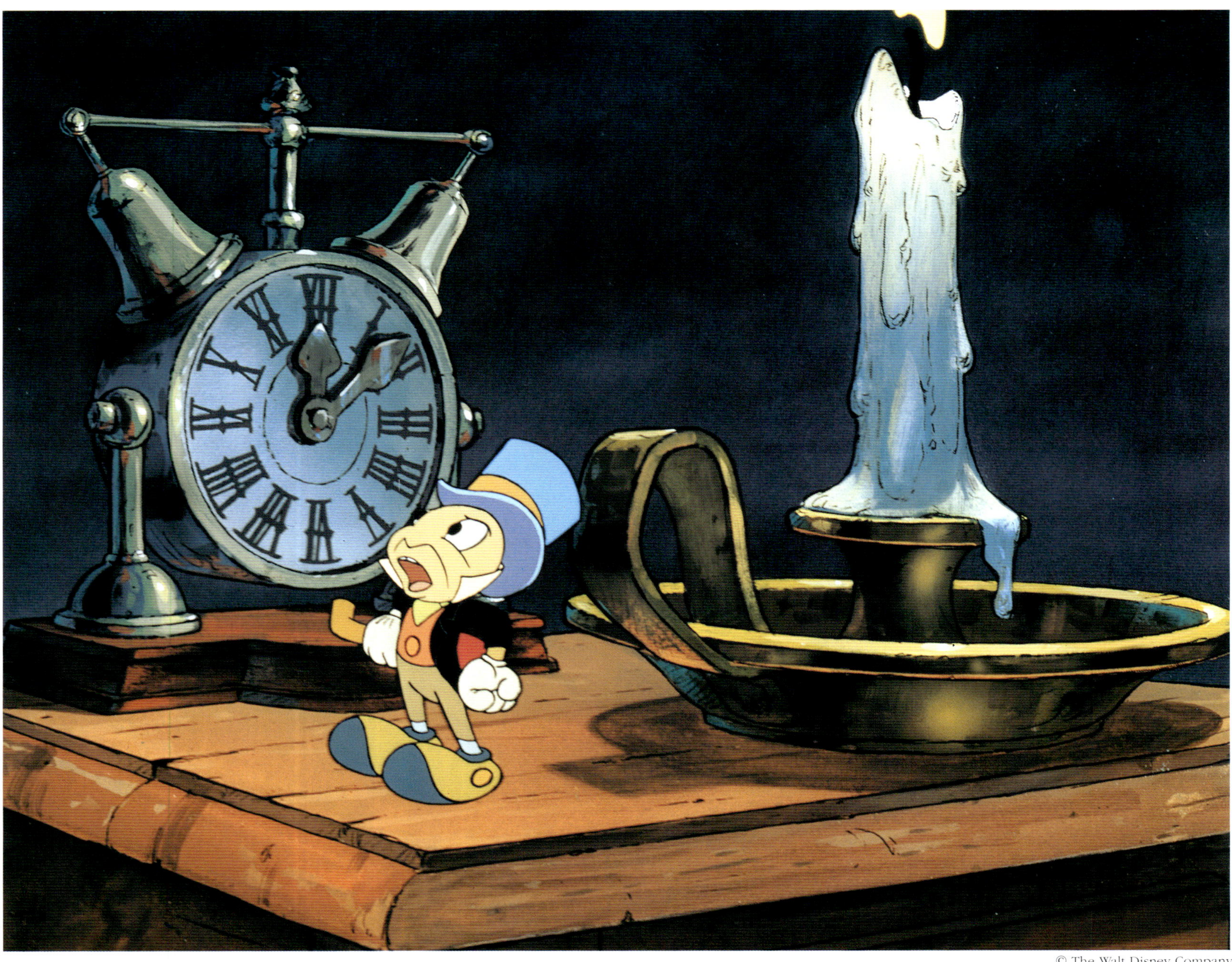

Mickey's Christmas Carol, 1983

"The entire movie of *Lady and the Tramp* was in a room down there," he says. "They told me to throw away all of the cels from the film except for three or four from each scene."

At the time, animation was going through a lengthy lull in the film industry. No one guessed that animation cels from Walt Disney pictures would one day fetch tens of thousands of dollars each. Coleman did as he was told and, much to the current dismay of animation collectors the world over, unwittingly threw away most of the original artwork for the beloved *Lady and the Tramp*.

The animation morgue wasn't the only room Coleman was asked to clean out in his early years with the company. Walt Disney died in 1966, and the family had his office at the studio sealed so it would be left untouched. Evidently, this decision was reversed a few years later, and Coleman and another employee were asked to enter the mysterious office and clear it out so it could be placed on exhibit.

"We were both kind of excited, and a little nervous, because he was such a legendary figure, and who knew what we might find in there?" Coleman says. "At first, it felt like we were treading on holy ground, or opening an ancient chamber in a pyramid. When we got in, it was much like any other

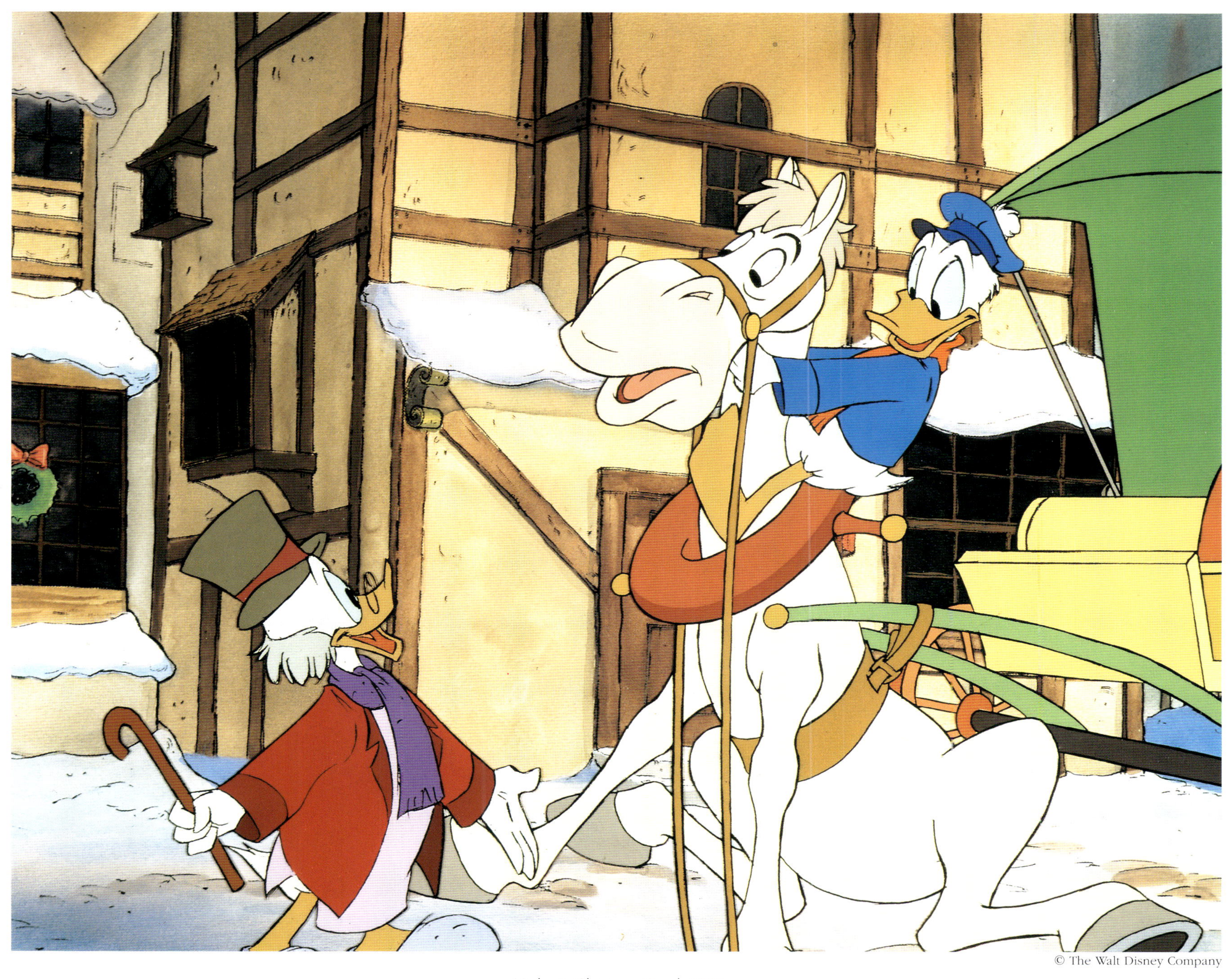

Mickey's Christmas Carol, 1983

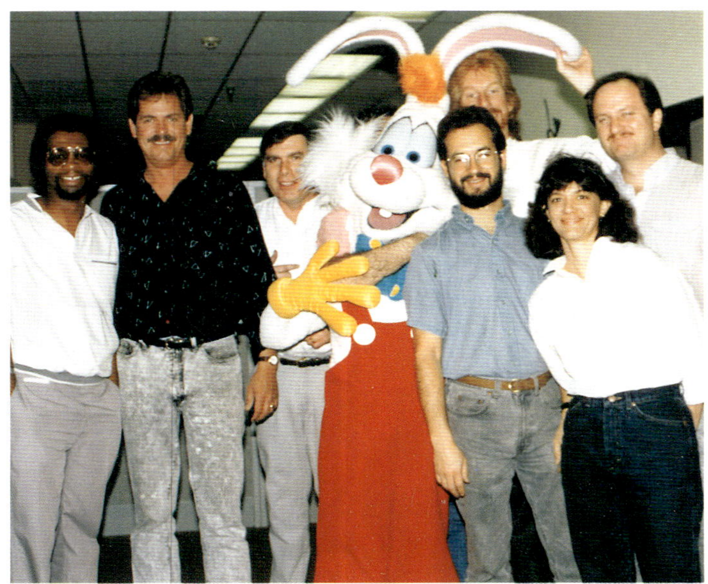

From the right – Bob Stanton, Christy Maltese, Brian Sebum, Dean Goren, Roger Rabbit, Phil Phillipson, James Coleman & Don

executive's office, with some pictures and a few items of Disney memorabilia here and there. He was a creative man with exceptional vision, but–as his office indicated–he was never pretentious, or garrish about his remarkable achievement."

There was a bright side to the cel disposal tragedy, though. The assignment enabled him to spend countless hours in the morgue, using his breaks and lunch hours to copy old animation backgrounds from the '30s, '40s and '50s. He was learning how to paint the way Disney artists used to do it.

It was much harder than he thought, but he persisted and finally mastered the style. When production was ready to begin on *The Rescuers*, the background artists saw what Coleman was doing and cleared a desk off for him in the Background department. They told him they didn't have the money to pay him, but that he could come up there and work whenever he wanted.

"In the meantime, they were about to start production on one of the *Winnie the Pooh* films—*Winnie the Pooh and Tigger, Too*," he recalls. "So I worked on some thumbnail sketches for that. I figured if I pinned them up on my desk, the director would come by and see them and maybe like them.

"Of course, that never happened," he snickers. "But, when they actually started production, they asked if I'd be interested in being an apprentice on the film. And I immediately said, 'Sure!'"

The man in charge of the film, Bill Lane, hurriedly assigned him a background to paint and then left for the weekend. "It was an old log in the mist in the forest, one of the hardest things you'd ever want to paint," Coleman says. "He just gave it to me without thinking I wouldn't know what to do.

"I started working on it, and I was just dying—I was so nervous. One of the older artists saw me and kindly offered me a different background to paint, and I didn't do much better on that. It was grueling, but I finally got the hang of it. In fact, once I did, I thought to myself that I might be able to get really good at this."

After the Pooh film, however, they moved him back to Art Props, explaining that they couldn't afford him when they weren't in production on a major film. This was the '70s, and animated movies were not receiving the fattest of budgets. In actuality, it wouldn't be until the phenomenal success of *The Little Mermaid* that animation, after a 30-year hiatus, would regain its rightful place in the film industry's boardroom.

Coleman was absolutely dejected. He'd worked at Disney for three years and didn't like taking steps backward. But he was far from defeated. He continued on his own to work on pre-production sketches for *The Rescuers*, the next film up. It was during this period that Ralph Hulett died, and Al Dempster, Bill Lane and many of the Hall-of-Famers decided to take their retirements.

"They told me they wanted a completely different style with *The Rescuers*, so I started coming up all these ideas and pinning them up on the board again," he says. "I hoped Wolfgang Reitherman, the director, would walk through and be impressed."

Strike two—"Woolie," as everyone referred to Reitherman, never stopped by to bestow praise on the young apprentice. It was a long shot, and Coleman knew it. He'd worked for the company long enough to learn some of its politics. There was a strict heirarchy in Animation, and a young artist would never presume he could just approach a director with his own ideas.

Sometimes, what one knows can use a little nudge from whom one knows. The legacy of Beth Coleman's 51-year career at Disney paid off once again for her talented son. An old friend of the family, Don Griffith, the art director for *The Rescuers*, had taken quite a liking to her son. He was someone Coleman could go to when he needed to talk to somebody, and his support had proven invaluable on more than one occasion.

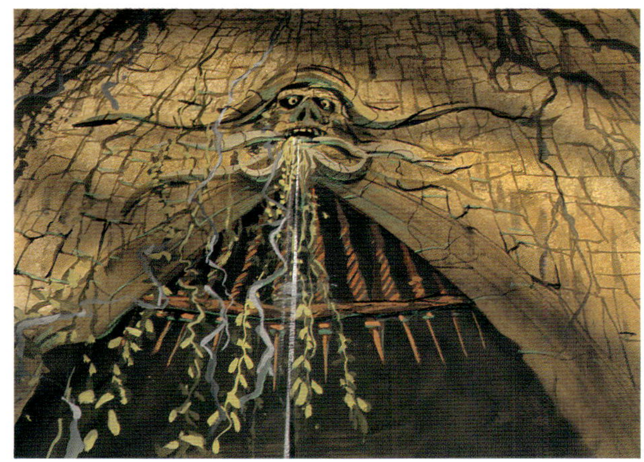

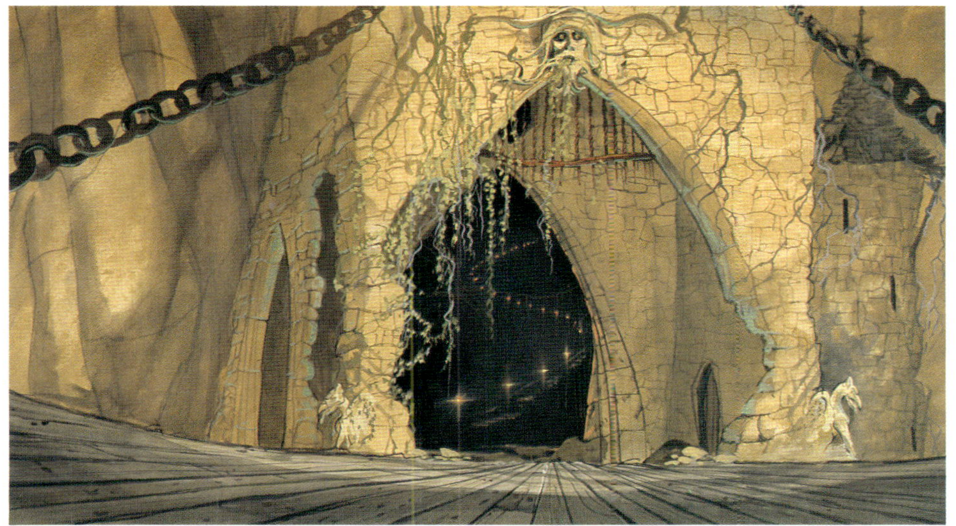

One of Griffith's thousand duties as art director was to critique the background scenes and make changes. Occasionally, he would take some of Coleman's background work in to Woolie and show him what the kid was up to. Woolie would say, "Yeah, yeah" and continue to puff on his big cigar. But Griffith was shrewd; at least Woolie started to become aware of who Coleman was.

When the department started rolling on *The Rescuers*, Coleman was called back up from Art Props to work on the film. He'd been there every day anyway, at the same desk where he'd been spending his breaks and lunch hours. The company had brought in a new man to run the Background department, and Coleman noticed right away the guy was going "out on a tangent" as it related to Disney style. He'd already been down that road himself.

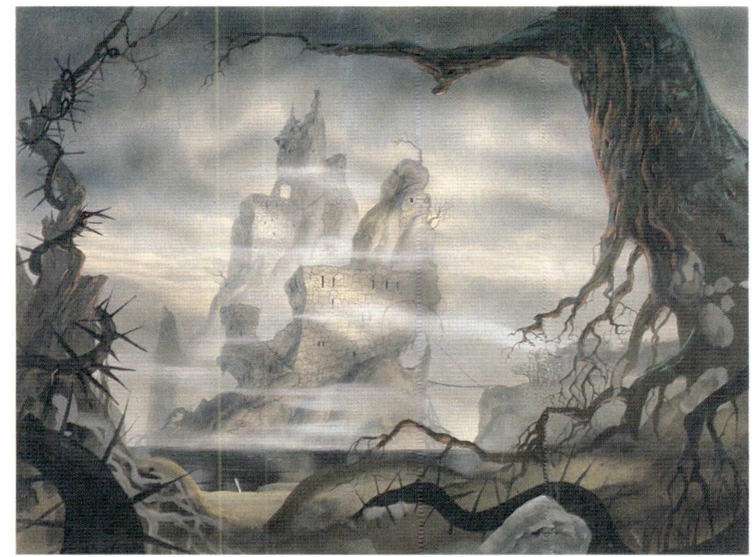

"He was thinking they were going to do the whole thing in transparent watercolor, and I knew it wasn't going to work," he says. "I'd heard the senior artists and art directors discuss what they wanted and, even at my age, I knew it was going to be unacceptable.

"So I started doing things on my own that were more traditional, and they took some of it up to Woolie, who said 'Yeah, yeah, that's the way we want to go. This is looking good!'"

One sequence in particular, the longest in the film, needed to be reworked, Coleman recalls. Half of it was painted in watercolor, the other half in poster paint.

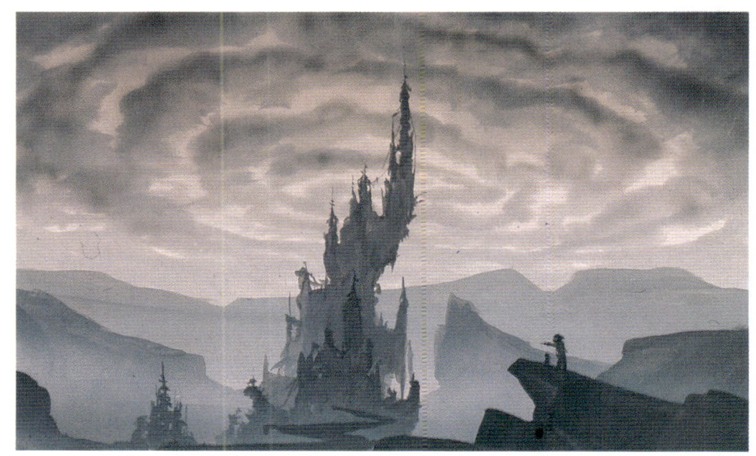

"None of it fit together, and Woolie wasn't happy with it," he says. "Even though I was a junior artisit, I went to Don Griffith and asked him: 'Don, if I come up with another color scheme and another way of painting this, do you think we can talk Woolie into just re-doing the whole sequence?'"

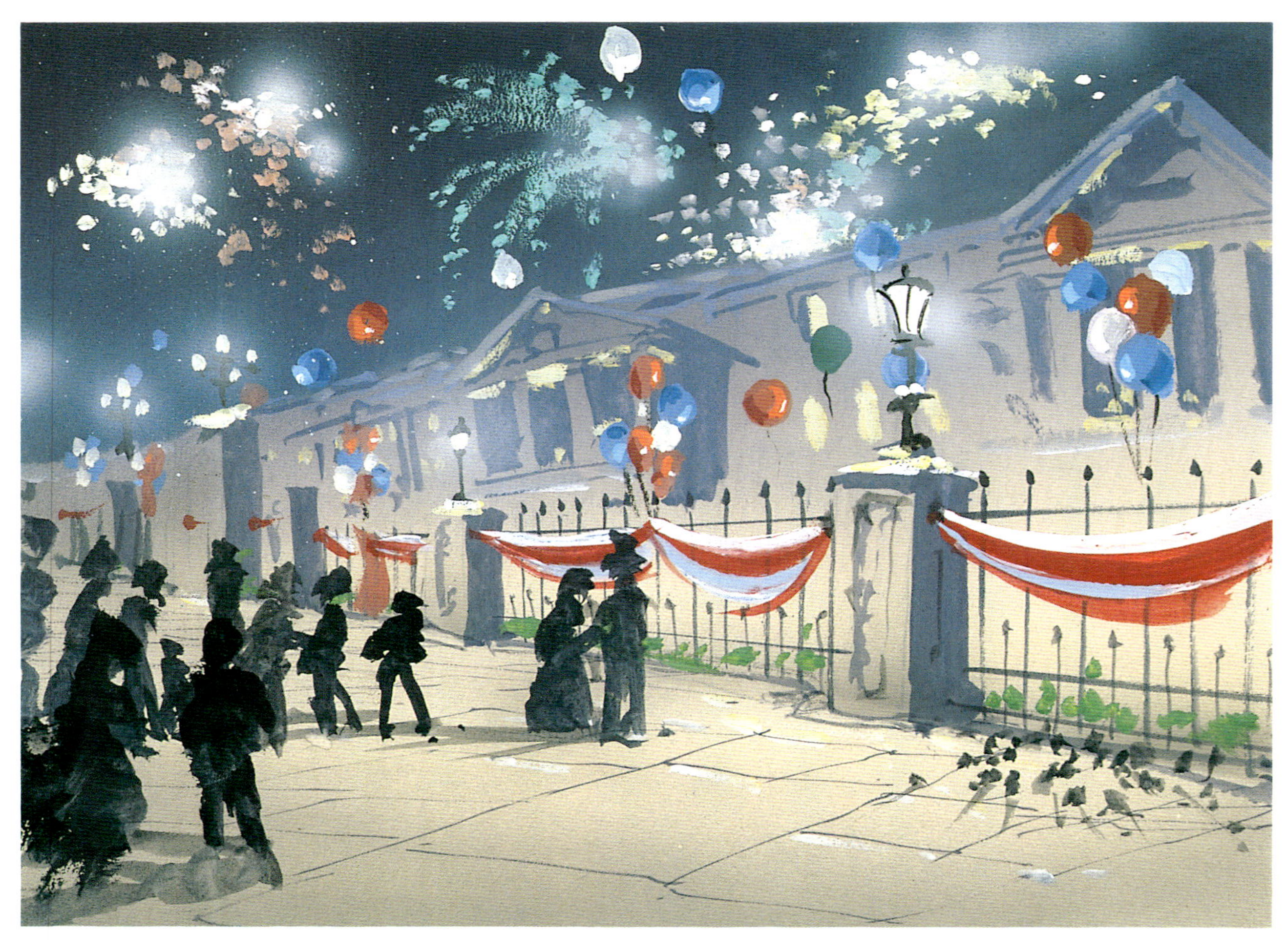

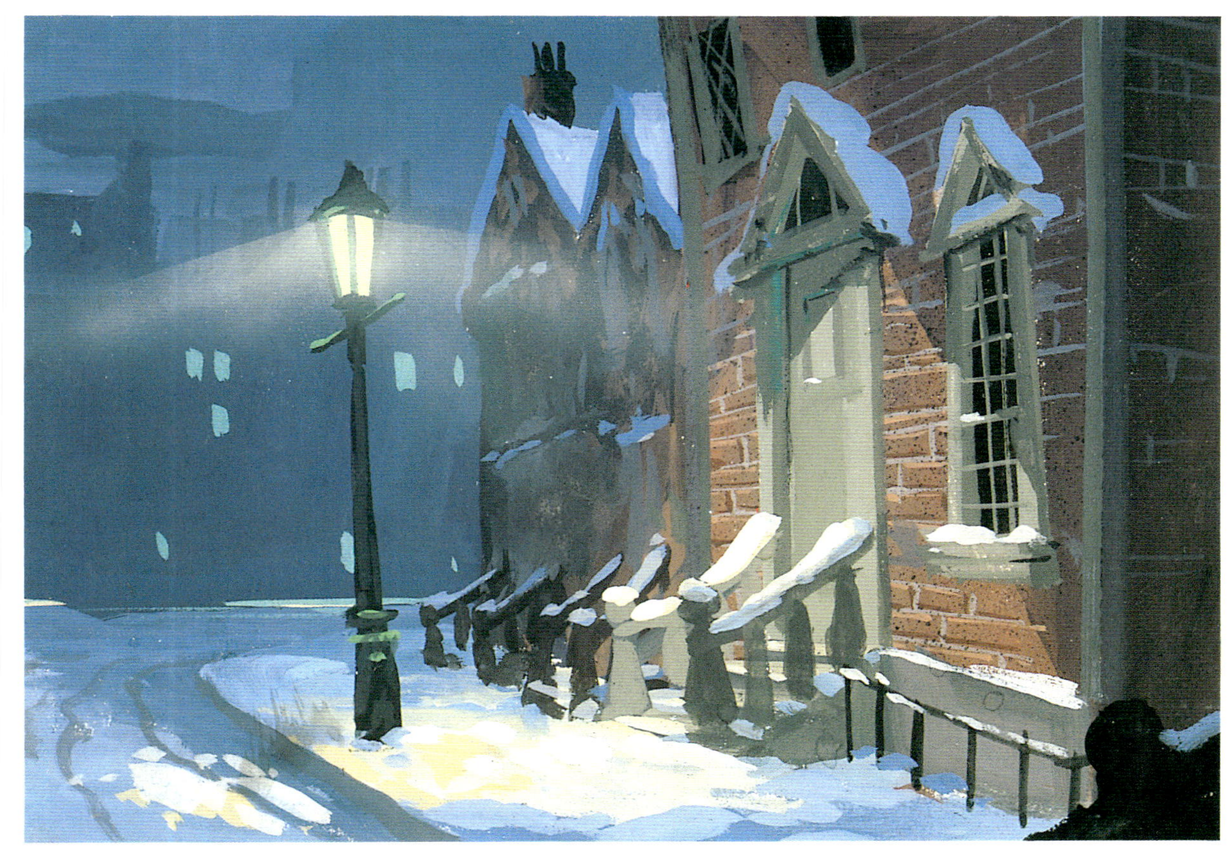

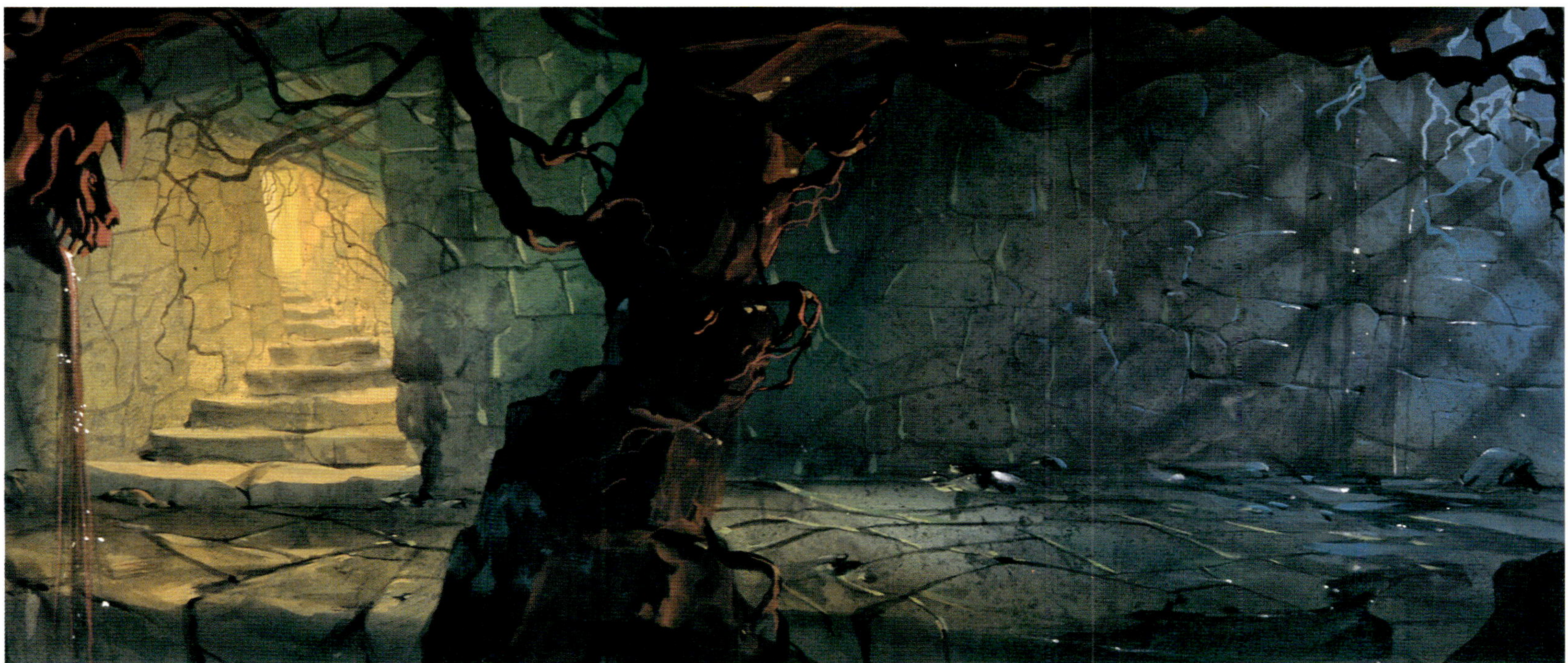

Griffith said, "Maybe," and told him to do a couple of backgrounds so they could show them to the director.

"I was scared to death because I recognized that this could be my big break," Coleman recalls. "And it was, as it turned out. Woolie liked it and told us to go ahead with it. Of course, I didn't realize it was going to require me to paint a couple of hundred backgrounds! It was a very long sequence. But I did it, and it looked pretty good. It was a great experience because it taught me a lot in a short amount of time."

When production for the film ended, the studio found that it needed to make deep slashes in its overhead. It was time for what Coleman calls "The Big Layoff." Most of the famous old-timers had taken their retirement so Animation was an easy target. One by one the background artists, and many others in other departments, were called in to the office and given their walking papers. Finally, it came time for Coleman.

"I just knew they were going to send me back to Art Props, or let me go," he says. "But when I went in and closed the door, they said, 'You're not going to get laid off. We're going to keep you here, and we're going to have you start working on the next film.'"

Suddenly, Coleman realized he had been chosen as the one to take over the Background department. He had been selected over numerous journeymen, all of whom had been let go.

"At this very same time, my wife was pregnant with our first child, and we'd just moved into a new home," he recalls. "They called me in and said, 'Well, buddy, you're it.'"

His first project was a movie called *The Fox and the Hound*, and he immediately started doing preliminary drawings. The film was placed on hold, however, and he was asked to design *The Small One*, a short subject film on which the Animation department wanted to try and nurture all of its young artists. It was to be the first time he would be completely in charge of all of the backgrounds for a film.

"Don Duckwall, the production manager in Animation, called me in and told me I could hire one person to work with me, which I did, and the two of us worked with Don Bluth on *The Small One*," he says. It also was the first directing assignment for Bluth, who later left Disney amid a well-publicized controversy, taking many of the Disney animators with him and starting his own company.

"Don Bluth had his own thing going on the side while we were working on *The Small One*," Coleman says. "In fact, I was working with him freelance to make extra money, and we made a film called *Banjo the Woodpile Cat*."

"I actually thought about leaving Disney and going with

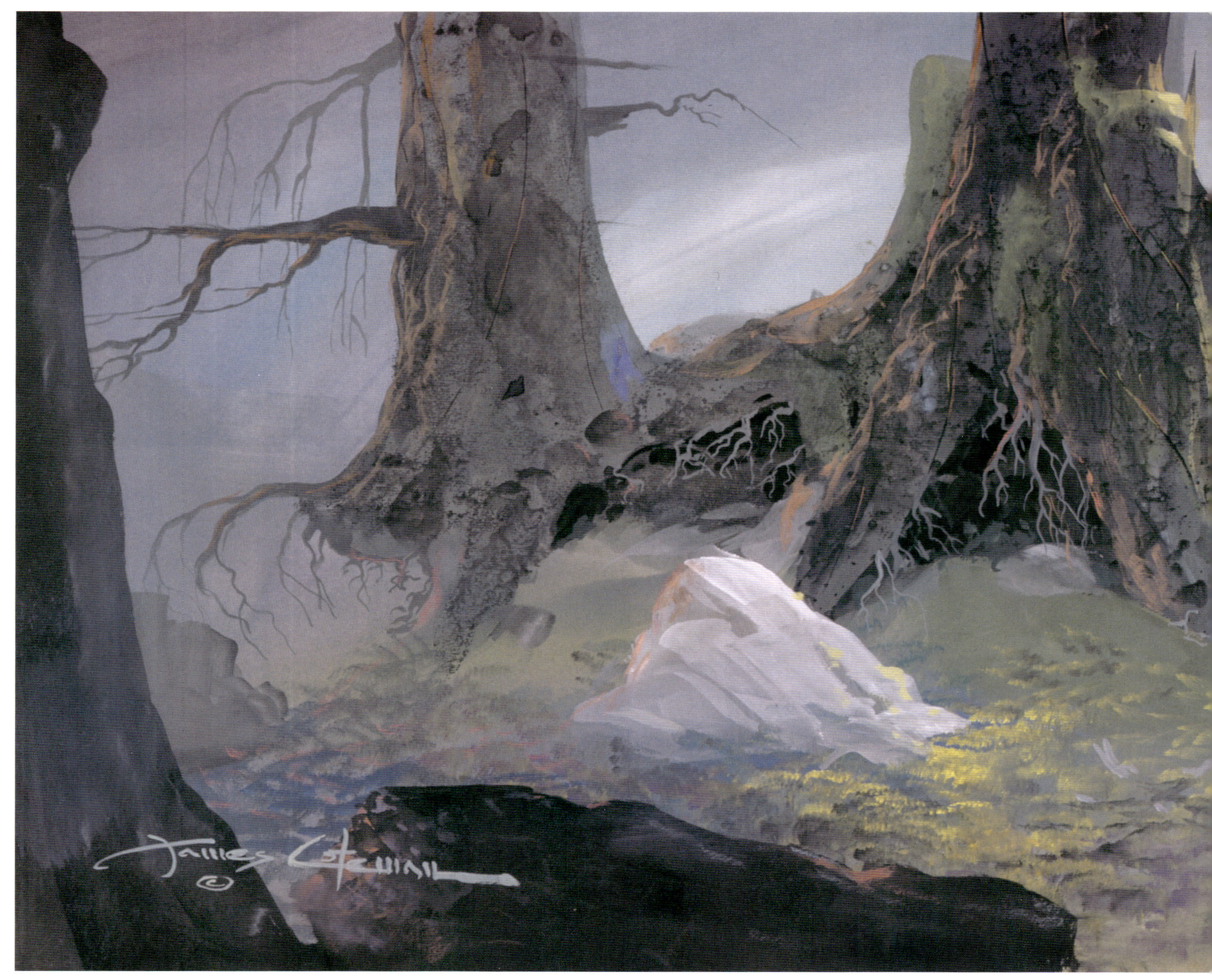

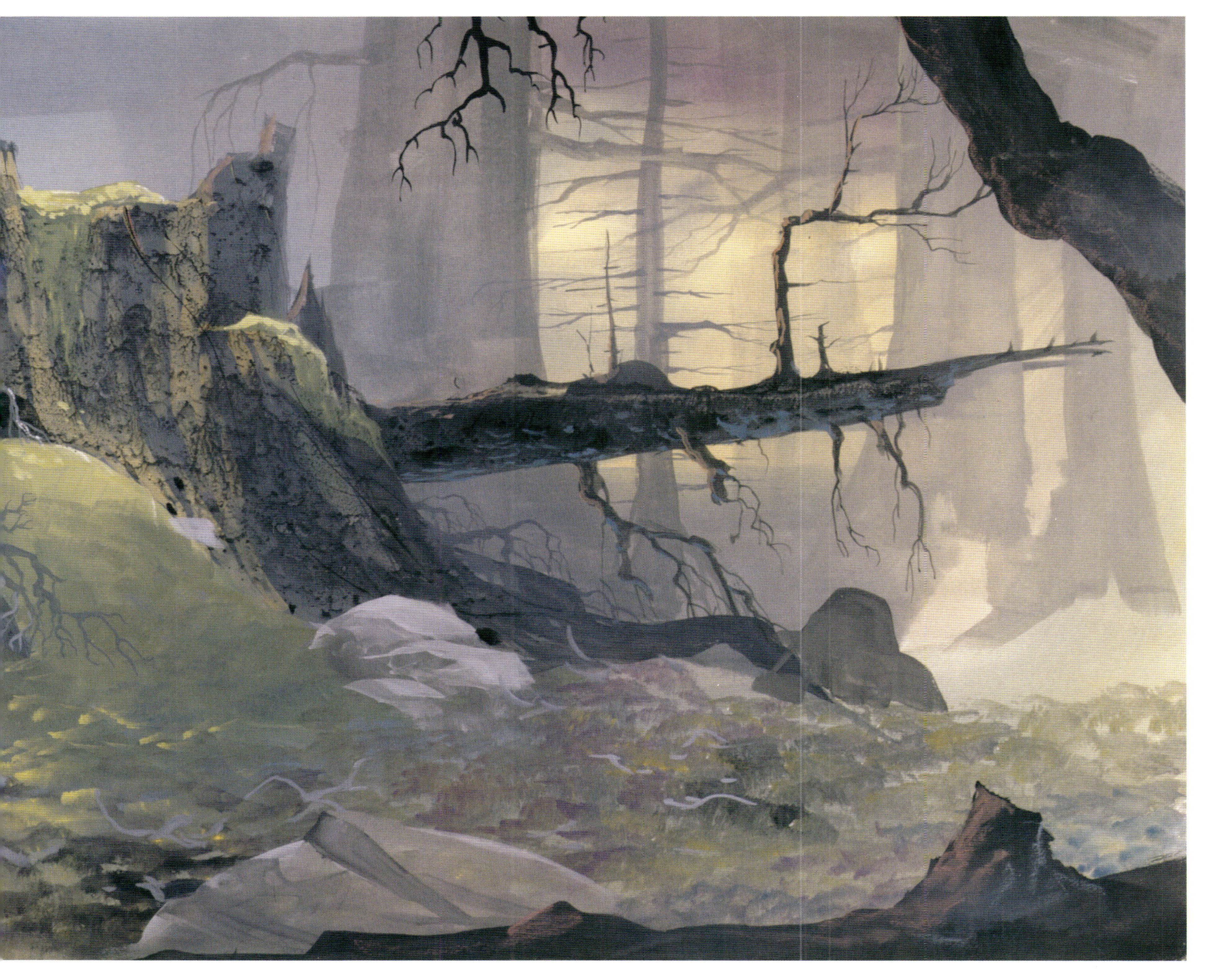

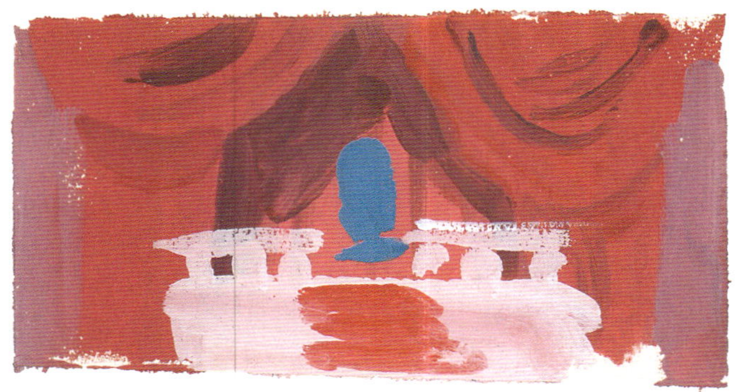

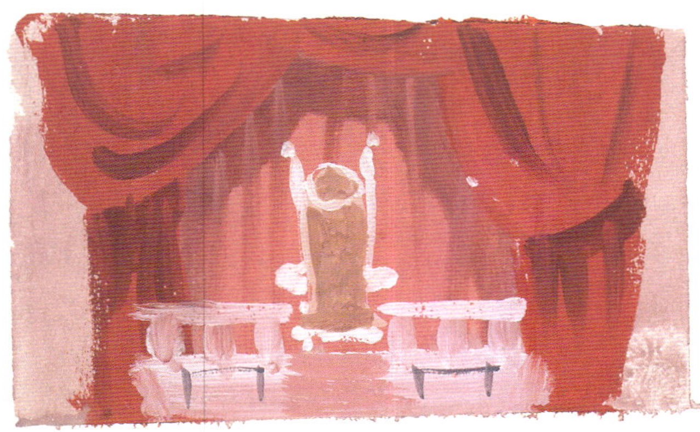

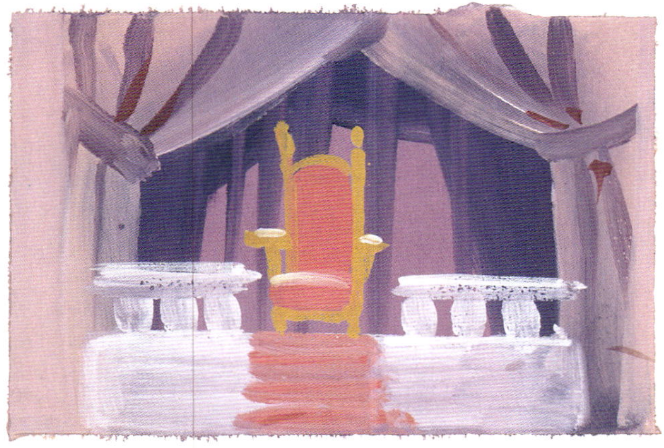

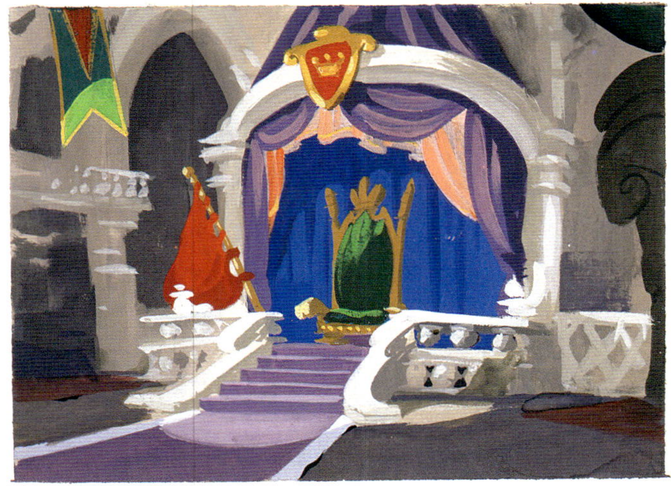

him," Coleman reveals. "Bluth was very charismatic, and the people who worked for him were mesmerized by him. But I wasn't. He knew I was talented, and I was interested in good opportunities. That, I think, is why we became friends."

Bluth offered him twice as much money as he was making at Disney to come to work for him, an offer hard to ignore. "I was young and struggling financially. . . it was just a major deal," Coleman remembers. "I had mixed emotions because I loved Disney and didn't want to leave. And I didn't want to be under Bluth's thumb. It was a major conflict for me."

He went in to see Joe Hale, who was being groomed by Disney as a producer for Animation, and told him he was leaving. "Everybody sort of knew what was going on when I went in there," he says. "I told Joe that Bluth had offered me all this money and that I had to go with him. 'How can I go home and tell my wife I'd turned something like that down?' I asked him."

Hale went to Ron Miller, the chairman of the board at Disney at the time, and told him about Coleman's decision, which resulted in his being called into Miller's office to repeat his announcement. Miller, however, wanted to hang on to his new Background head.

"He made me a counter-offer and told me they really wanted me to stay. It was a good offer, though not nearly what Bluth had offered me. I wanted to be with Disney, and I never felt right about leaving because I knew we were going to make some good films. So I decided to stay."

After finishing *The Small One*, Duckwall told Coleman it was time to start building a department. It was time to get ready for *The Fox and the Hound*. So Coleman started looking for candidates to hire and train.

"I decided that the best thing to do was to train new artists the same way I was trained," he says, as if it were that simple. "First, they needed to learn how to copy backgrounds the way Disney has always done them, and then get more creative as you go. I hired people from the Art Center School of Design who were well-trained anyway as painters, so it worked out really well."

The next film up was *The Fox and the Hound*, which he claims was a tremendous learning experience. A very talented concept artist named Mel Shaw had talked the director into giving the film a different look with pastels.

"It was just impossible to do," he says. "I spent so much time trying to find a way to give the film that look without actually

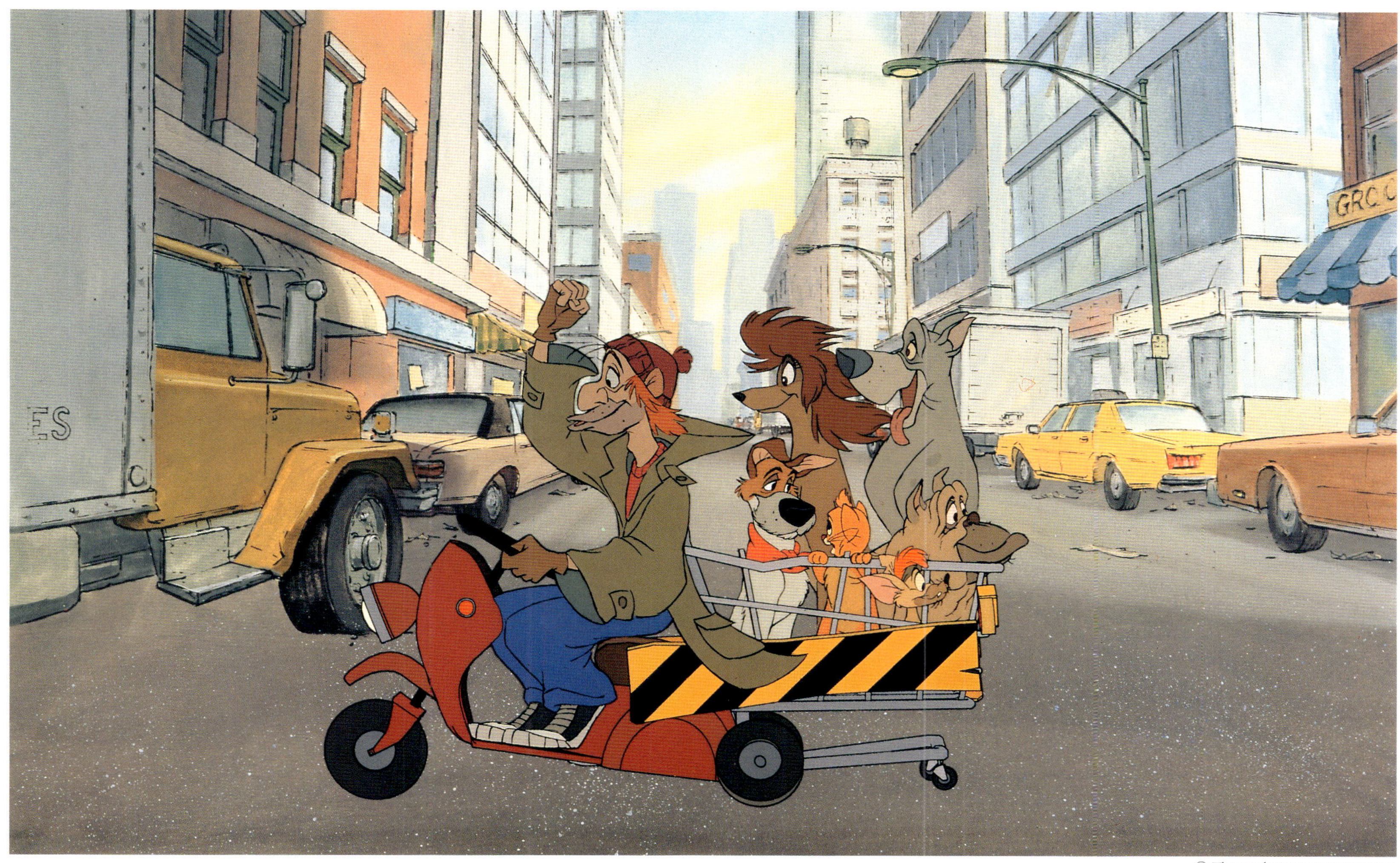

Oliver & Company, 1988

using pastels. Ultimately, we ended up going back and repainting all the sequences the regular way.

"I have to say, though, as upset as I was with Mel at the time, I learned so much from him. If I could run into him today, I'd tell him how much I appreciate the contribution he made to me personally. He was a master of color and design."

The Fox and the Hound was the first feature whereupon Coleman, from beginning to end, was the lead painter, designer, color stylist and department head. "It was the first time they gave me total control of the budget, told me to hire so many people and that it was basically my 'baby.'"

In a sense, he'd become an artist in management, as well as a creative leader in the color, look and design of the films he would work on for the next seven years. He was on his way—his daughter, Kim, was a toddler, and his wife was pregnant with their second child, Scott. They moved from the Valley and settled in Thousand Oaks, California. Disney was taking very good care of him financially, an arrangement that eventually made him one of the highest-paid artists in animation.

"That was because I was in a position where I had knowledge no one else had," he explains with genuine modesty. "I was fortunate enough to have been exposed to some of the great masters of animation before they retired, or died. And everyone else had either resigned or been laid off. I was the only one left. I was in the right place at the right time."

Fortunate timing? Maybe. But it was talent and old-fashioned hard work that propelled Coleman to top of his field. "Virtually anybody who is a real success has put their heart and soul into whatever it is they do," he says. "They go 10 steps beyond what they had to do to get there, and they work far harder than anyone can imagine just to get the break. Then, they do whatever they have to do to make it all work."

After *The Fox and the Hound*, he did *Mickey's Christmas Carol*, another short. By then, his staff had been through a full-length feature together and had jelled as a team. His theory of hiring good artists out of art school and training them his way was paying off, and the crew had a lot of fun, he says, working on the half-hour program. He had, in actuality, established a new training method that Disney was still using in the early '90s when he left the company.

It was not merely a training ground, either. The team stayed together for years and worked on a lot of films together. "Most of them went on to either head the department or to other studios where they did very well," he says of his crew. "They were people who were good artists in their hearts, and that's why I chose them. I think they liked working for me; we were like a family."

Coleman didn't waste time in making his mark. As soon as he took over the Backround department, he set about resurrecting some of the old Disney magic.

"If you remember back to films like *Robin Hood* and *The Aristocats*, and even *101 Dalmatians* for that matter, there was a look to them, but it wasn't the old rendered Disney look," he says. "I convinced them early on that we could do a film without that Xerox line, which cheapened it as far as we were concerned. We didn't have the money they throw at films today, but I managed to talk them into recapturing some of that old Disney look, and do it within budget."

One of the films that had the right look was *The Black Cauldron*. Management felt this picture was going to be the project that would revive the public's interest in animation. But, dark and brooding, it failed miserably at the box office.

"I don't know if it was the story or what," Coleman says, shrugging. "Maybe it just needed to be brighter and more fun, I don't know. For me, though, that film had more of my effort in it than any of the others, start to finish."

He worked for a year and a half just on preproduction sketches, some of which were huge. Much like he does today with his fine art, he painted very large pieces of artwork for the film, whereas, usually, the backgrounds were rendered on a much smaller, thumbnail scale.

"I loved it. . . painting larger, canvas-size scenes really sparked my imagination," he says with excitement.

At 35, he'd not only mastered his job, he'd begun to transcend it. He'd reached the pinnacle in background animation; the next step would have been to become a director.

"Everything sort of came together for me," he reflects. "But I wasn't really satisfied. Then this film came along and, all of a sudden, it sparked a realization in me that I could really paint. People would walk into my office and see the paintings leaning against a wall, and they were just blown away. They were so much larger than what they were used to, and very powerful."

It was a turning point for the artist. He began to think: "What if I put more effort into my art, my own art?" He was making a great living at Disney, and still painting on the side, even showing some of his work from time to time. Yet his fine art was still deep in the back seat compared to his career in animation.

"With *The Black Cauldron*, something hit me that there was a potential here I wasn't realizing in my own work," he says. "Part of it was that I was trying to do two different things. I didn't want to use what I was doing with background art in my paintings at home. I wanted them to be completely separate. Then I discovered that was what was stifling me. I found out that a lot of what was coming out in the Disney work was me!

"It was at this point that I decided to make a commitment—I was going to spend the rest of my life focusing on my own art."

Within 10 years, he figured, he would be established as *a name* in the fine-art community. He set up easels and oil paint in his office and started once more spending his lunches and spare moments pursuing his goal. He'd go home after work and, after the kids went to bed, continue to paint. Eventually, the work he was doing at Disney started to flow with his art at home.

"I began to focus more and more on my own paintings—the Southwest, mountains, the redwoods, that sort of thing," he says. "Then there was a big changeover at Disney. [Michael] Eisner and the new management came in and took the Animation department out of the Animation building,

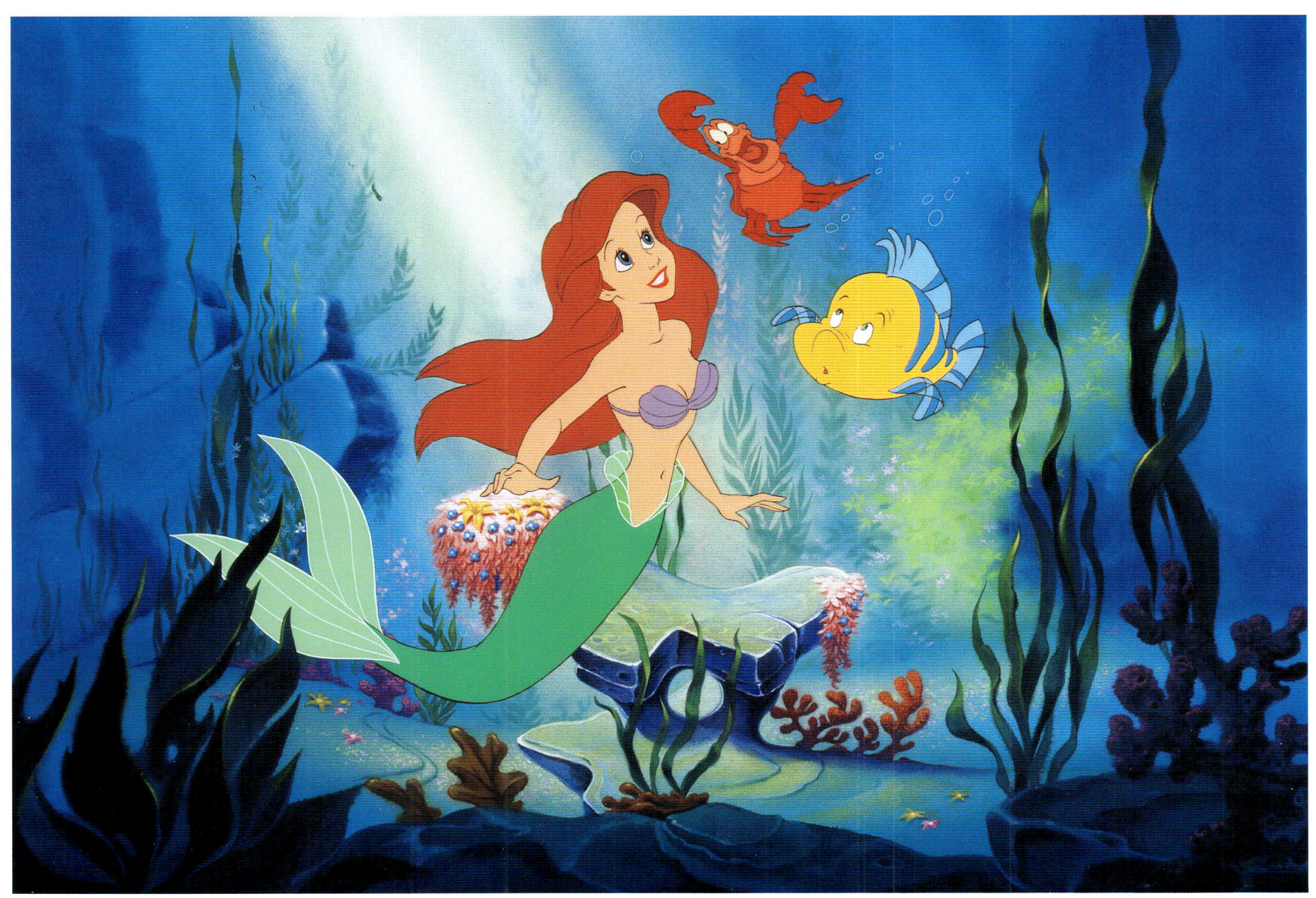

The Little Mermaid, 1989

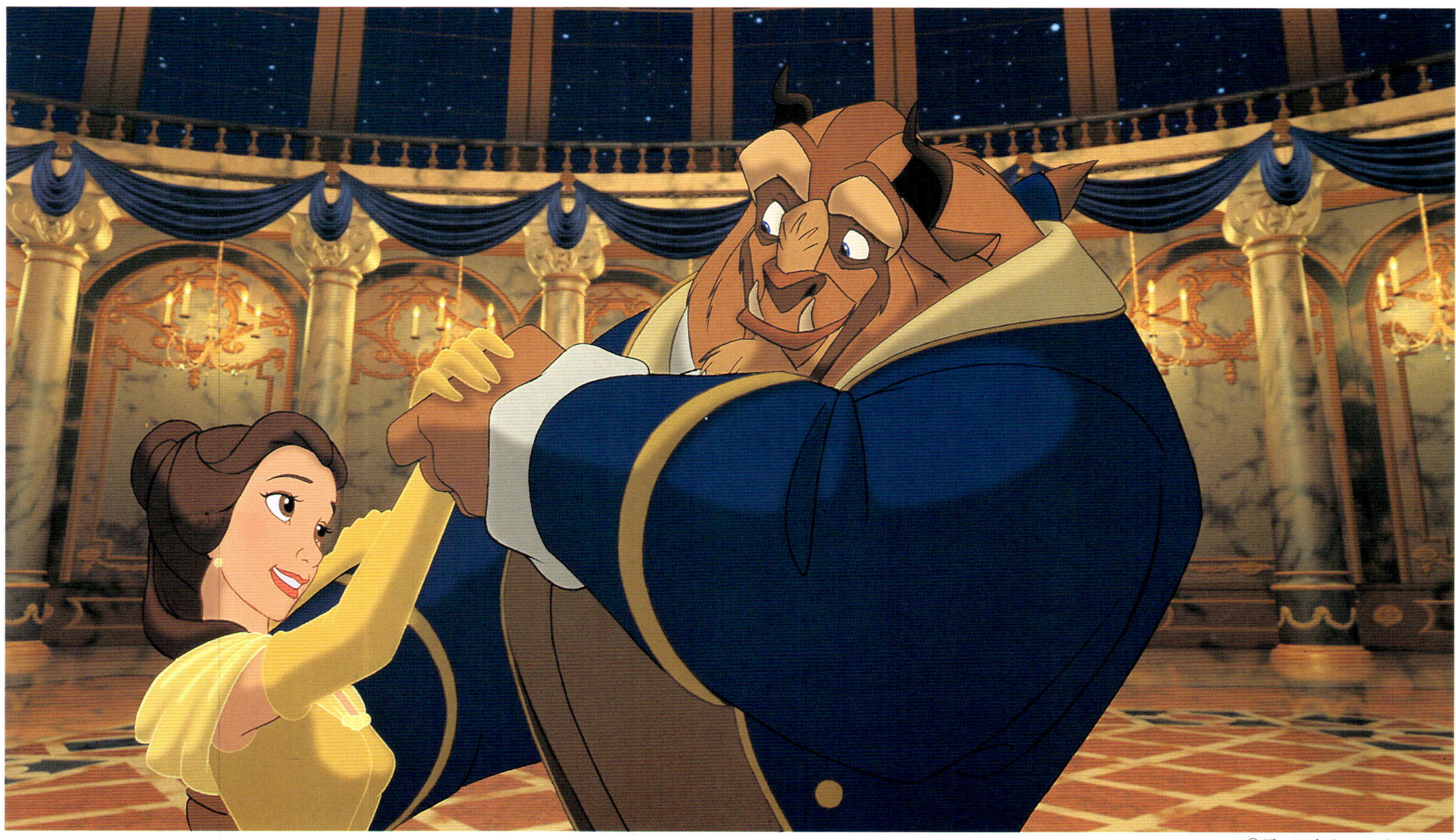

Beauty And The Beast, 1991

which had been built specifically for animation, and put us in warehouse space in Glendale.

"That really stunned us," he recalls. "I remember thinking I'd better start to work even harder on my own art. . . they could close this whole thing down any day. They knew what they were going to do—they were going to produce an explosion of live-action movies."

Even though their workspace had been relocated, Animation started a new film, *The Great Mouse Detective,* which Coleman loved because of its Victorian scenery. And then came *Oliver & Company,* which, like *The Black Cauldron,* was touted as the film that was going to revive interest in animation.

Meanwhile, Coleman had immersed himself in his fine art to the point where his work was being shown in 17 art galleries throughout the Southwest. Exhausted from keeping up with the demand for his original paintings at the galleries, he felt that if he could "just get over the hump" and make enough money with his fine art, he could cut back his hours at Disney. And that's exactly what happened when *The Little Mermaid* came along. He went in and told management he only wanted to work a few days a week.

"They said 'OK, whatever you want, but we don't want to lose you,'" he recalls. "We made a good agreement, and I worked several days a week on this film."

Interestingly, the Background supervisor on *The Little Mermaid* was an artist named Donald Townes, whom Coleman had hired and trained years earlier. "In many ways, I still see Jim as my boss and look to him for direction," says Townes, now working at Rich Animation. "He was the bridge to the old Disney, the last guy to have direct access to the old artists. I always knew I was getting the best instruction.

"He was very nourishing as a boss, but more importantly, he was extremely gifted. He could sit down at a blank canvas and just stir up images. My interest in the animation field was through Jim Coleman. His sense of color was so fascinating—simple and fresh, yet full of imagination and feeling."

On *The Little Mermaid*, Coleman worked on the underwater scenery, particularly the organic backgrounds and castles. "I liked working on the underwater castles," Coleman says, "but I didn't want to work on the castle above water. I didn't like working on the more realistic structures.

"*Oliver* made money, but it still wasn't the breakthrough film for animation. Thank God *The Little Mermaid* came along. We saw right away that this was going to be a project with some depth. First, there was the music, far better than they'd had in many, many years. The management was smart because they didn't hire just anybody off the street to do the music. They went to Broadway and brought in heavyweights."

In a sense, the new management brought their best to the film, as did the Animation department. The artists continued toward using the old Disney style, and the company brought something to the project that hadn't been done for a long time—using top talent from other fields to work on the film.

"They used to do that in the early Disney films," Coleman says. "Walt hired all the top people. But, of course, he could afford to do that because after the Depression, everyone needed the work."

Coleman, on the other hand, had more work than he could handle. As *The Little Mermaid* opened and shattered box office records, Walt Disney Studios was about to lose one of the best backgound artists it ever had.

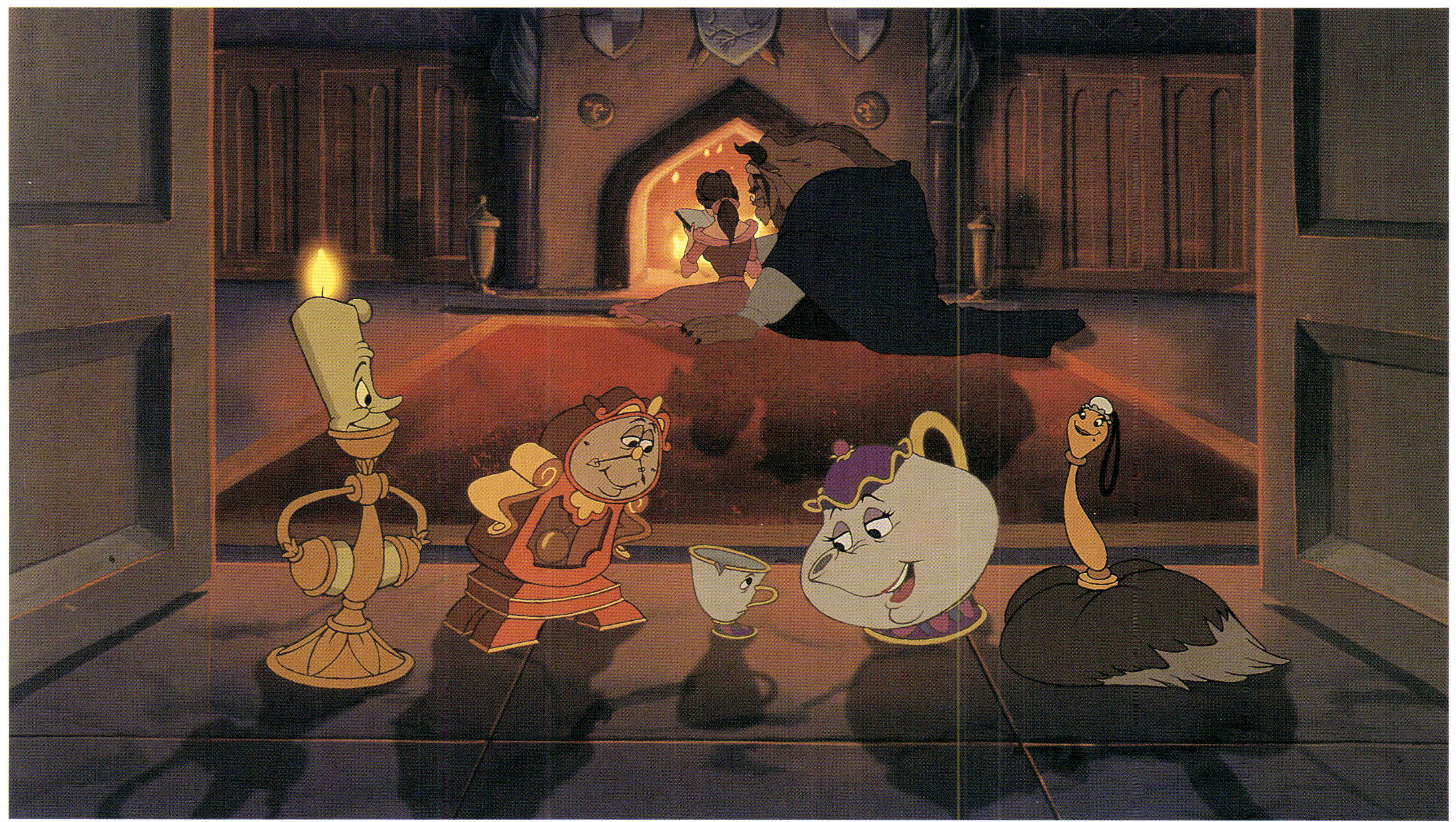

Beauty And The Beast, 1991

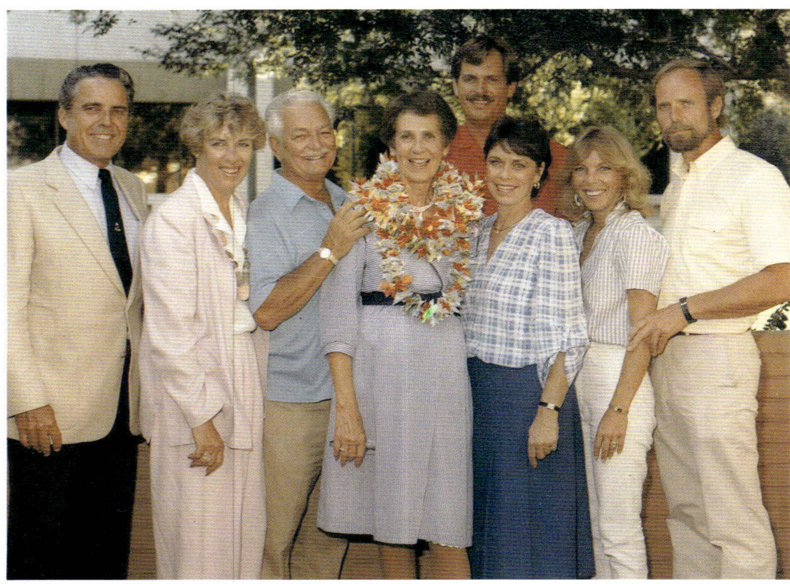

Beth Coleman's retirement from Disney after 51 years. From left Ron & Pat Wilkinson, Frank & Beth Coleman, James Coleman, Judy Nixon, Bobby Coleman and Jeff Coleman

"Here we were, about to go through a renaissance in animation, something I'd hoped would happen my whole career, and I wanted to be part of it," he laments. "At the same time, I was hitting my stride in fine art, which I knew was my future. I loved both of them, but I had to let one of them go."

Hot on the heels of *Mermaid* came *Beauty and the Beast*. So Coleman stayed on, working only one day a week on the new film. By then, he knew in his heart which way he was headed. Another artist he'd hired and trained, Lisa Keene, who was in charge of backgrounds for *Beauty and the Beast*, was very supportive, allowing Coleman to work whenever and on whatever he wanted for the film.

"We were lucky to still have his involvement," Keene says. "He was the link between the old Disney and the new. It was very sad when he left because it was the end of an era. He created such an easy atmoshere when he was here, and we've never been able to recapture that feeling of family.

"Jim's still an inspiration around here, though," she continues. "As a fine artist, he's realizing what for many of us is a dream. We're all huge fans, and I'm so happy for him."

Conversely, Coleman takes great pride in his former colleagues' success. "It's like a father seeing his children realizing their greatest dreams," he says of Townes and Keene. "It was so exciting to go in there and see them where I used to be. And they were working on these beautiful films, with real budgets. I couldn't have been prouder."

After *Beauty and the Beast*, Coleman reached his moment of decision. "I went home, sat down and realized I might not ever work on another Disney film," he says, his voice dropping. "I'd worked out a deal with them so I could stay with the company on an extended leave basis. Then I rented an apartment and turned it into a studio. I was ready to paint."

A short time later, in 1991, Coleman began publishing his paintings as fine art posters and lithographs. The demand for his work soared. Almost overnight, he became too busy to work, even one day a week, on another movie.

Disney called him anyway and asked him to work on *Aladdin*, which was very tempting, he admits. "I went in and looked at *Aladdin*, and I just knew there was no way I could find the time to do it," he says with a tinge of regret. "I had to stay focused on my fine art. I'd been working for six or seven years toward that goal, and I was right where I wanted to be."

Coleman's tenure at Walt Disney Studios spanned 22 years. He recently was asked to work on a new film, the animated version of *Pocahontas*, which he felt he had to turn down. To this day, however, he has not received anything in writing officially stating that he no longer works there. Perhaps one day he'll lend his talent to another animated classic. He intends to be around for a while.

"I always figured if I could just paint the rest of my life—never retire, just keep on painting—I'd be happy," he concludes. "But you never know. . . they still haven't sent me a pink slip."

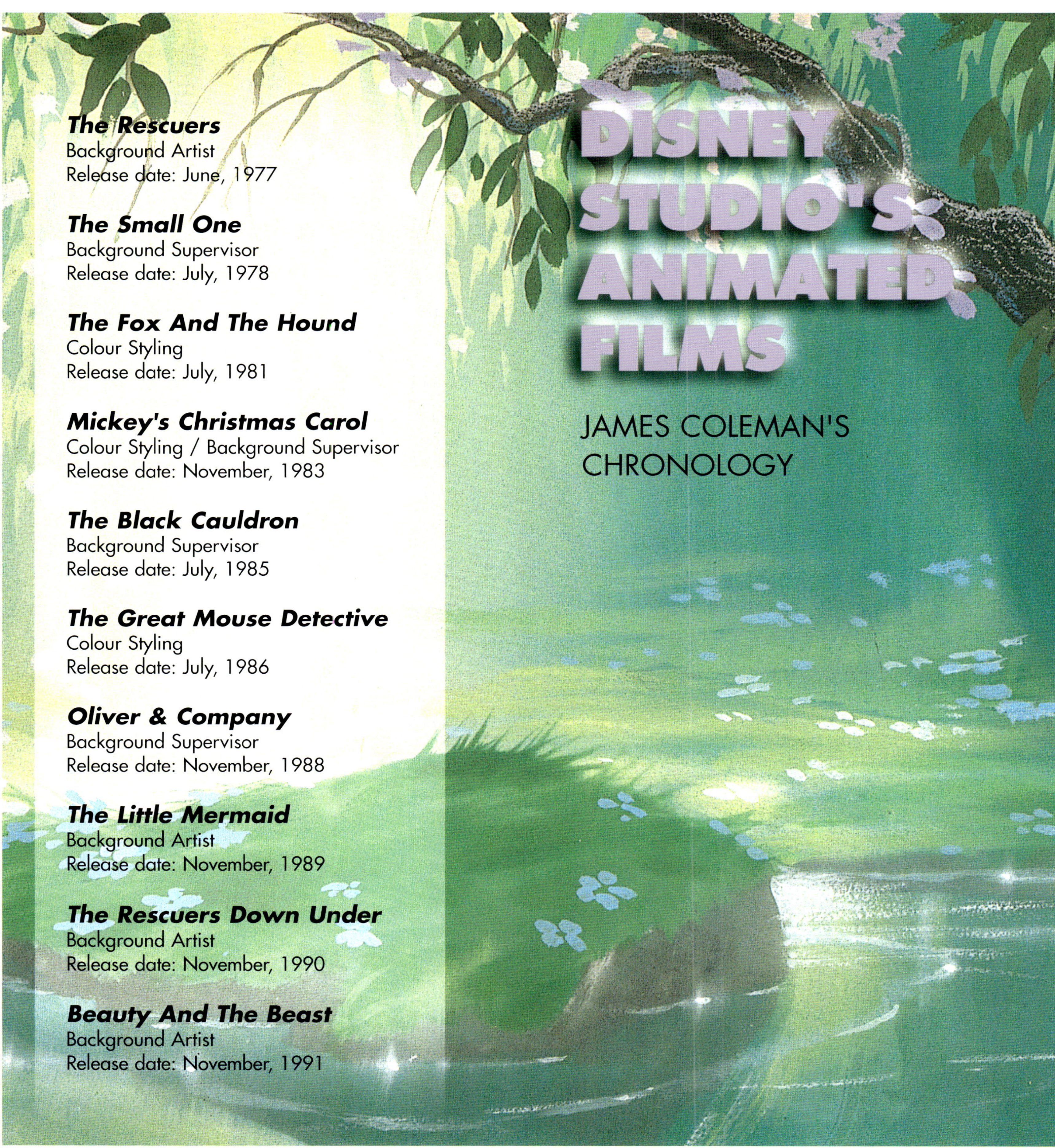

DISNEY STUDIO'S ANIMATED FILMS

JAMES COLEMAN'S CHRONOLOGY

The Rescuers
Background Artist
Release date: June, 1977

The Small One
Background Supervisor
Release date: July, 1978

The Fox And The Hound
Colour Styling
Release date: July, 1981

Mickey's Christmas Carol
Colour Styling / Background Supervisor
Release date: November, 1983

The Black Cauldron
Background Supervisor
Release date: July, 1985

The Great Mouse Detective
Colour Styling
Release date: July, 1986

Oliver & Company
Background Supervisor
Release date: November, 1988

The Little Mermaid
Background Artist
Release date: November, 1989

The Rescuers Down Under
Background Artist
Release date: November, 1990

Beauty And The Beast
Background Artist
Release date: November, 1991

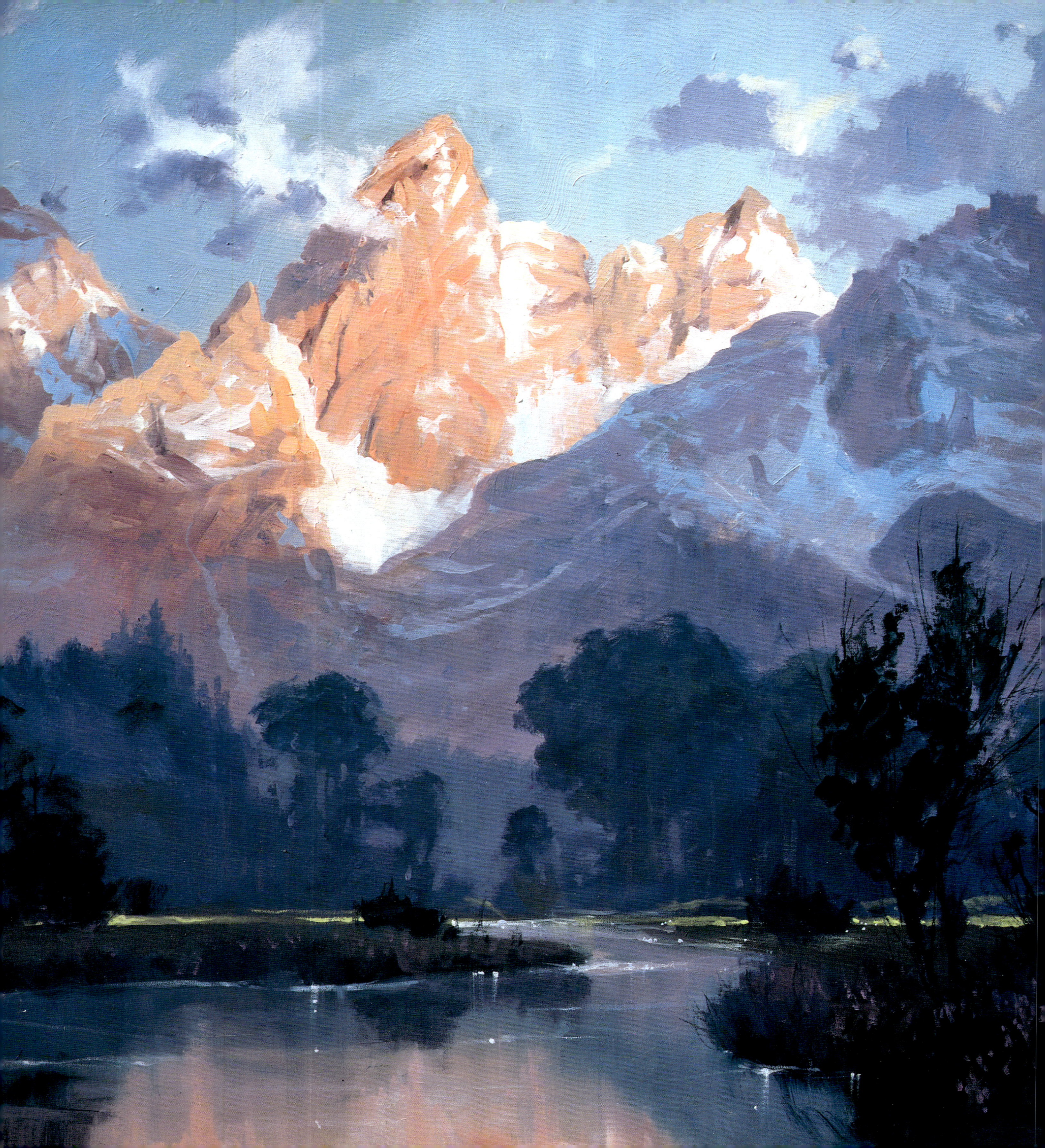

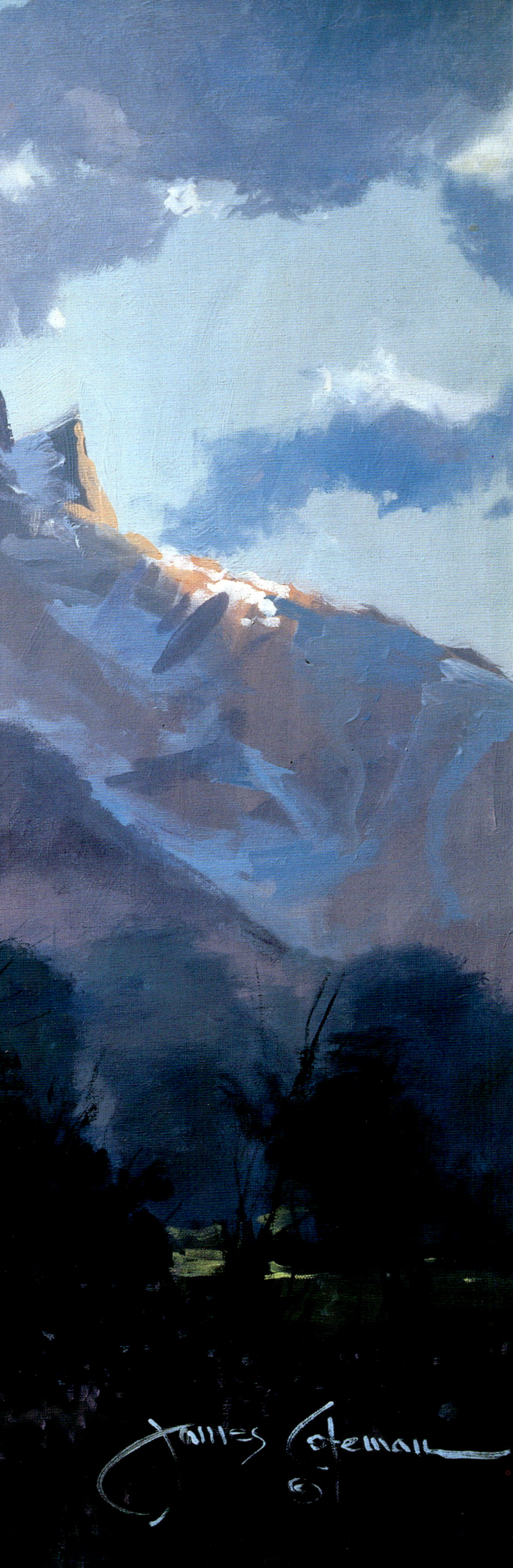

4

Fine Art

Two decades of painting magical worlds for Disney had provided James Coleman an opportunity to avoid the traditional life of a starving artist.

There were no long periods of subsisting only on wine and French bread. There was no alcoholism or strange, erratic indulgence searching for his soul in the South Pacific. And he didn't cut off any body parts to convince a girl he was in love with her.

But there were no assurances. Leaving a successful career and shoving off to sail the world of fine art on his own took a huge leap of faith for a man with a wife and three children. Fortunately, he'd paid his dues and prepared well. There were many nights of eating grilled-cheese sandwiches as he and his wife navigated through the lean, early years at Disney. Every spare dime he made from selling his own work was reinvested in paint and canvas, which he stretched himself—not out of preference or pretentious artistic nostalgia, but out of simple financial necessity.

When his paycheck grew, relieving him of 10 years of stern frugality, he still had to juggle a demanding job with his painting at home. He'd come home from work each day and wait until his wife and children had gone to bed before disappearing into his studio to paint, often working until the sun came up. It was a hard habit to break, and today he still does most of his painting after 10 p.m.

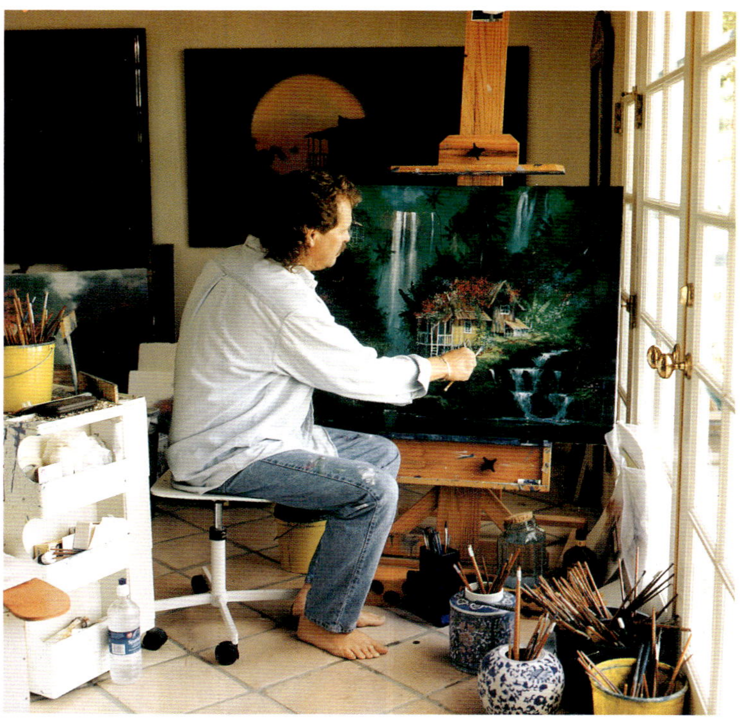

James working in his studio in Thousand Oaks, California

As his work started to sell on a more regular basis, Coleman began to recognize his potential. He was so encouraged that he worked even harder to produce more paintings.

"For people to come into a gallery, especially in towns considered to be art communities, and then choose my work over that of other artists, just blew me away," he explains. "I knew how hard they worked for their money, and for them to part with it to buy one of my paintings meant that it had really touched their hearts. It was the highest compliment I could ever receive, and still is."

Compliments aside, the proceeds from his paintings made a difference in the Coleman household. "It really surprised me," he says. "And it surprised my wife, too. She was thinking: 'Hey, now I can get that new washing machine we've been needing.' And I was thinking: "Yeah, and I can buy that new easel.' These weren't luxury items or anything—they were things we needed and would have had to borrow money to get.

By the standards of most struggling artists, Coleman had "done it right," waiting until his art was selling before quitting his day job. "It wasn't a total leap off the cliff," he admits. "I held probably a half-dozen one-man shows while I was at Disney. Then I had my first big break at a gallery in La Canada, where many of the artists at Disney showed their work. Al Dempster and Ralph Hewlett encouraged me to try and get a show there, and I did."

It was actually an art store called White's Art Store Gallery. "Just a little hole-in-the-wall place," he says. "But a lot of wealthy people would come in there because of the Disney artists.

"I had a show there every year for four or five years, sometimes selling 50 watercolors in a single show. I framed everything myself because there wasn't any money."

He was asking $40-$50 for an original at the time, and people were buying them. This convinced him he needed to expose his work to a wider audience. "I figured that if I was going to do this, I was going to do it in a big way," he explains. "I had to cash most of my stock options at Disney to pay bills. But I cashed the last one—$3,000—to buy paint supplies and start my business.

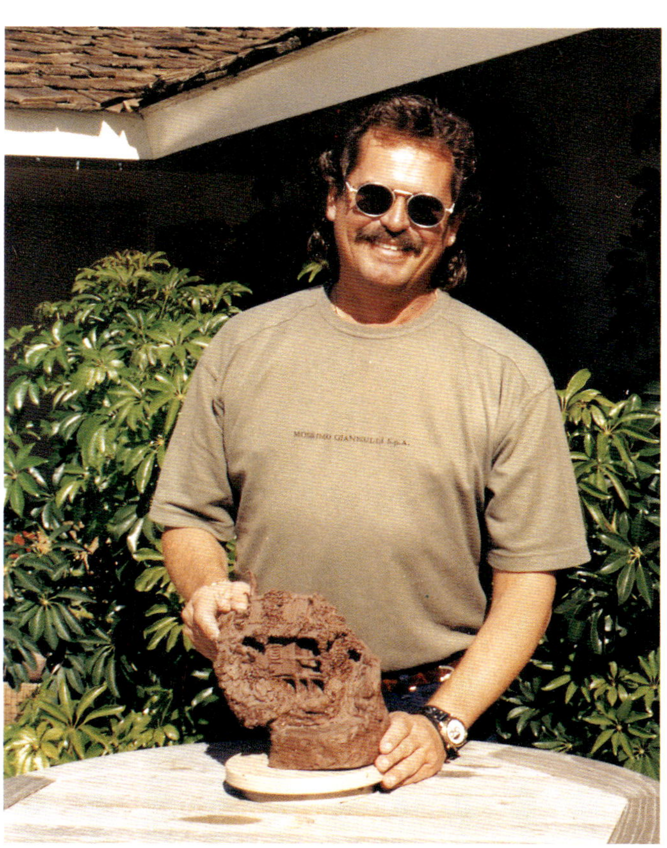

Jim with his first sculpture

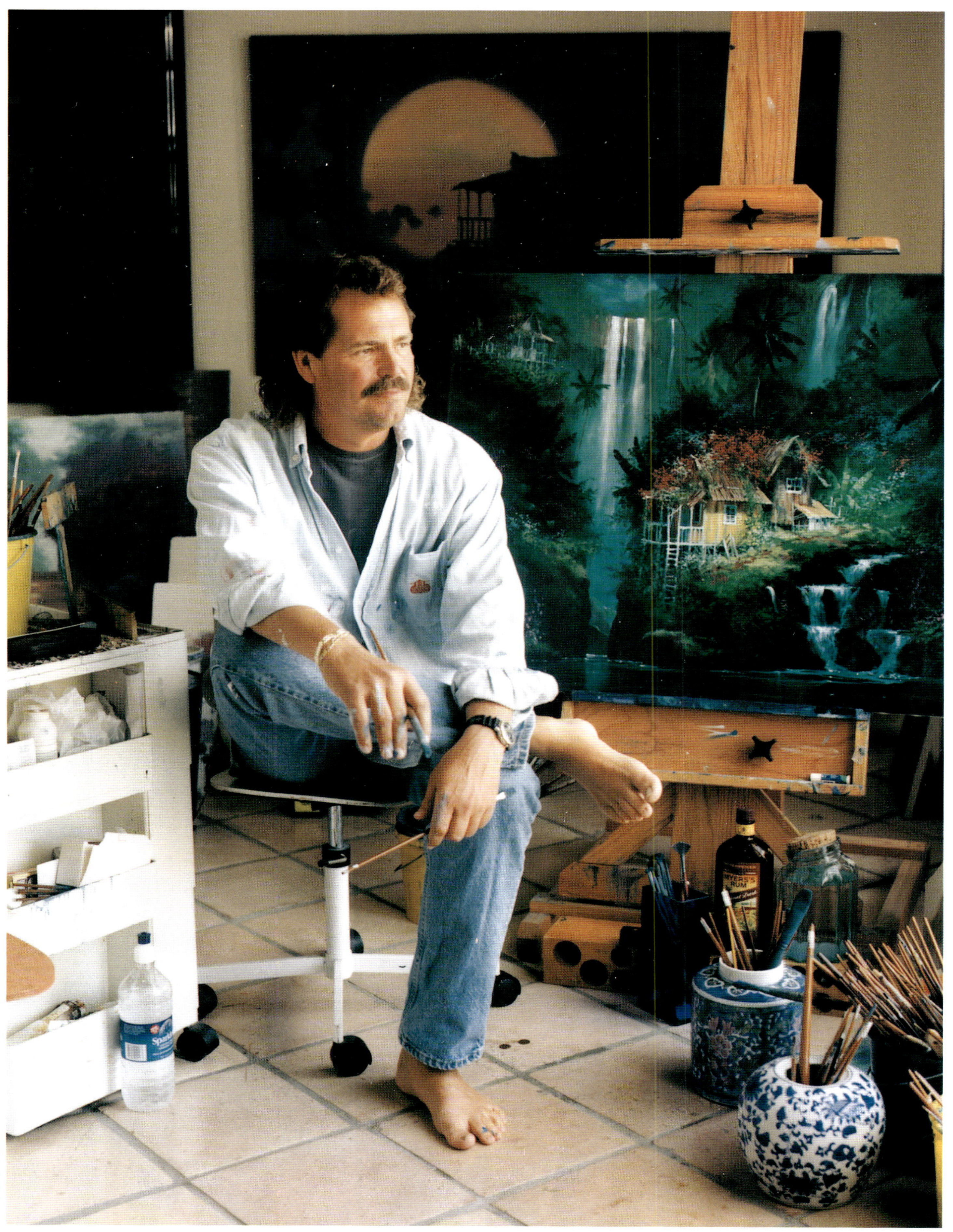

In December of 1993, my wife and I completed a room addition to our home which required a large vertical showpiece above our new fireplace.

Living close to Laguna Beach, the art capital of Southern California, we believed that this would be an enjoyable evening shopping spree. As we sampled the variety of artists in this seaside community we soon realized we had very demanding tastes. We were very frustrated and ready to call it a night when we walked in to the Wyland Galleries. We were asked if we were familiar with the works of James Coleman. The name caught my attention. He shared the same name as my brother-in-law who is the President of the Crystal Cathedral Ministries and a graphic artist.

The first painting I saw was a moonlight Hawaiian sea with the light bouncing on the water like a bag of illuminated marbles dancing on a shining onyx table. The shadows from the steep cliffs of the coast-line gave incredible depth to a single dimensional canvas. A lacy white waterfall and a swaying palm tree gave life and movement so that this surreal painting came to life. The effect on my spirit was exactly what I needed to come home to. . . peace. I felt like I had been miraculously transported into the most tranquil spot in all Hawaii. I could feel the tensions of the day fall away.

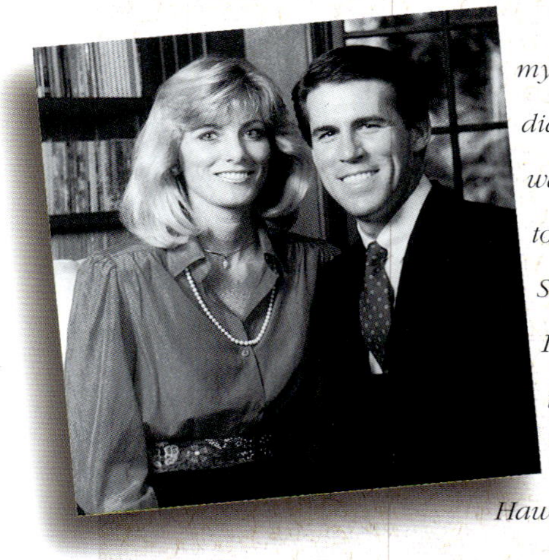

This is what I wanted to display in my house. Unfortunately the dimensions did not fit, so I commissioned the piece I wanted. In January 1995 it was delivered to our home. Our piece is entitled "Beside Still Waters", taken from the 23rd Psalm. It gives me the feeling I need when I step through the doors and into our home. It has turned our home into a tranquil Hawaiian paradise.

Rev. & Mrs. Robert A. Schuller
San Juan Capistrano, California

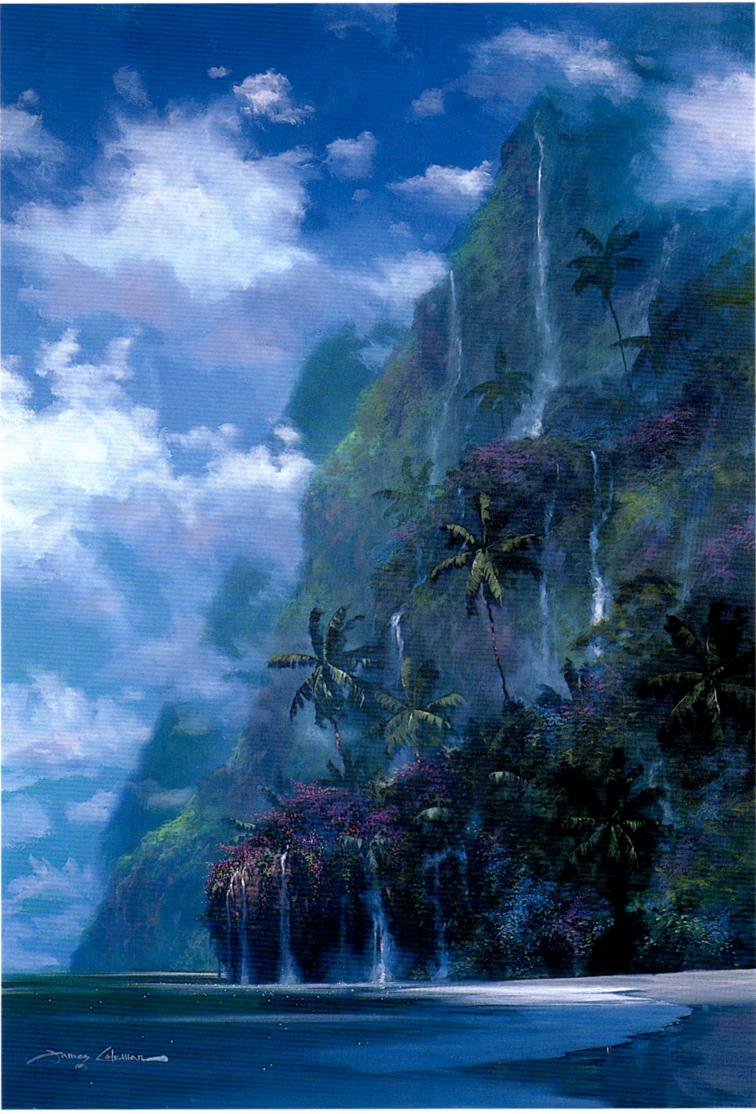

Beside Still Waters, Oil 60 x 40 inches

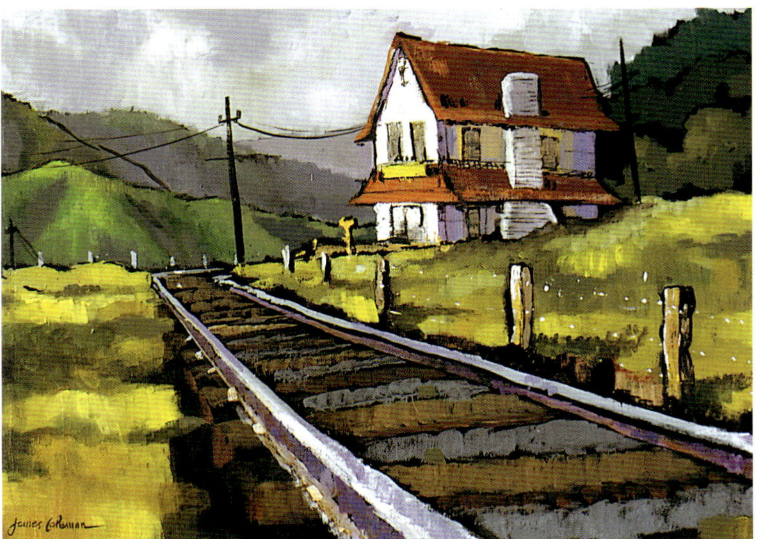

Early paintings shown at the White's Gallery and at the Disney Library

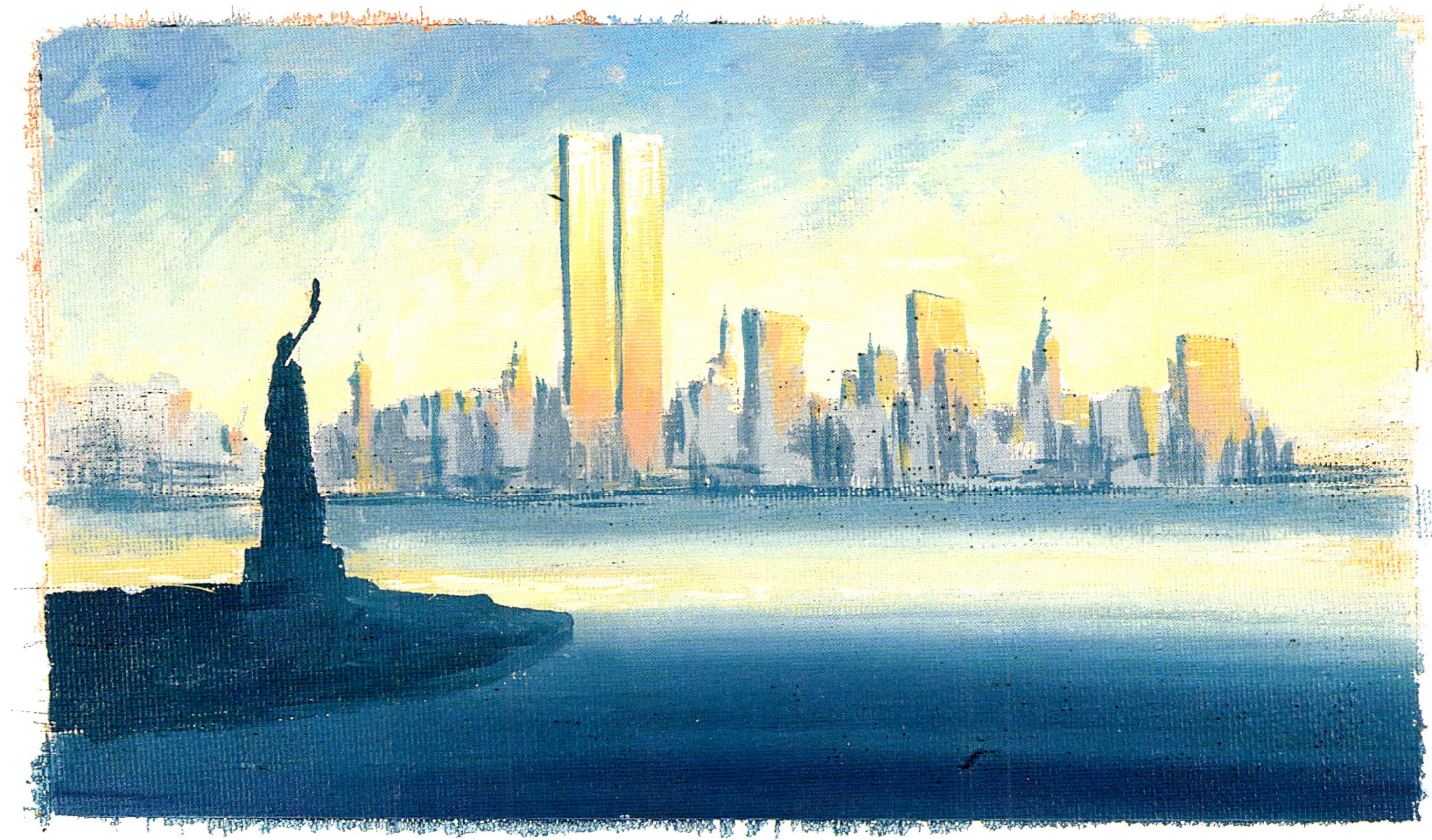

Liberty, 1981

"I remember one night, after painting until 2 or 3 a.m., I went out in the back yard and looked at my house. I thought about my family in there, and I knew that this hand. . . had paid for all of it.

After White's Art Store was sold, Coleman, as well as many of the other Disney artists, started showing elsewhere. He was called by the Burbank Public Library, which wanted to display his work, and soon after he was featured in a large show in Monterrey Park.

The name of the game, however, if he wanted to make a living as a fine artist, was in art galleries. He managed to get picked up by the small but prestigious Fireside Gallery, and then by Gallery Americana, both in California.

He also had begun to take trips to Hawaii, where he started searching for galleries where he might want to show his work. At the same time, he turned his attention to the Southwest, focusing his work more on deserts, redwoods, coastal scenes and Indian reservations.

"I started mailing photographs and letters to galleries all over the Western United States," he says. "The people at Disney would laugh when they saw me come in with dozens of envelopes. I had my own little mail-order business going. And, to my surprise, I received quite a few responses. Pretty soon, I was in galleries in Colorado, Arizona, Wyoming and California."

His work had found a market. But there was something about Hawaii he couldn't get out of his mind. He felt a connection with the Islands he didn't fully understand. In 1989, he finally figured out what it was.

"I was on Kauai, and I started to really look around at the landscape," he recalls. "Then it hit me. Nobody was painting the farms. The local people lived there, and this was the real Hawaii—not lava and tiki torches."

As luck would have it, Coleman's father walked into the Shipstore Gallery in Kapaa, Kauai. One of the art consultants told him the gallery might be interested in showing his work.

"I called the owner, who told me they might be interested and to send him a few paintings," Coleman recalls. "When I got home, I painted seven or eight scenes—a few with tin roofs, and others with rain forests. I didn't want to do the traditional palm trees and tourist attractions."

When the gallery received the paintings, they didn't display them at first. But several months later, the owner called up and said, "Hey, can you send over some more of

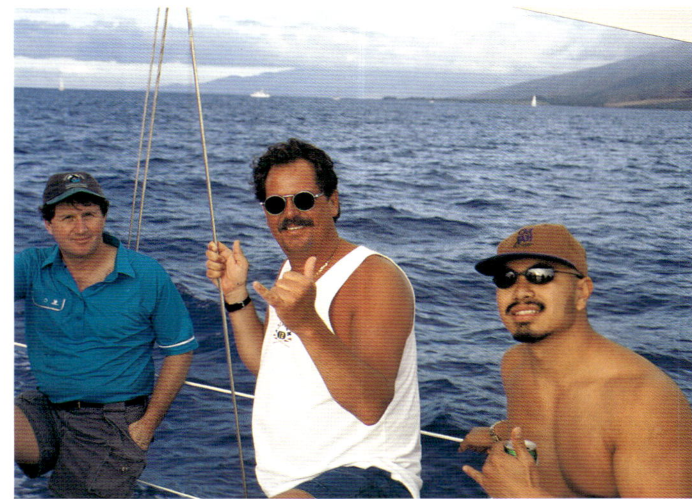

Mike Maiden, James Coleman & Walfrido, Maui, 1993

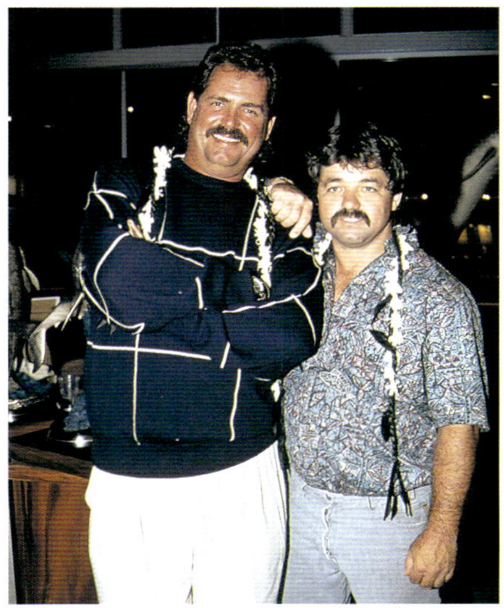

James Coleman & Bill Wyland at Aloha Towers Gallery opening, Oahu, 1995

those? You're not going to believe this, but they're all gone!"

"Hawaii started working," Coleman says. "And not only was it working, it was insane! Everything I sent over sold out right away. I couldn't send them enough. And what made me realize I'd touched on something was that the local people were buying the paintings.

"A year later, I held my first one-man show in Hawaii, and we sold 30 or 40 originals just like that. So I started to have three or four shows a year on Kauai. It was crazy! I was selling more out of that one little gallery on a neighbor island than in all of the other galleries combined."

He then started looking for galleries on other islands. Lahaina Galleries turned him down, as did another gallery on Maui. But, a few days later, he received a phone call from Bill Wyland, the brother of the well-known marine artist.

Coleman had been familiar with Wyland's work and had seen him in a magazine article years earlier. Now, here was his brother, calling and offering him an opportunity to show at Wyland Galleries, which operated five or six high-profile galleries throughout Hawaii.

It was a tempting proposition, but this was a big gallery. He wondered how he could produce enough paintings for such a large operation when he wasn't even able to keep up with the demand at Shipstore. But the Wylands were persistant, and soon he was sending paintings to their gallery on Oahu's famous North Shore. "At first, all I had was originals," he says. "But Wyland convinced me to publish some of my paintings. And once I did, things really took a turn. Almost overnight, sales for my work just. . . exploded."

Coleman started publishing more of his work after that, and was soon selling out of limited edition prints and cibachromes, which, in turn, helped sell his originals. Suddenly, he was on a rocket ship to the stars.

"I was originally against publishing," he admits. "It seemed to be just too. . . commercial. Then I realized not everyone can afford an original work of art, or get to a gallery or museum to enjoy it. By publishing my work, many more people would be able to see and even purchase a piece of art they couldn't have afforded before."

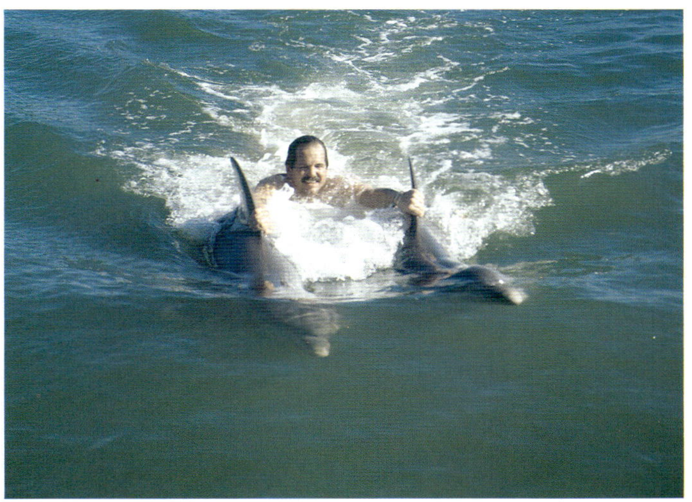

Jim swimming with dolphins, Dolphin Research Center, Key West, Florida

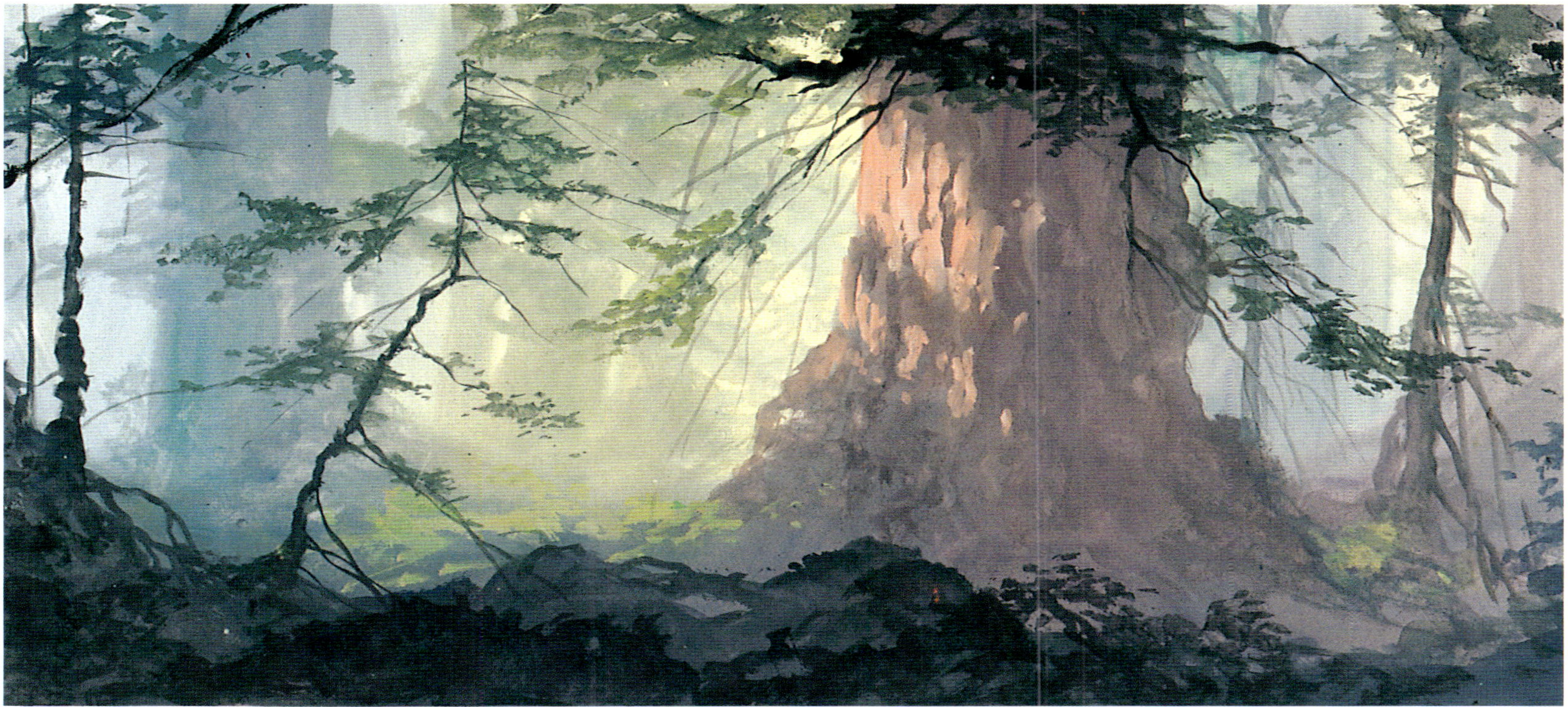

The world of fine-art publishing has grown dramatically in just the last three years, with computer graphics creating a host of multimedia capabilities. The selection of limited edition fine art posters and museum-quality lithographs have been augmented by high-grade cibachromes and seriography. Coleman now has more than 50 images available in cibachrome, ranging in price from $750 to $3,500, far less than his original paintings. And they sell out consistently, with galleries and collectors waiting impatiently for more to be produced.

In 1991, when Wyland opened galleries in Laguna Beach and San Diego, Coleman agreed to show his work in both. "That turned out to be just unbelievable," he says with genuine astonishment. "After a year and a half there, the shows were getting so packed you couldn't even get in the door, especially at the all-artists shows, where Wyland, myself and Roy Tabora would make a rare appearance together."

Coleman's one-man shows were packing the house as well. "That was shocking to me, that I had that much impact," he says. "But it was fun, and I really liked being in the galleries because you got to meet people and listen to first-hand feelings about what my paintings meant to them. What I'd always hoped for was to be able to touch their hearts and minds and imaginations. That's what every artist wants to do."

In one sense, Coleman feels a tinge of guilt when people tell him they've given up their vacation to buy one of his paintings. "If their hearts have been touched, people will give up almost anything to keep that feeling," he says. "When that happens, I find myself telling them: 'No, no. . . please don't do that. You need your vacation, you need to get away.'"

One such couple, he remembers, responded: "Yeah, but this painting will last forever. Vacations come and go."

It's particularly exciting, he says, when someone who has already purchased one of his paintings tells him, "You don't know what this means to me," or, "We have this painting in our bedroom because it's so romantic."

Coleman is aware that people purchase his moonlight tropical paintings for their bedrooms. "I know they do because they tell me," he laughs. "And why not? I'm a romantic. It's fun to make a living showing that romantic spirit I see in nature to other people. If they put one of these paintings in their bedroom, it just proves that some of these husbands know what they're doing.

"What I'm trying to do is make the viewer feel, and long

When I first saw the work of James Coleman, I was on tour with Ice Capades in Scottsdale, Arizona. Then I saw his work again at a Wyland Gallery on the Island of Oahu in Hawaii while performing there.

When I first saw his work it instantly drew me into such a beautiful peaceful world. I could feel the power and yet the serenity of this private hide-away. I have such a strong picture and feeling of what paradise is and James Coleman took me into that sanctuary within myself through his expression.

I decided to commission his piece "Peaceful Rythym" as a gift for myself. As I reflect upon my career as a professional Ice Skater, I look upon these years with such happiness and fulfill-ment that I then asked Mr. Coleman to place a pair of ice skates hanging from the railing of the cottage in the painting. For me this brings together the joy of this paradise with my love of skating, making it such a special union.

Greg Bonin
Olympic Gold Medalist

to feel, not just fantasy, but real fantasy," he says. "That's what I like about Steven Spielberg's films—he uses these great fantasy scenes, but they're images that are possible. And that makes them even better."

Something Coleman often hears is: "Well, this looks real. . . but how could it be?" If they've been in the redwoods, he maintains, they know the scenes are real. It's the tropical paintings they're not sure about, he says, because most people haven't been to the rural and coastal valleys and seen the tin-roofed houses for themselves.

"There is some fantasy in my work, but what is so incredible is that these places are out there!" he exclaims. "Every time I feel like some of my work is starting to go over the edge, I remind myself that it's nothing as spectacular as the real thing."

What Coleman tries to do is capture the mood of a moment in nature, and then convey his impression of it on canvas so that it will create an emotional impact on the viewer. In the studio, he tries to go back to the moment and ask himself: "Now, what time of day was it? And why did that touch me so much?" He might even change it, deciding it would have more impact at night. Or, he might decide the scene would be more effective if that bush of flowers were toplit.

"In some of the moonlight scenes I've done," he says, "the moon was basically behind a house, but I have the shadows such that the moon appears as if it's above the house. People ask me why I would do that, and I tell them that if I do it exactly true to nature, it's not going to have the same emotional appeal.

"That's what I learned at Disney. Sometimes you have to manipulate things to get the most out of the artwork."

As a color specialist and designer for Disney films, Coleman's job was to create mood within sequences through the use and design of color. "The trick is to take a composition and enhance the power of the piece and maybe bring more life and light to it," he explains. "That can mean, for instance, transposing a group of colors into various times of day. When you change something from morning to afternoon, they're the same basic colors, but they take on a completely different temperature."

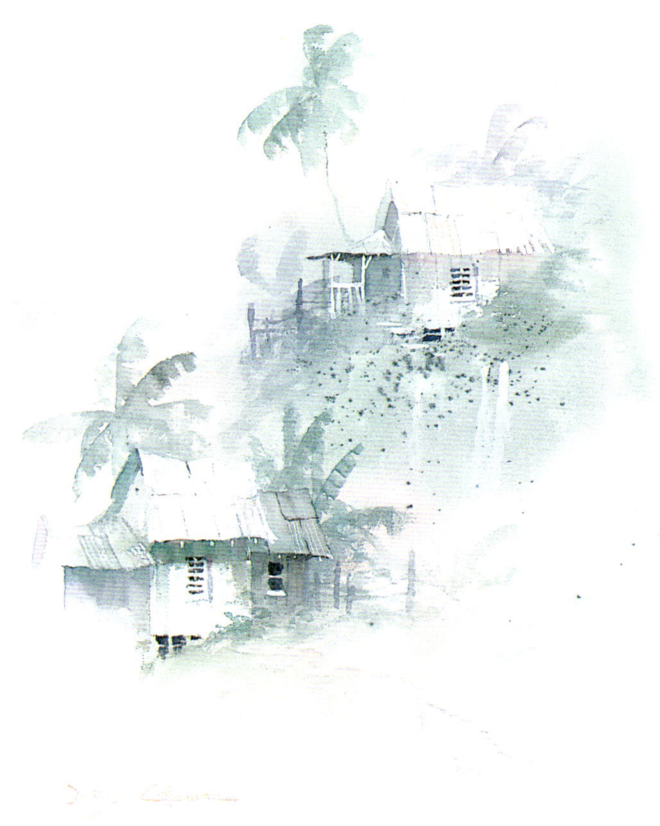

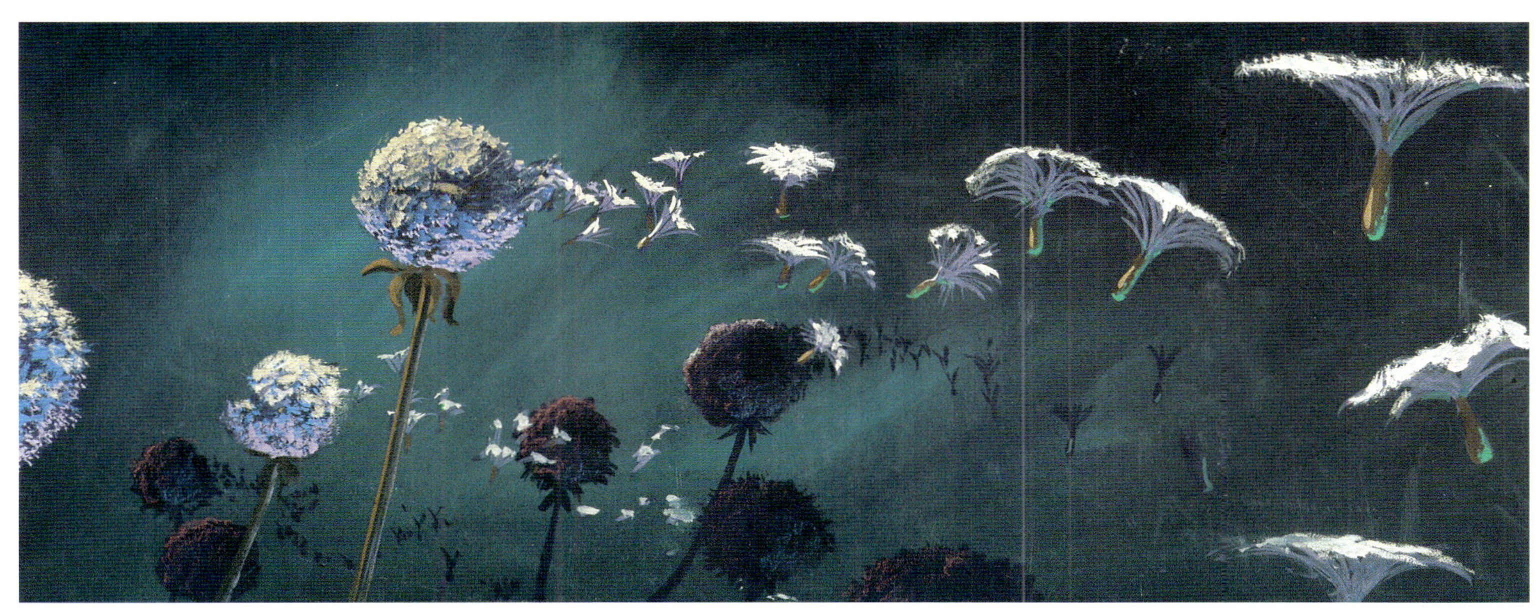

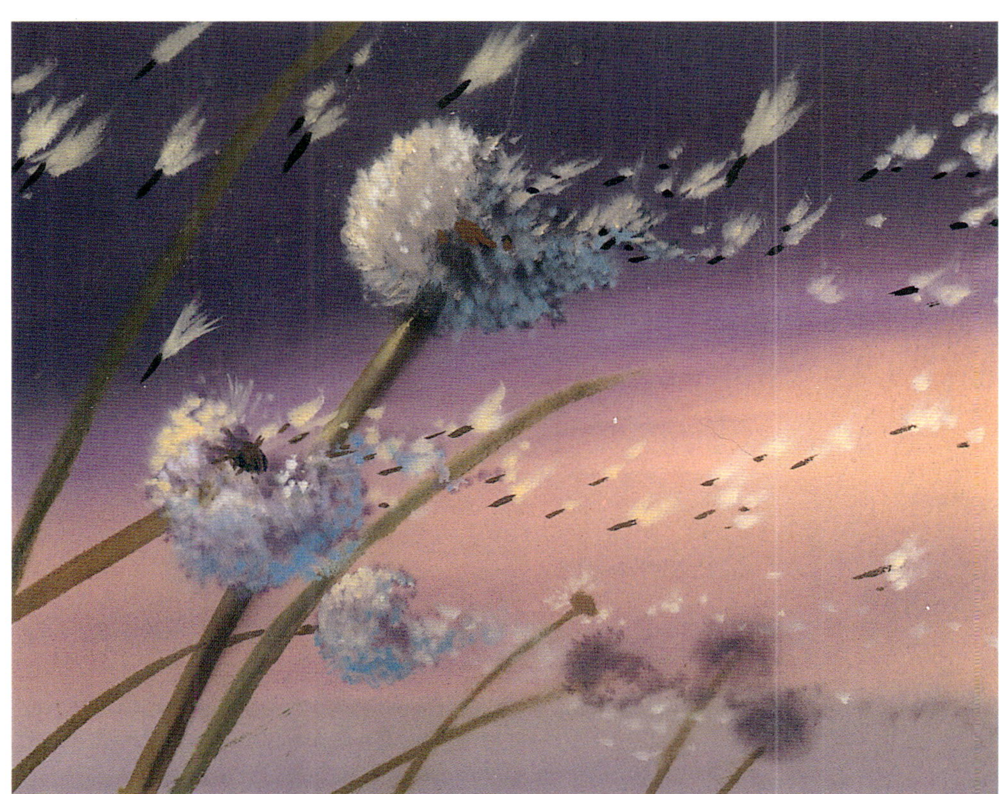

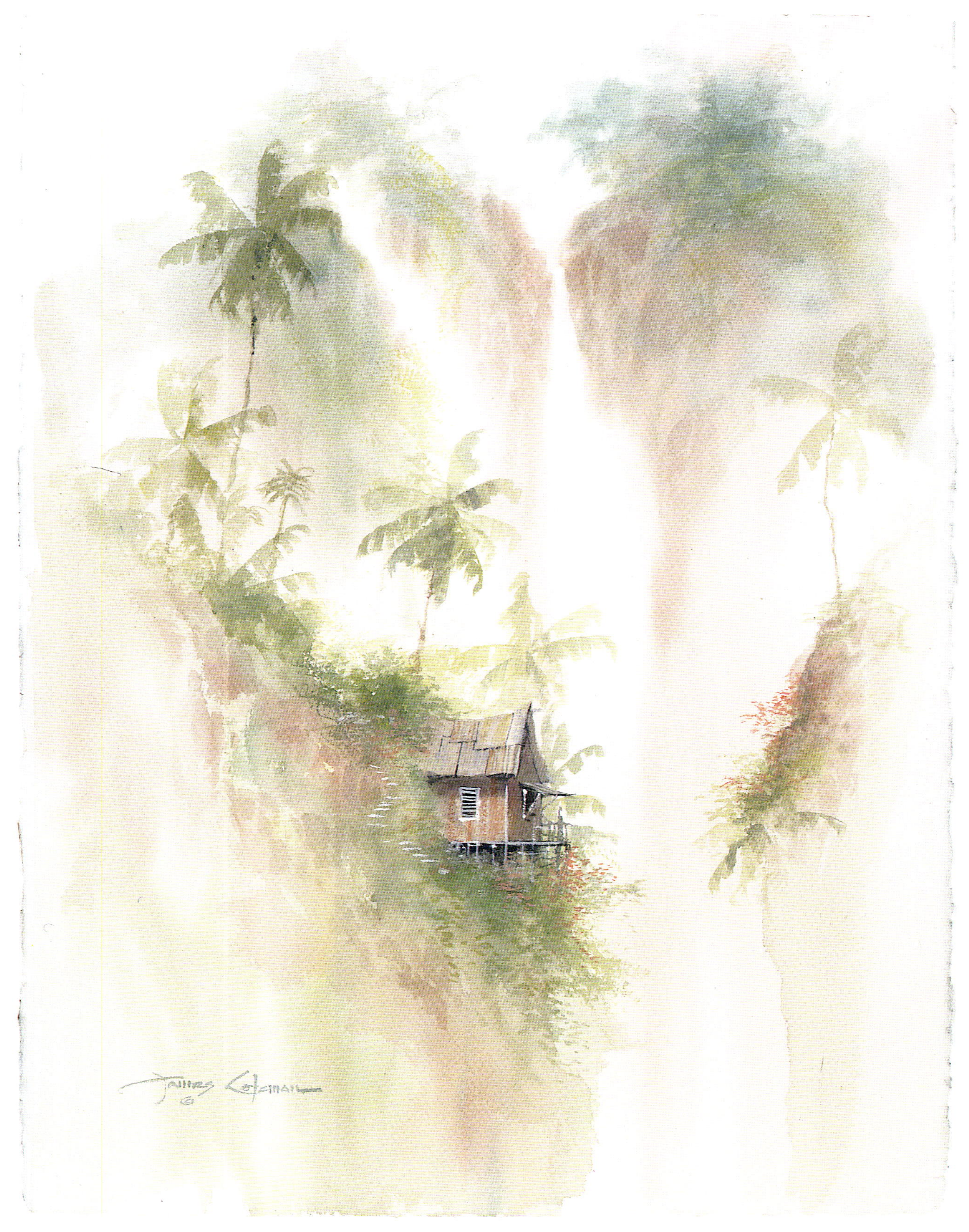

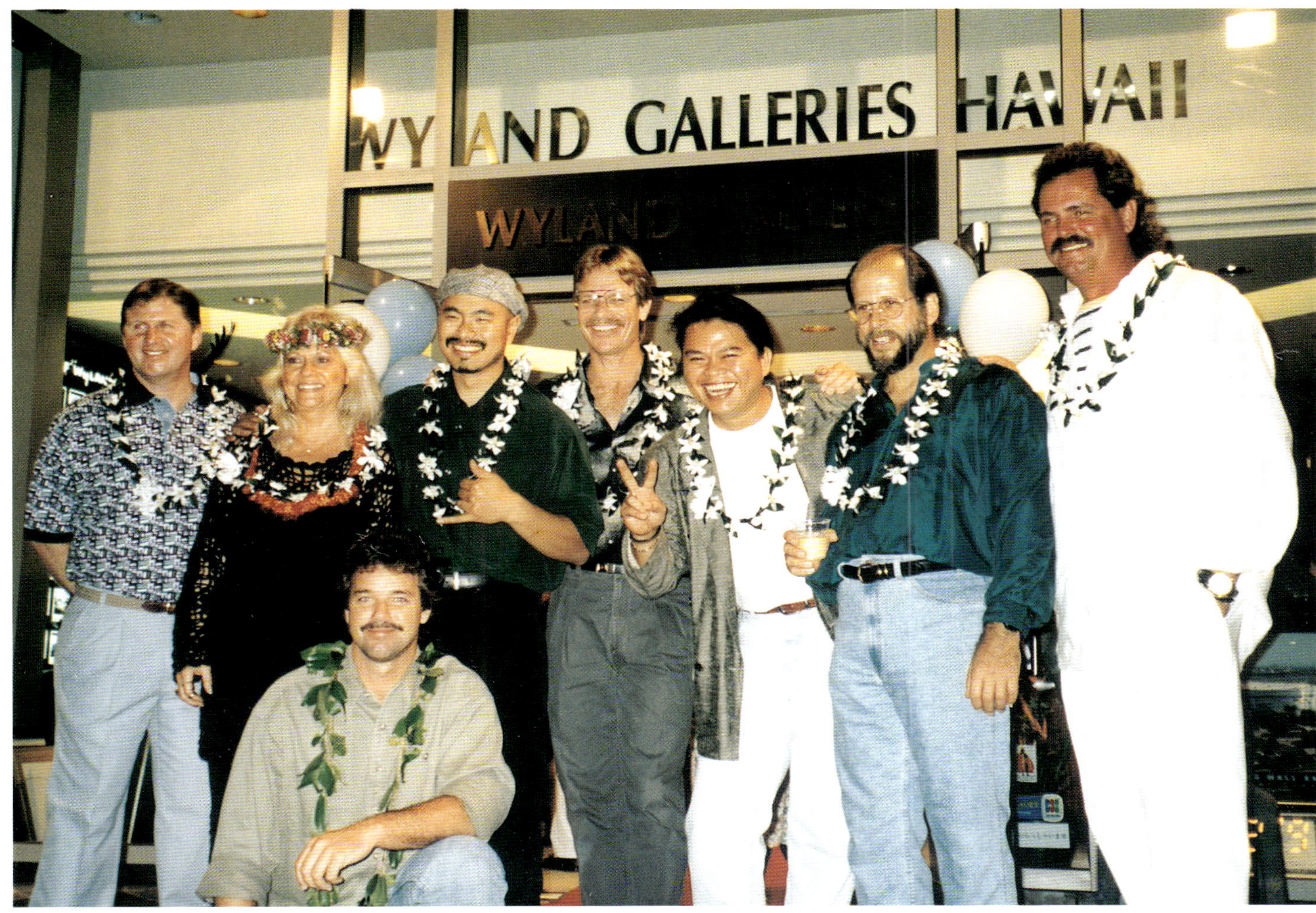

Mike Maiden, Janet Stewart, Wyland (kneeling), Walfrido, Scott Hanson, Roy Gonzalez Tabora, John Pitre & Coleman at Wyland Galleries, Waikiki, 1995

Much of Coleman's work today contains the cooler colors—blues and greens accented by magentas, soft violets and others. But he doesn't overanalyze his use of certain colors, except to say it has everything to do with feeling.

"From an analytical point of view, I guess you could say that certain colors make people feel a certain way," he concedes. "But rather than doing that, I just choose colors and groups of colors that feel right to me.

"When I transpose reality into a painting, obviously I twist the ranges of colors to suit what I feel works best. It's almost a personal thing, just as all paintings are. When you paint them, they're a personal statement; and when you buy them, they're a personal aquisition."

Color, form, mood, emotion—it's all dictated by light, a subject Coleman doesn't mind analyzing at length. "Light, as we know, is the key to life," he begins. "If you take it all the way back, from the standpoint of creation, everything comes from light."

When people look at a painting, they don't always realize why it "catches" them, or doesn't. The reason, Coleman asserts, is because it either has a luminous quality and looks alive, or it's flat and has no life whatsoever. Of course, there needs to be objects, he adds, like trees, mountains and tin-roof houses. Otherwise, it would be a stage without an actor.

"There are people who are geniuses at painting the human figure or wildlife," he points out. "But for me, I made a decision that I wanted to represent nature, and I ultimately realized that the only way to do it was to use light in creative ways.

"Everything, in that sense, is the same. I can take it apart and put it back almost like a puzzle, with the initial impact

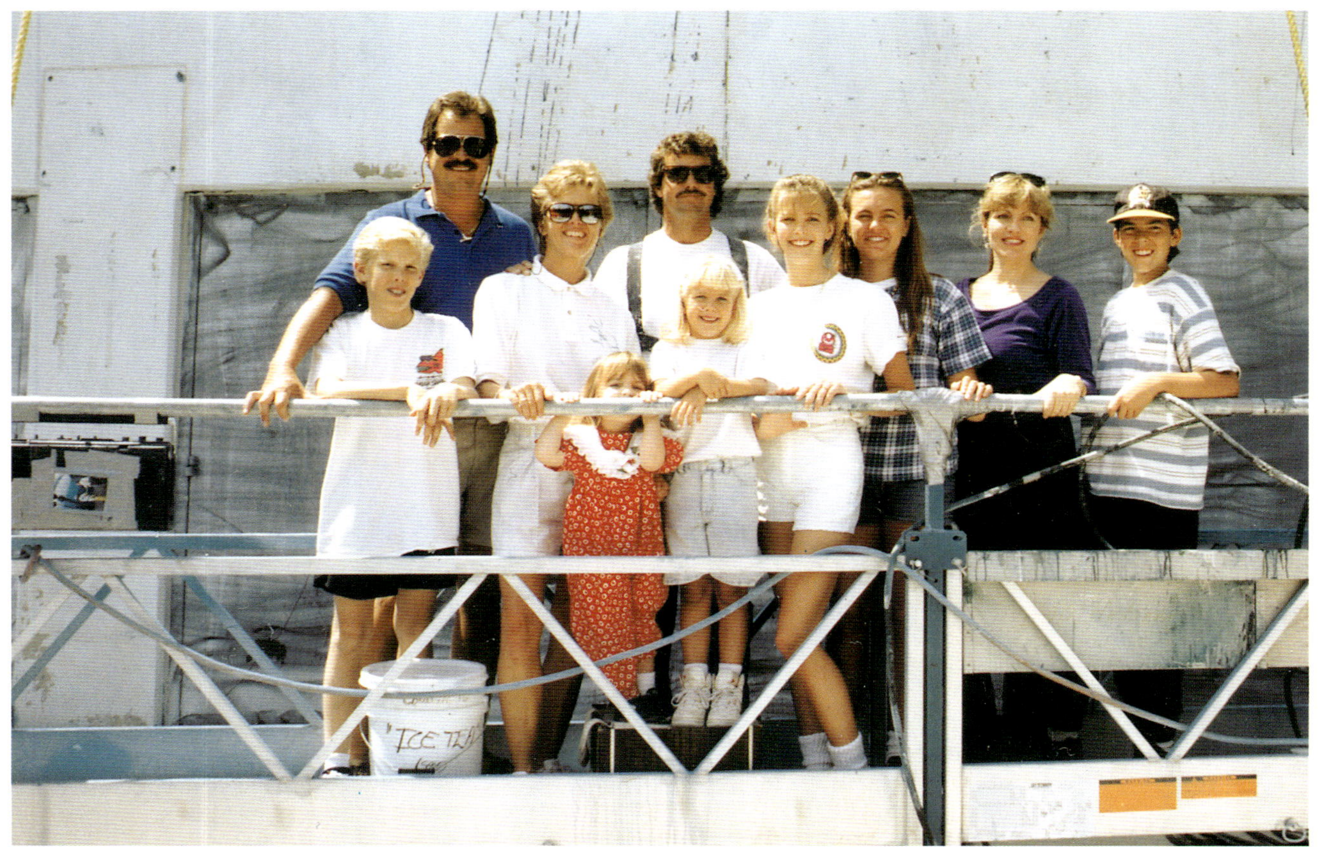

Coleman's family on a scaffold as Wyland paints his largest mural on the Long Beach Convention Center, Long Beach, California, 1991.
From left – Scott, Jim, Cathy, Madelin, Wyland, Kadie, Kimberly, Christina, Joanne & Patrick

being the light source and how it affects everything else."

As analytical as that sounds, Coleman is anything but procedural about his work. "I know artists who'll do thumbnails, sketches, and then do a small mock-up before they do the actual painting," he points out. "By the time I would get to the painting, using that technique, all the soul would be gone."

Everyone has seen, heard or smelled something that takes them back to a feeling they've had in the past. Often, it can trigger a flow of memories. Coleman says he tries to help that flow by painting places people have either experienced before, or have always wanted to experience.

People sometimes tell him they've experienced one of his scenes first-hand. "I know that path," they'll say. Or, "If that path is in the redwoods, I've been on it." This is especially true in Hawaii, he adds, where people who grew up there tell him things like: "I've seen that little house," or, "I grew up in a house like that."

Coleman paints moments in nature that reach in and touch people's hearts, yet no people can be found in his scenes. Or can they?

"I've found that if you put people in the paintings, it immediately causes the viewer to see another person, rather than to place themselves in the painting," he says. "I try to draw viewers all the way into the painting so they'll be participants. I want it to be something they can add to, or dream about. I want them to get completely lost in it."

The artist must be the first participant, however. "It's not just a job—it's your life," Coleman says authoritatively. "It becomes the essence of everything you're doing and thinking about. Each time you look at something, you look at it from that point of view—why does this look the way it does? How does that tree bend? How does that wave in the ocean fold over the foam? When do you have that glittery effect on the water from the moon? It's like taking pictures in your brain constantly."

Again, with Coleman, it's not about merely taking images back to the studio. It's what you do with them when you get there.

"I saw an old tin-roof house on Kauai recently," he says. "The back half of it had these huge cascades of flowers growing right out of the windows. Obviously, the people who lived there had closed off that part of the house, and it just filled up with vegetation.

"It doesn't matter if I paint the house exactly the way it was. What matters is that it spurred my imagination to say: 'My gosh, these plants could be literally growing inside these people's living space! That, in itself, starts to open up other windows for how I can get the essence of these people's existence on canvas. I don't have to actually put them in the scene. You know what they're like by looking at the spirit of their home."

When you get right down to it, everything Coleman paints is about spirit. Whether it's a tin-roof house, a waterfall in a deep tropical valley, a mountain framed by a sensational cloudscape, or majestic redwood trees towering over a path in the forest, it's a look into a spiritual moment in nature.

"The most rewarding thing for an artist is to know that you've touched a person's soul with something you've created," he says, a smile starting to form. "I believe it's like an extension of creation, no matter what the artform—painting, music, writing, whatever. God created everything, and what the artist does is an extension of that creation.

"What I'm doing is taking the way in which I see and feel the world and putting that on canvas. And, to me, the world is full of peace, tranquility and serenity."

I discovered James Coleman's work on the island of Maui. What struck me most about it was an immediate feeling of wanting to be in that picture, in that place.

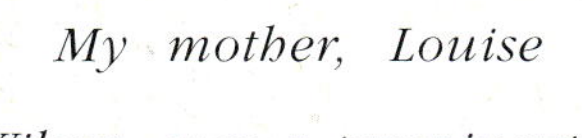

My mother, Louise Wilson, was a prominent artist in the pacific northwest, and I grew up with, not only an appreciation of her work, but with all the artists in the Seattle area with whom she traded. Now appreciating someone's work, and actually buying it are two different things – but after returning from Maui I still had a strong enough feeling to track Mr. Coleman down and commission a painting.

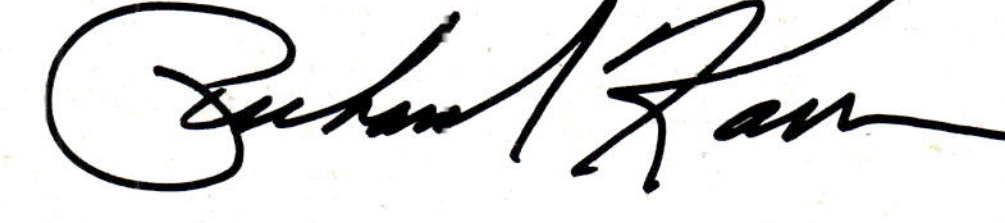

Richard Karn
ABC's Home Improvement

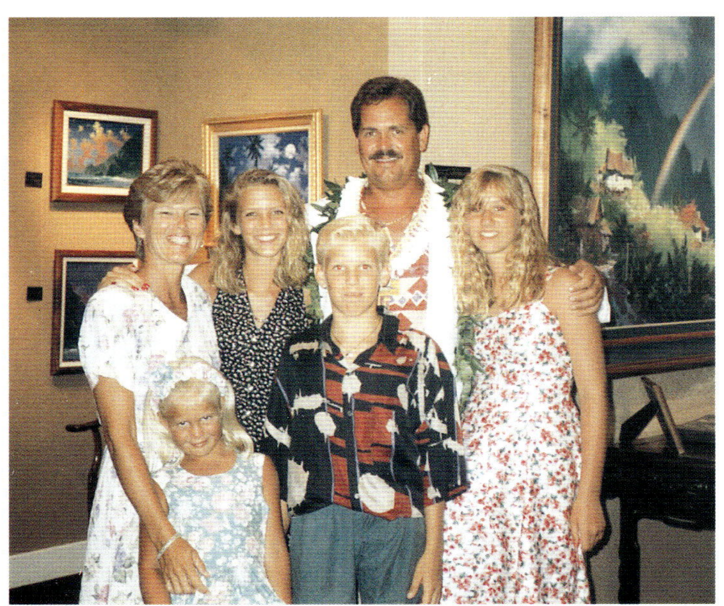

James with his family at an art show

Coleman draws great satisfaction from the fact that he has touched the souls of so many people with his work, which can now be found in Europe, Asia, North America and Hawaii. His paintings have had a profound effect on some.

"People who have lost loved ones have told me: 'Your painting has made such a difference. . . It's time to start loving again.'

"Another time, a man and wife whose house had burned down bought one of my paintings and told me: 'This is the start of our new home. We're going to build our entire house around it.'"

When people come up to him with tears in their eyes, he knows he's using his gift to its fullest potential. It's all part of the spiritual aspect of what he does, and how he lives. It's what keeps him at the easel.

"I have to paint," he says. "When I stay away from it for more than a day, I feel empty. But when I'm painting, it's like a glass being filled with water."

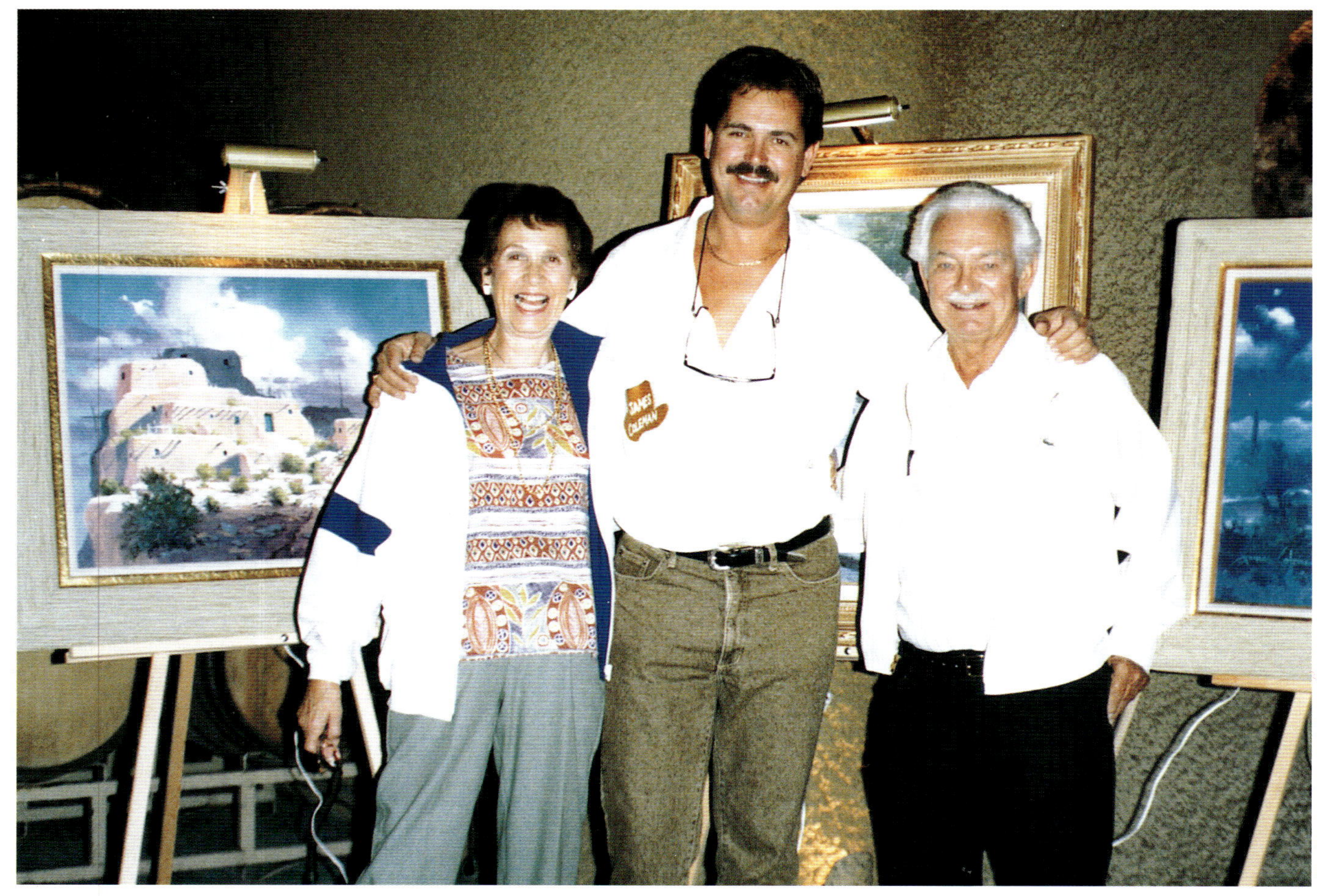

Jim with his parents at an art show

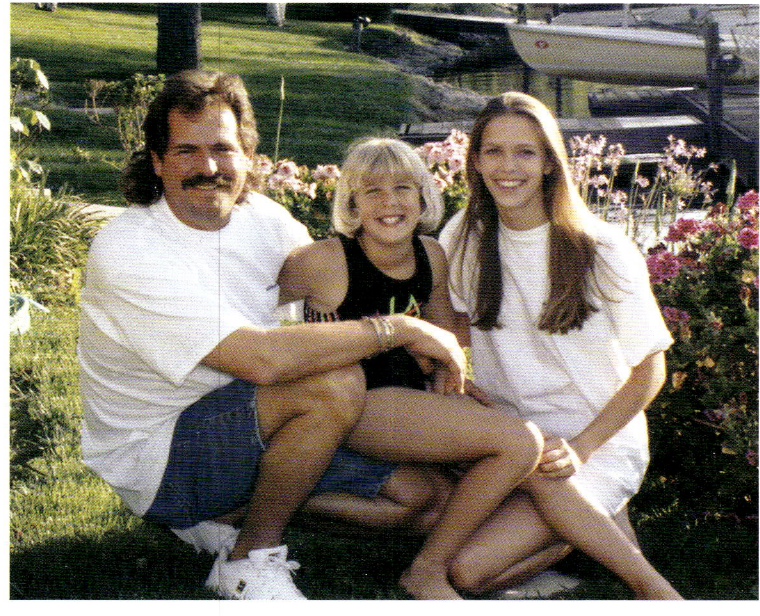

Jim with his daughters, Kadie and Kim

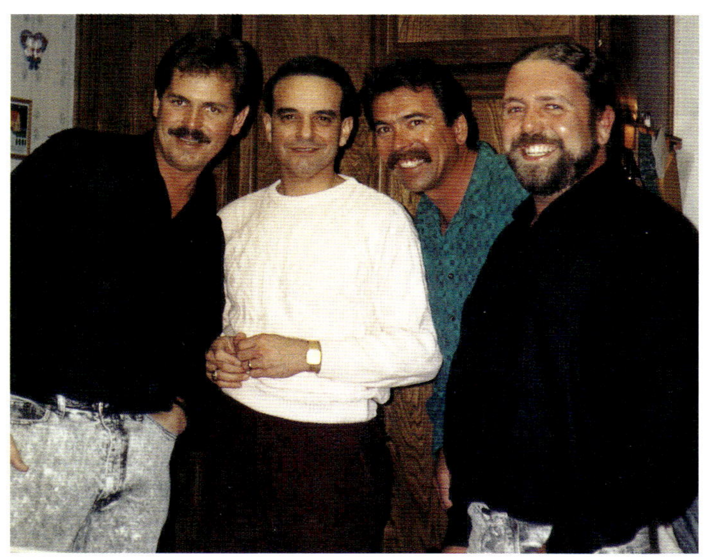

Jim's 40th birthday party. From left, Jim, Dr. Dennis Maceri, John Freeman and John Coleman

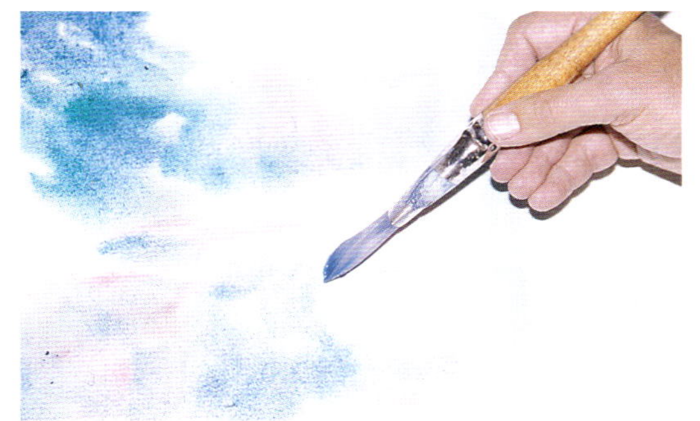

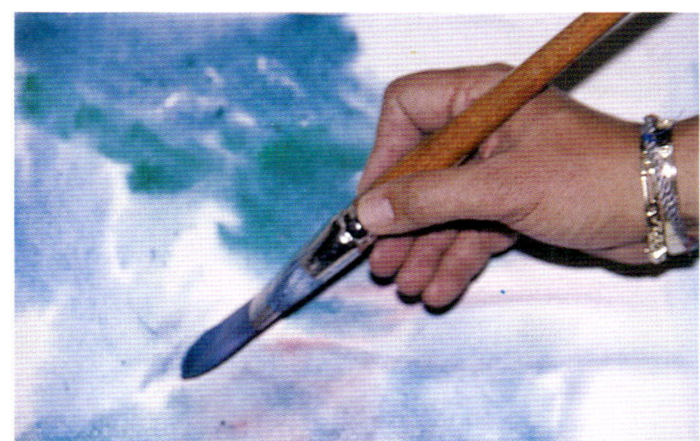

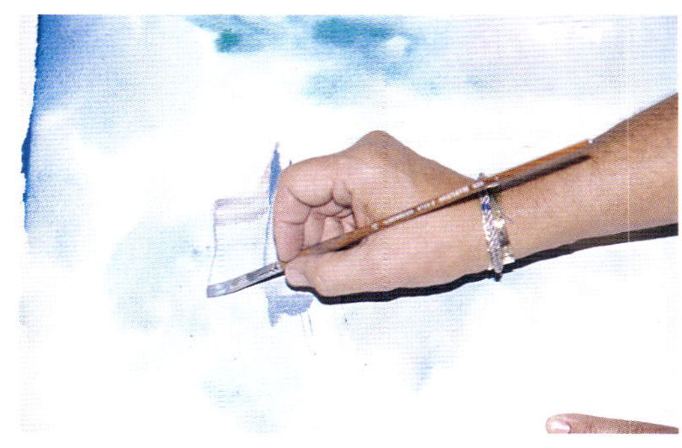

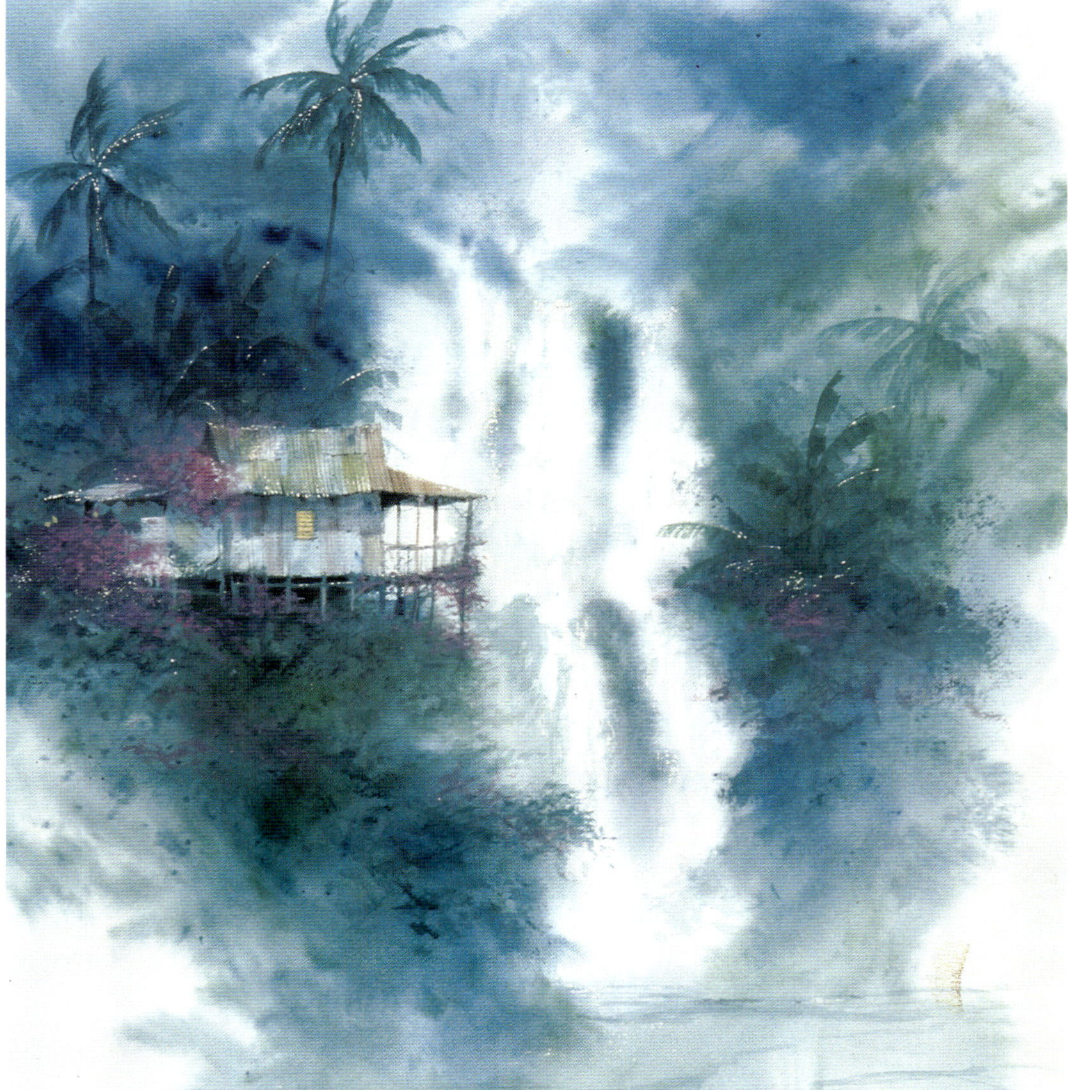

Development of a Coleman watercolor

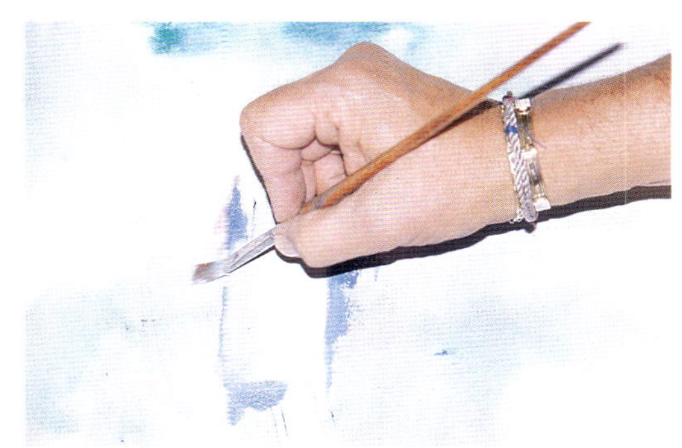

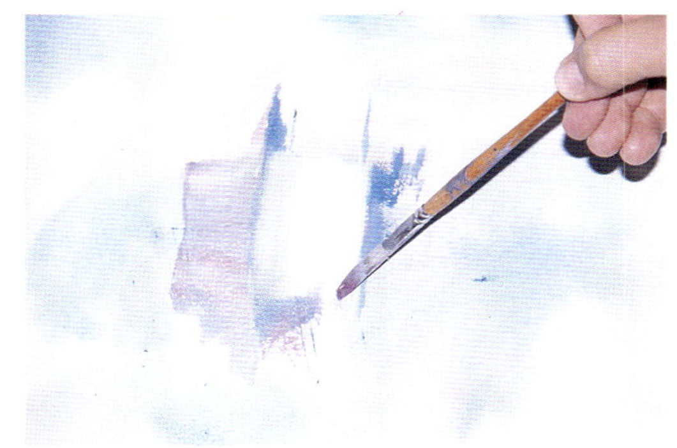

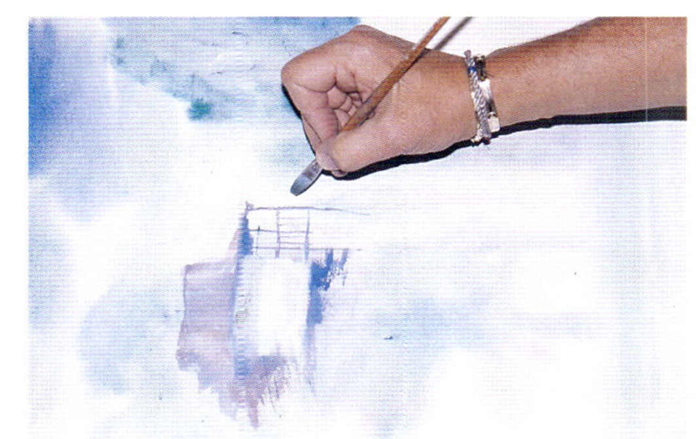

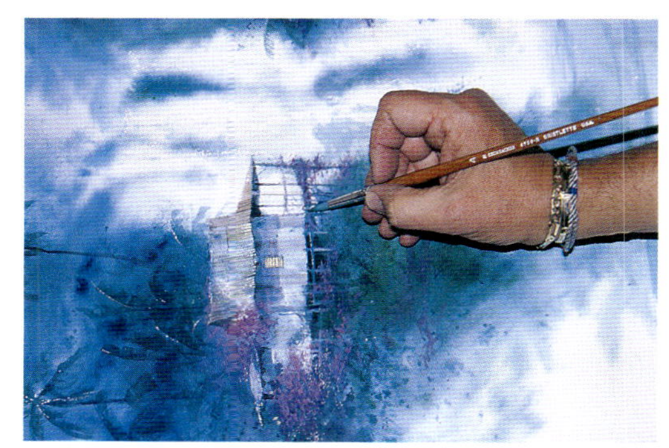

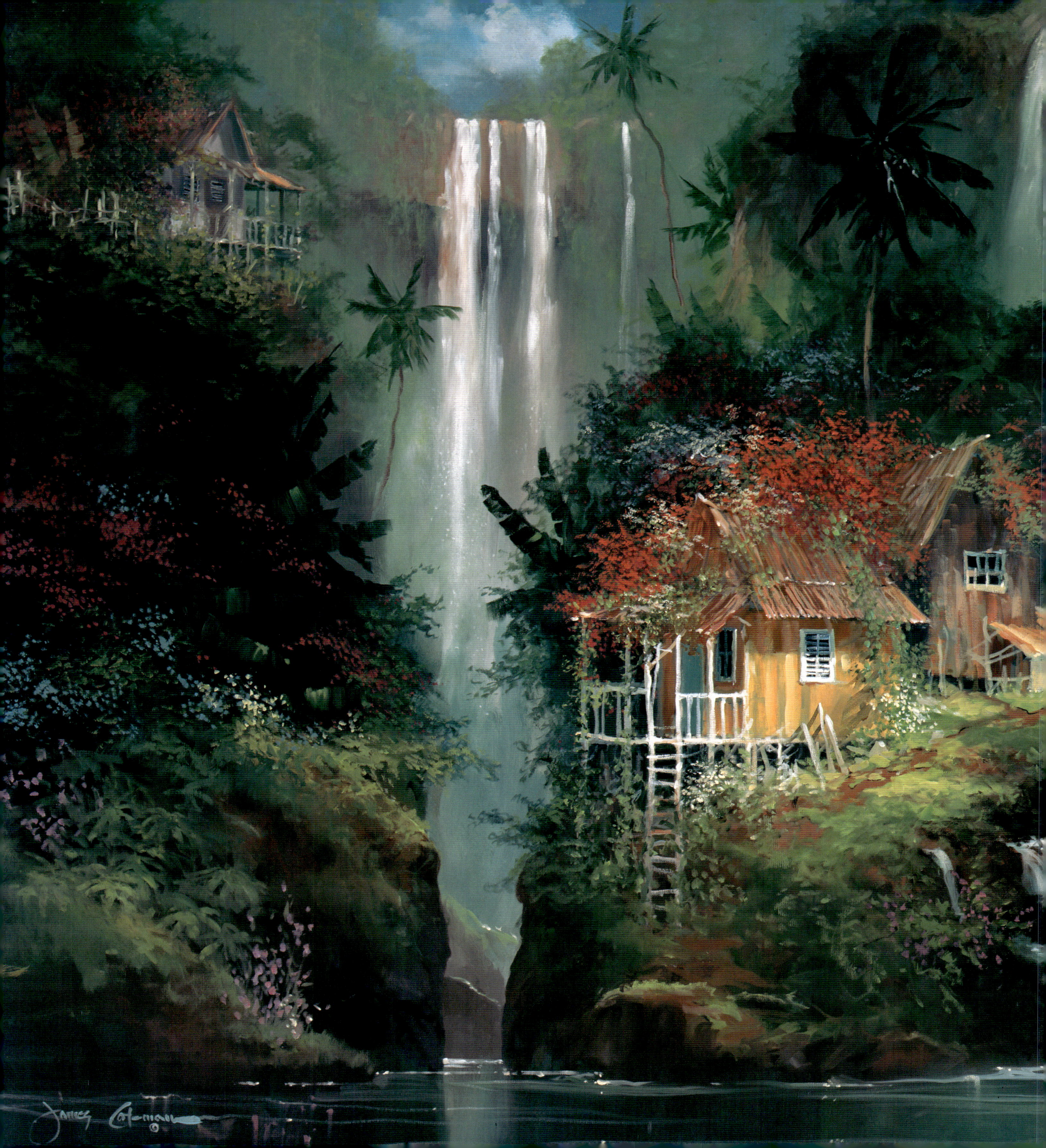

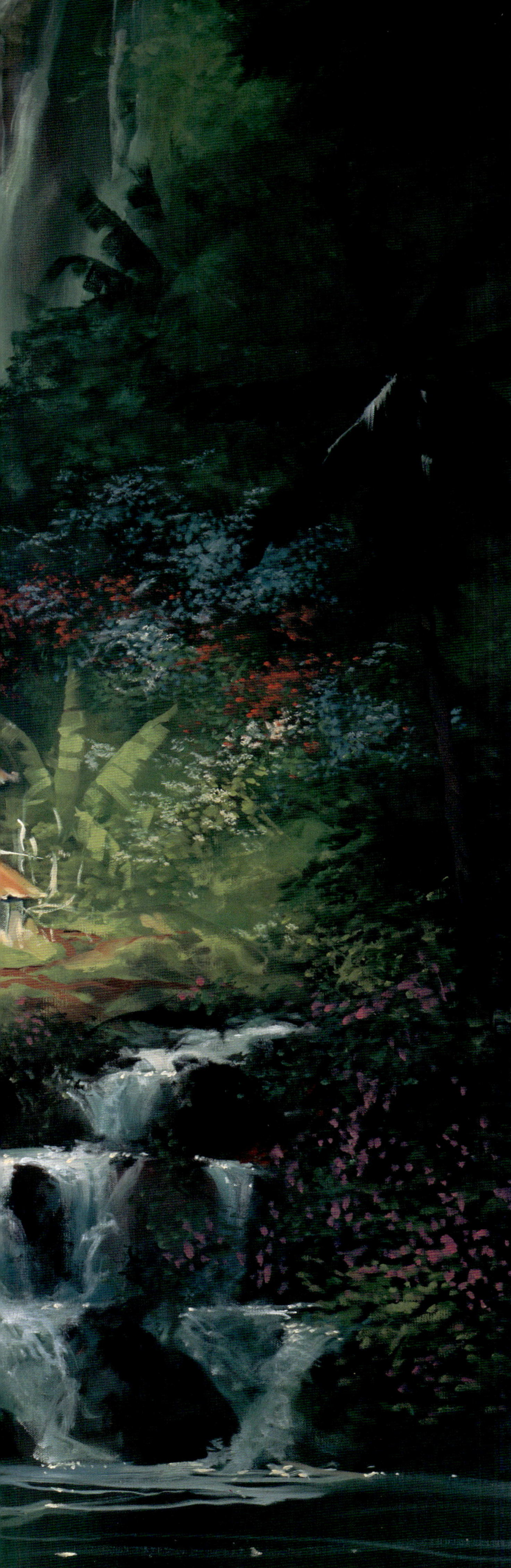

5

Tropical Dreams

The old gentleman stood in front of the painting crying. Coleman, surrounded by a throng of people, watched him out of the corner of his eye as he shook hands and circulated among the fans who had flooded the gallery to meet him.

It seemed as if the man had been standing there for a long time as the artist, curious, excused himself from the crowd and slid over next to the man.

Coleman said nothing because the man, his eyes full of tears, was obviously lost in the painting. Sensing someone was next to him, sharing the piece titled *Mystical Falls*, the old man started to weep. Without looking at him, he said to Coleman: "You can't imagine what I'm feeling when I look at this painting. I was in Viet Nam during the invasion of Cambodia. I can smell it, feel it and breathe it. It was one of the most beautiful places I've ever been in my life, and the most terrifying. "When I look at this, I love it and hate all at the same time."

Coleman didn't know what to say. When he painted this tropical piece, full of long, graceful waterfalls pouring into a lush green valley, he had thought nothing of the Viet Nam war. But this wasn't the first time someone had told him his scenes looked like Viet Nam, Cambodia, Thailand, Malaysia, Tahiti or Samoa. In fact, people have told him they've seen his tropical fantasies all over the world.

"A woman came up to me once and said, 'I lived in that house in Cuba.' When I told her I painted the scene she was

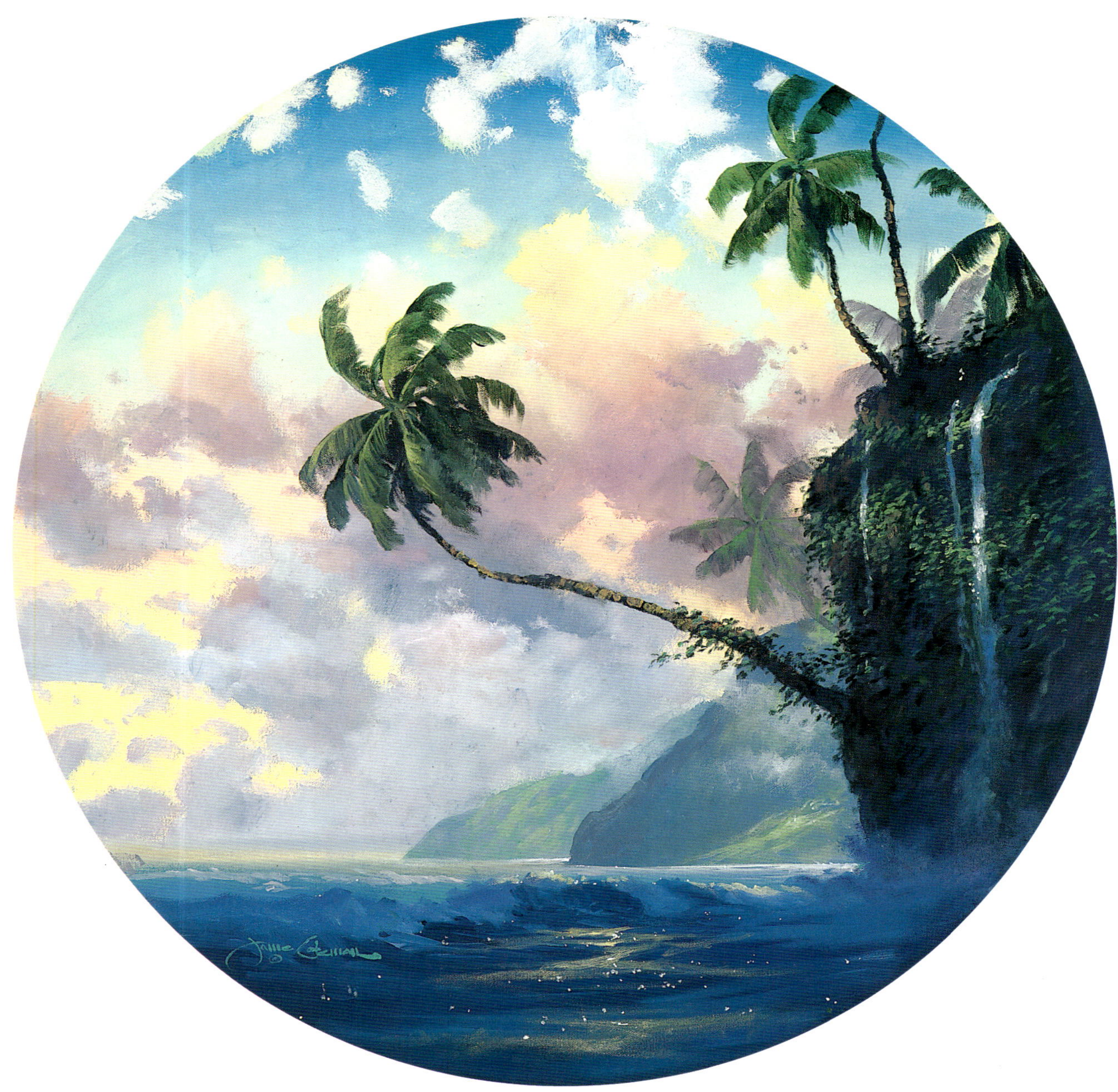

Trade Winds – Oil, 30 inches round

looking at from places I'd seen in Hawaii, she said, 'I don't care. I grew up in that house.'

"I met a man in Hawaii who said he owned one of the largest hotels in Tahiti," he continues. "He said one of my paintings looked just like Tahiti, and that if I came over there, he'd show me places I've never dreamed of."

Coleman doesn't doubt it a bit. He's used to being more and more astonished each time he visits Hawaii, and he immerses himself in the hidden treasures of the Islands' countryside. He feels he hasn't even scratched the surface in terms of exposing himself to the rich tropicana the globe has to offer.

"I didn't even think about painting anything tropical until I'd visited Hawaii several times," Coleman says. "When we first went there, my wife and I, we did all the tourist things—Waikiki and all of that. Now that I've been there so often, I've found that the real Hawaii lies off the road, where most people don't take the time to go."

In a sense, he seems to have captured the essence of something common to perhaps every tropical region in the world. The spirit conveyed by these paintings seems to be reaching people everywhere.

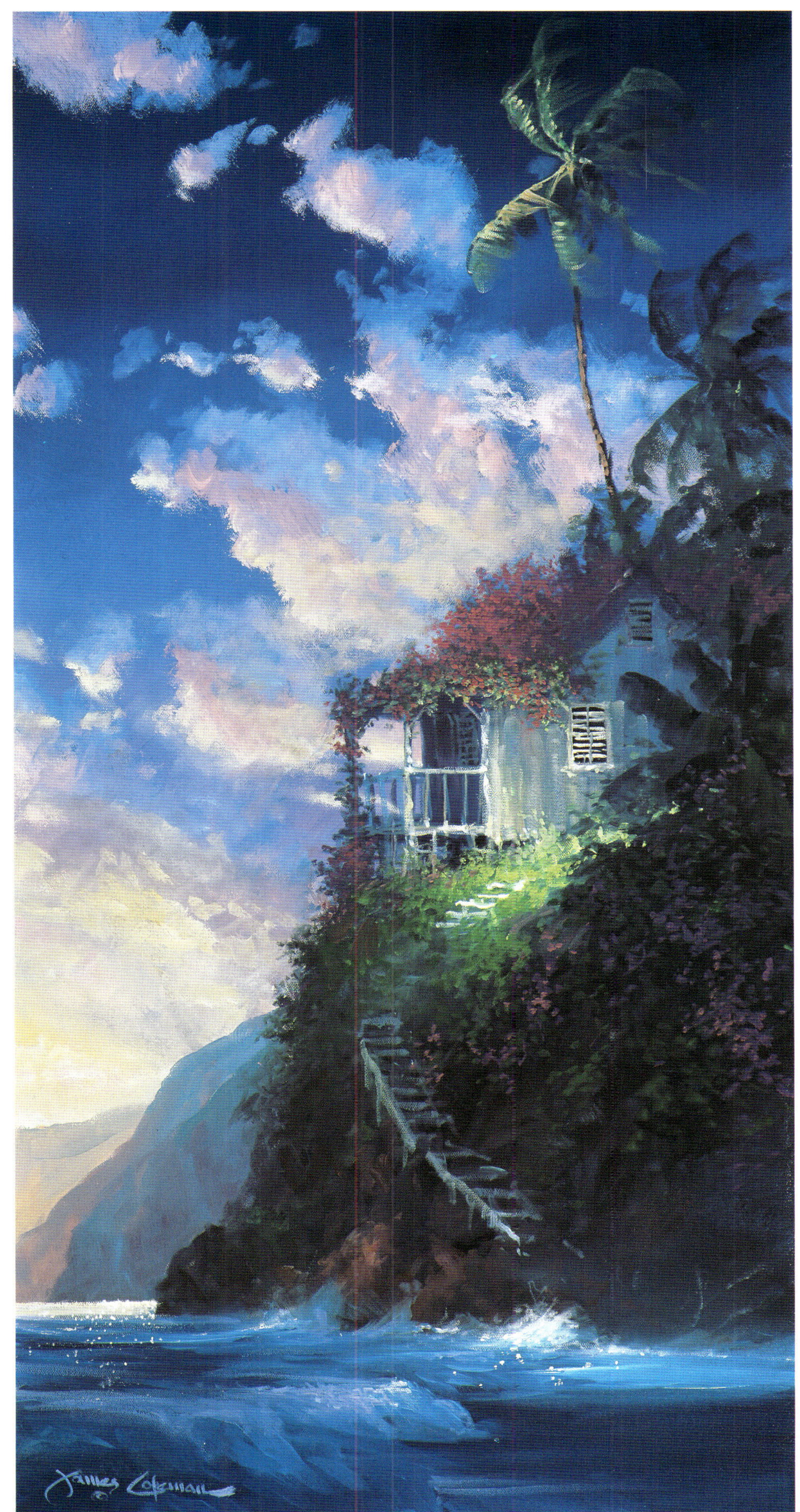

Afternoon Breezes
Oil, 36 × 18 inches

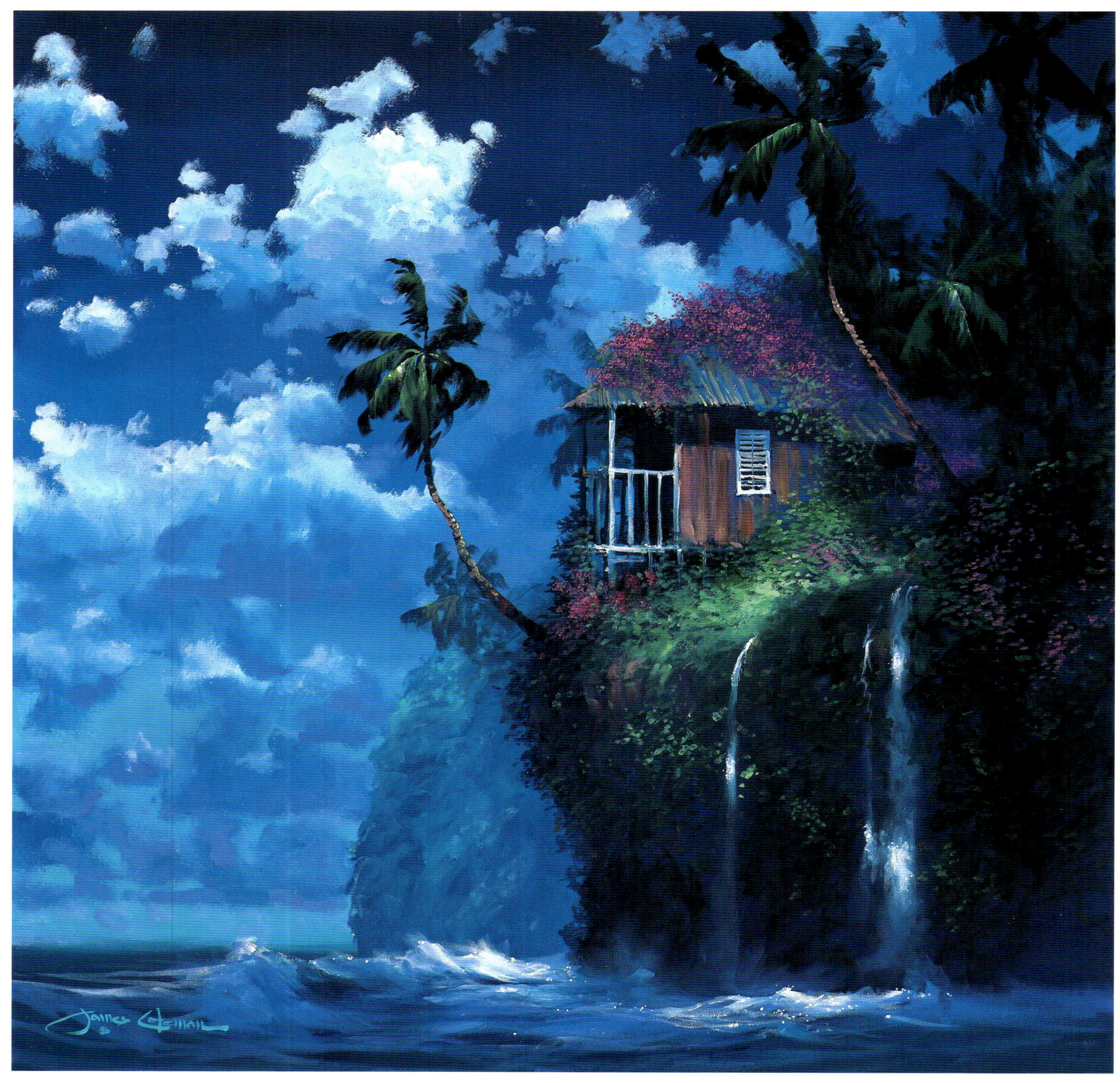

Tropical Hideaway – Oil, 36 x 36 inches

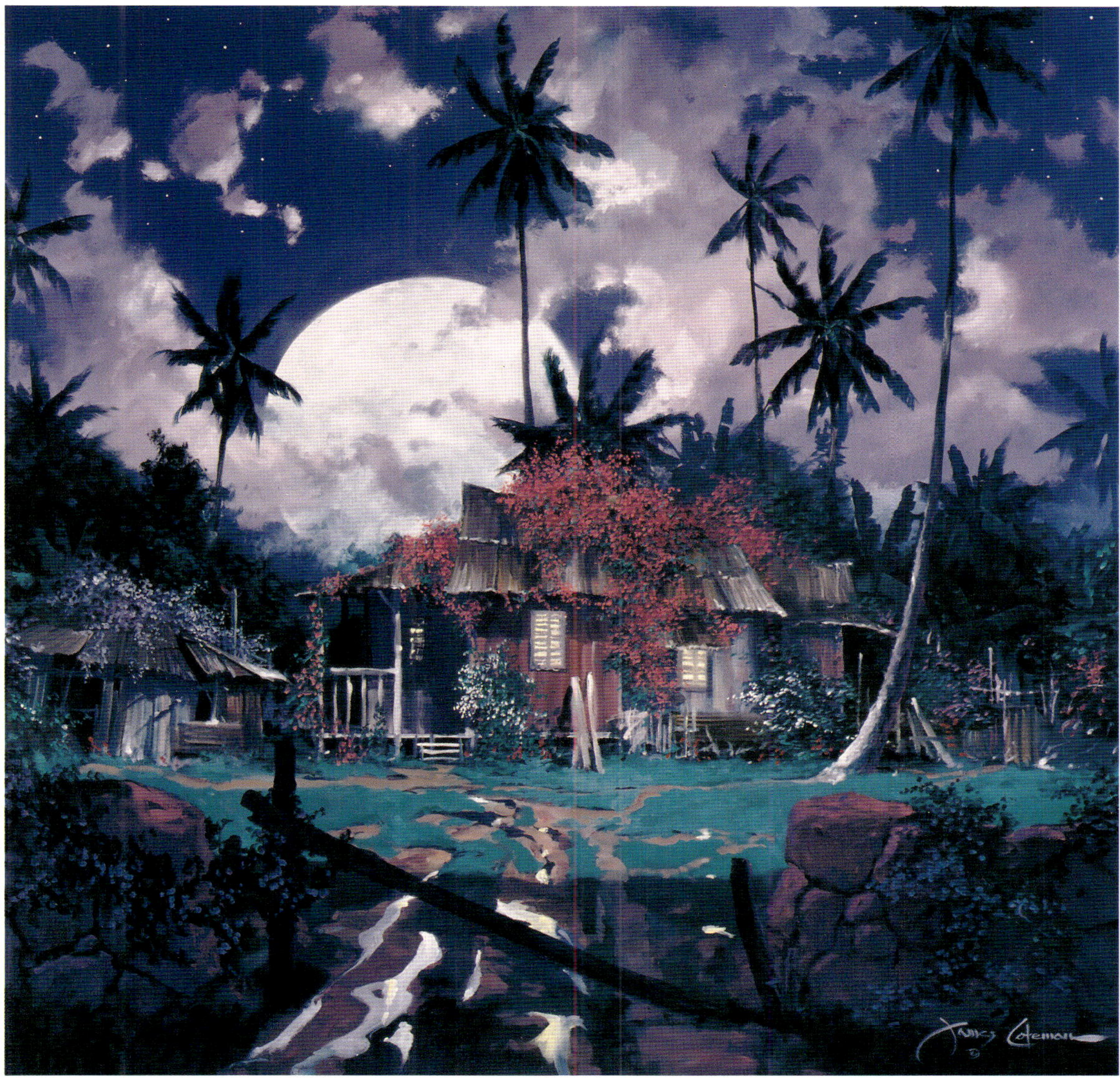

Full Moon Rising
Oil, 48 x 48 inches

"That's what I try to do with all my work," he acknowledges. "I'm a person who feels things, and I believe my spirit connects with everything in nature, and always has. I feel like God gifted me with that connection, and I think I've used the gift properly."

Coleman says he wanted to paint something from Hawaii that was different than what had been done before. Seascapes, beaches, mountains, palm trees—those images had reached a saturation point. After a few more visits to Hawaii, he started seeing the deep valleys with stunning waterfalls, and the little pathways that led up, or down, to small tin-roof farmhouses nestled in misty rainforests.

"The first tropical scenes I did were mostly cloudscapes because that was what impressed me initially," he says. "It was seven or eight years later before I started seeing the other things. It took me that long, I think, to really crystallize my feelings for Hawaii.

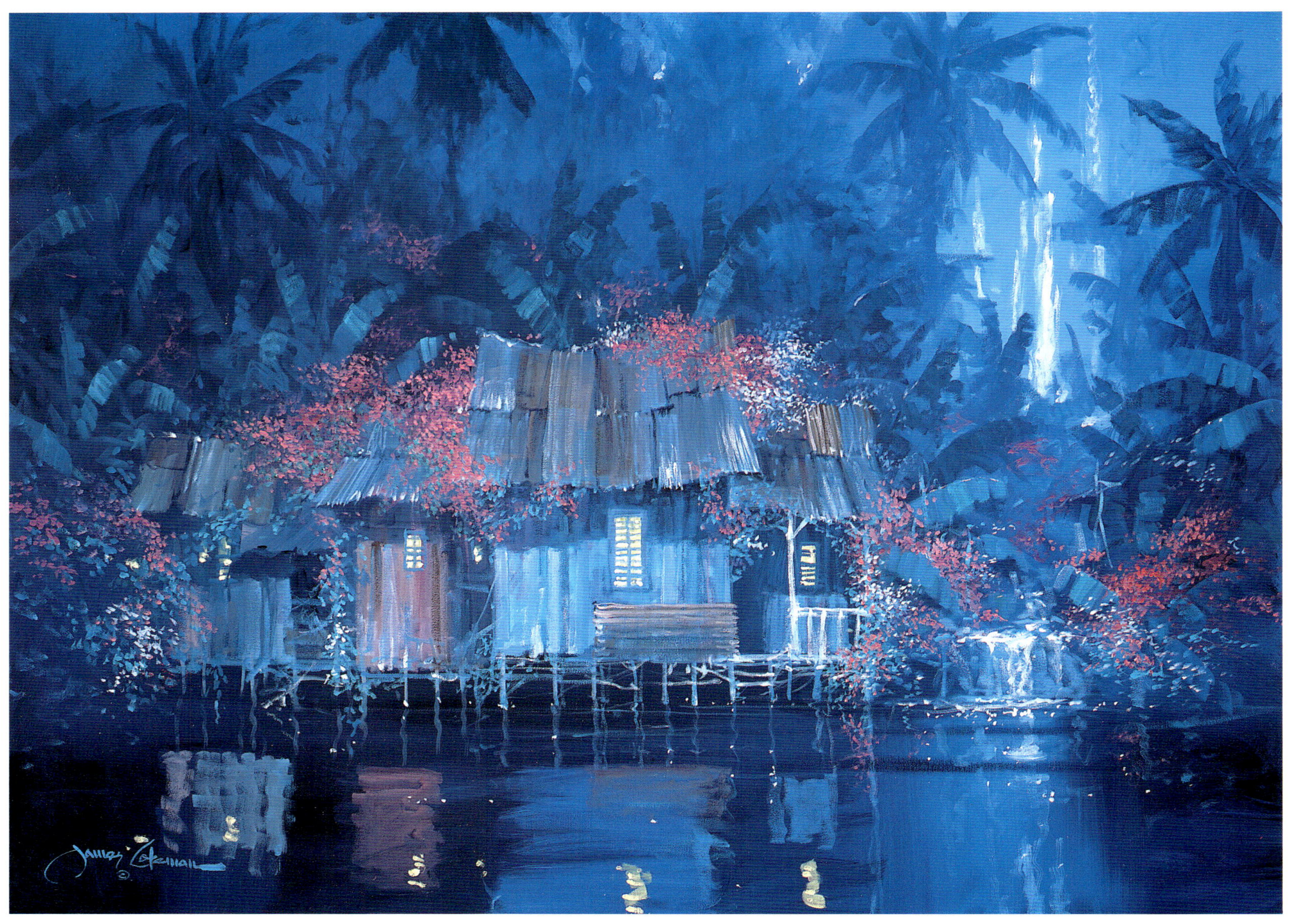

River Magic – Oil, 30 x 40 inches

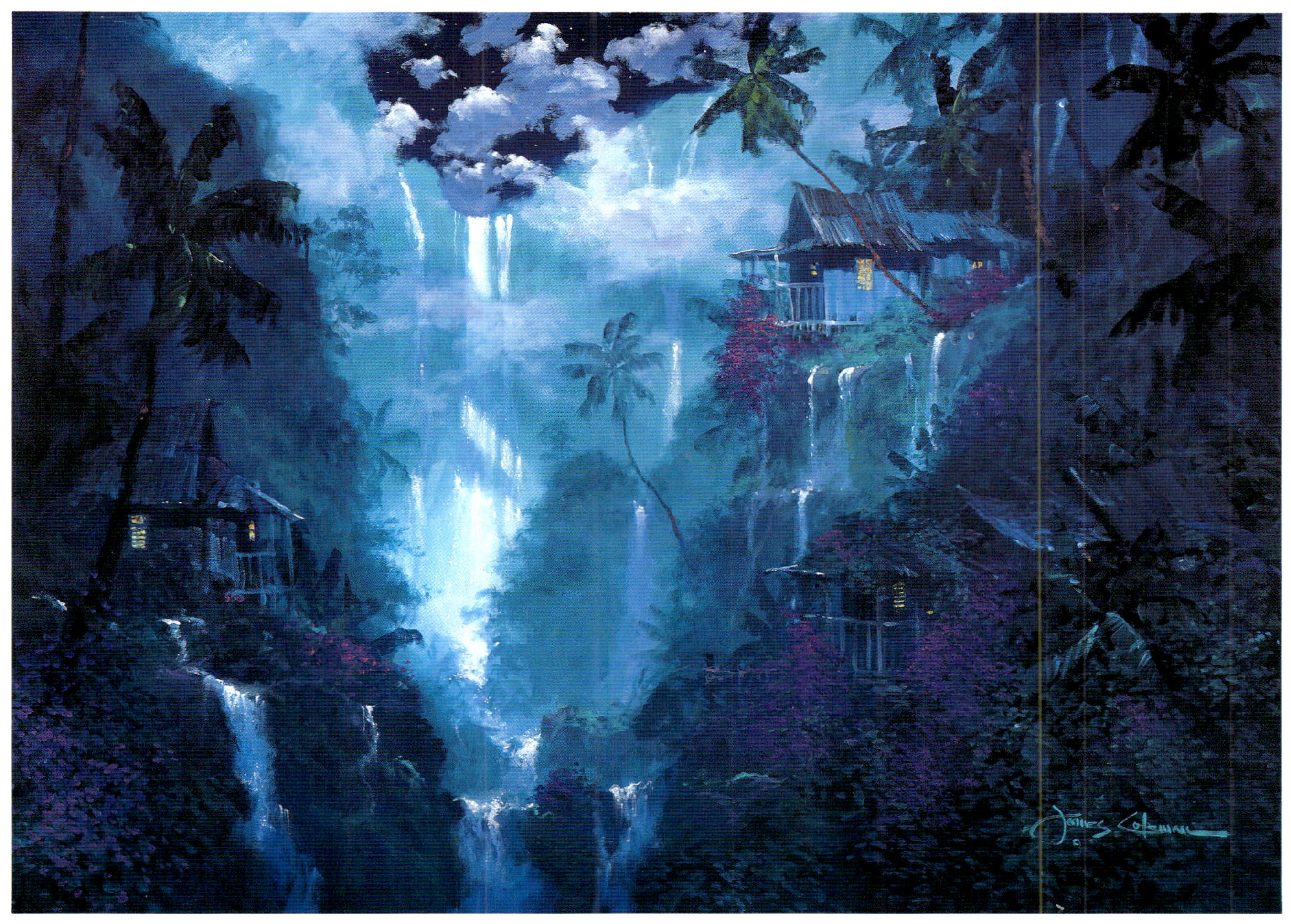

Majestic Falls – Oil, 36 x 48 inches

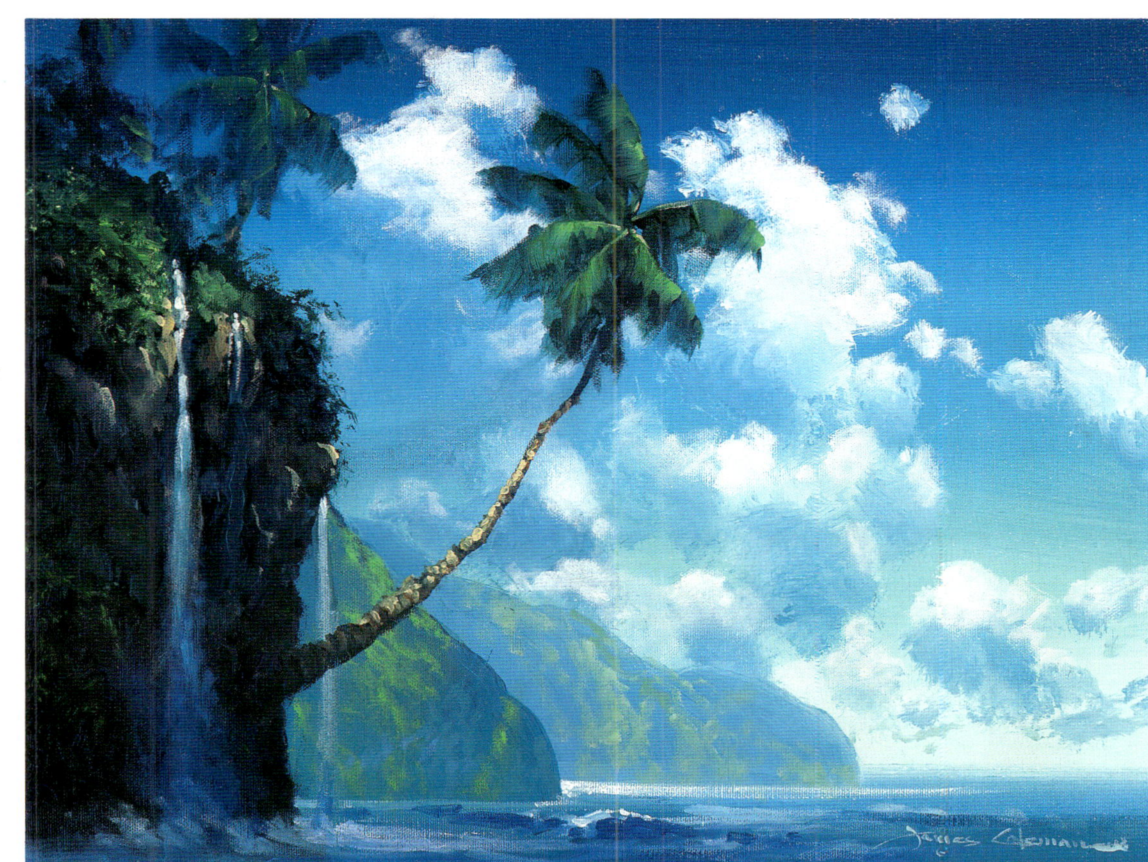

Paradise Surf
Oil, 20 x 24 inches

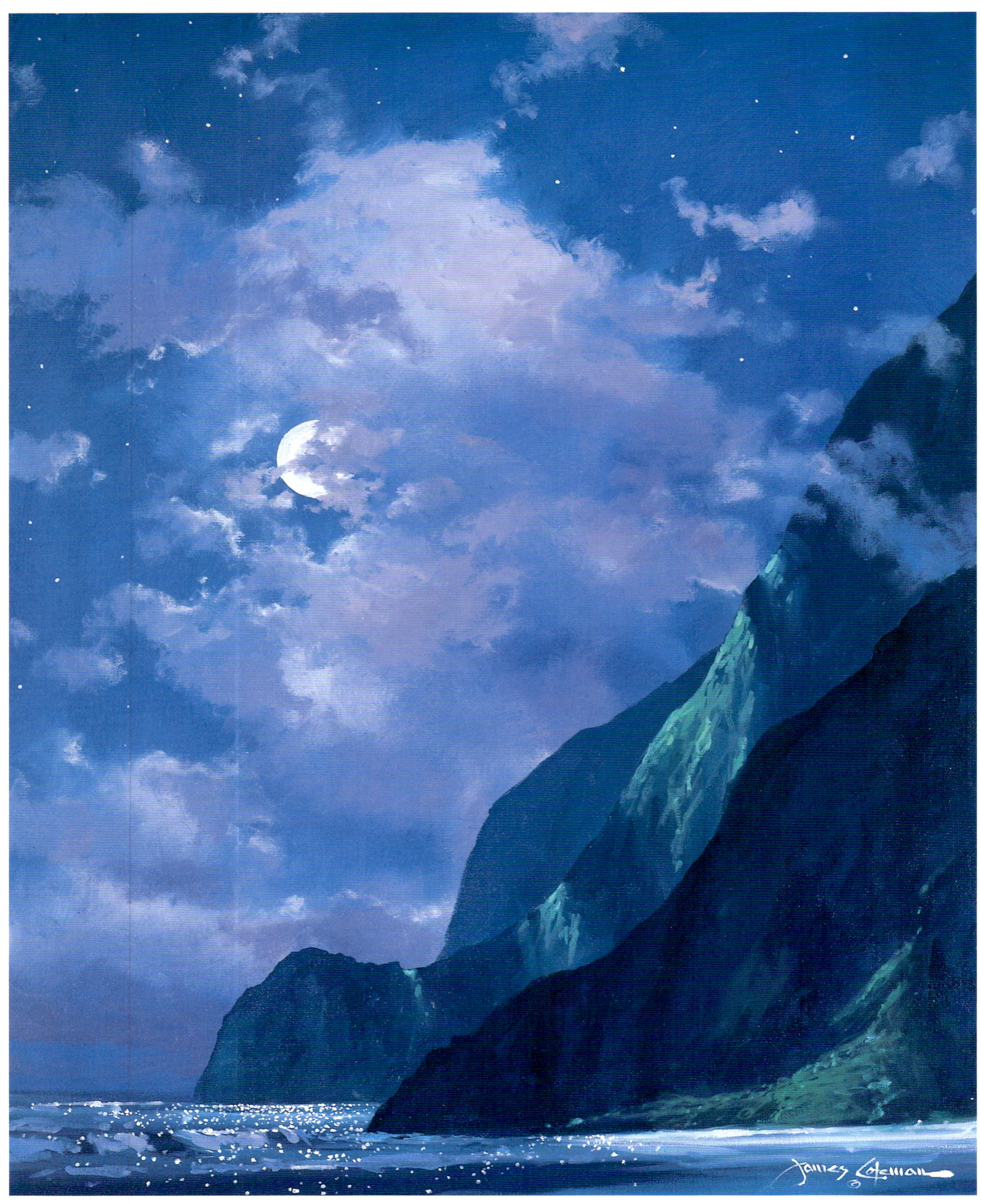

Moon Shadows – Oil, 30 x 24 inches

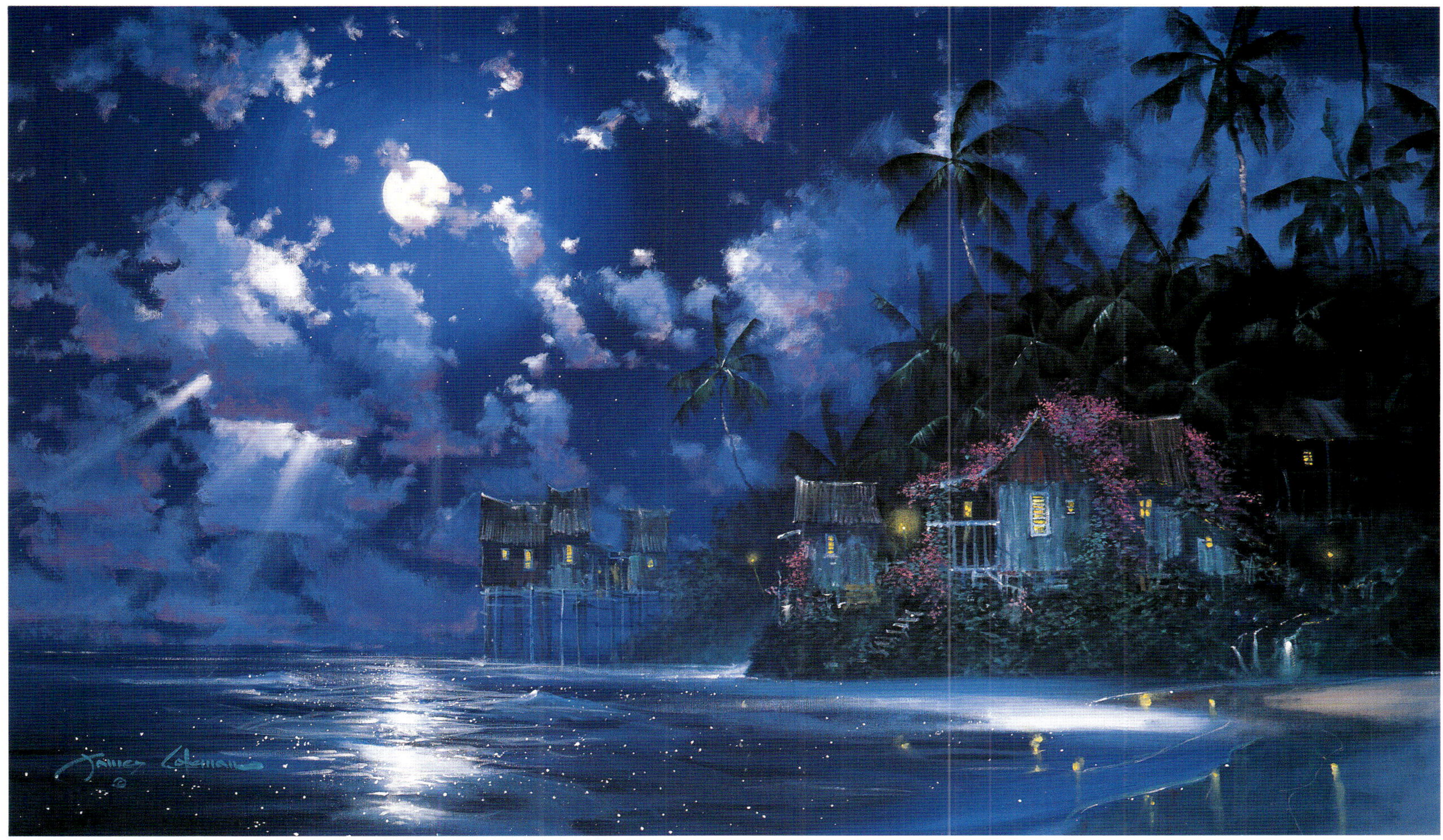

Magical Evening – Oil, 36 x 60 inches

"I actually loved the seascapes and all of that, but there was something I felt about the spirit of Hawaii and the people who lived there. And I wondered how I could capture that spirit without painting the people."

He tried painting people at first, but it didn't work. He felt he was an outsider looking in, and it didn't feel right. So he searched for another way to capture the essence of what he was seeing in the Islands.

"I finally realized it was the farms and the country life of the people who lived there that represented the true nature of Hawaii," he explains. "There were tin-roof houses and little rural farms that had been that way for a long, long time. And they were so much a part of the landscape, as were the people, that it all came together as one spirit. I tried to reflect this spirit by painting these houses and farms in their natural environments."

Naturally, he embellished them somewhat. In some cases, he combined two worlds to achieve the effect he wanted. "I remember taking helicopter rides over Kauai and saying to myself: 'Wow! What if somebody lived down there, which they probably did at some point, right in the middle of this deep tropical valley with these waterfalls near their homes.'"

So a little fantasy started creeping in. He'd learned at Disney that by taking reality and, through a little molding and changing, he could add some fantasy to it that opened people's minds.

"No one ever saw a place like that, but they want to, and they're close enough to reality that they could," he says. "Then I started realizing that these scenes were not that much of a fantasy after all. I've met a lot of local people in Hawaii, older folks, who come up to me with tears in their eyes and say: 'I lived in a house just like that.'"

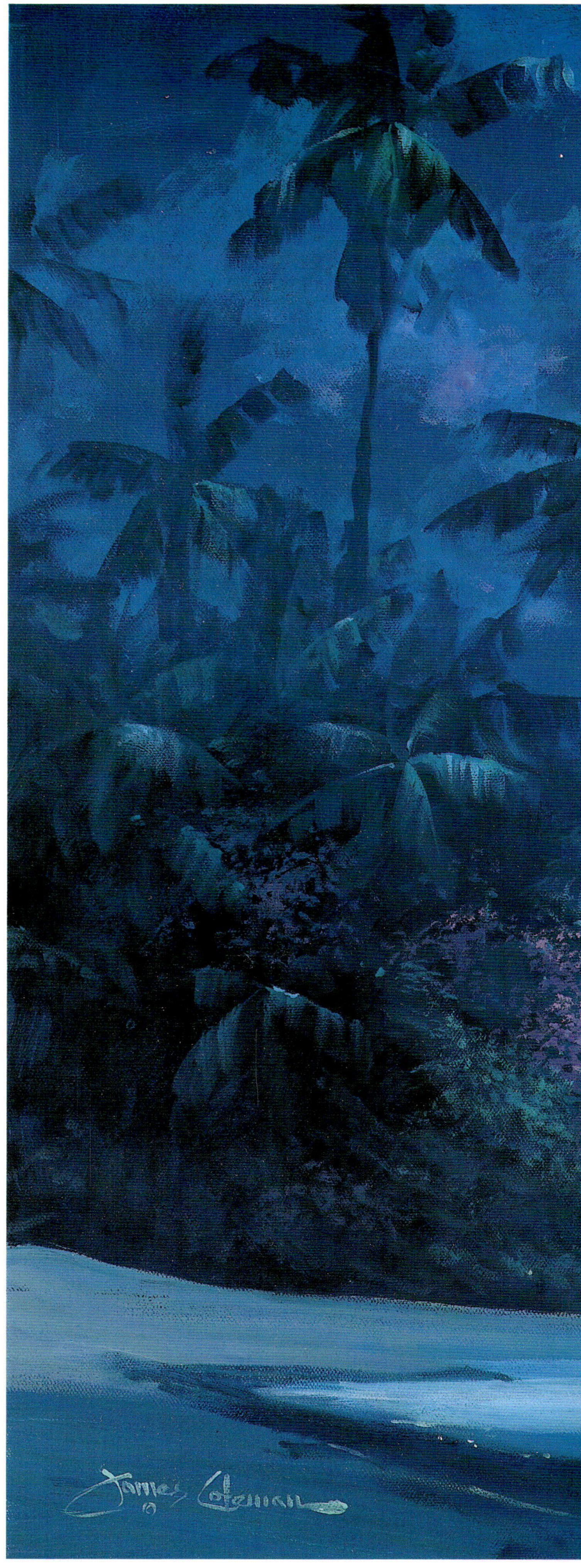

Midnight Surf
Oil, 24 x 30 inches

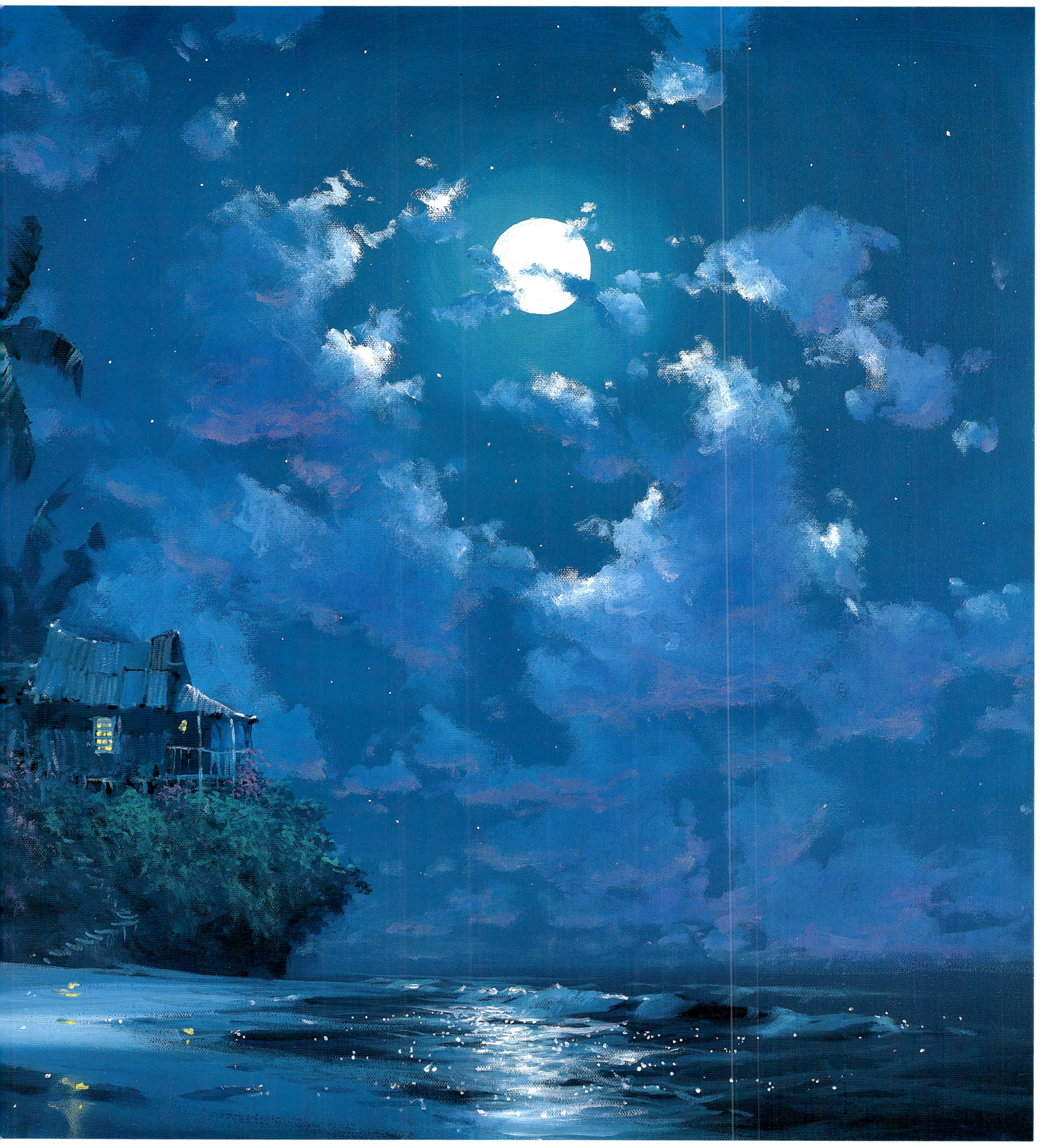

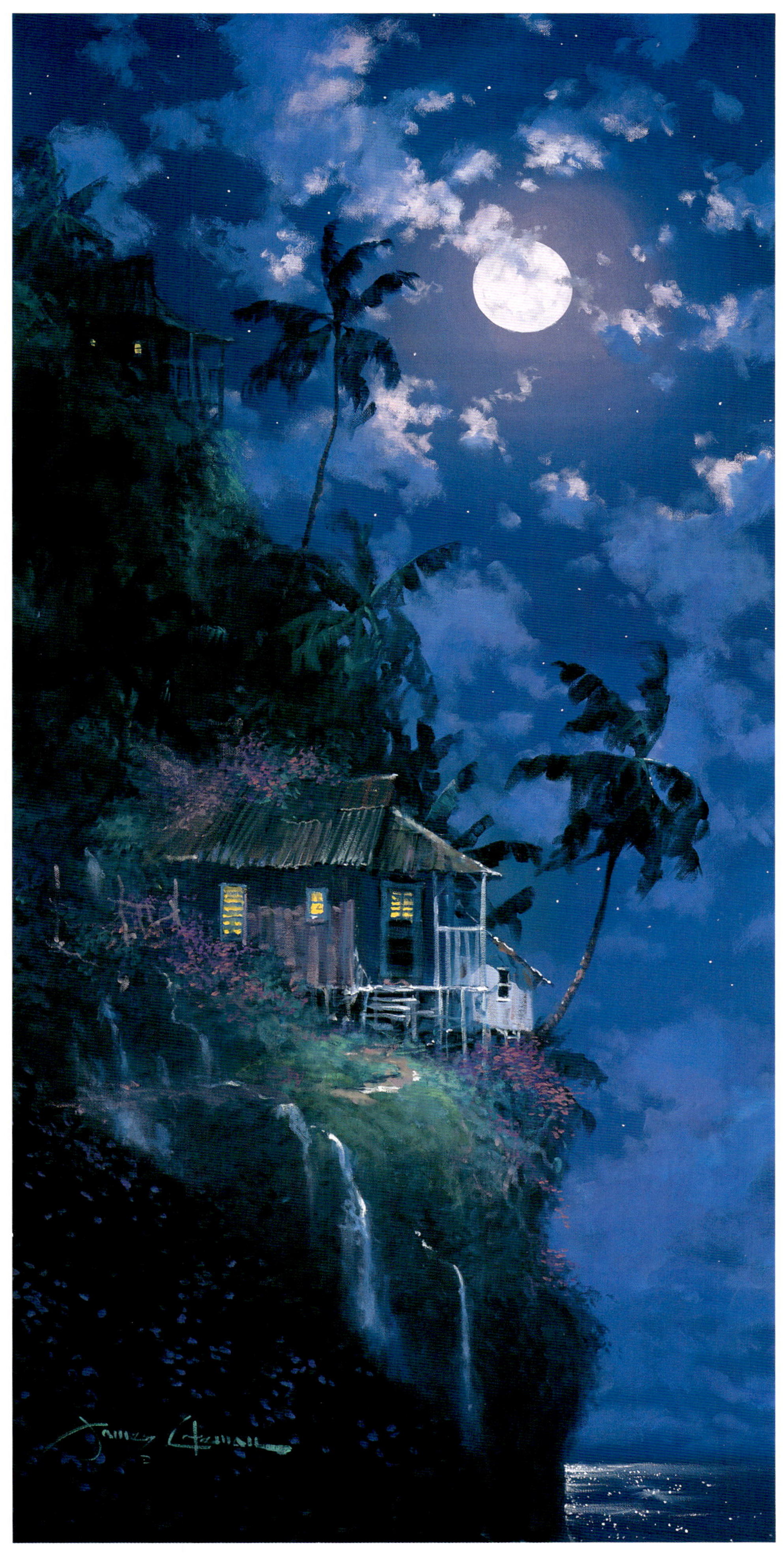

Midnight Peace
Oil, 48 x 24 inches

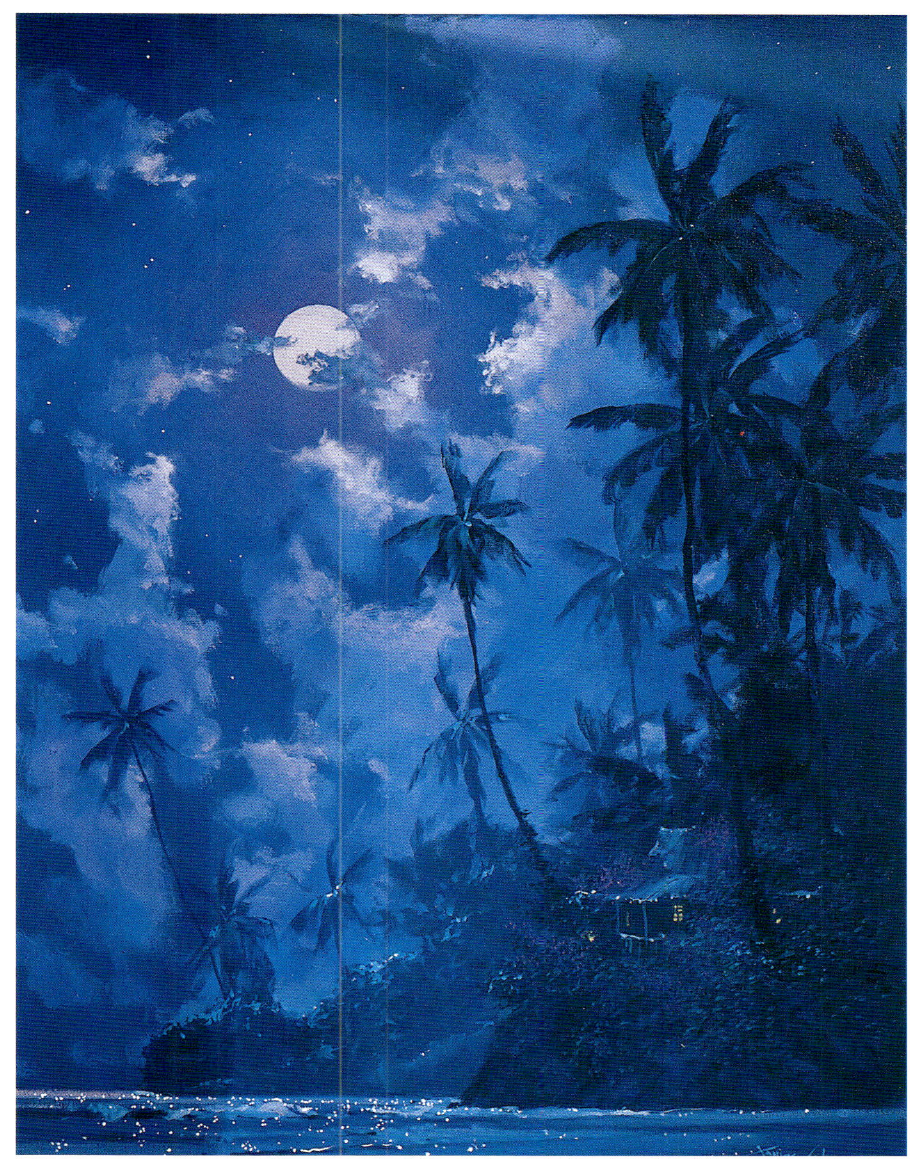

Night Enchantment
Oil, 36 x 18 inches

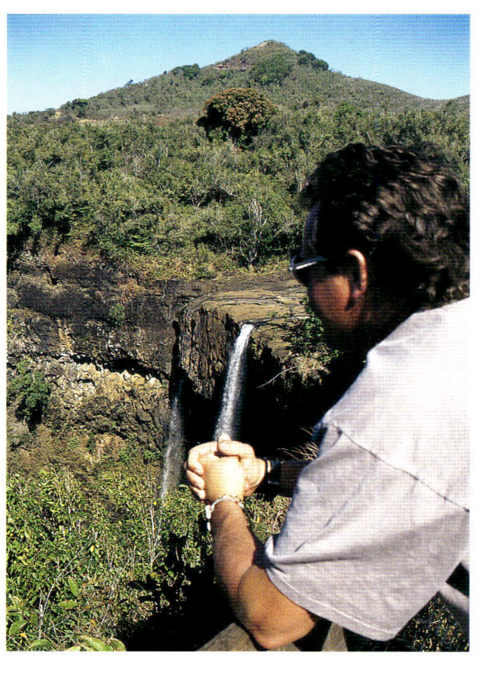

In addition to structures and form, much of the emotion that appears in Coleman's tropical scenes is the result of the way moonlight and shadows affect these forms. *Majestic Falls*, for example, portrays shadows falling across a waterfall he'd seen on a moonlit night on Kauai.

"When I saw that, I realized that, just like you have shadows from clouds in the daylight, you also have them at night—moonshadows. In fact, I have a published piece called *Moonshadows*, which shows the clouds casting shadows from the moon on the NaPali Coast, and the moon is reflecting off the ocean."

Moonlight, Coleman feels, has always afforded him the best opportunity to translate mood because it's something you have to feel. Seeing it is not enough.

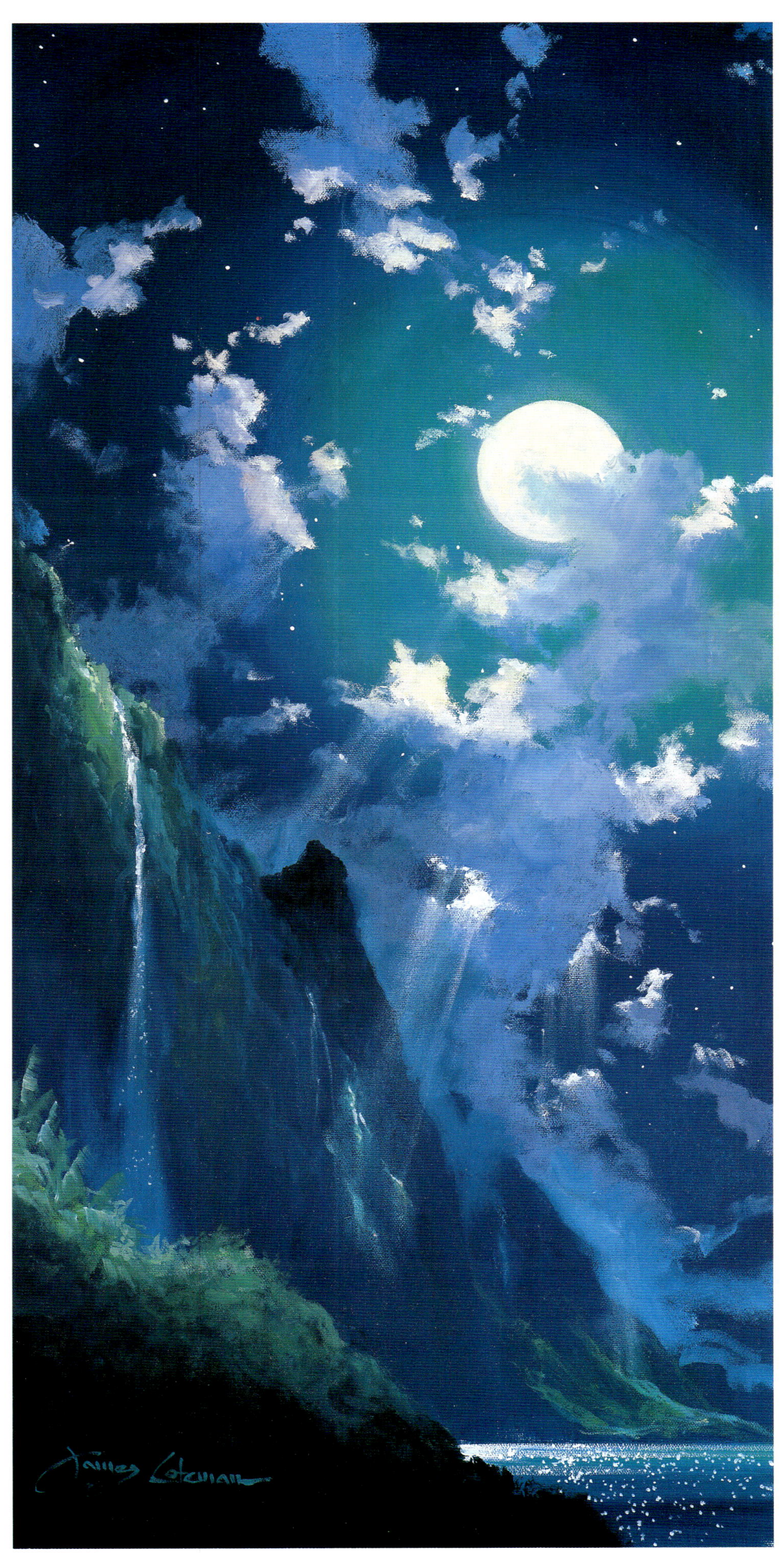

Moon Dreams
Oil, 30 x 15 inches

Rhythms in Blue ▶
Oil, 30 x 24 inches

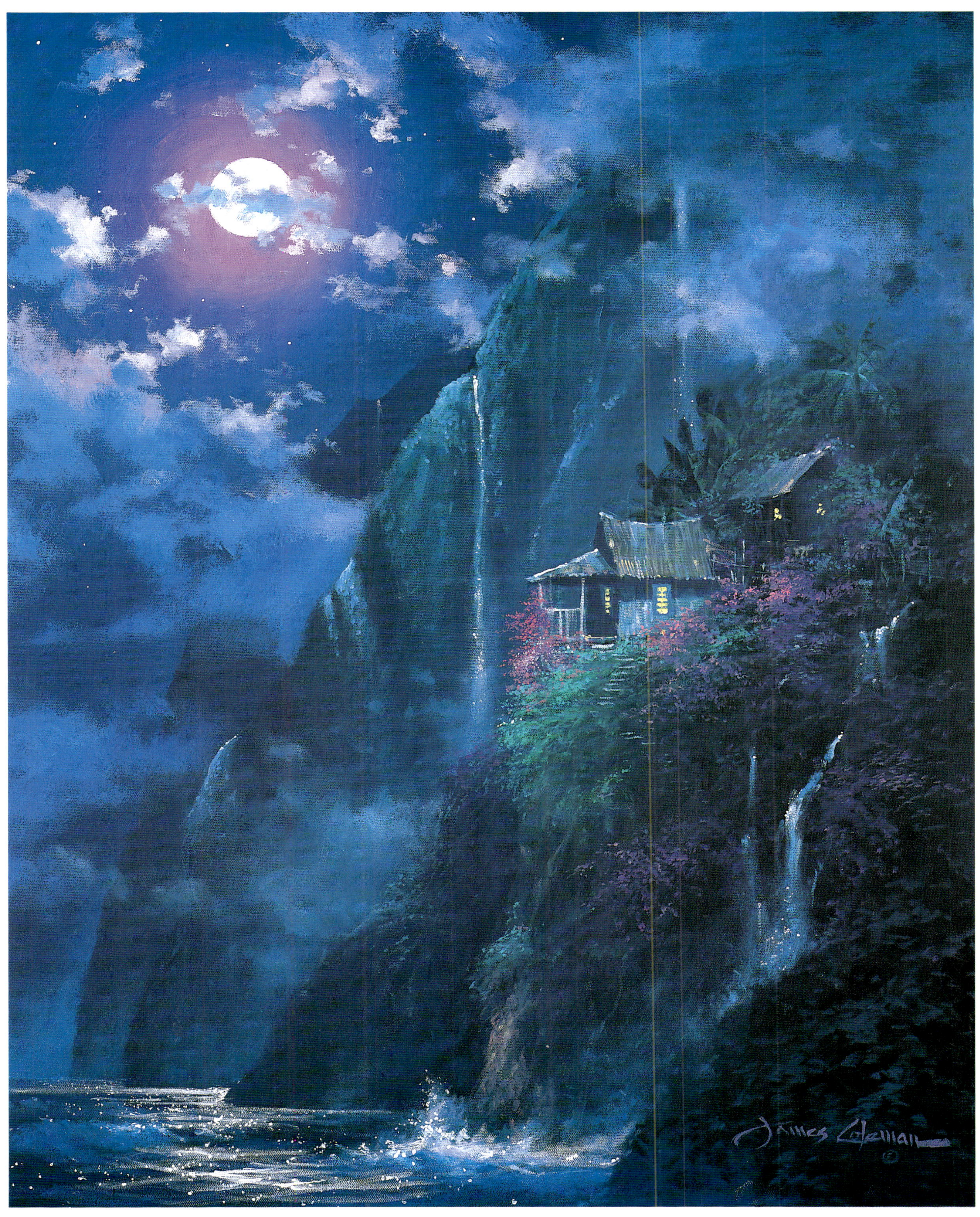

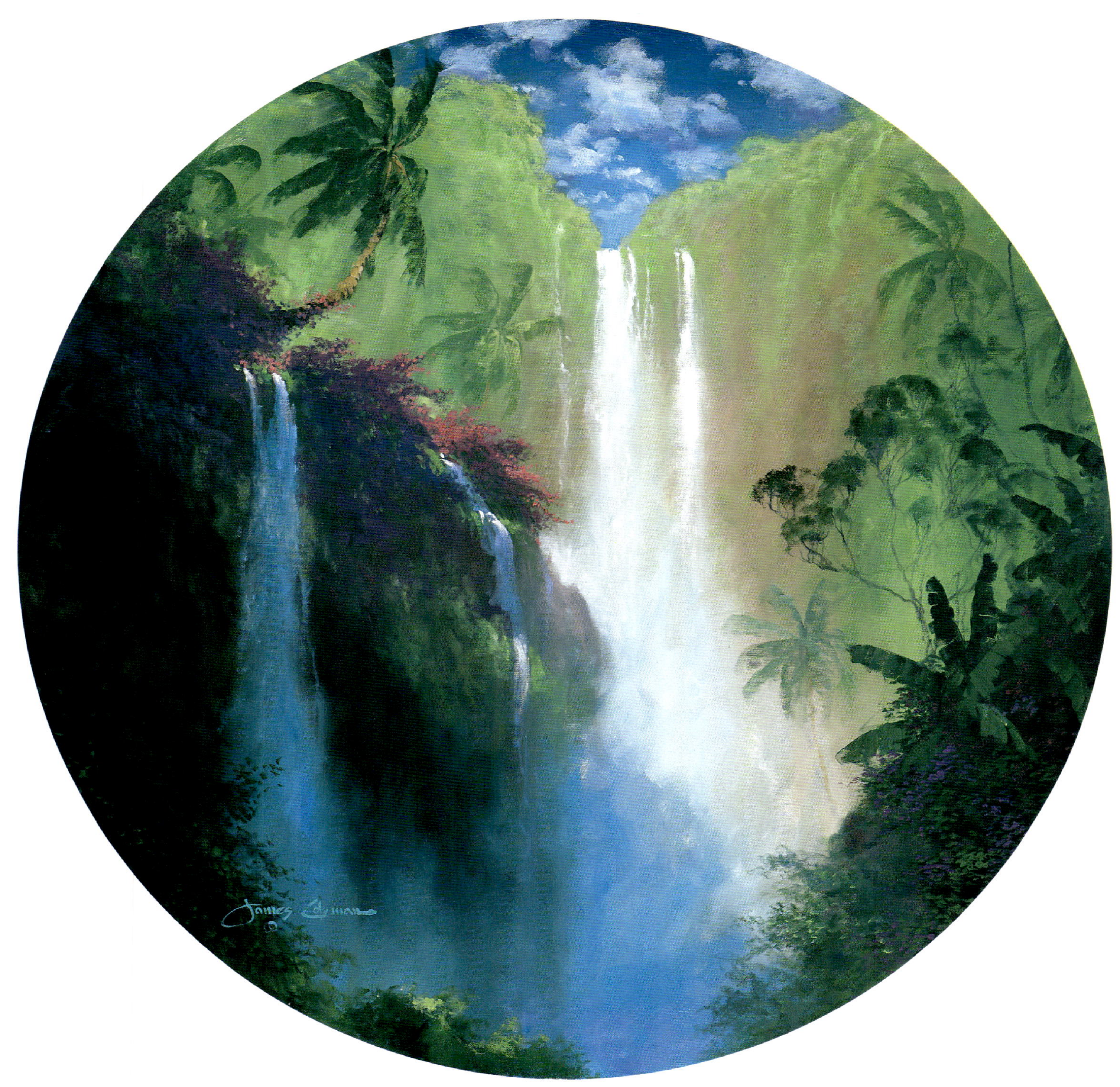

Waters for Life – Oil, 36 inches round

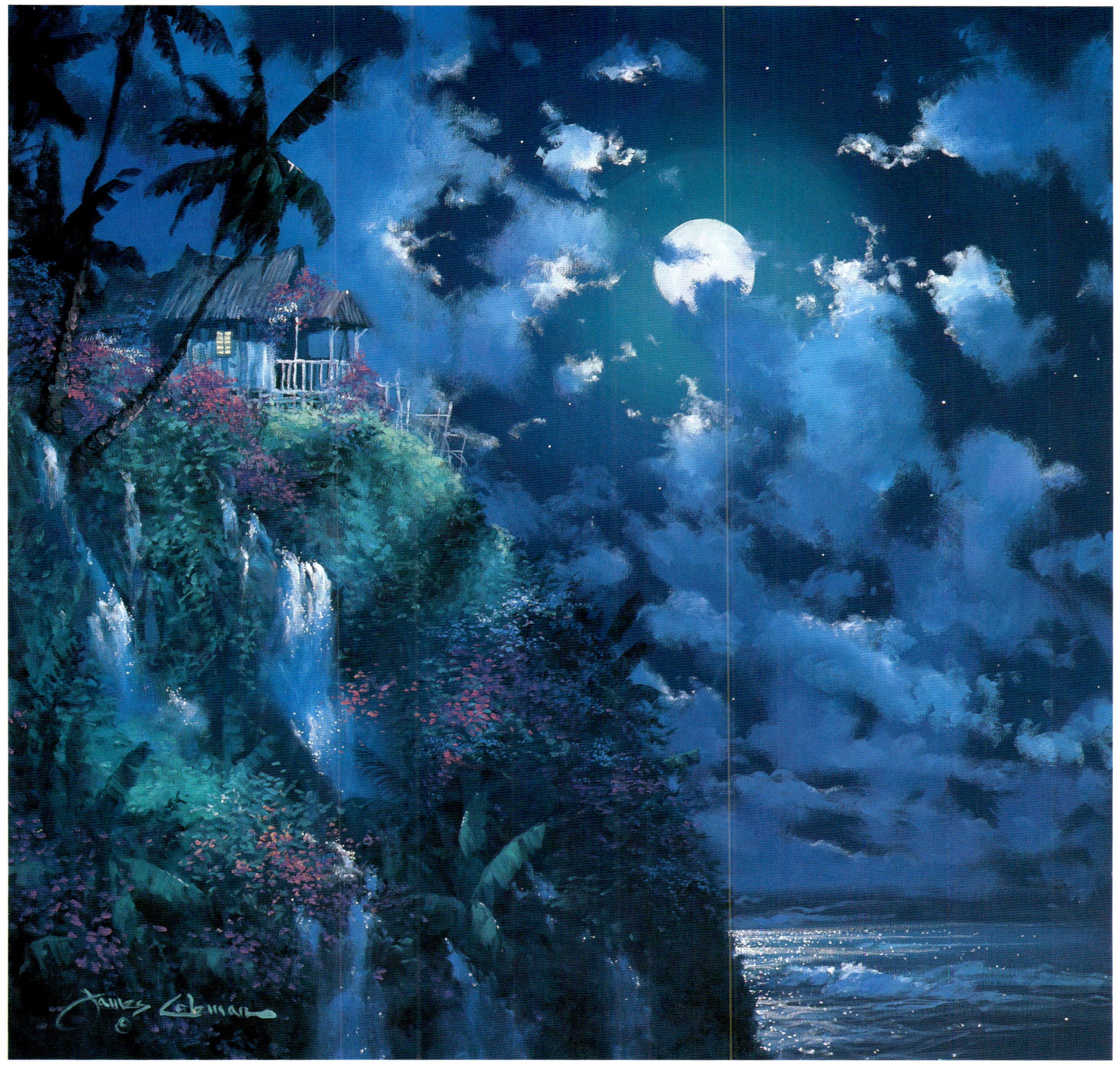

Moon Magic – Oil, 30 x 30 inches

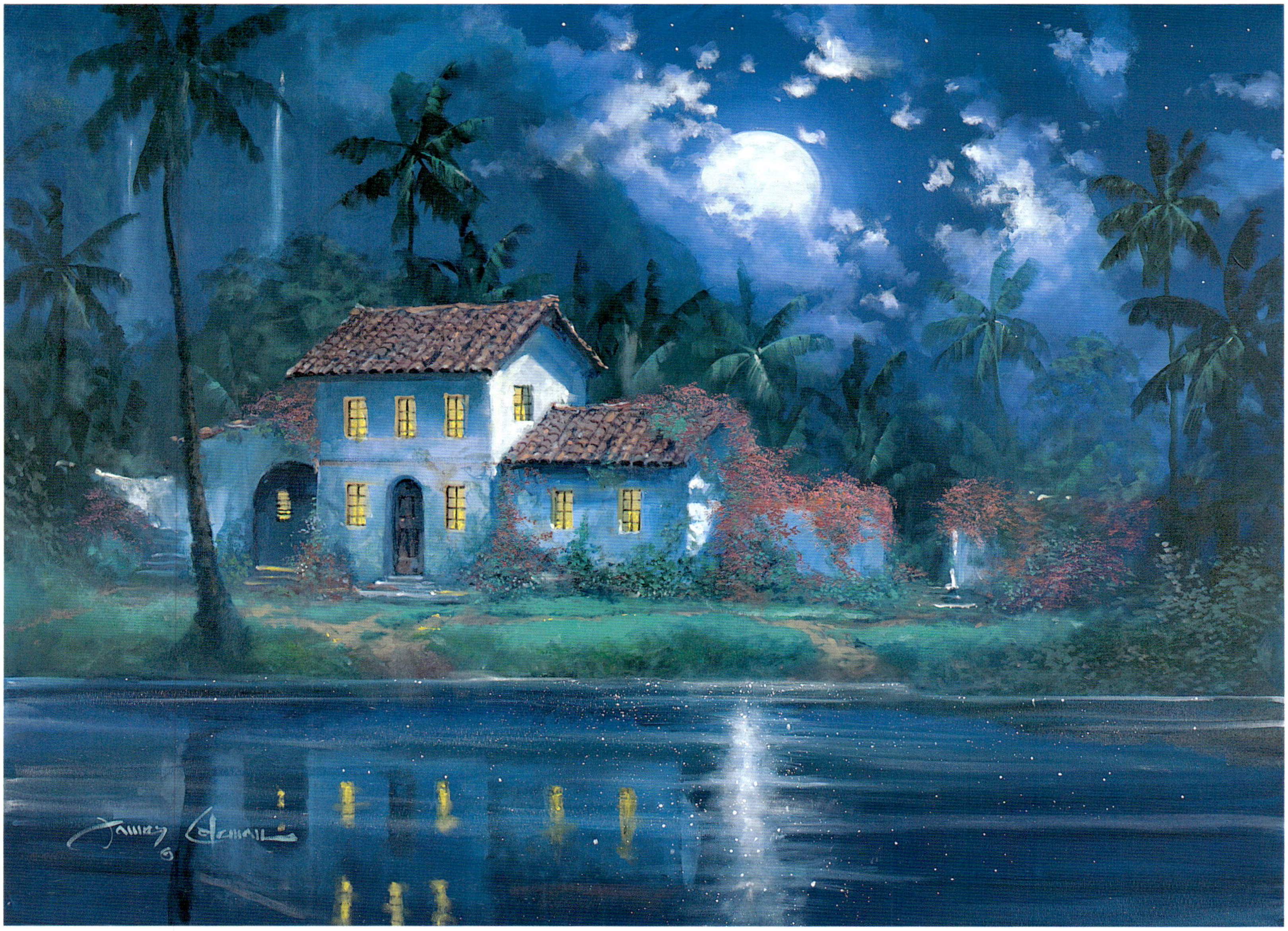

Ancient Evening – Oil, 30 x 40 inches

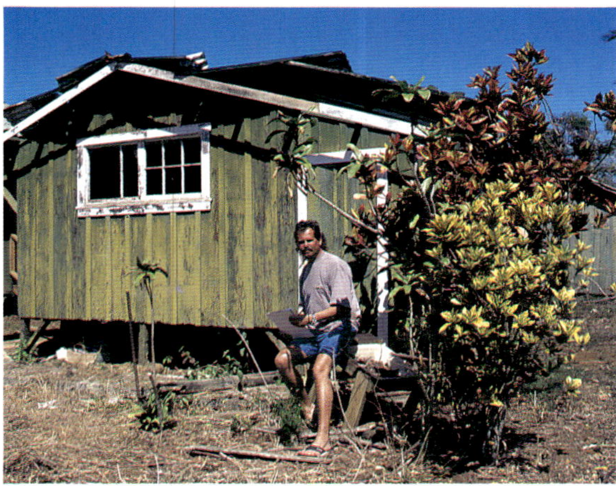

Jim in Kauai studying his subject

"It's one of those things you have to do blind," he explains. "You can't just walk out with your easel like you would in the daylight and start painting. You have to mix your colors, and you have no way of seeing color in the dark. Moonlight distorts color; it doesn't look the same as it would under normal light.

"Basically, moonlight is an illusion, just like painting. You trick people's eyes into seeing something they're not really seeing. So, when you say there's a certain light in a painting, there's really not. It's just putting different colors together so that it appears there is light.

"Moonlight probably carries more emotion than any other light, but it's also very difficult to create a believable illusion with it. That's why not many artists paint it."

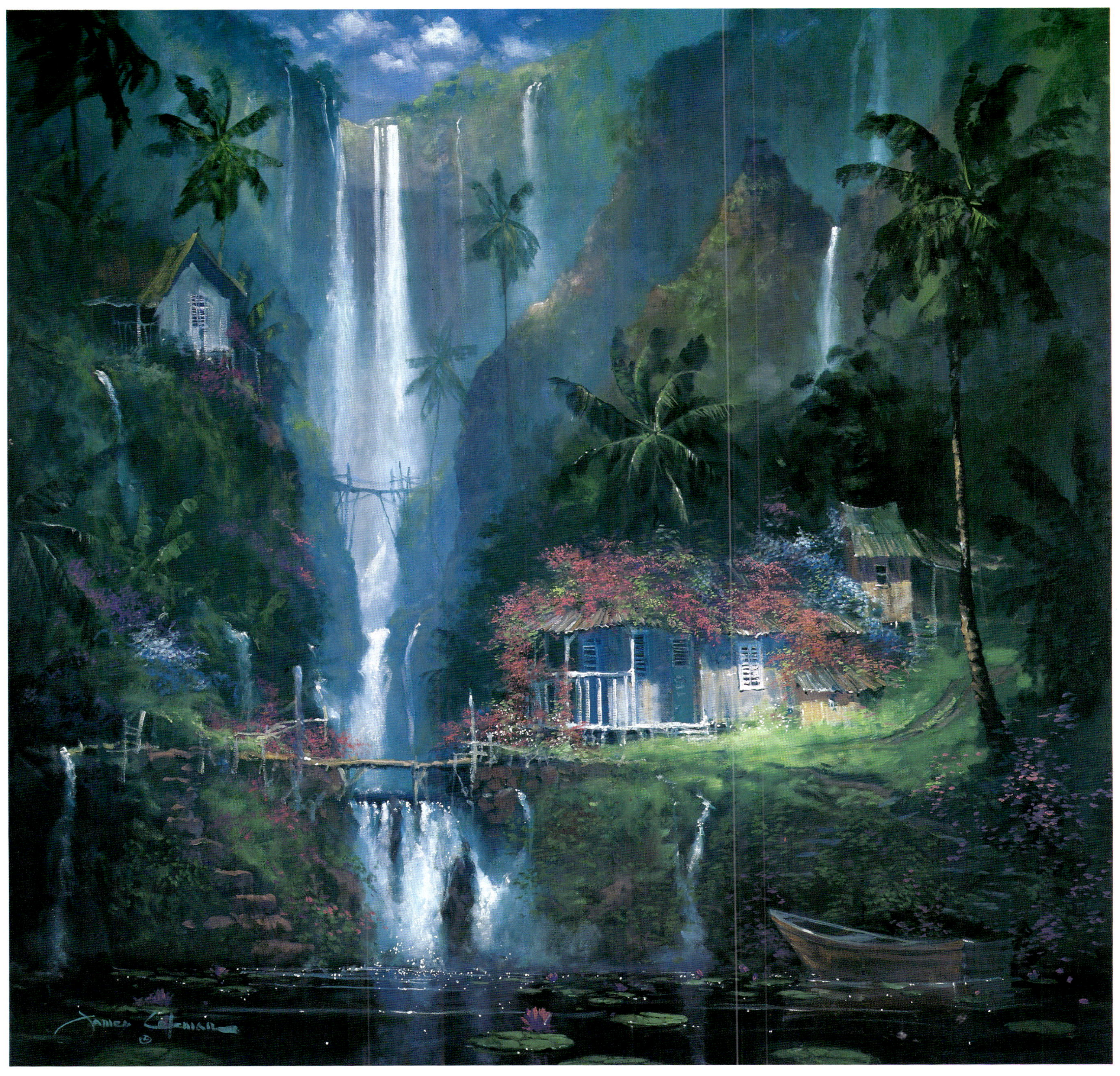

Peaceful Rhythms – Oil, 48 x 48 inches

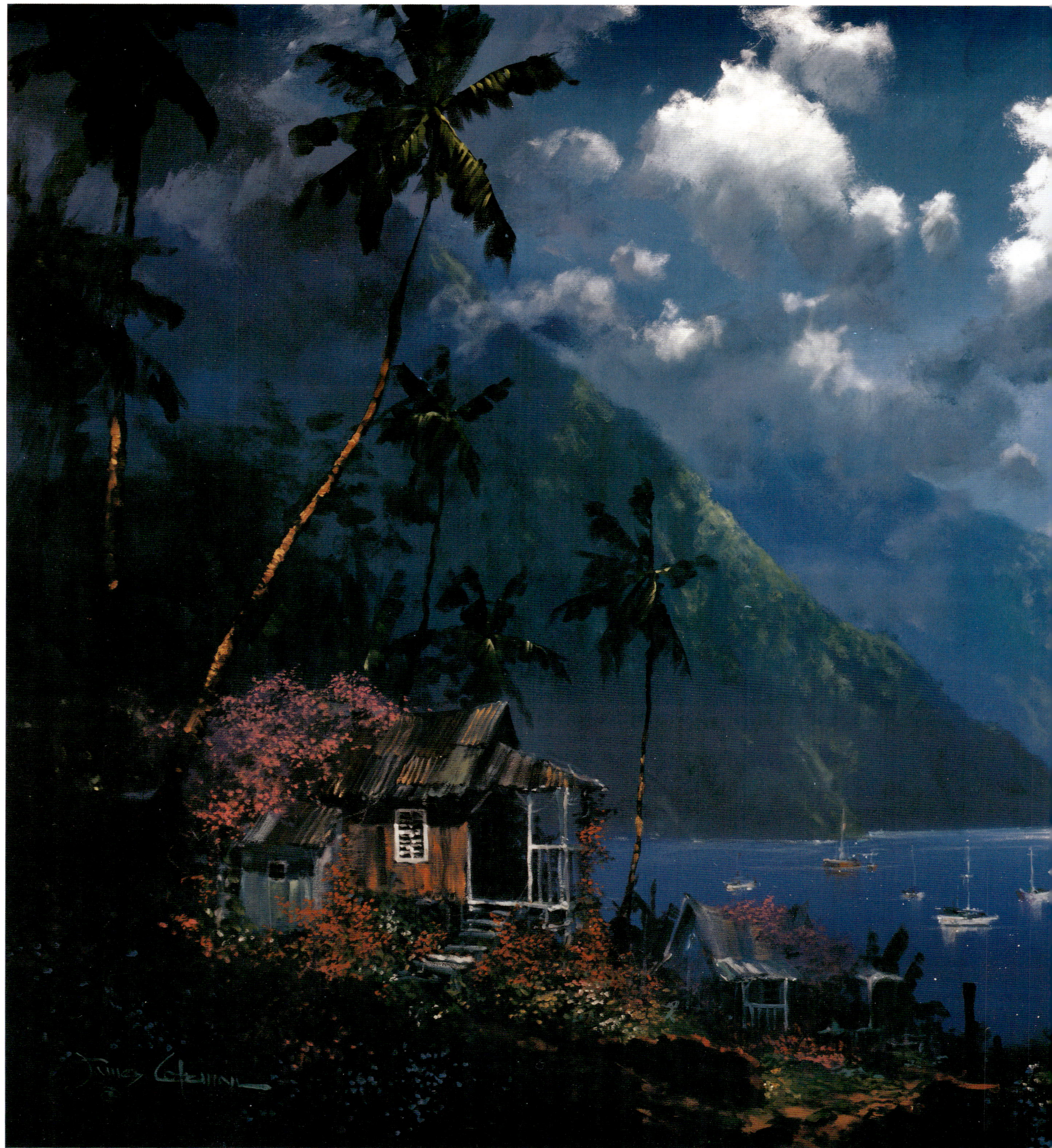

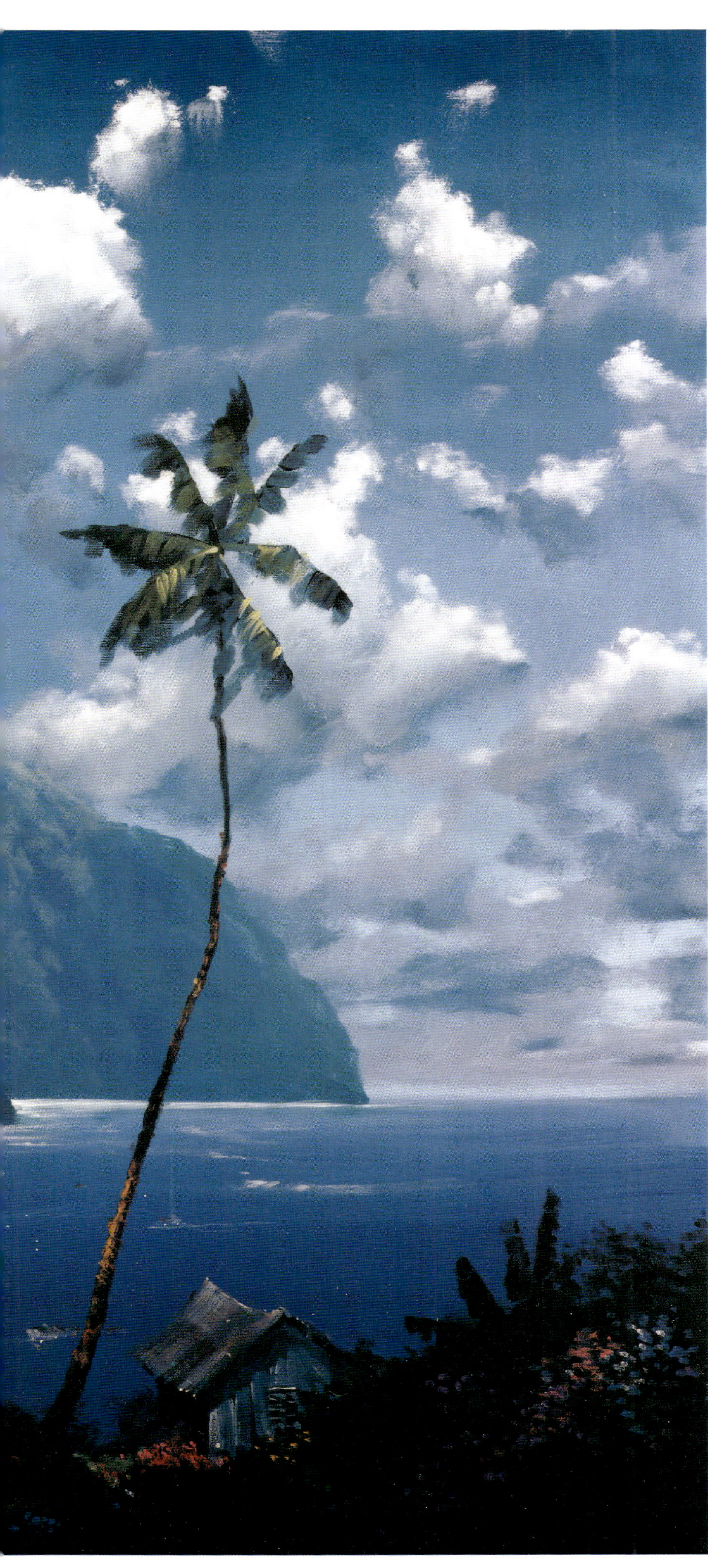

Memories of Paradise
Oil, 36 x 48 inches

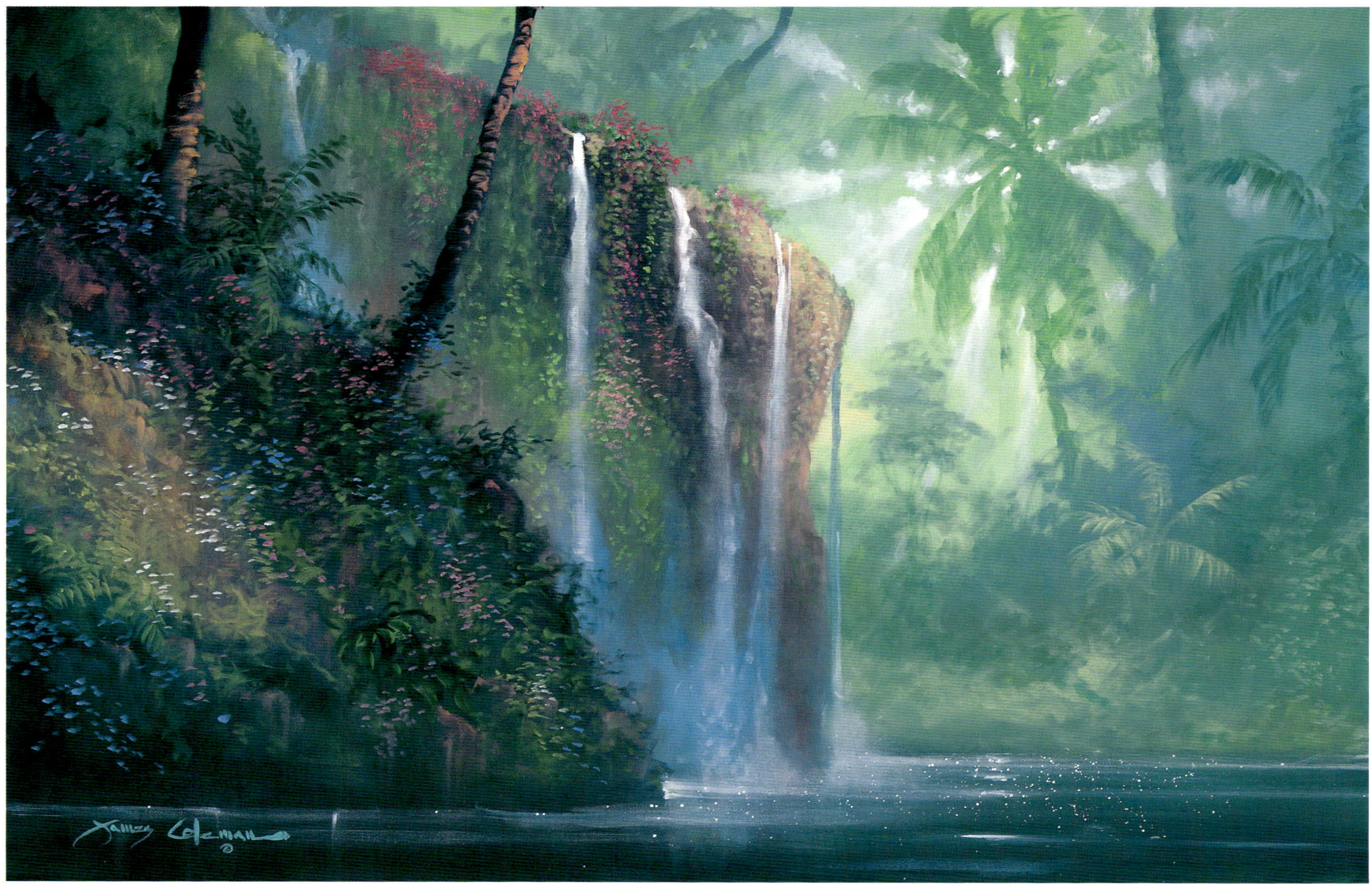

Misty Melodies – Oil, 22 x 28 inches

Coleman will often see something that strikes him, and he'll use it in a different setting that has more impact. In *Peaceful Rhythms*, he has painted a small waterfall with a footbridge above it near a house. It was something he just happened on when he was on Kauai that charmed him enough to use it later, but the waterfall was nowhere near as large as it was in the actual setting.

Coleman's work with tropical scenery often has been characterized as being Oriental in nature, though he says he makes no conscious effort to achieve that effect. "I've always been drawn to that style, just as the great masters used to be—like Van Gogh and Gauguin," he says, curious about it himself. "Maybe I've seen something I'm not aware of that has steered me a little in that direction, I don't know. But it's nothing I try to do. It could be the subject matter. A lot of the paintings look like they could be scenes of Asia."

Evidently, his work has struck a chord with art collectors in that part of the world. The princess of Thailand has purchased two of Coleman's original tropical paintings.

Some of his paintings have been inspired by his own desire to experiment, such as *Memories of Paradise*, which has a small bay and boats anchored in it. "Something I've always wanted to do is sail and be able to dock in a little port like that," he reveals. "I had done a painting called *Rain Over The Bay*, which was made into a lithograph that sold out fairly fast. So I realized there are other people out there who like boats and bays and would like to spend some time there."

In *Evening Serenity*, however, a painting of a number of tin roofs on a river at night with waterfalls, the scene is not, he says, a place where one would necessarily want to live.

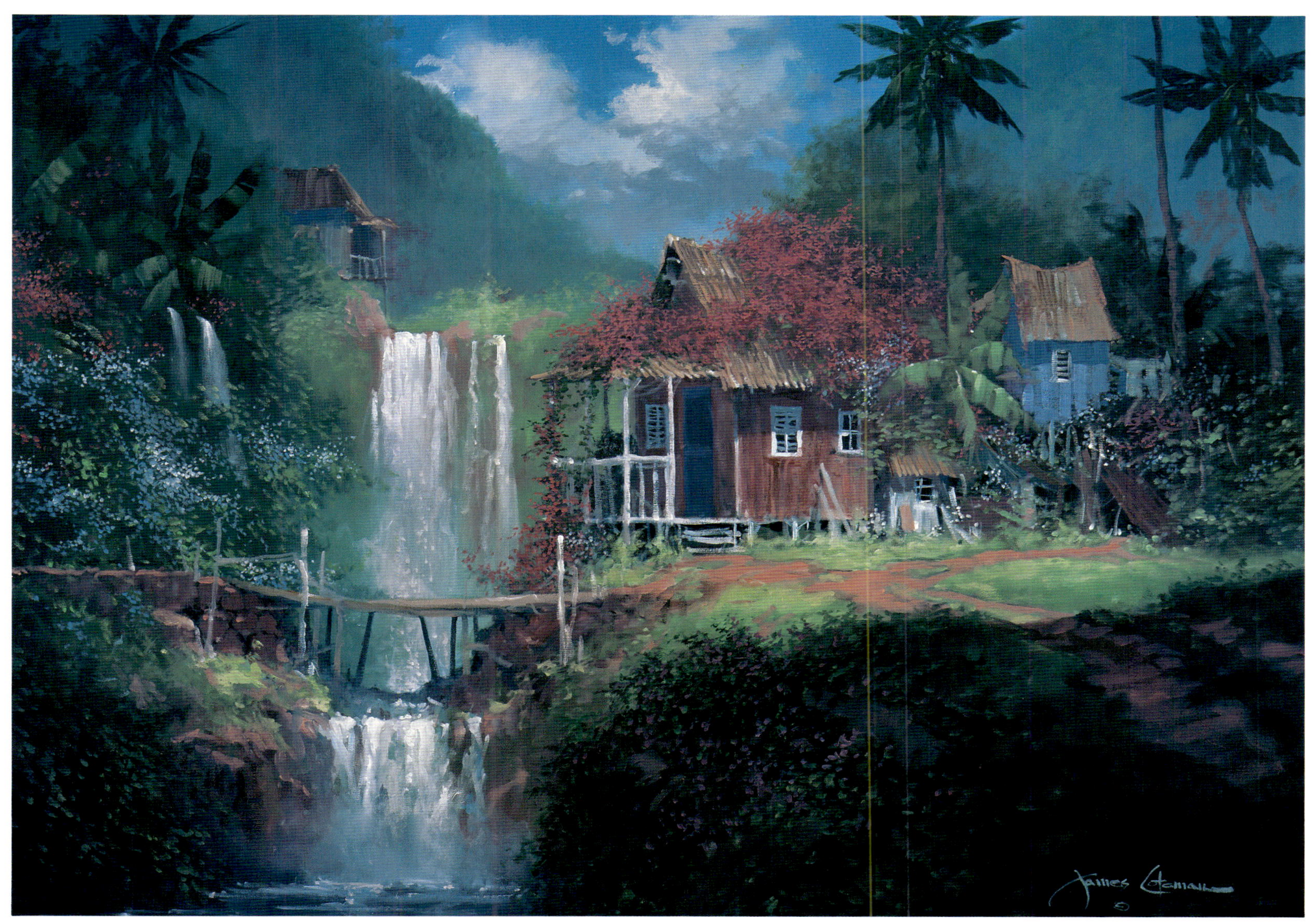

House of Flowers – Oil, 36 x 48 inches

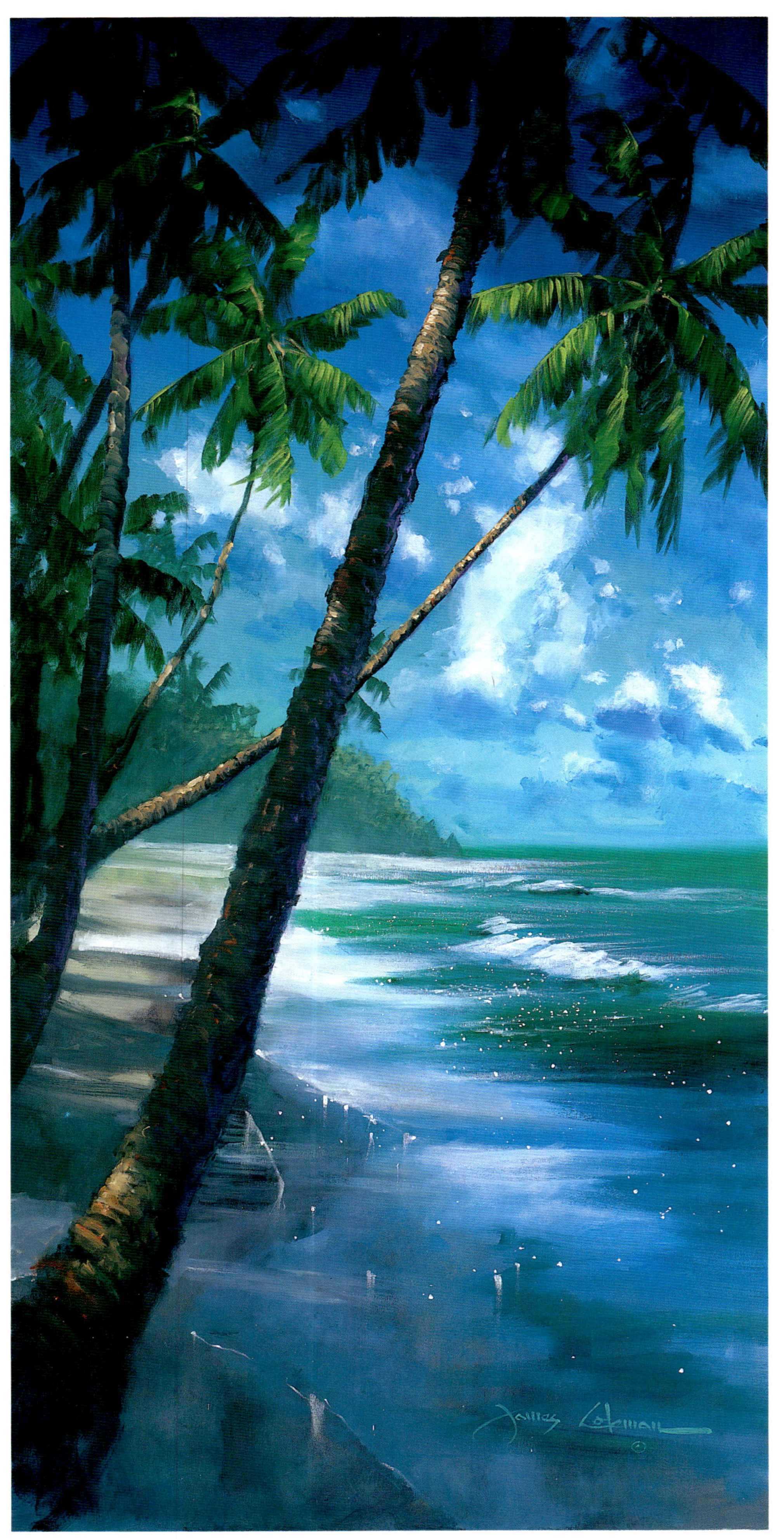

Radiant Surf
Oil, 48 x 24 inches

Misty Peace ▶
Oil, 48 x 24 inches

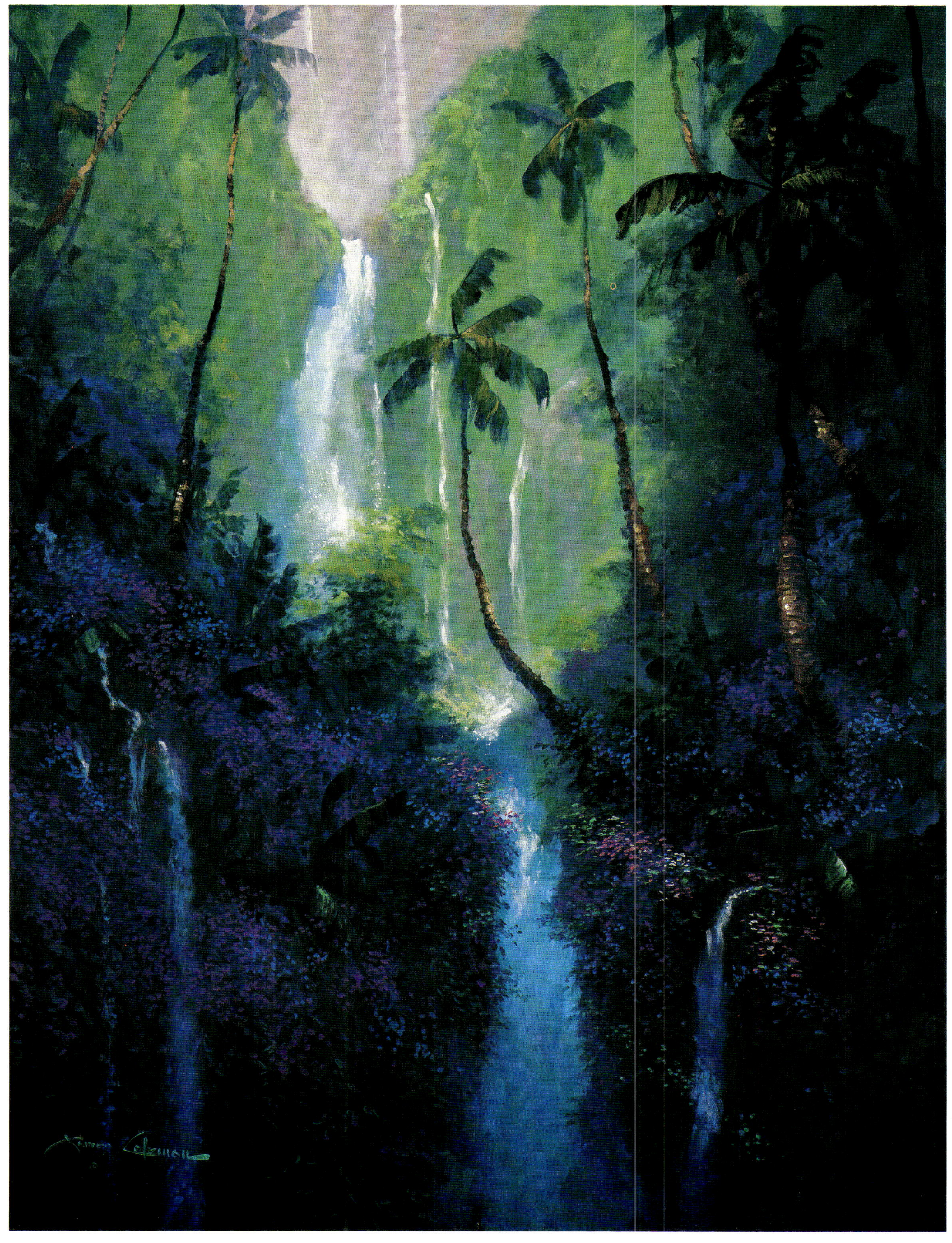

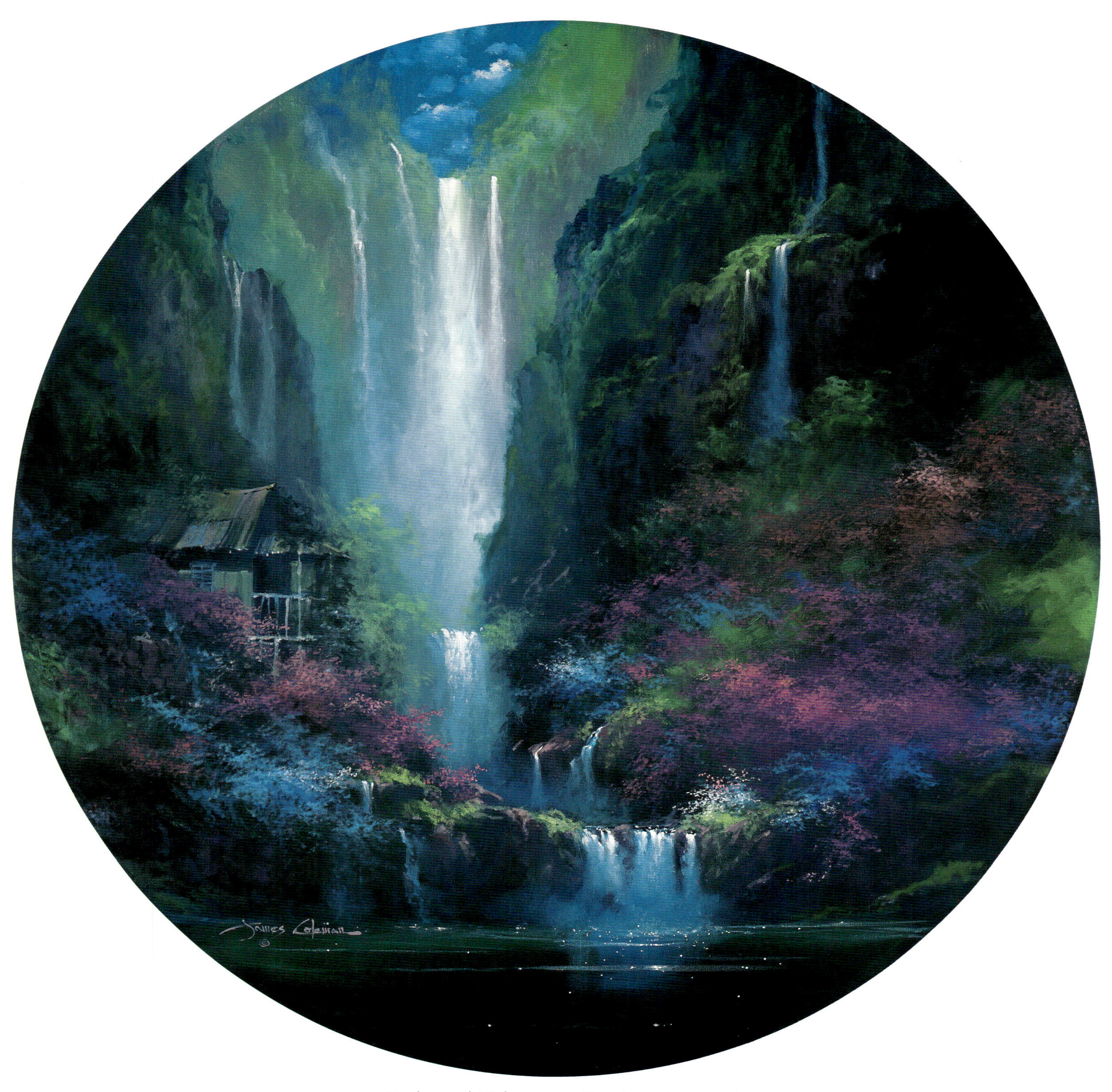

Enchanted Hideaway – Oil, 44 inches round

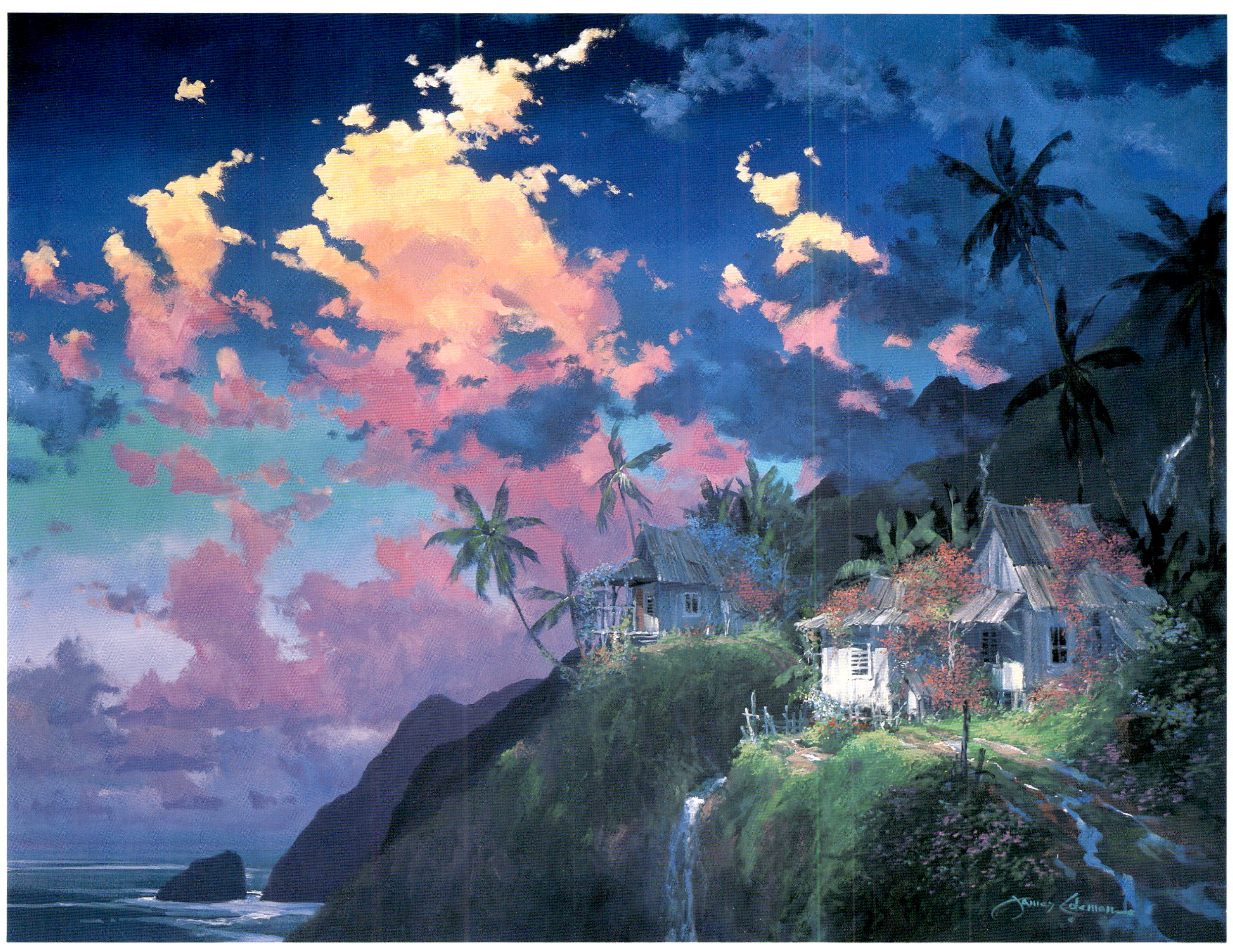

Escape to Paradise – Oil, 48 x 60 inches

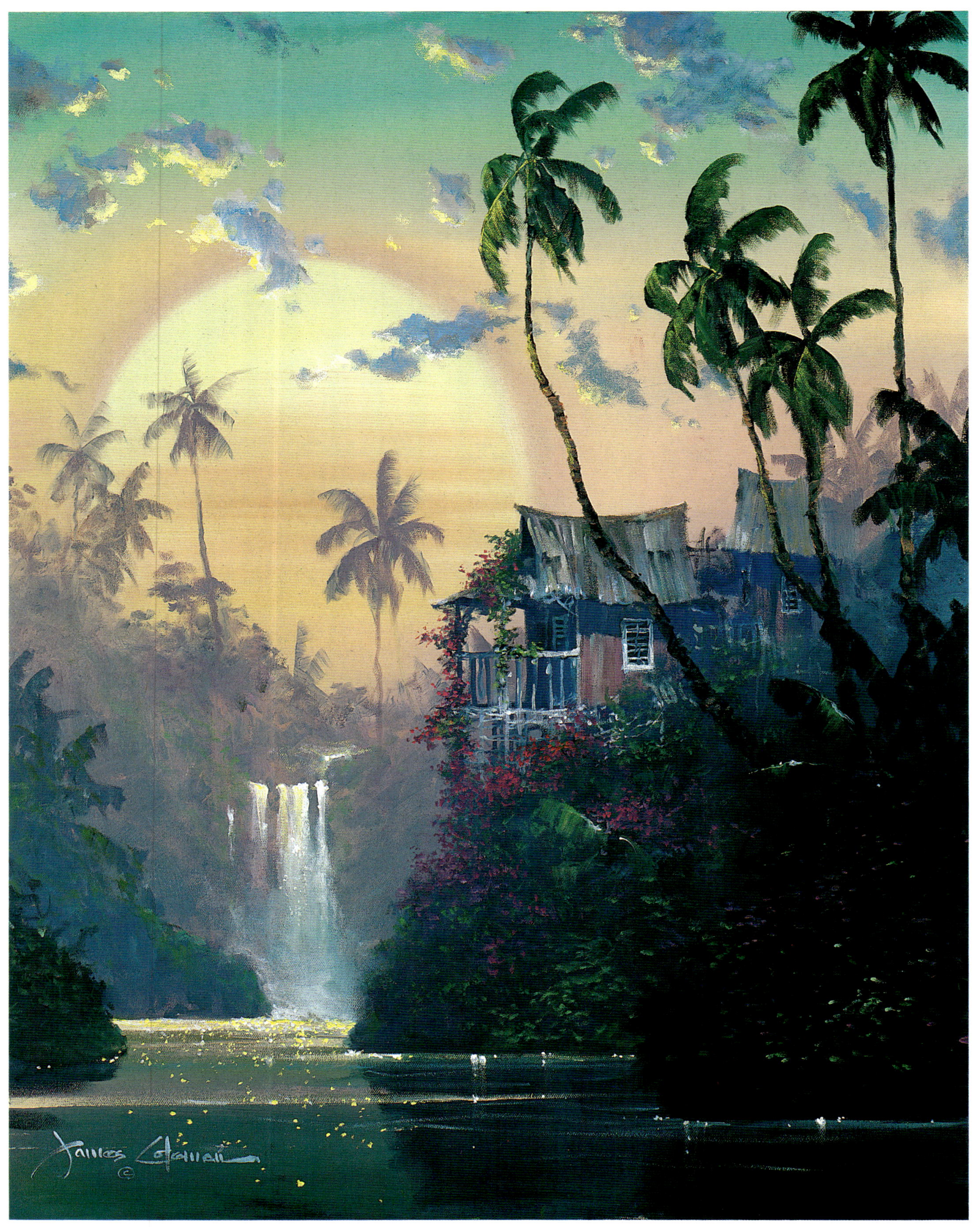

Afternoon Splendor – Oil, 36 x 24 inches

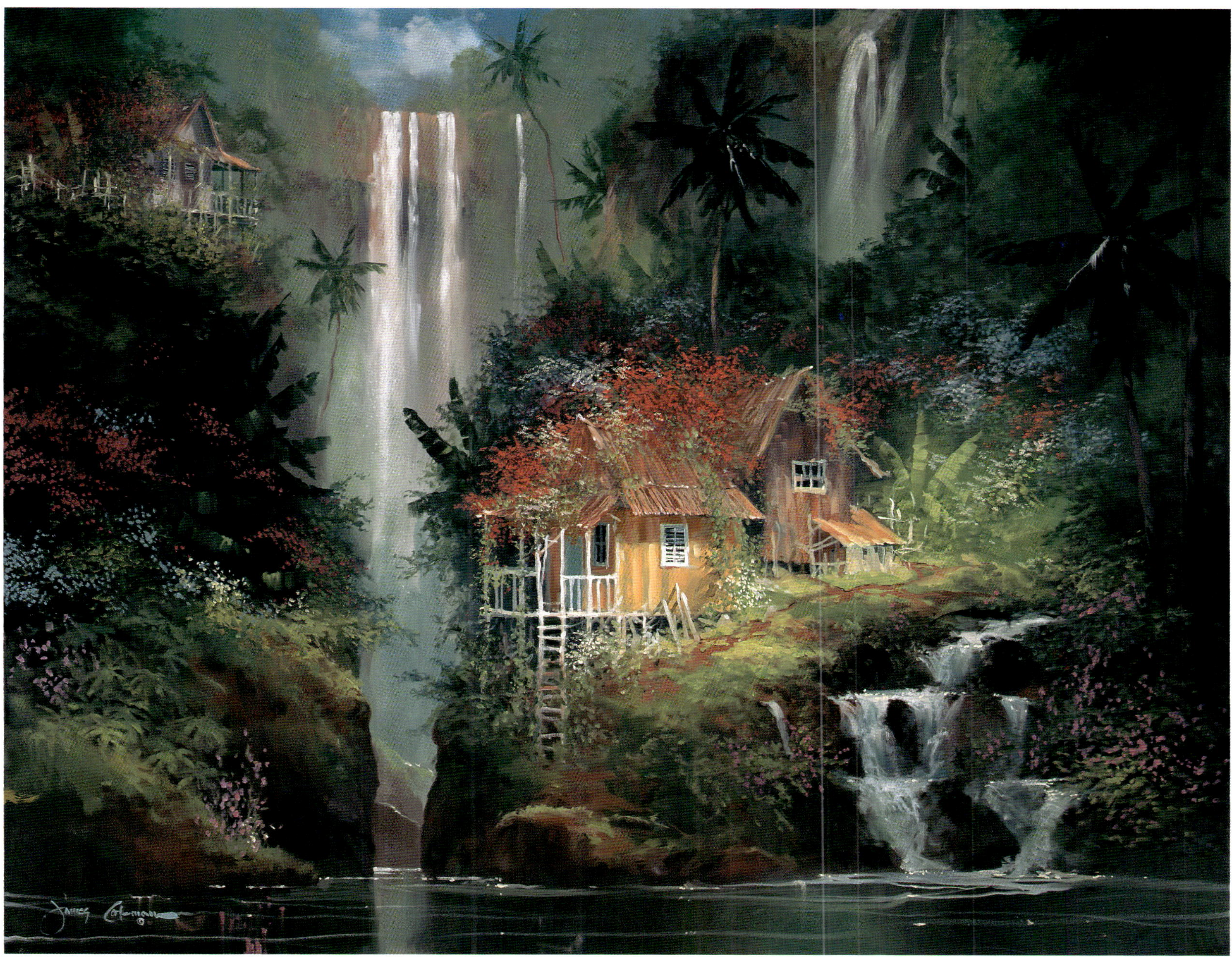

Living Aloha – Oil, 48 x 60 inches

But it represents other places that have been romanticized to the point where people want to look at it and be part of it somehow.

Some of the most important elements in Coleman's paintings are clouds, especially in tropical settings like Hawaii, where they hover so low. "I've always been impressed with the clouds in Hawaii," he says. "They carry so much emotion and color, and people sometimes overlook them, just like the stars I put in the night scenes, or the glitter on the water.

"These are sort of subliminal things, I guess, but they're so important. They're part of the reason that most people don't get bored with my paintings. They spot these features after they've been looking at the painting for a while."

"As long as they continue to touch people, I'll continue to paint them," he says. "I love these places myself, and never get tired of painting them. I would, however, like to find the time to travel more and see other tropical places around the world. Every time I visit the tropics, I see something new that astounds me beyond comprehension. I get the feeling there's a lot more out there."

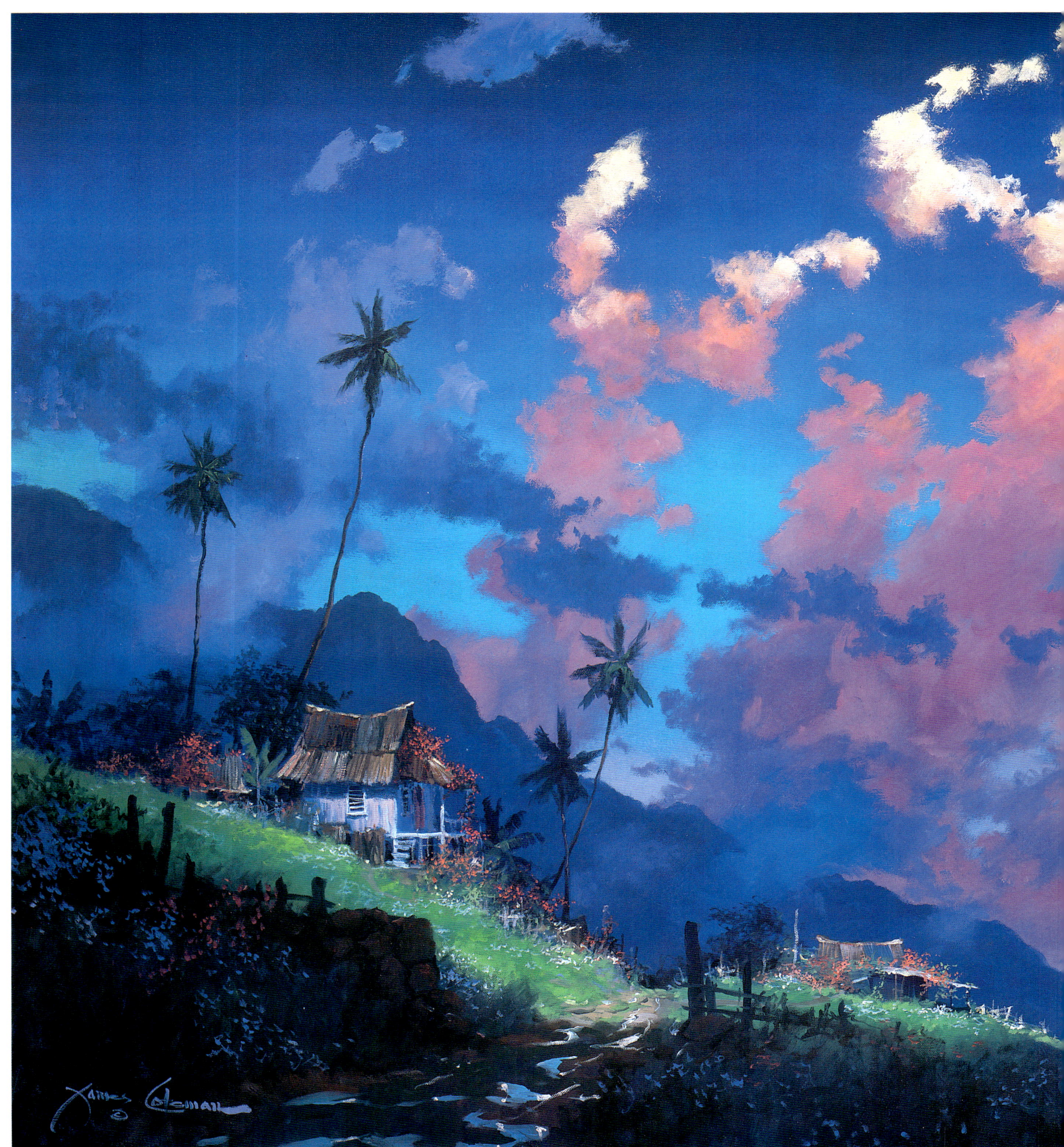

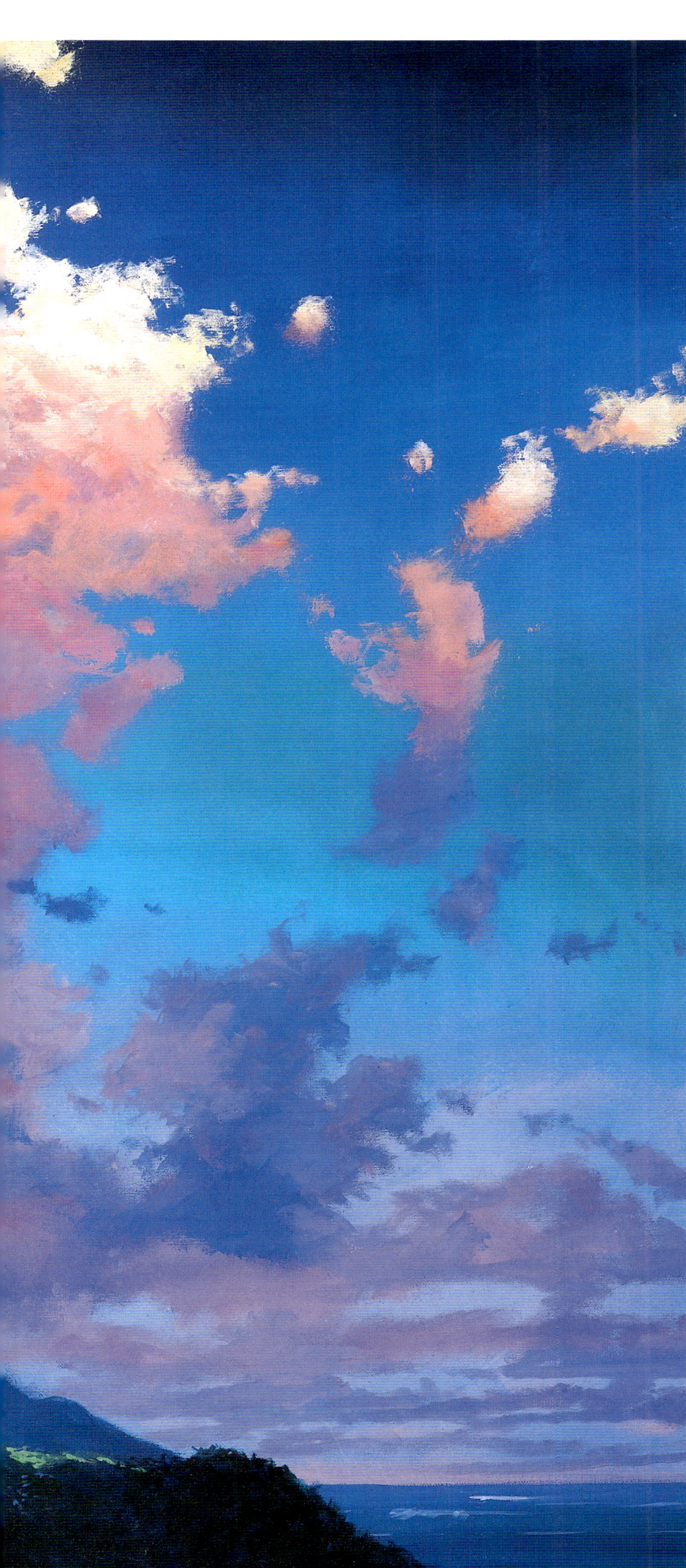

Impressions of Paradise
Oil, 36 x 48 inches

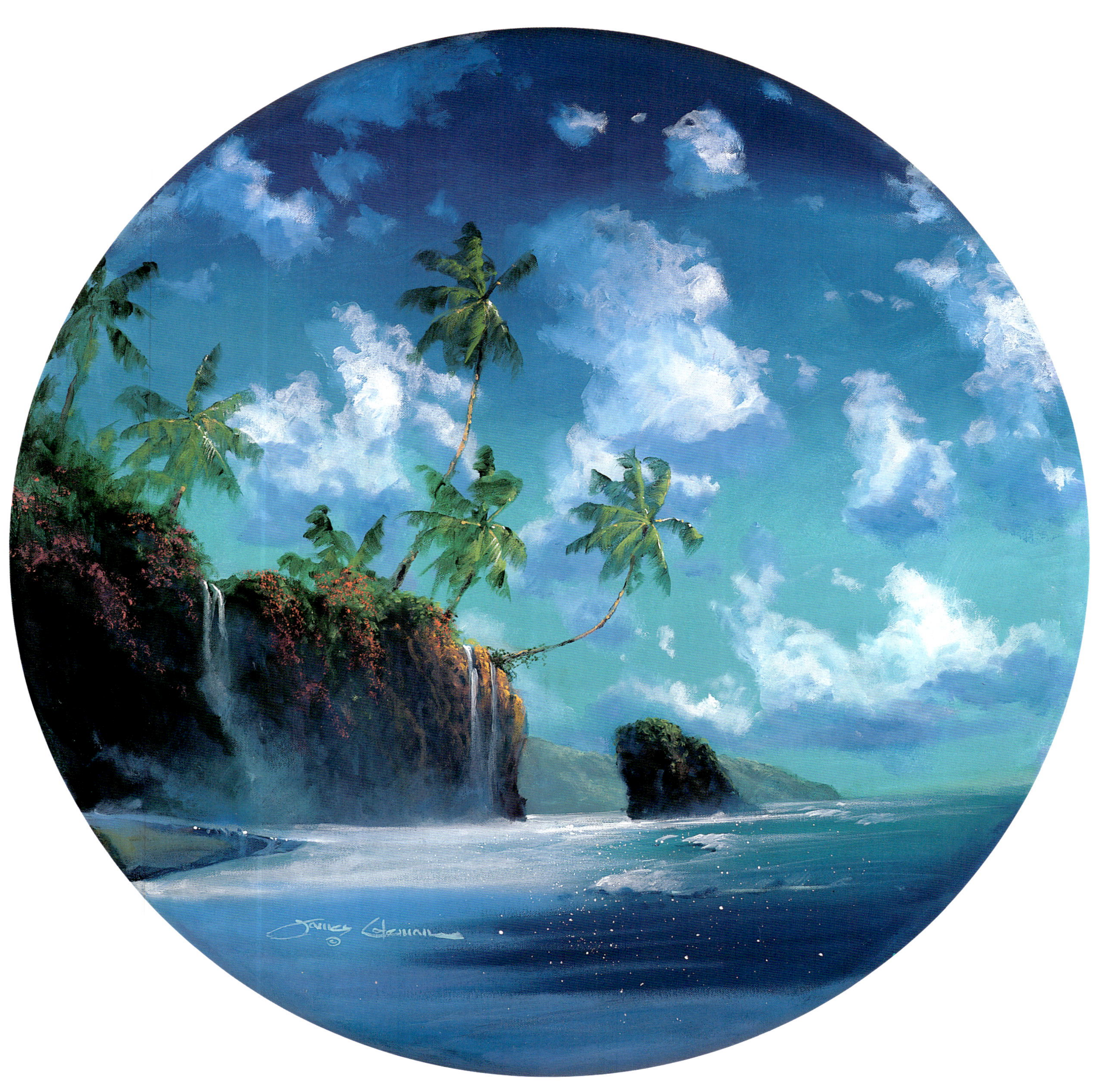

Welcome to a Dream – Oil, 30 inches round

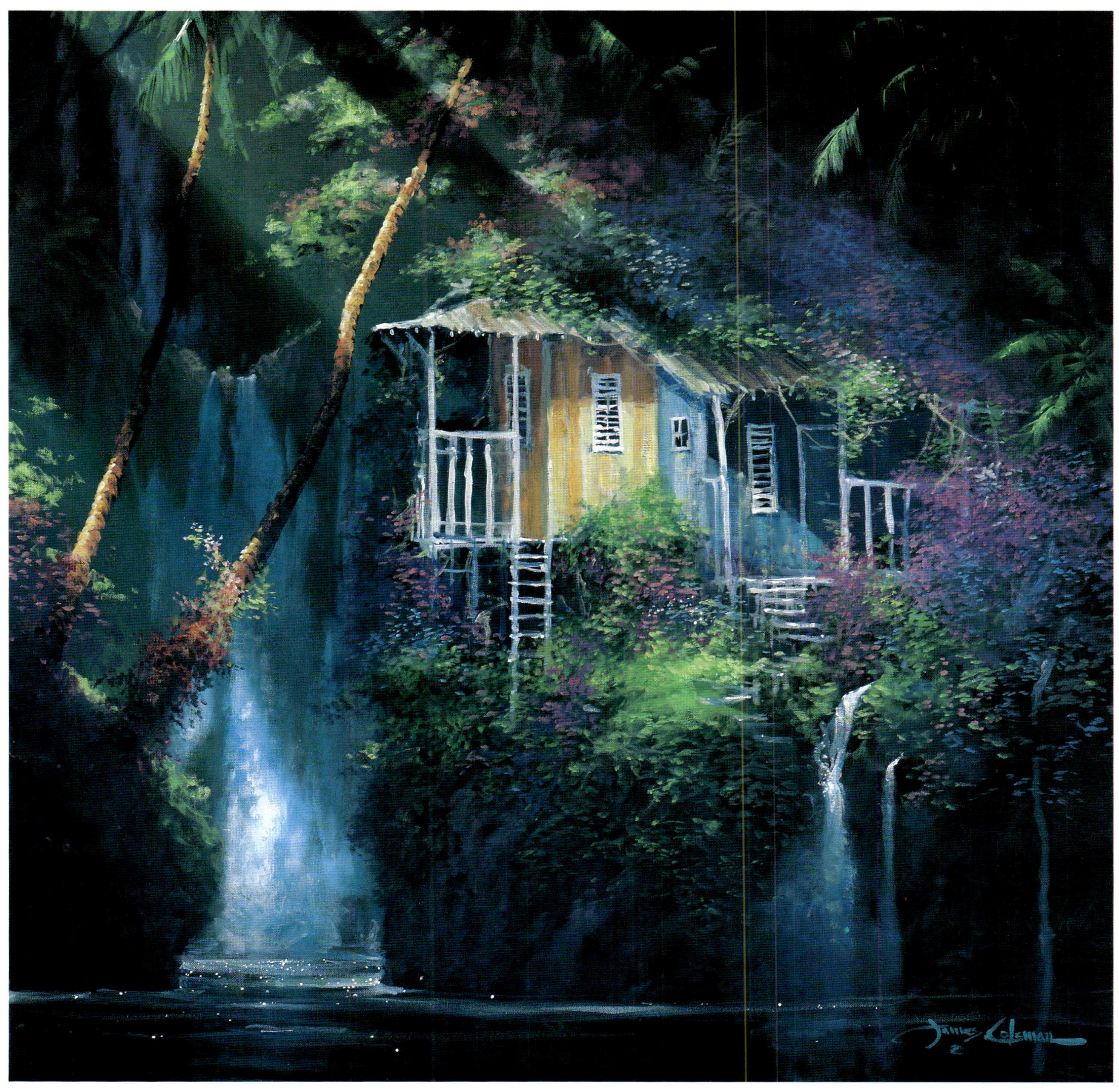

Peaceful Seclusion – Oil, 36 x 36 inches

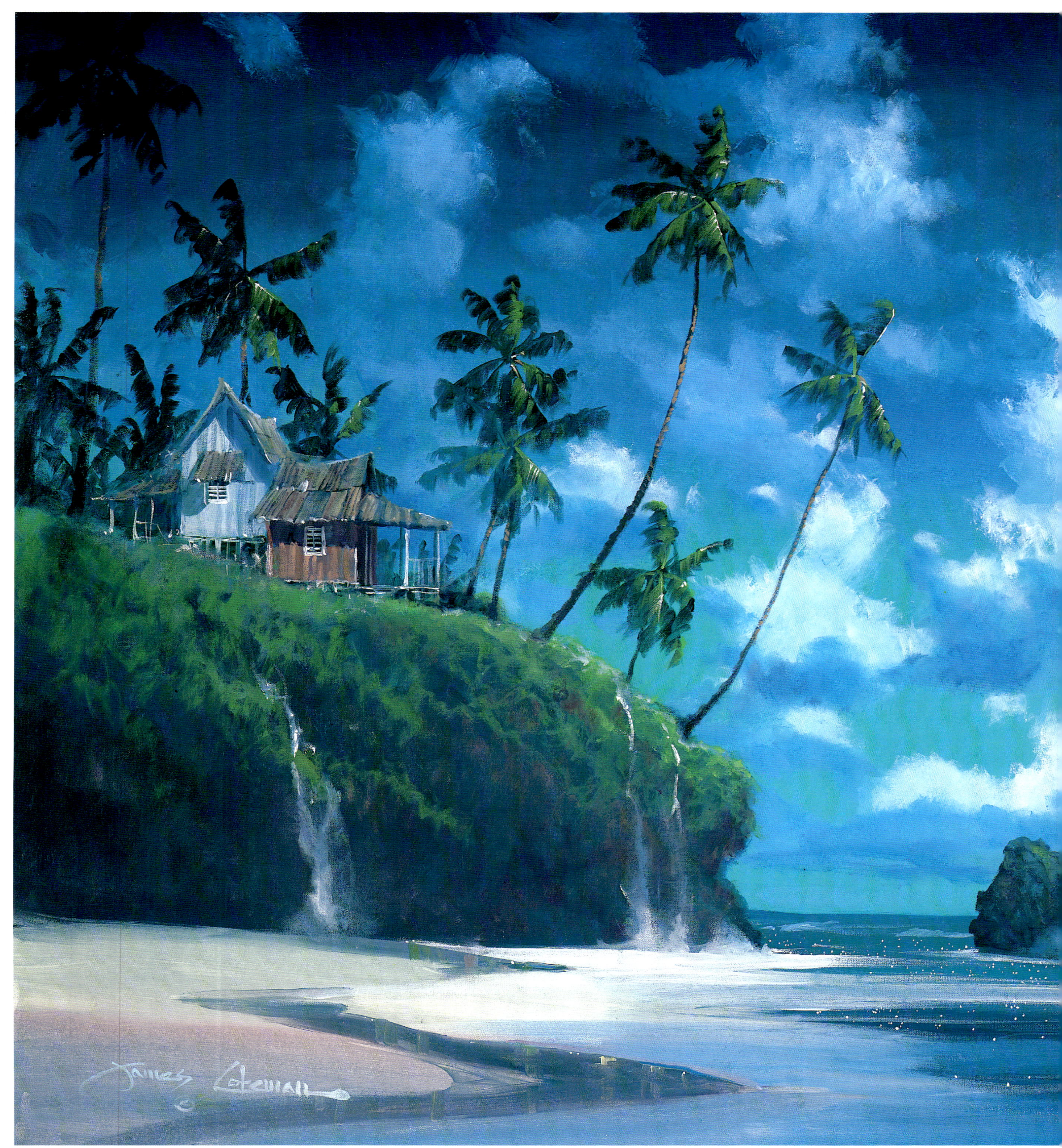

Sunlit Beach
Oil, 36 x 48 inches

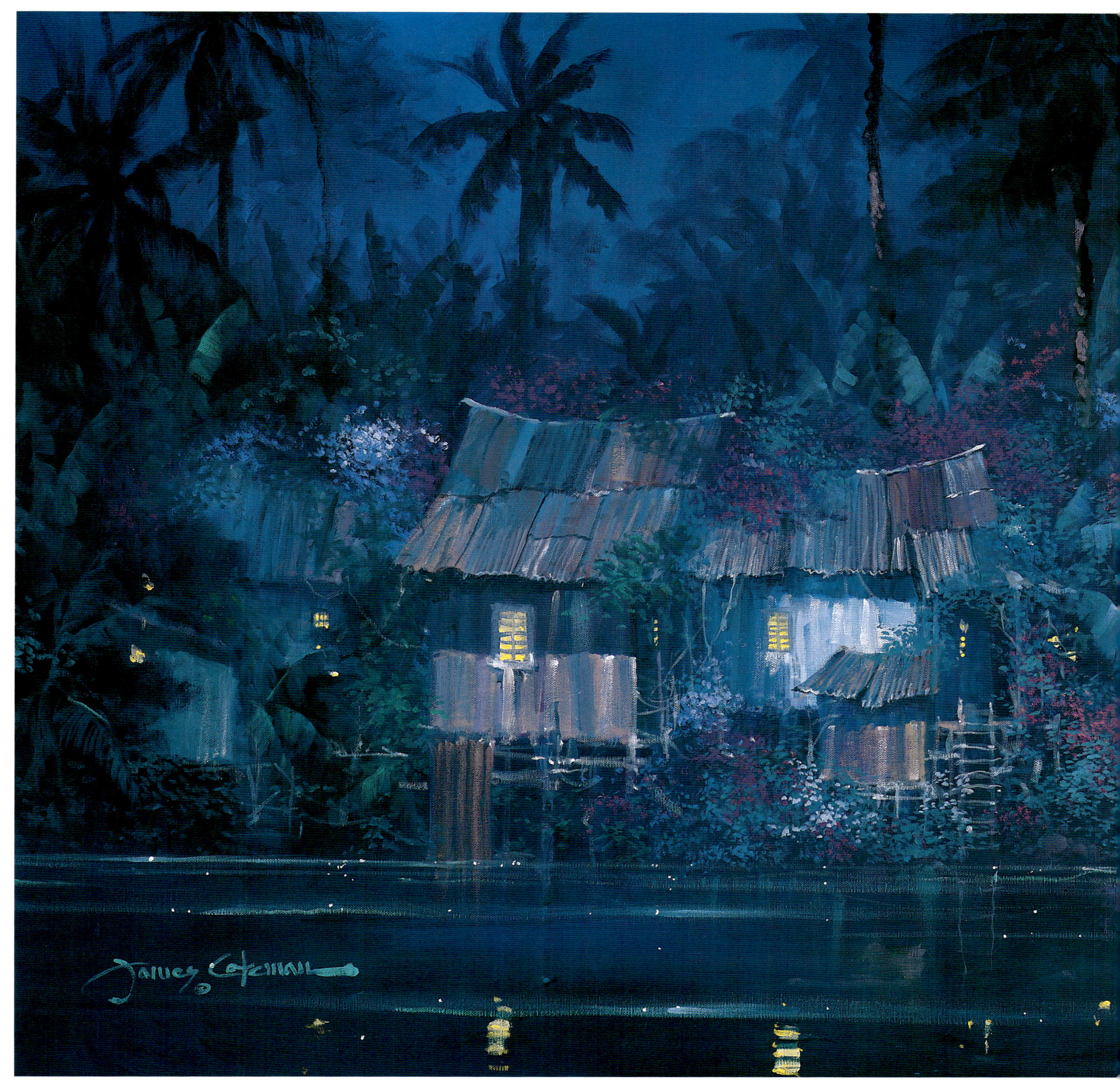

Evening Serenity – Oil, 30 x 60 inches

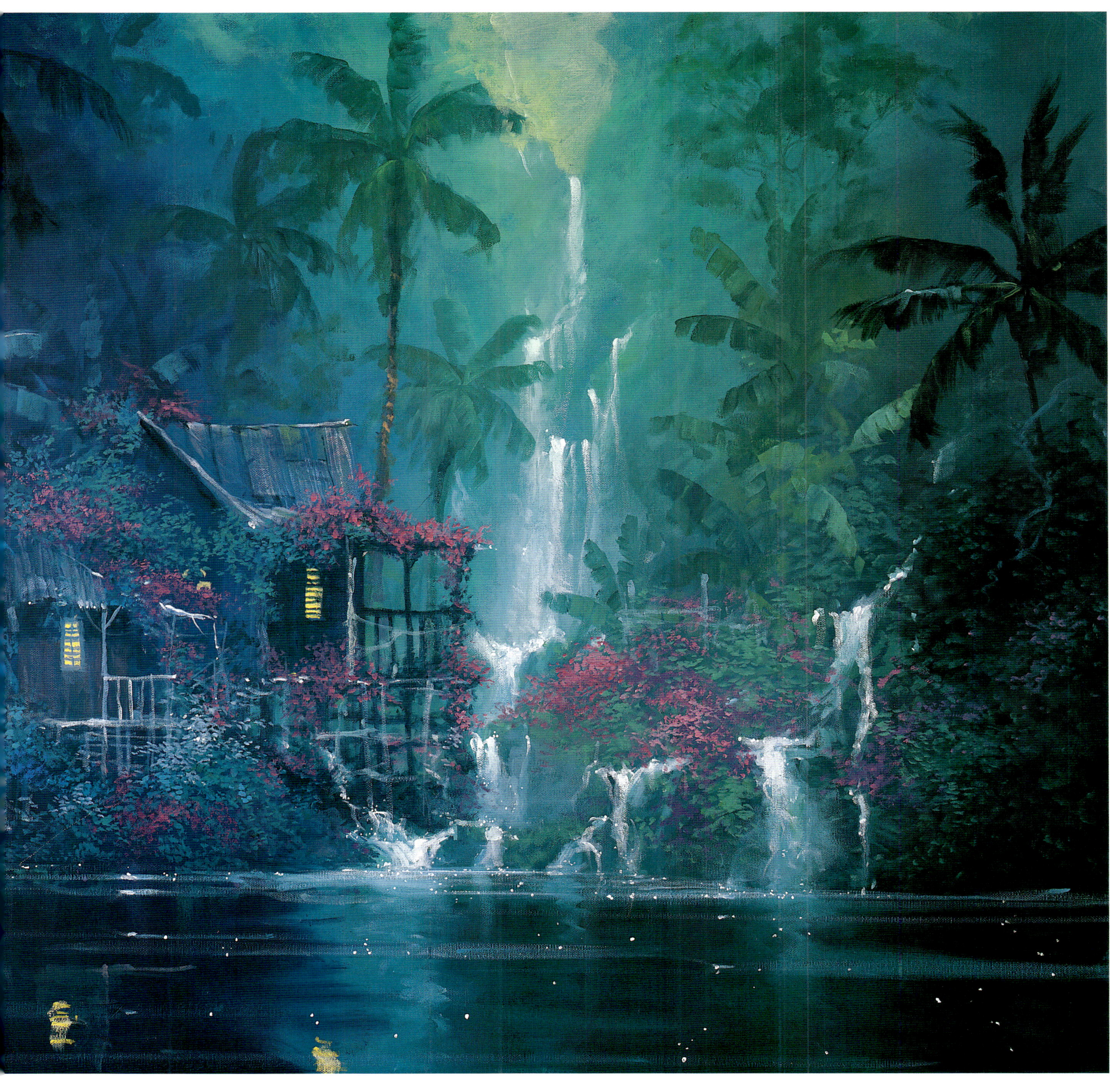

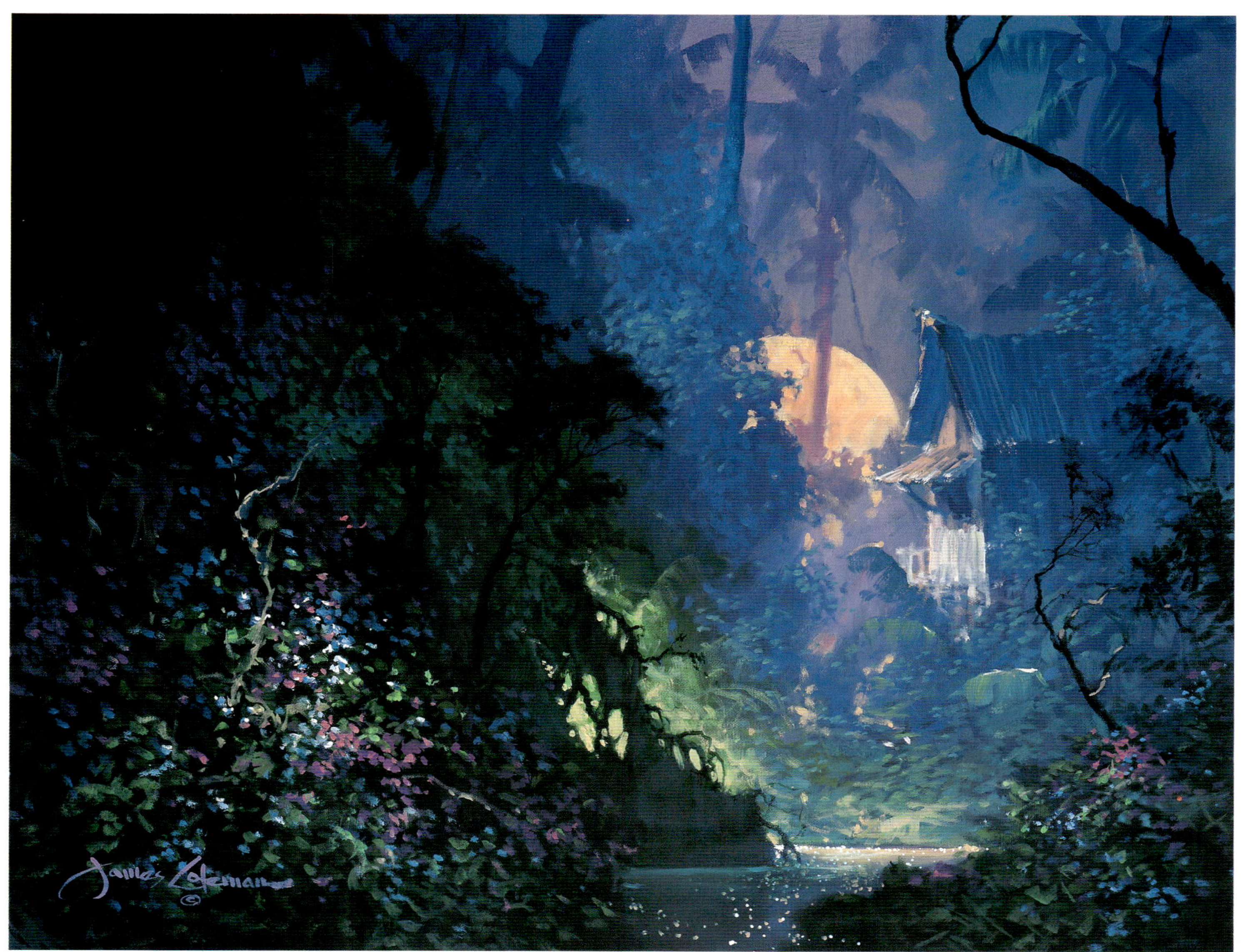

Misty Enchantment – Oil, 24 x 30 inches

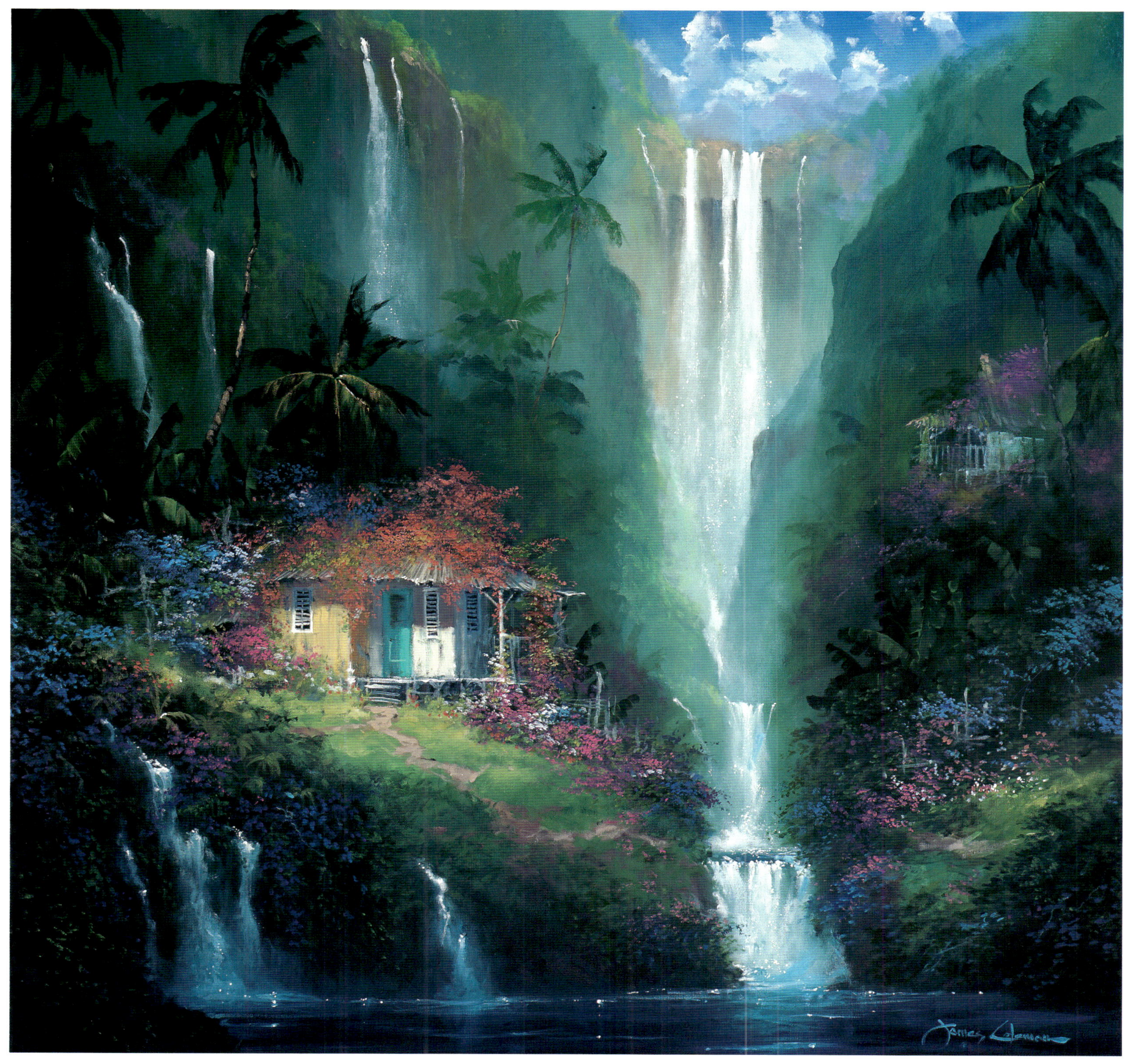

Surrender to Paradise – Oil, 48 x 48 inches

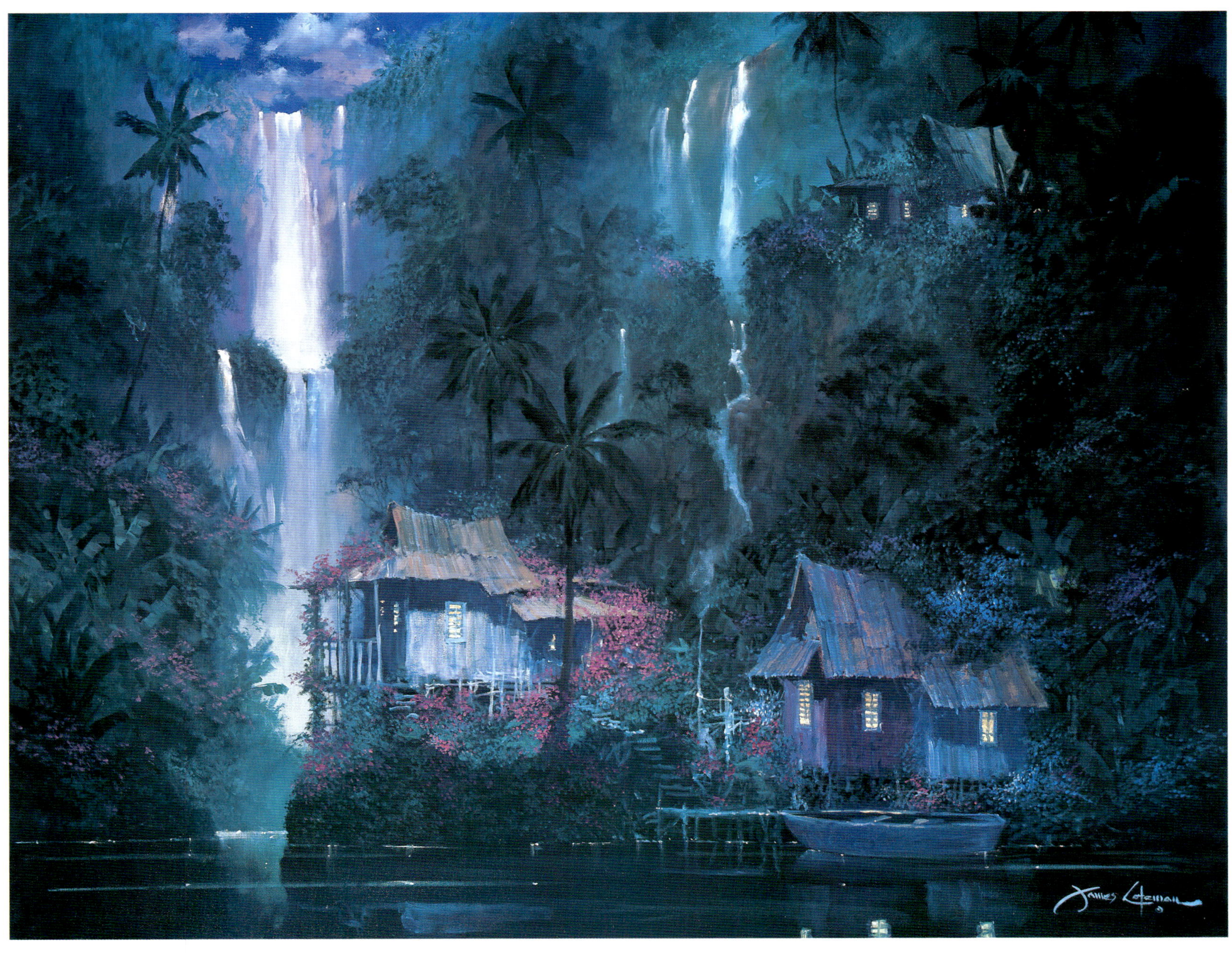

Tropical Dreamscape – Oil, 48 x 60 inches

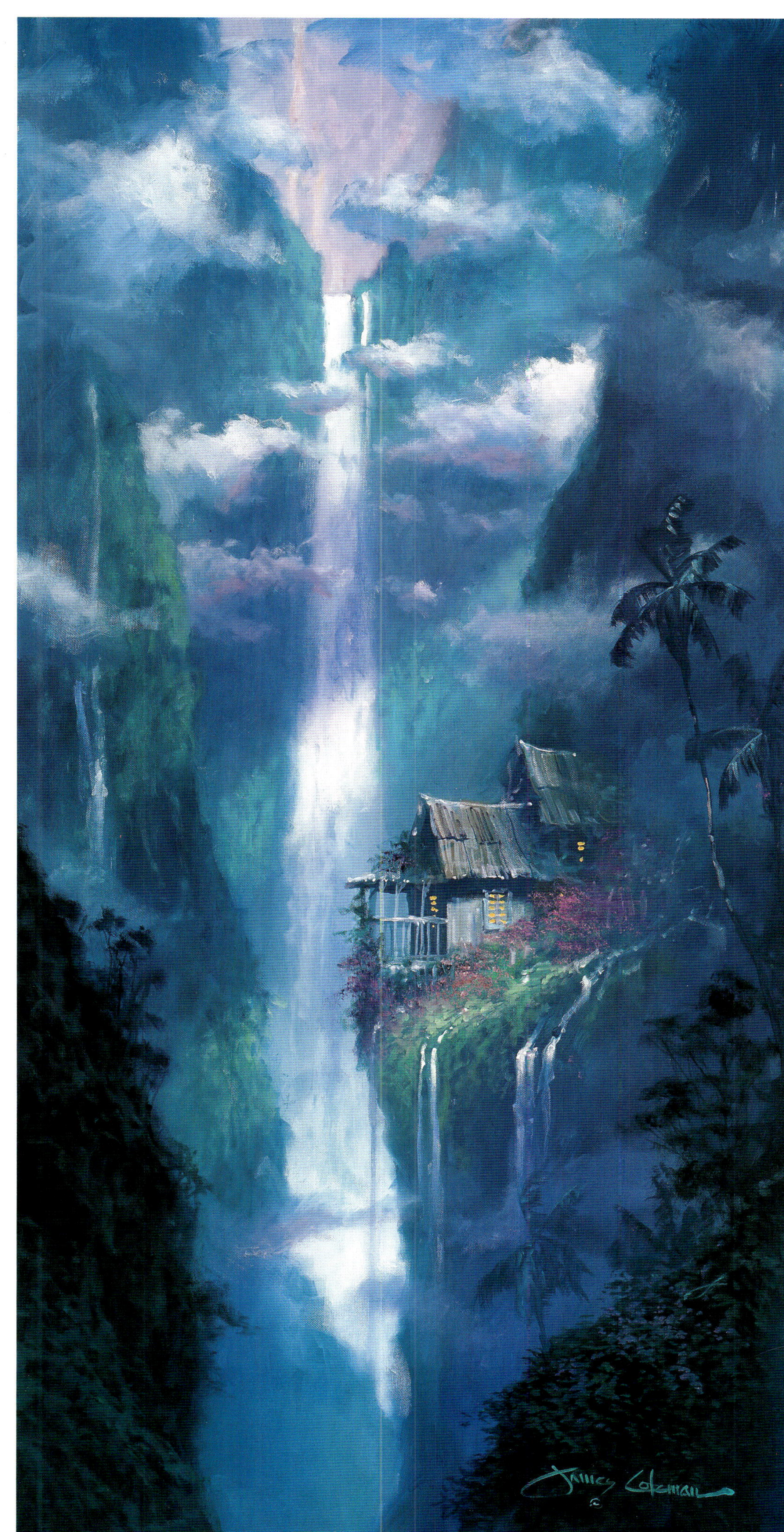

Never Ending Spirit
Oil, 36 x 18 inches

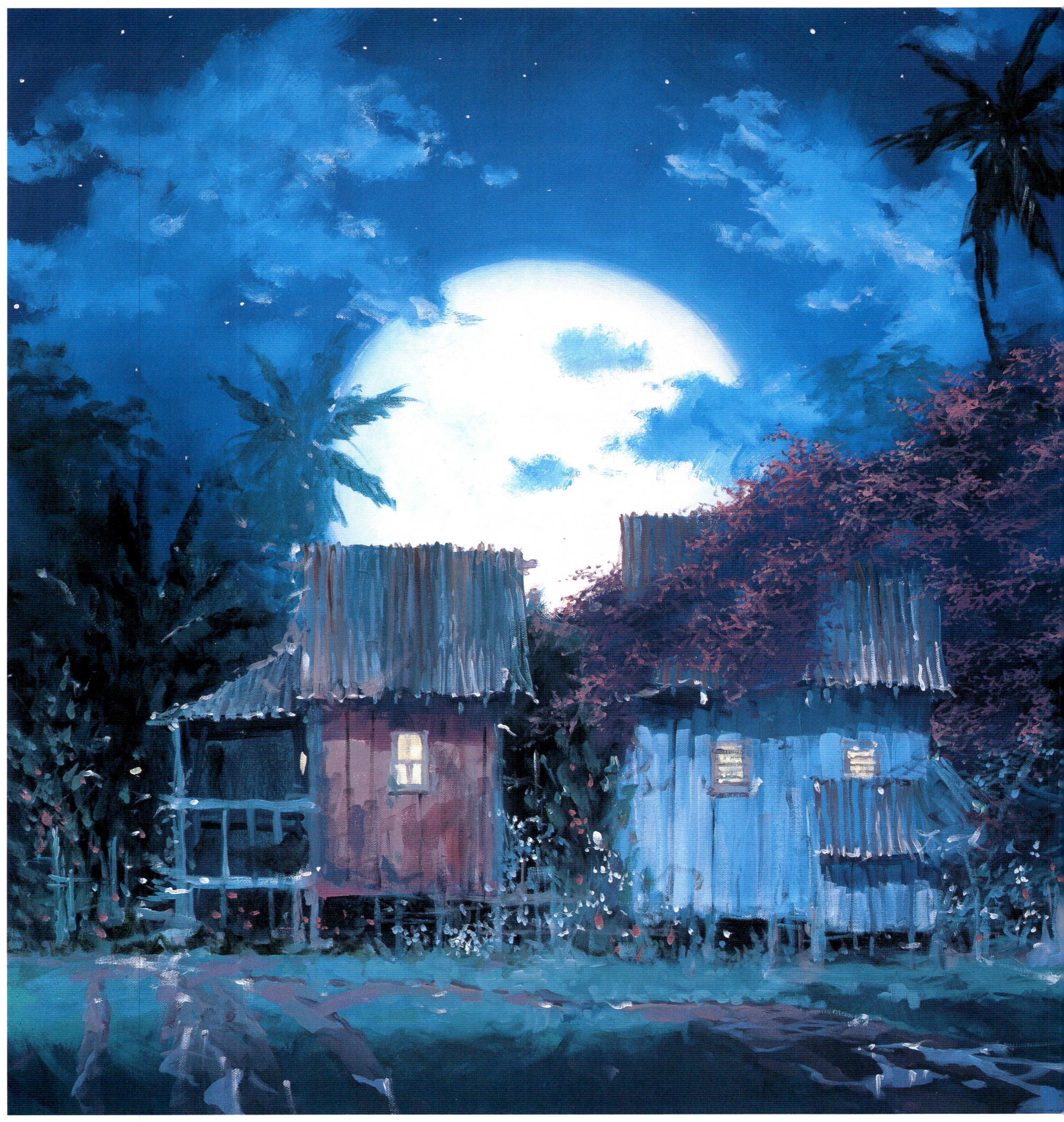

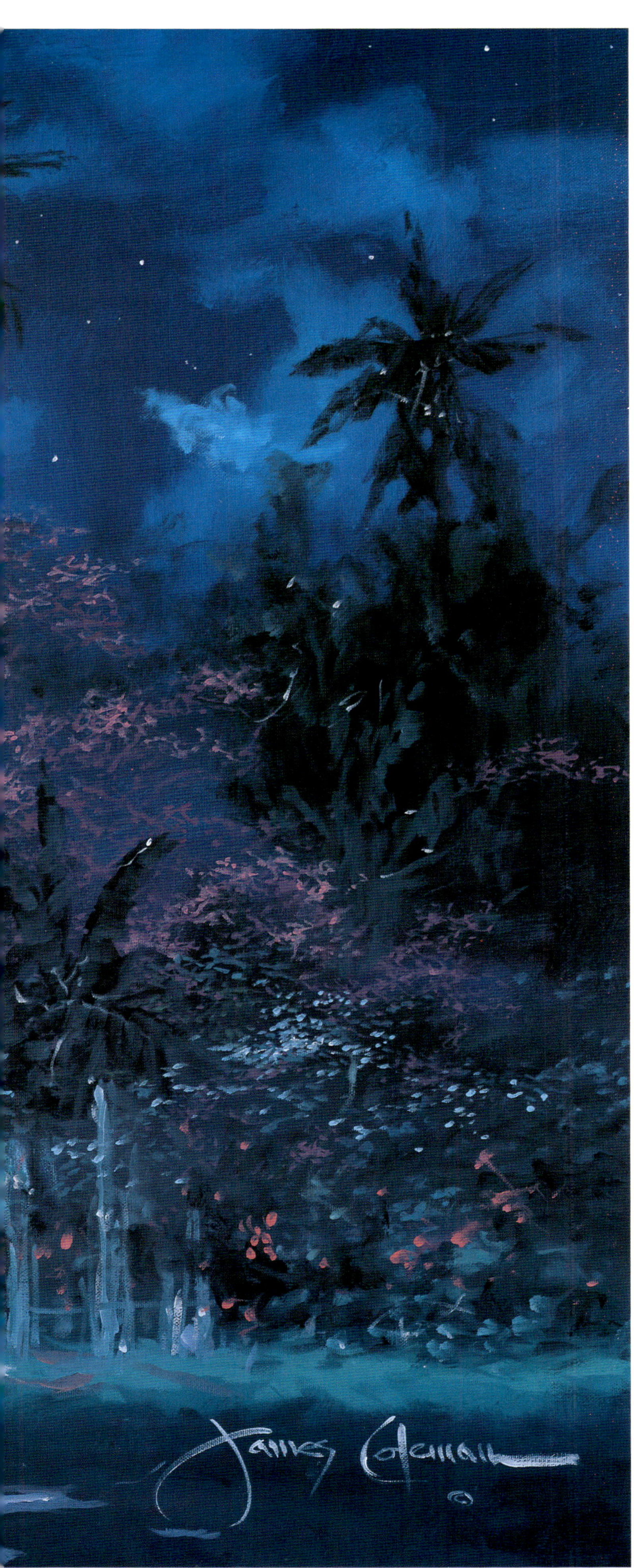

Paradise Moon
Oil, 30 x 40 inches

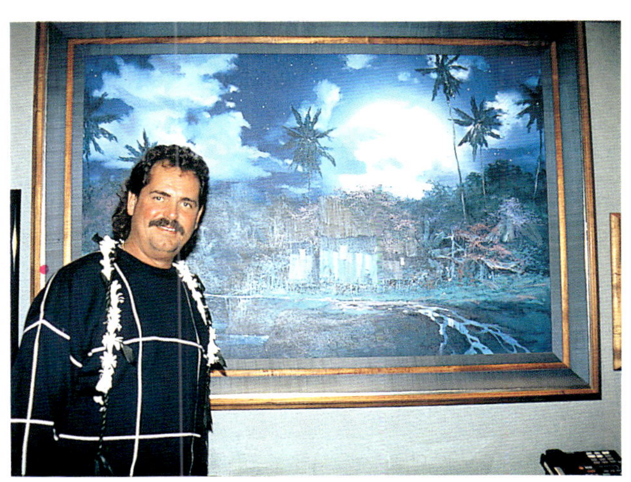

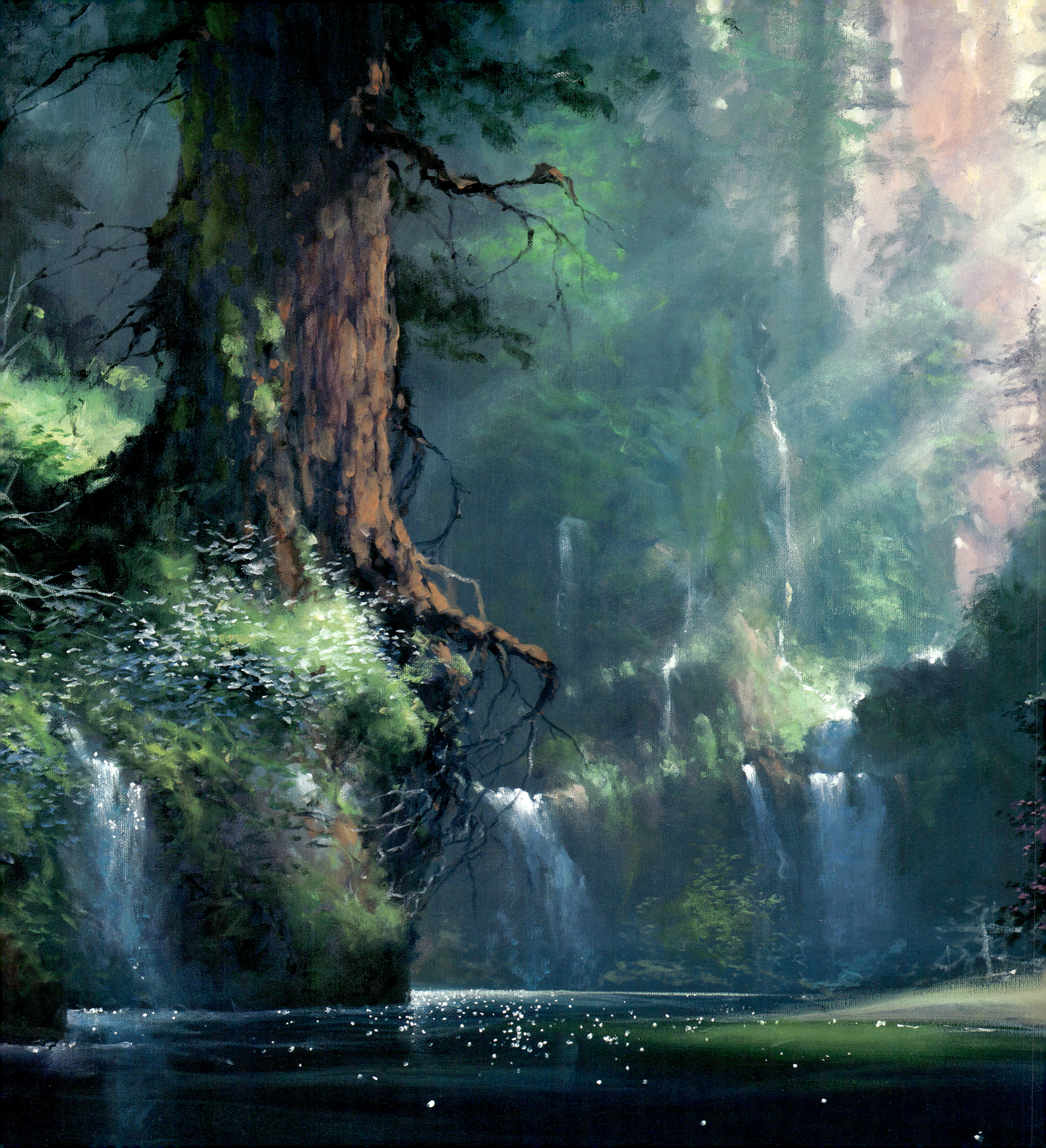

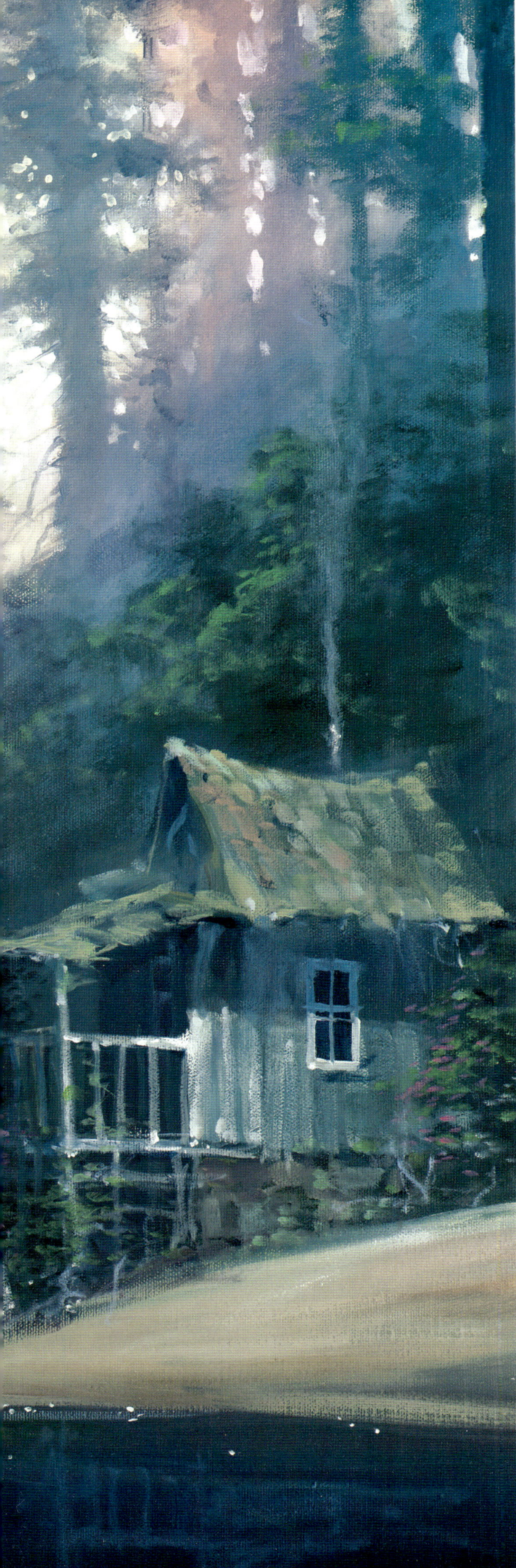

6

Enchanted Forests

"How do you do that?" the other kids asked him, their 8-year-old eyes wide open and their little mouths agape. He was the same age and same size as they were—how could he draw trees so "good?"

Coleman just smiled and bore down even harder on the leaves and branches of the oak trees their elementary teacher had told them to draw. He couldn't have answered them if he'd wanted to. He didn't know why he could draw them so well. He just could, that's all.

"I loved to draw, I know that," he says today. "And I drew trees, I suppose, because I was good at it and they interested me."

He remembers trips with his parents to see his older brother in Bishop, California. The trip up from Los Angeles took them along the eastern edge of the Sierras, which is mostly high desert, but the countryside was lined with all kinds of trees, from desert shrubs to oaks and aspens and, as they climbed in elevation, pine trees.

"I remember being inspired by the mountains rising up out of the high desert with trees up against them, especially in fall, when the colors were changing," he says. "These were easy subjects for me to start out with."

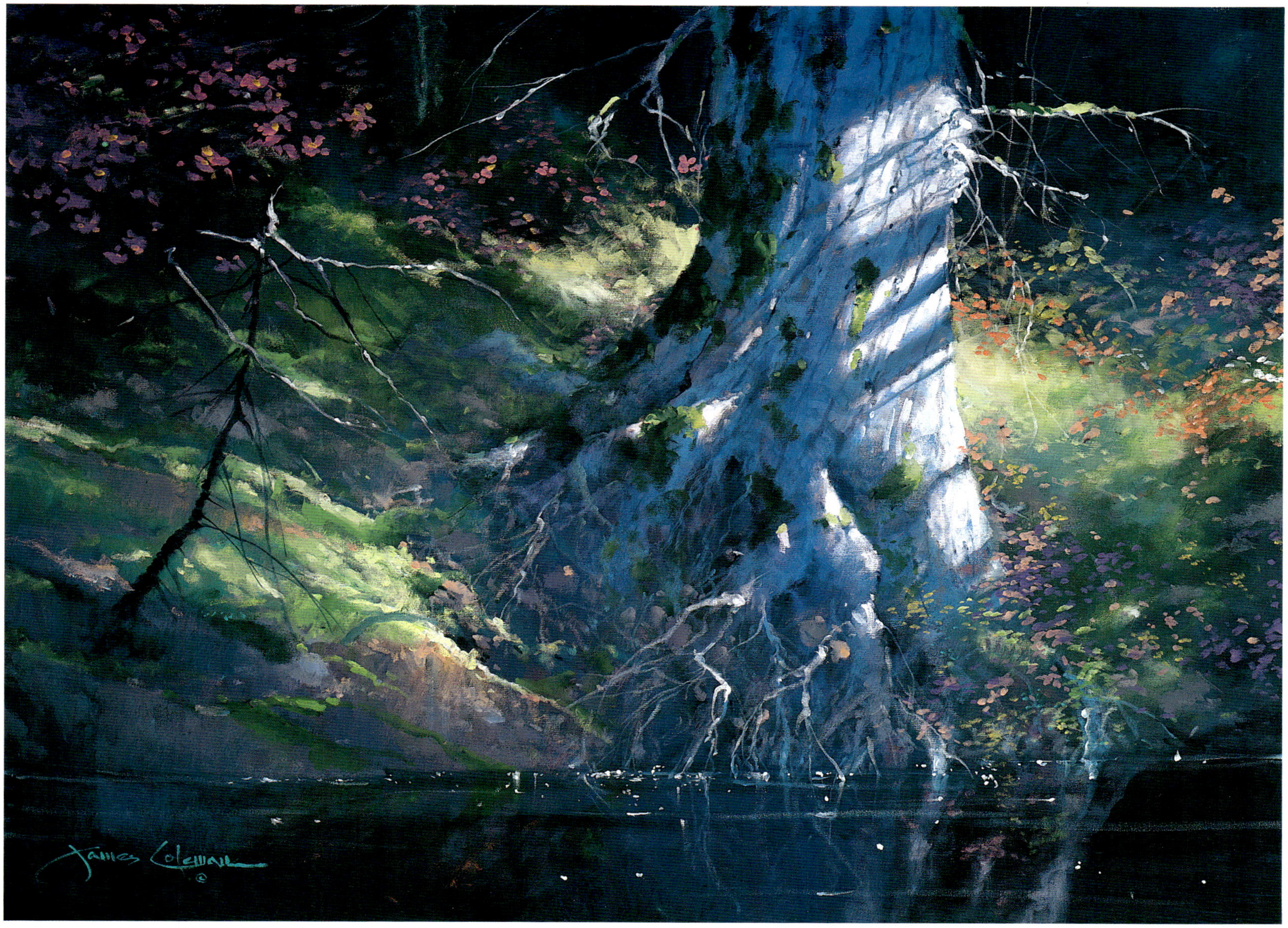

Quiet Light – Oil, 36 x 48 inches

Serenity ▶
Oil, 48 x 36 inches

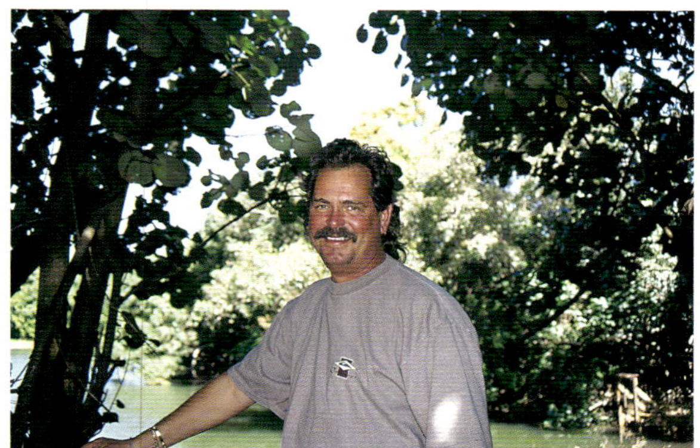

Through his adolescent years and into early manhood, Coleman painted trees, mountains, redwoods and deserts almost exclusively, with the exception of some coastal scenes and cloudscapes. Earlier on, he would take a sketch pad or pastels with him on hiking and camping trips, and sometimes he would take photographs and then paint when he got home.

Eventually, he just started taking pictures with his eyes, his mind and. . . his heart. He'd see something that interested him and made mental notes of it, committing it to memory. Spending hours looking at a subject, he'd absorb everything he could, so that when he returned to his studio, he could recall

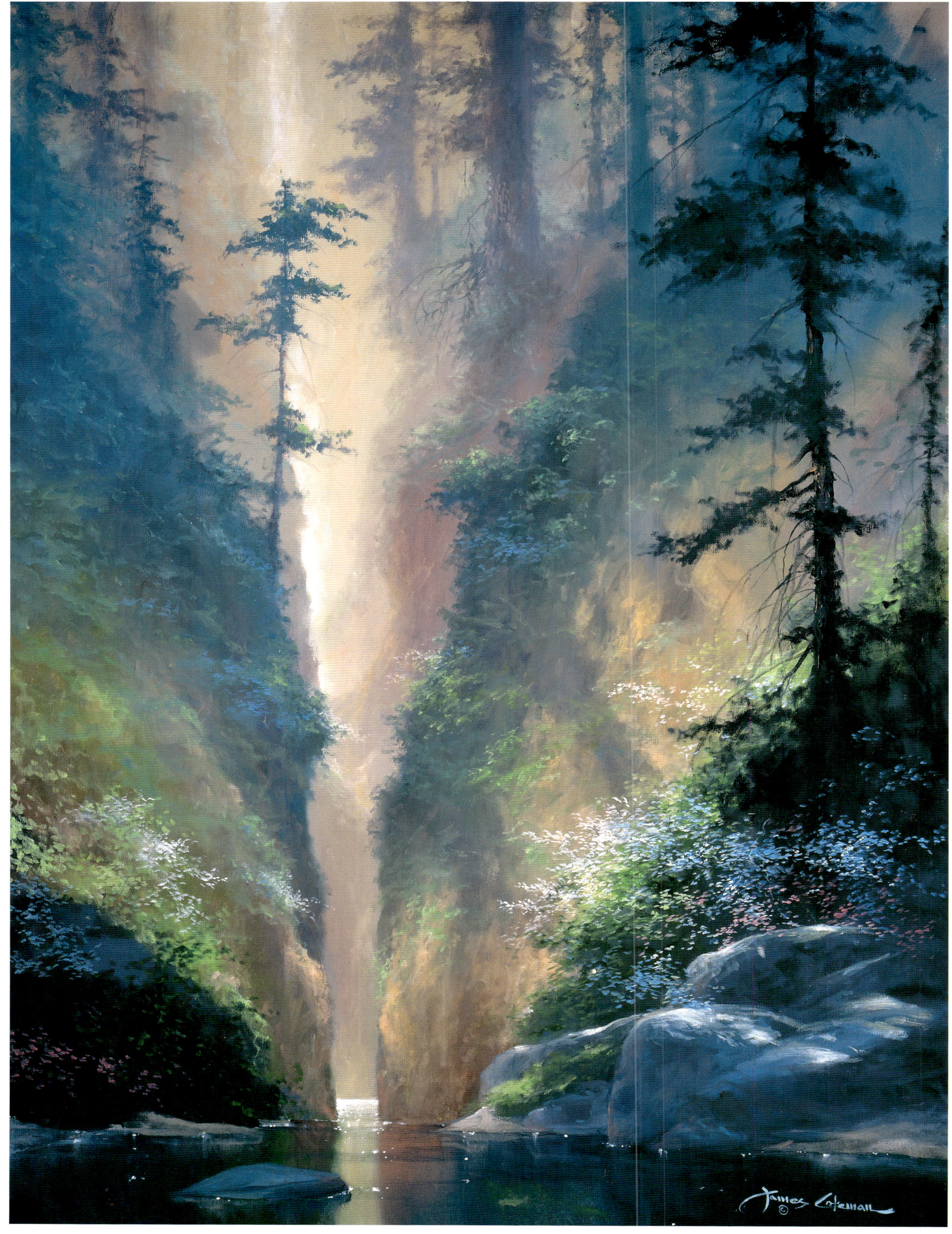
James Coleman ©

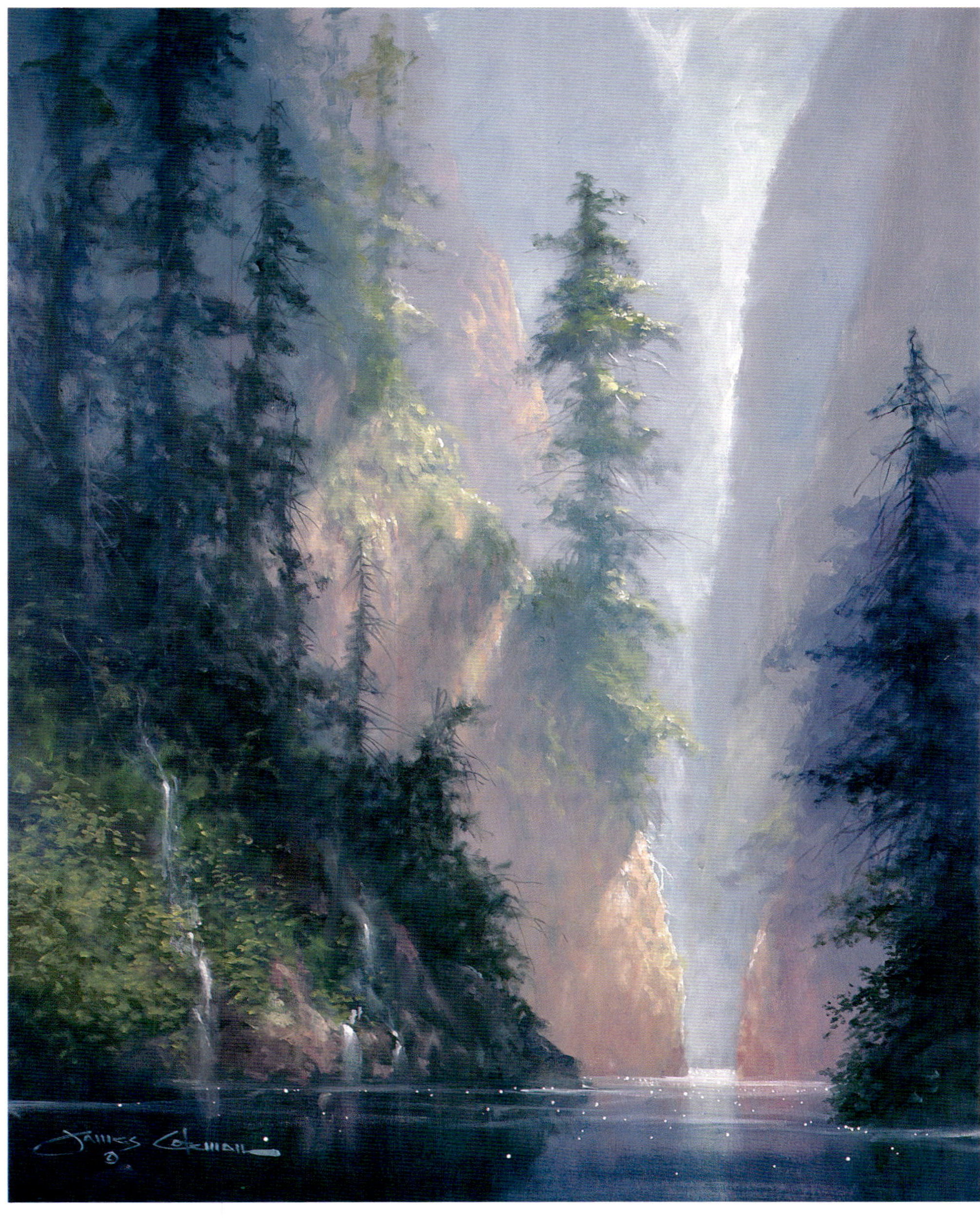

Mountain Sanctuary
Oil, 30 x 20 inches

Silent Mood ▶
Oil, 30 x 24 inches

what it was that moved or inspired him. Other times, all it took was a brief look, like in *Silent Surrender*, a haunting image of a small snowdrift against a sunlit tree in the mountains near Park City, Utah.

"I was skiing and happened to stop at this little spot," he recalls. "There was this tree at the edge of the woods, and the snow around it hadn't been touched. The sunlight, which is low in the winter, was shining across it, and it was absolutely beautiful. It would have made a great photograph. Part of the trunk was covered with snow, and the light patterns showcased this one tree, even though there were other trees around it.

"It was a simple image, a close-up, and that's what I was looking for at the time, something simple but intimate."

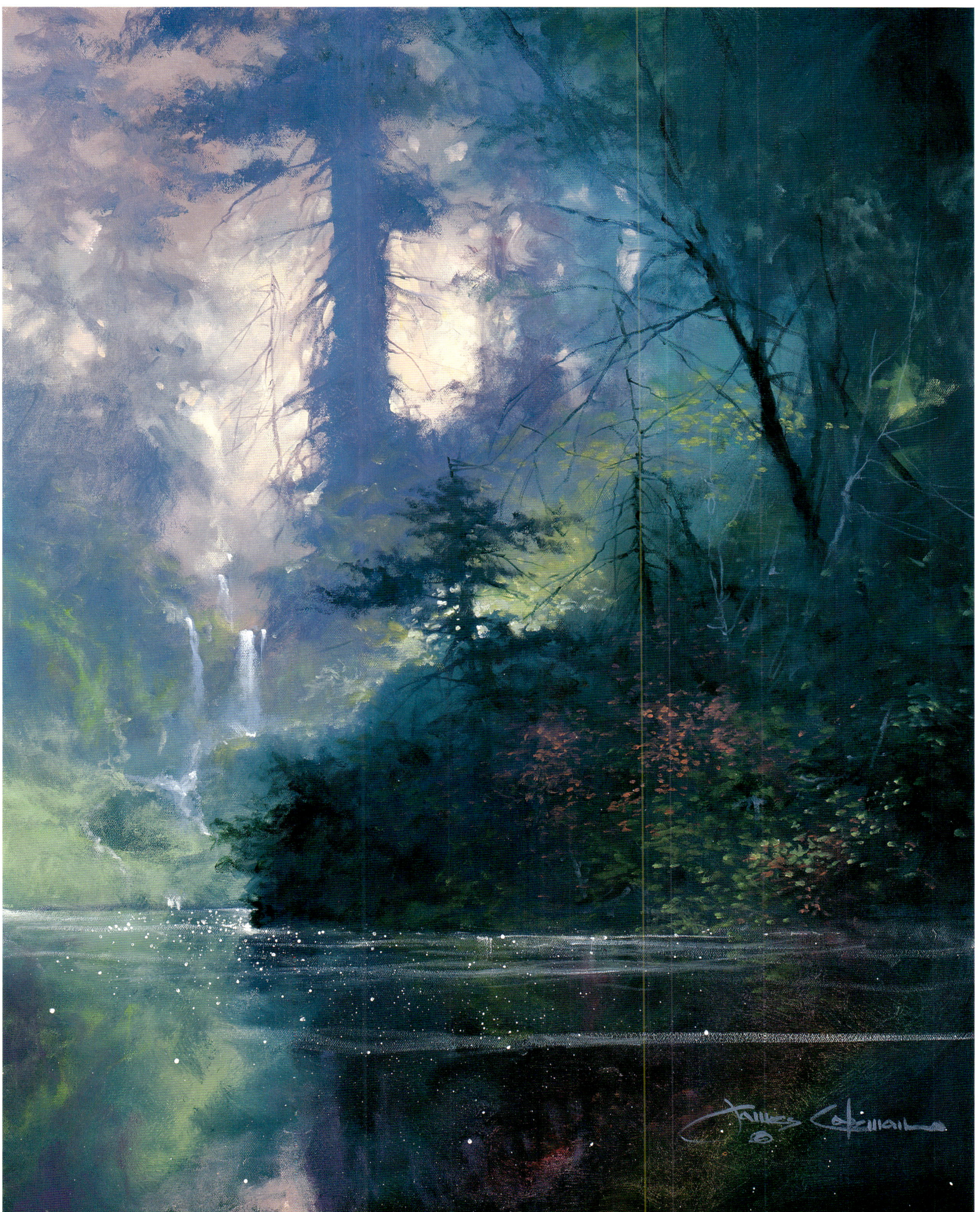

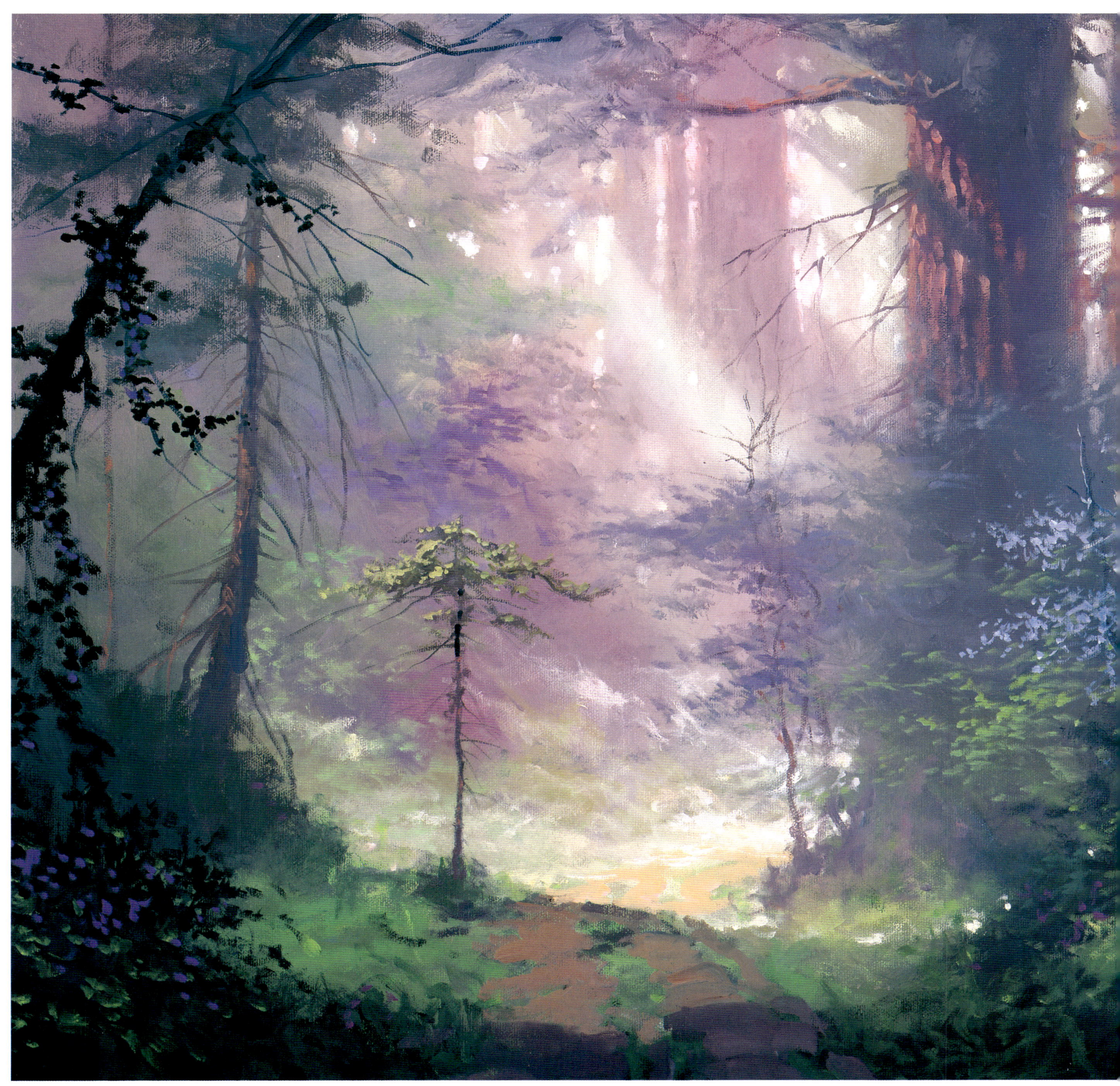

Misty Morning – Oil, 18 x 36 inches

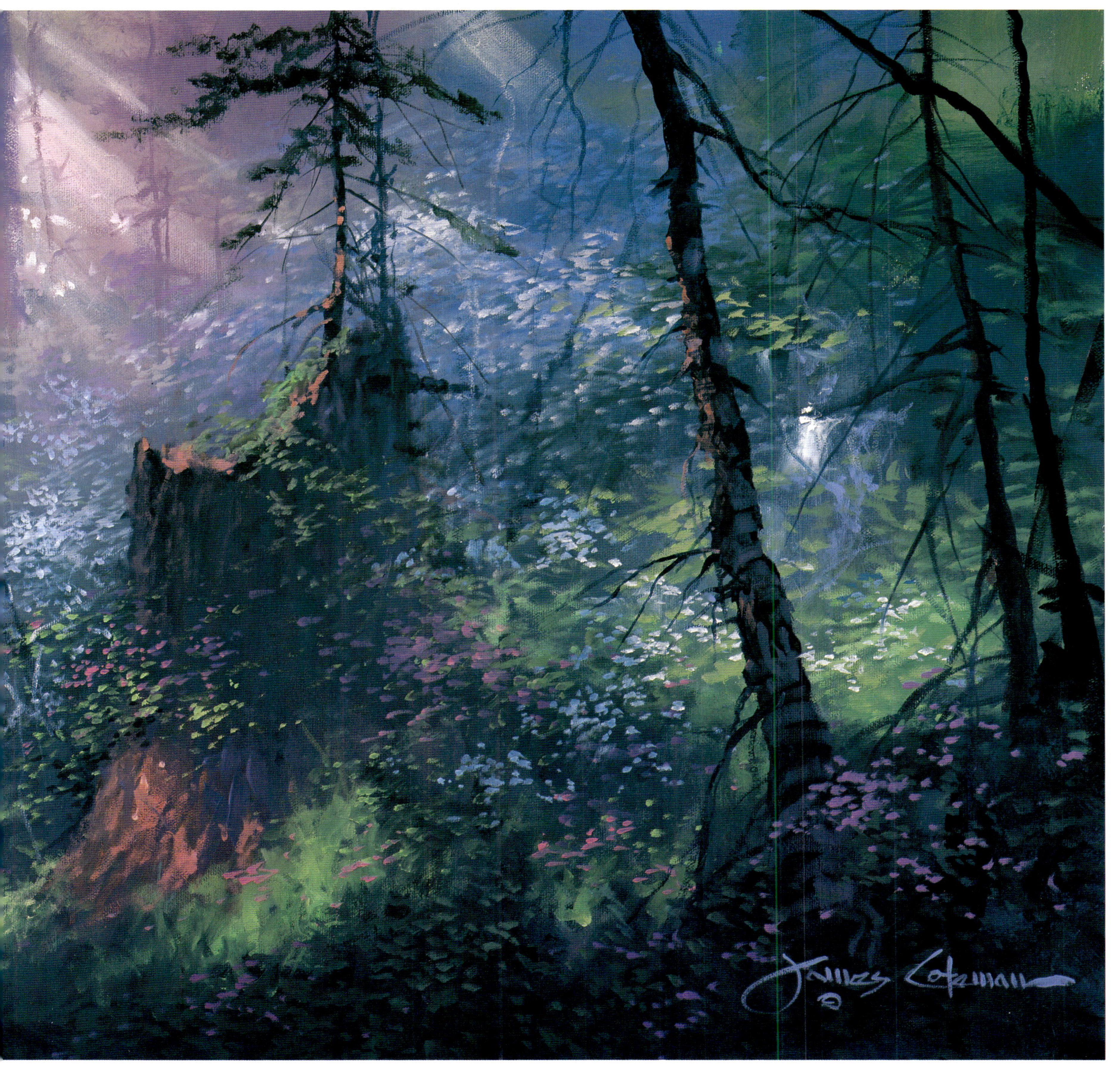
James Coleman

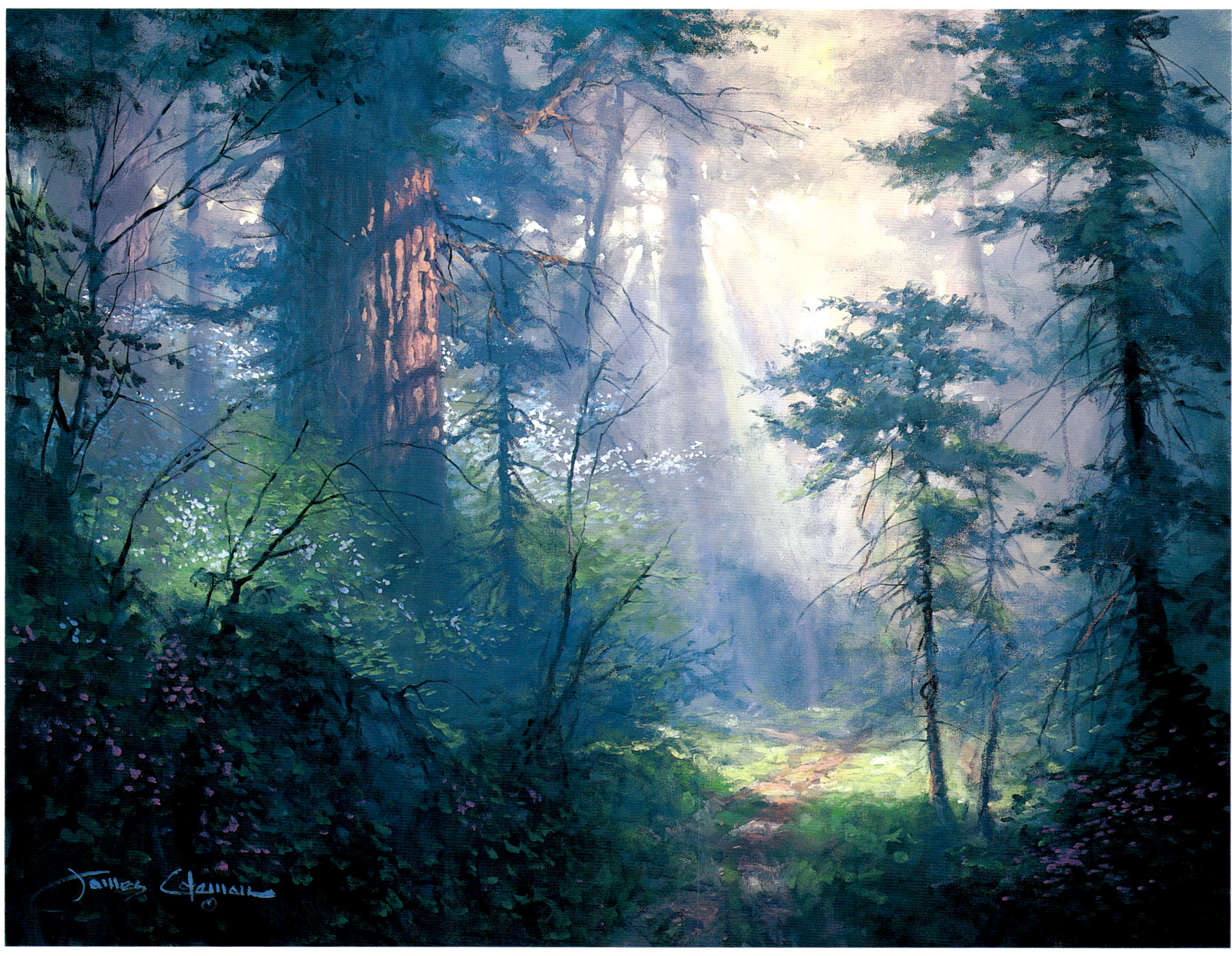

Streams of Light – Oil, 24 x 30 inches

The artist says that on some paintings he will have a basic composition in mind when he goes into the woods looking for something he'd like to paint. But, like the tree in *Silent Mood*, images often just jump out at him. A similar thing happened with *Misty Morning*. This time, he was out hiking and came across a downed redwood tree in Sequoia National Park.

"I was walking down a pathway and saw this stump with little trees growing up out of the top of it," he says. "It just stopped me in my tracks, so to speak, and I realized it was a very powerful image.

"It was very early fall, and the light coming out of the forest was kind of hazy. At first, I thought I could just paint the tree because it was so interesting. Then I thought about the way the light rays were coming through the forest and how peaceful it made everything look."

Streams of Light has a similar effect. There are not as many elements in the painting, but the rays of light filtering through the trees cast a soft glow along a pathway in the woods.

"What I like to think is you can take the simplest of subjects," he asserts. "And when you have the right light, and the right

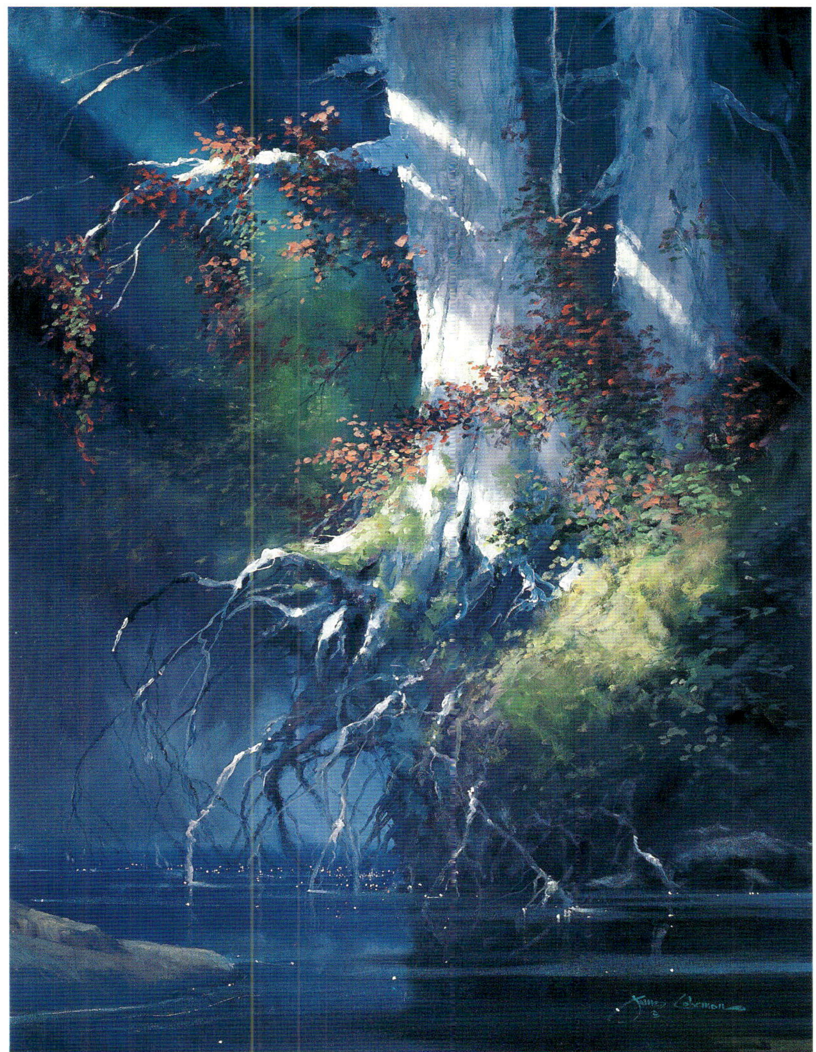

Tranquil Dream – Oil, 48 x 36 inches

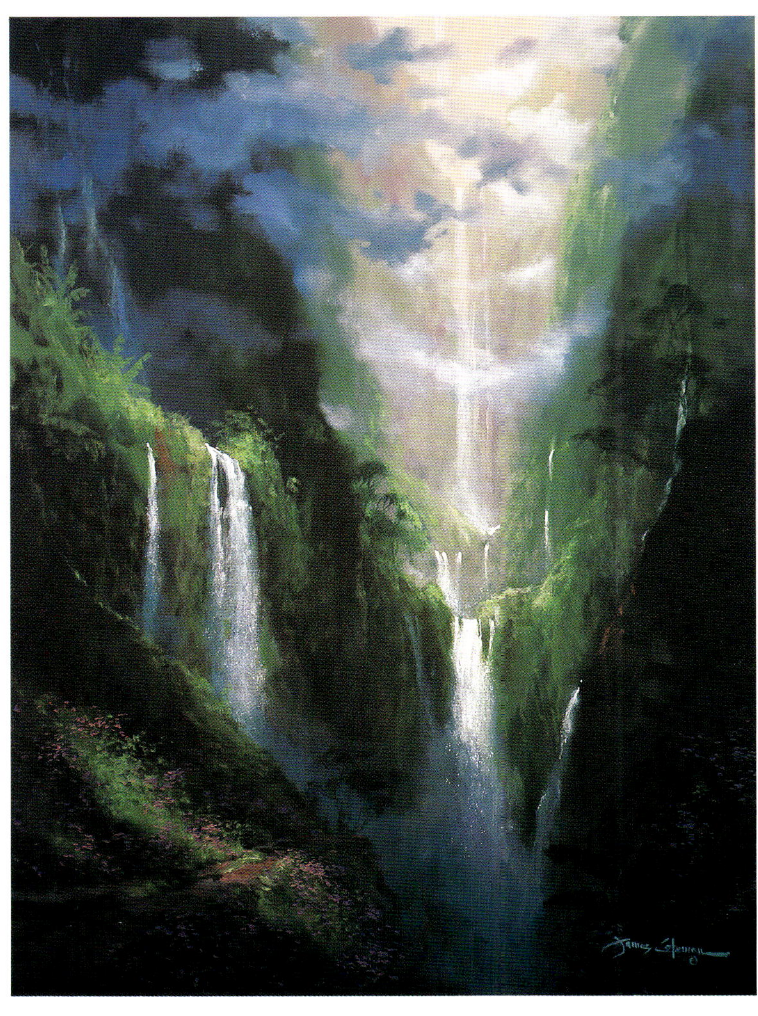

Eternal Mist – Oil, 48 x 36 inches

use of it, you're going to be able to cause people to be drawn into it. They're going to say, 'Oh yeah, I've seen that,' or, 'I saw that same thing when we were. . .'

"It actually could have been anywhere in the world. In a sense, it doesn't matter where you are, there's always someplace like it, or almost like it. That's probably why I don't remember places or names of trees and things—it's not important. There are differences, but I'm not as interested in showing those in a painting as I am in creating a mood for people, wherever it is."

Indeed, Coleman's forests are not limited to the redwoods of California or the misty Pacific Northwest. They could just as easily

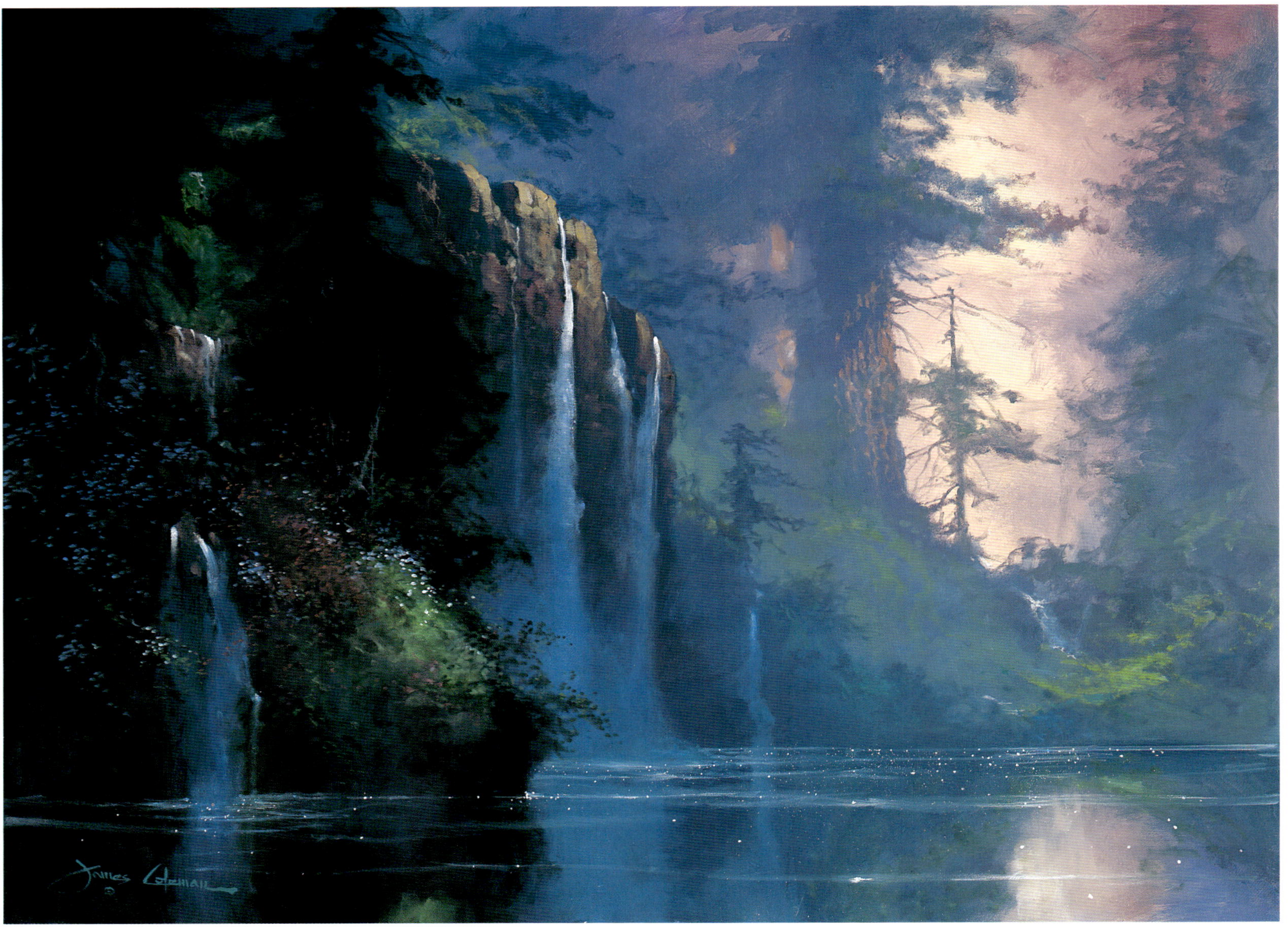

Natures Symphony – Oil, 30 x 40 inches

Thundering Falls ▶
Oil, 40 x 30 inches

be found in Canada, Alaska or in mountains and wooded areas in other parts of the world.

"Hopefully people add their own information to one of my paintings and make it a place they're familiar with," he says. "That way, the viewer becomes part of the painting. They're not just viewing it, they're actually living inside of it. I think that's the secret to what I do."

When he first started painting forests, he painted them more as a naturalist, he says. Then, as he moved into impressionism, the lines became much softer. His forests today are still impressionistic, but with a little more detail than he once used.

But not much detail—Coleman concerns himself much more with the emotion of a scene rather than re-creating exactly how a tree or pond looked when he saw it. Some artists who paint as many forest scenes as he does are extremely knowledgeable about the trees they paint, capable of recognizing and reciting the names of dozens of species. Not Coleman.

"I don't think in terms of categories or titles," he explains. "It's all just an experience, and trees are the same way. I know some of them because I've been hiking and fishing for such a long time. But I've never made a study of them, like this is an ash, or that's an elm. They're just trees, with different shapes,

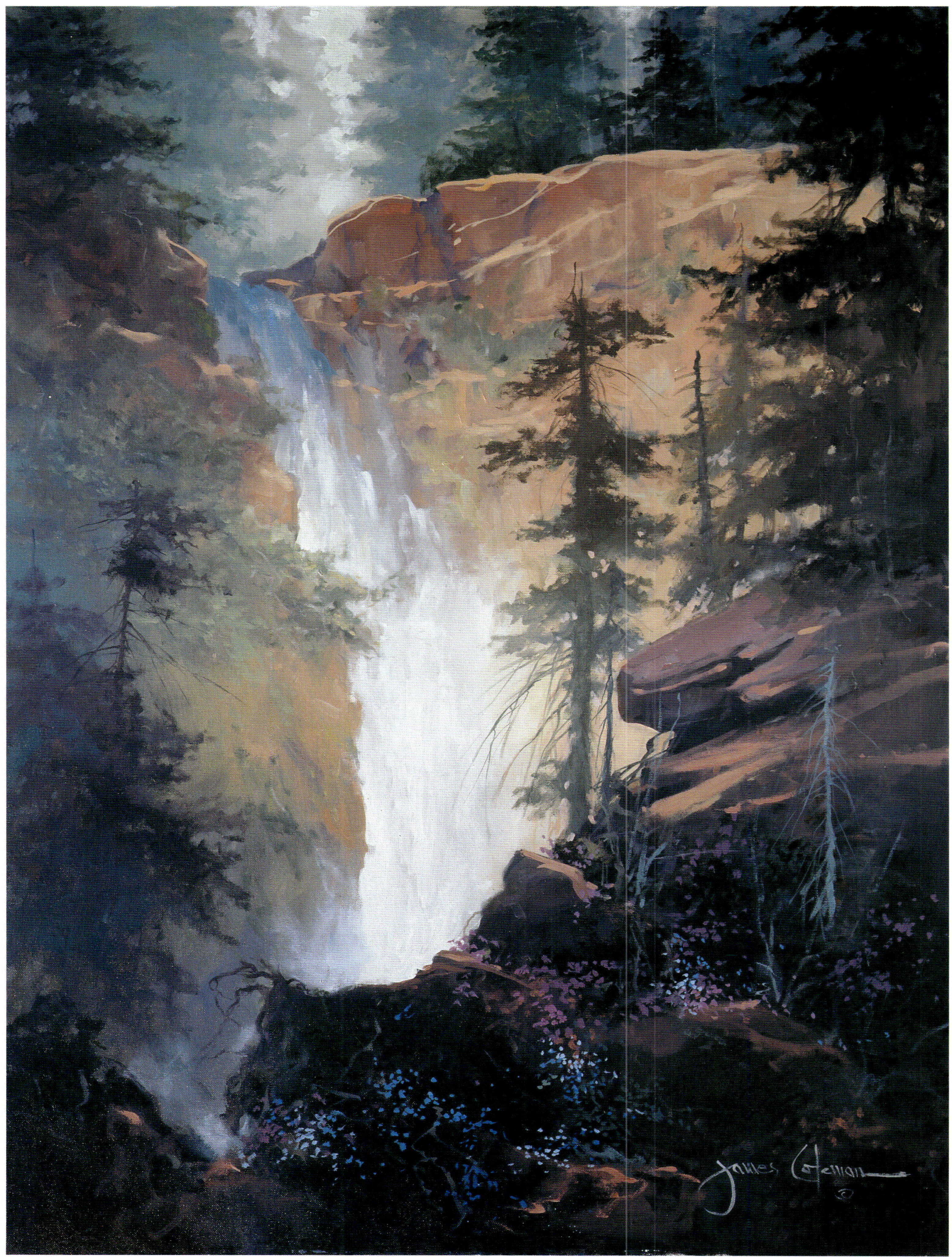
James Coleman

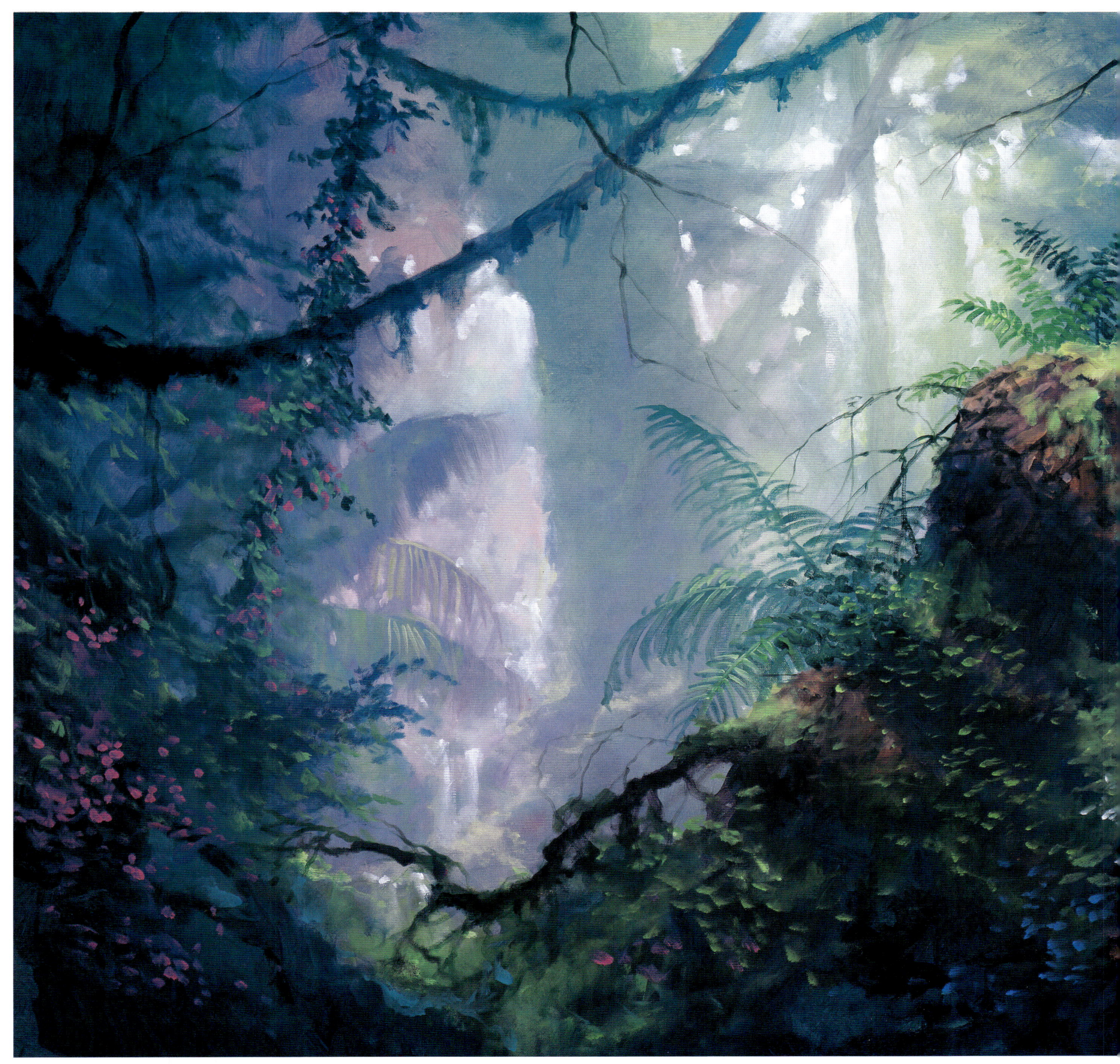

Timeless Illumination – Oil, 24 x 48 inches

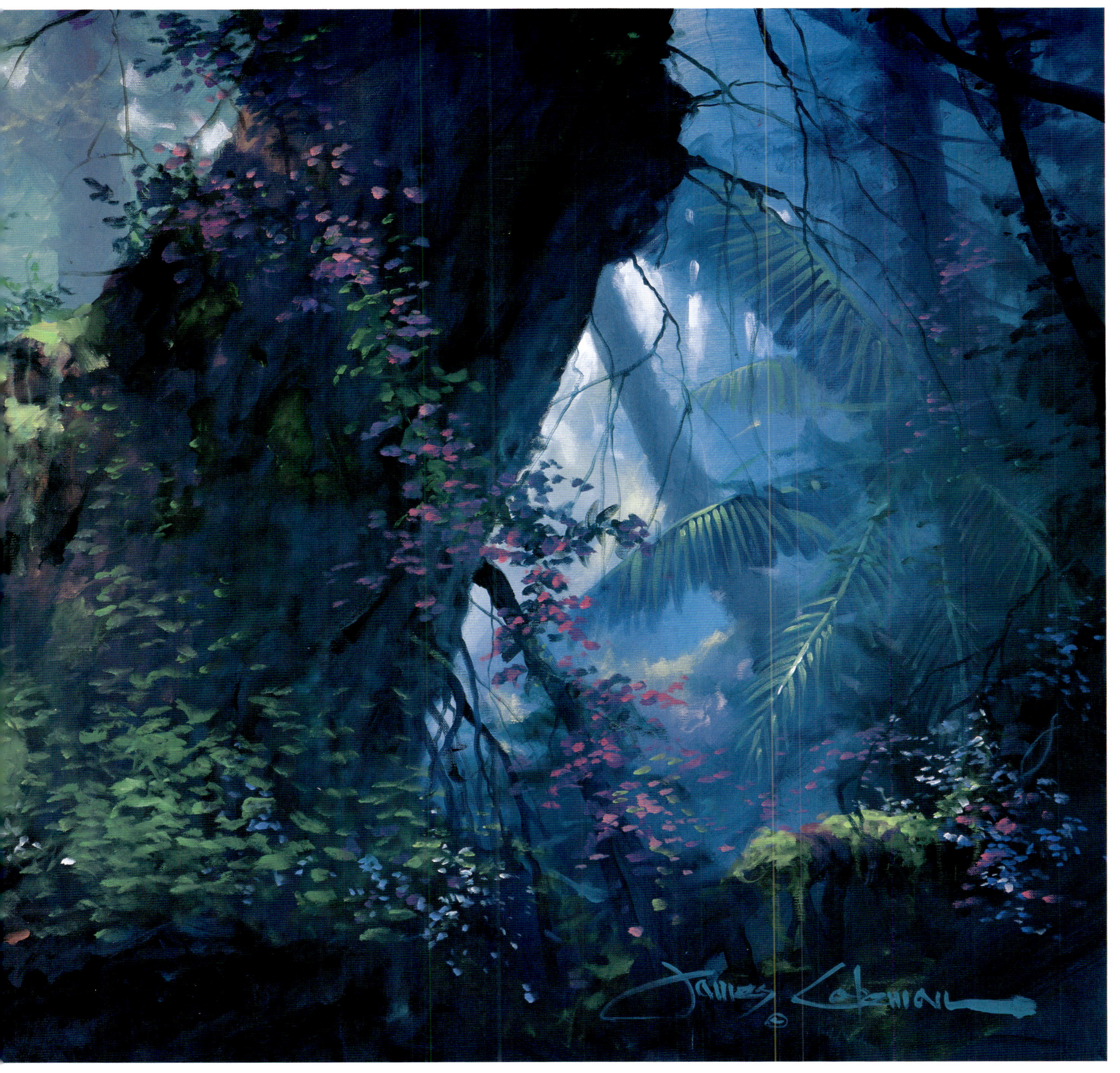

colors and spirits. And that's how I identify them."

Many of Coleman's mountain and forest scenes were inspired by backpacking trips in the Sierras, and, most recently, while fly-fishing in Wyoming. Most of the time, he will focus on a single intimate moment or subject during these trips.

"In *Serenity*, it's different," he points out. "It has a lot more scope. The way it's painted, it drops back into an almost endless succession of canyon-like formations, going back. . . back. . . back. In my mind, it causes people to imagine what's back beyond those different levels of vision.

"This painting includes water, air and land along with trees, foliage and flowers. It has all of the things that, to me, have a spiritual connection with people. The still water, for instance, with the light reflecting off of it, causes people's minds to melt into that image.

"*Serenity* started out as a tropical scene, and I knew I had to start adding some palms or ferns or banana trees. Then I stopped and said, 'Why?' This could be almost anywhere. I've had collectors ask me if I painted it in Tennessee, the Northwest and other places. I actually saw this scene when I was hiking in the high country, along Yosemite Creek. But I painted most of it from my imagination."

Nature's Symphony, Coleman says, is a good example of how he sometimes uses similar colors in various paintings. "There's a lot of crossover," he says. "I used to paint mostly coastal and Pacific Northwest scenes, with a lot of fog. You can find some of those same colors in the mountains. In fact, I took some of the same theories of light and color from the trees and redwoods and used them when I went to paint the desert."

Another common theme in his forests is the thick, prominent tree with its roots climbing down the bank of a river or creek. The trees in *Quiet Light*, *Peaceful Solitude* and *Tranquil Dream* are specific trees Coleman has seen in the woods, more than once.

"There's a tree on the bank of the Merced River I've seen for years," he says. "It's been dead so long it's totally bleached out white, with its roots hanging down into the river. I used to hike along the river several times a year, and I would always stop by the tree to see how it looked during various times of the year."

Although trees are the first subjects Coleman ever painted, and are still the most prominent figures in most of his art, there are many other elements that make them work. Rather than a mere reporter of what he sees in nature, he takes elements that already exist and arranges them much like a composer would with musical notes.

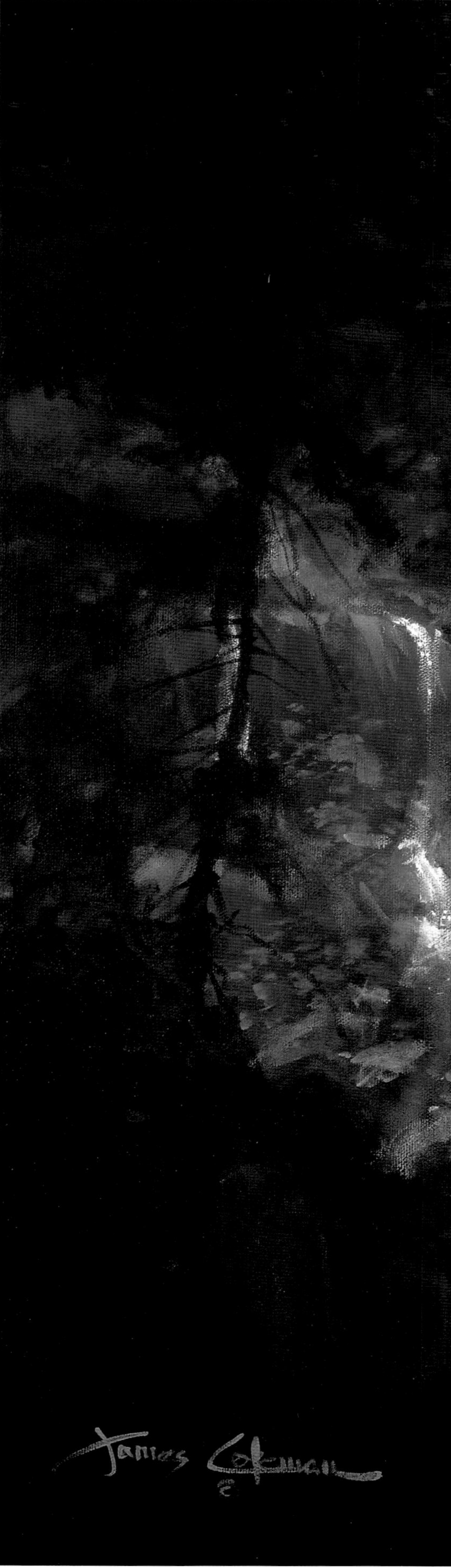

Mountain Hideaway
Oil, 24 x 30 inches

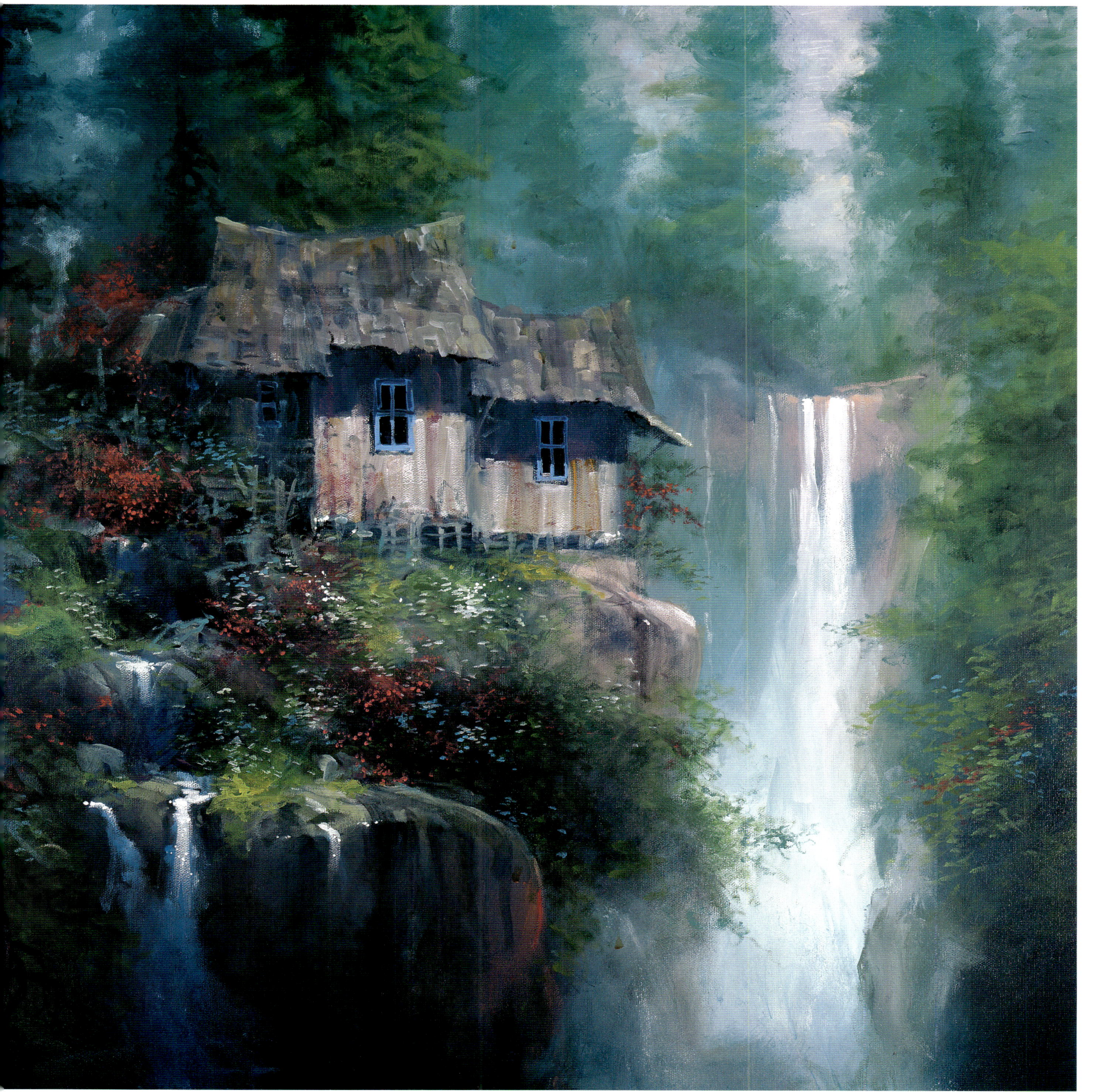

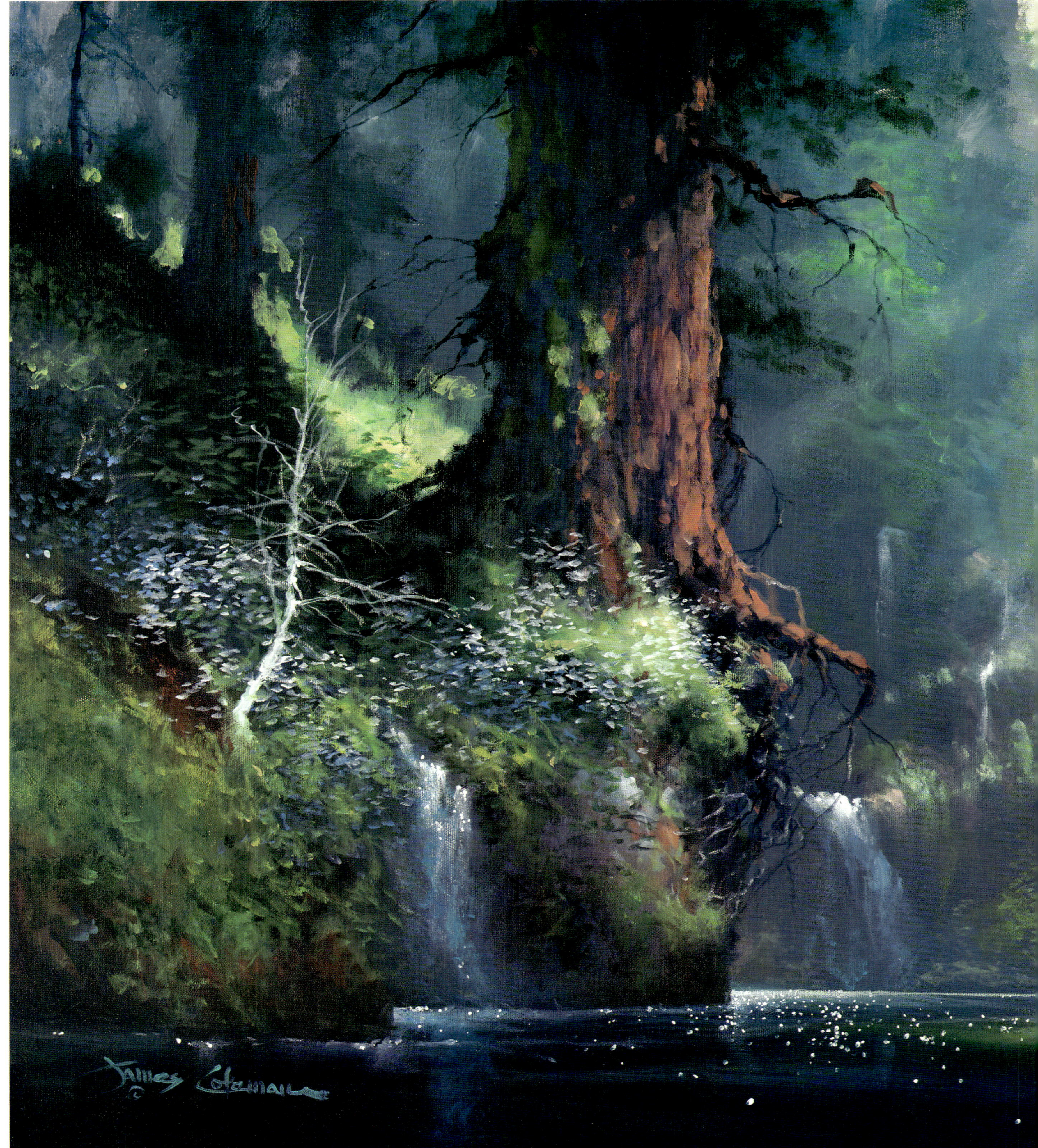
James Coleman

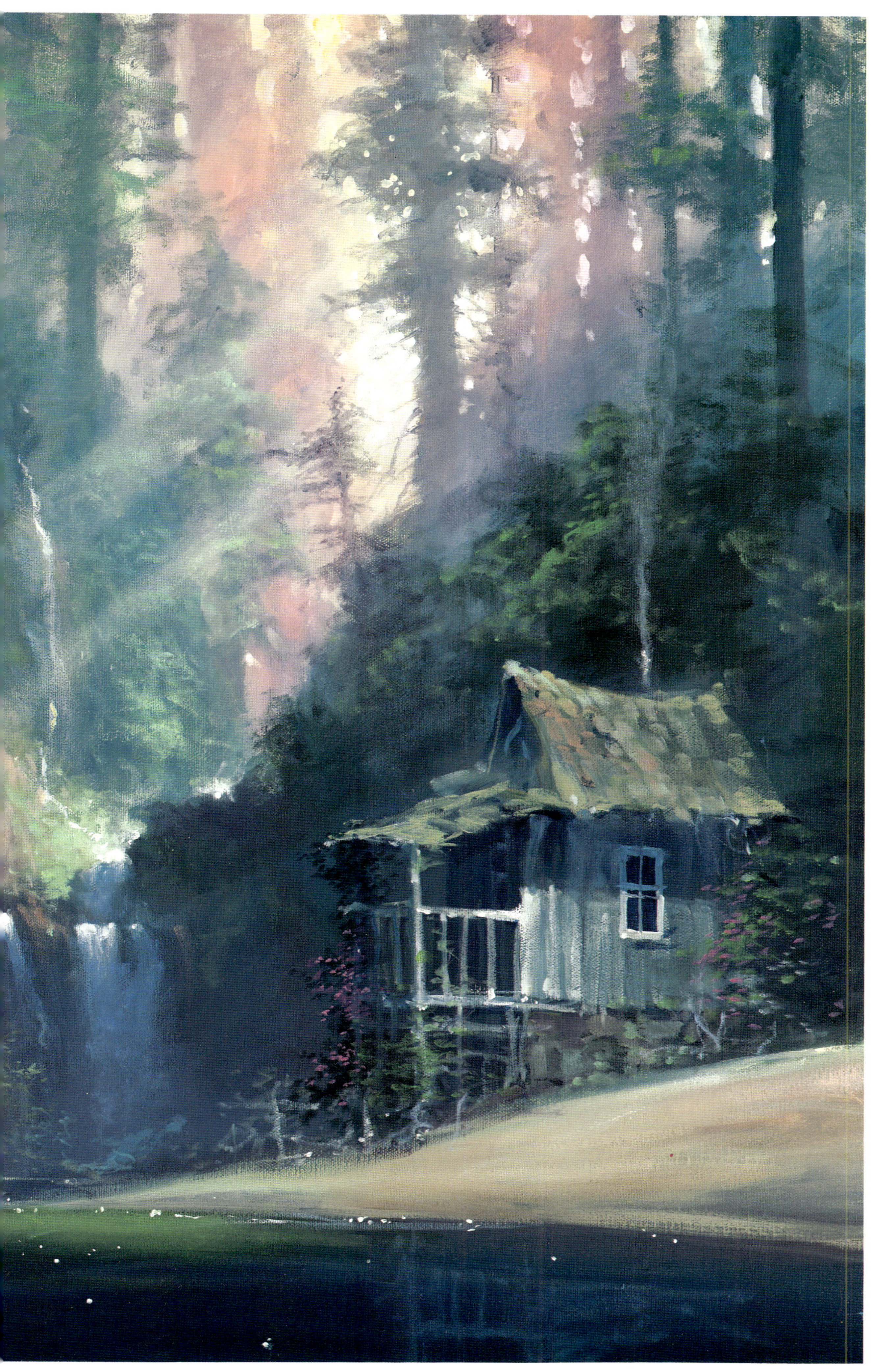

Peaceful Solitude
Oil, 24 x 36 inches

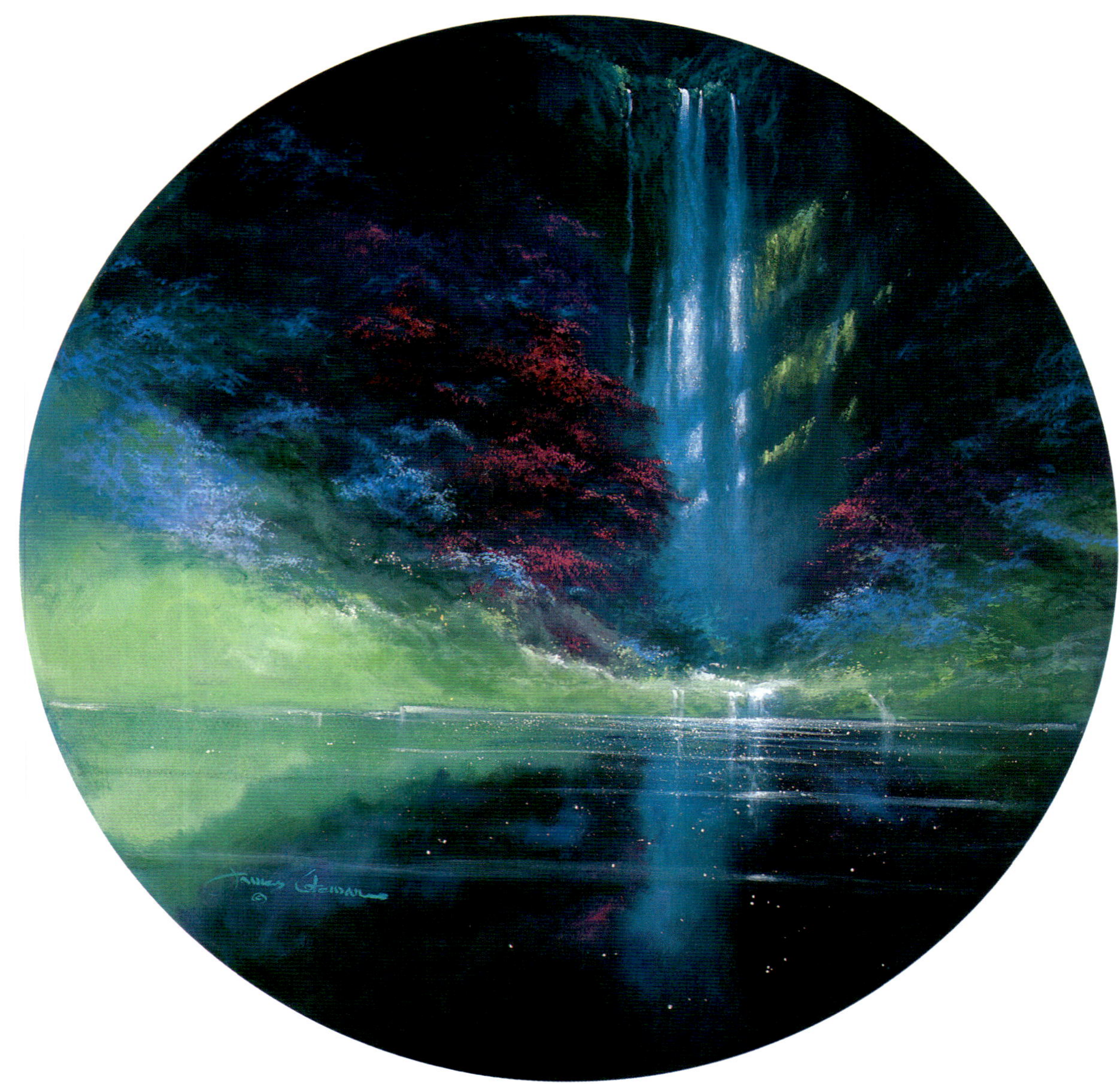

Reflections – Oil, 44 inches round

"I arrange them in such a way that they have an emotional effect," he agrees. "These are real elements—they're not total fantasy. But I stretch and mold and change them to get the most out of every image."

Sometimes, he adds, a painting will end up with an image that just isn't very strong, and he'll have to shape it and add to it. Other times, the process just comes together on its own.

"When that happens, and the entire painting is right where I want it, I'll look at it and say, 'Wow! I like this.' I won't know how it got there because it was a living, growing thing. It wasn't just a commentary on rivers in America."

That statement notwithstanding, Coleman has, in fact, made a strong commentary on rivers in America, and on forests, mountains and other treasures that lie within America's great national parks.

Since 1990, he has entered his work in the United States' National Parks Art Contest, repeatedly placing very well in the contest. "I don't enter the contests to compete," he clarifies. "I'm just a strong believer in preservation, and I've spent a lot of time backpacking and fishing in our national parks. As long as the proceeds from the contest go toward their improvement and protection, I'll continue to participate. I want my kids to be able to enjoy them the way I have."

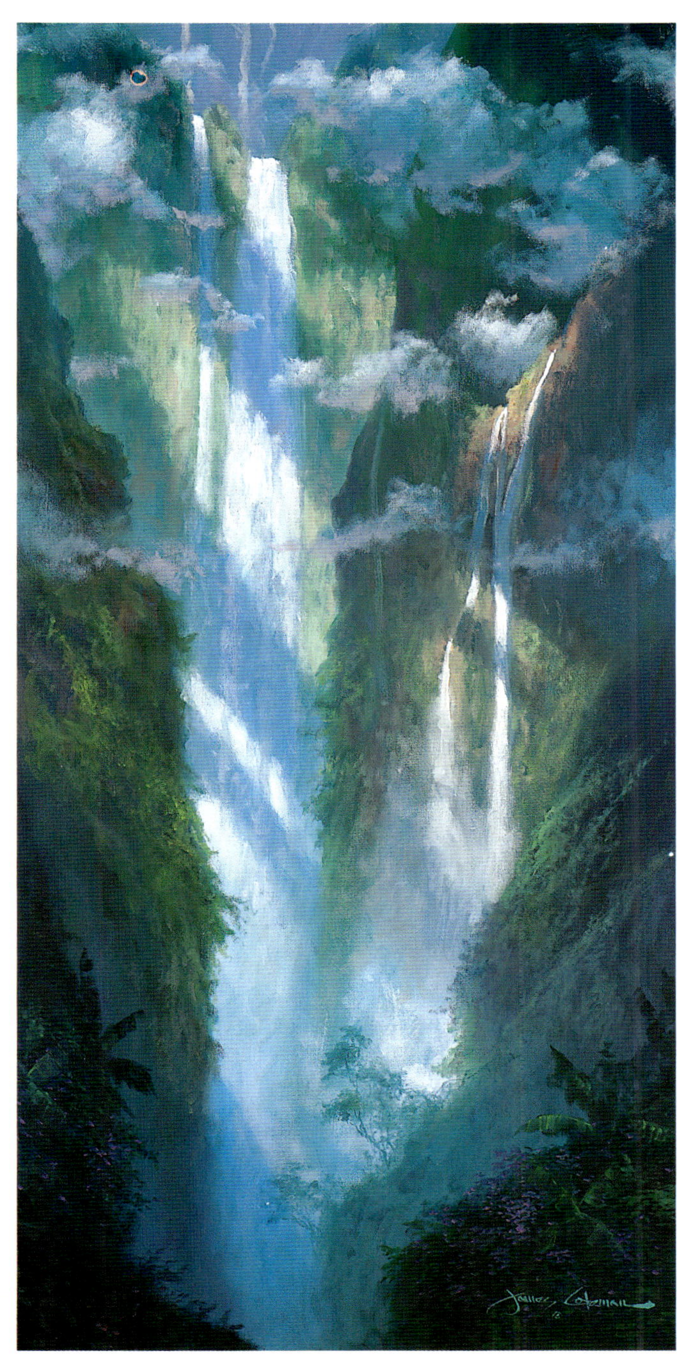

Radiant Waters – Oil, 48 x 24 inches

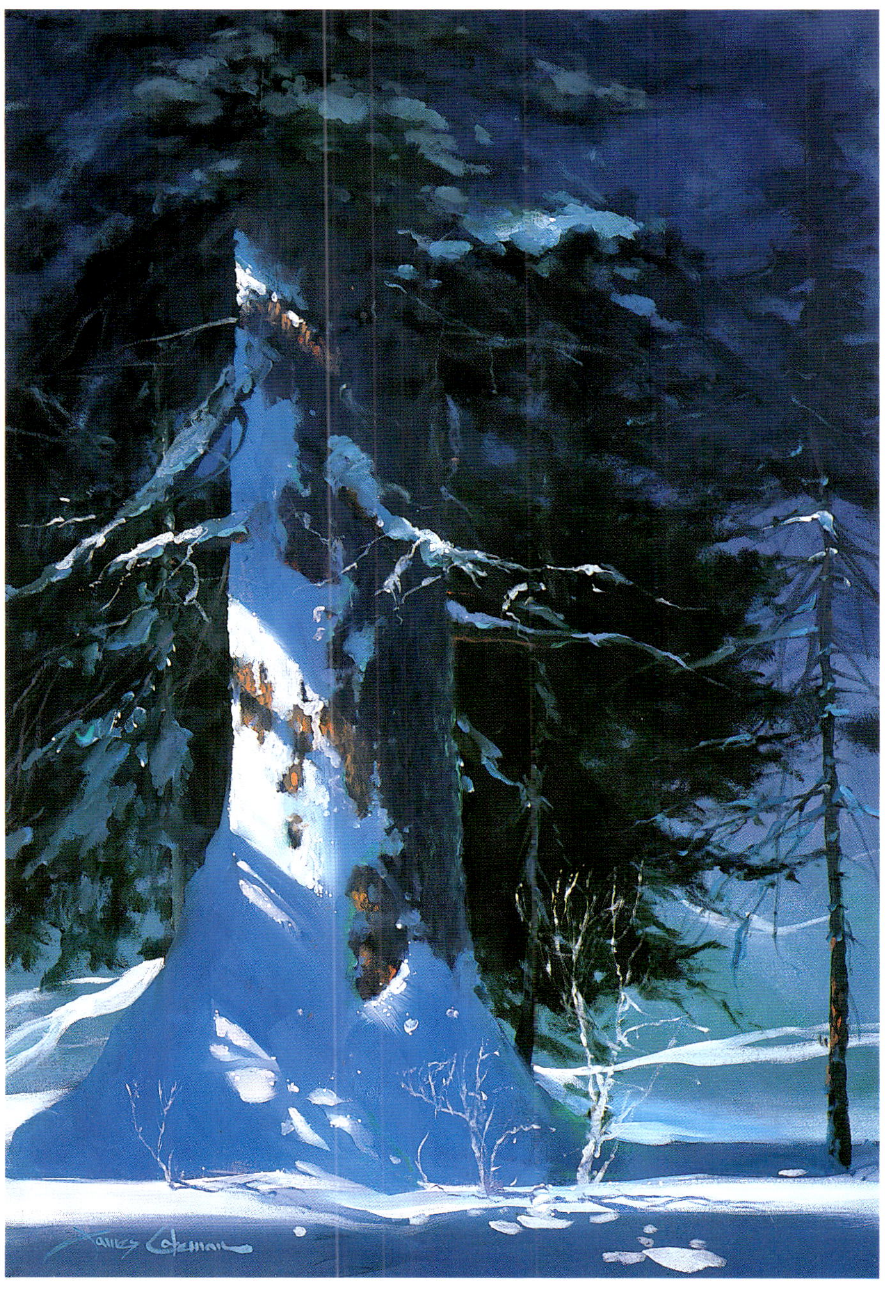

Silent Surrender – Oil, 40 x 30 inches

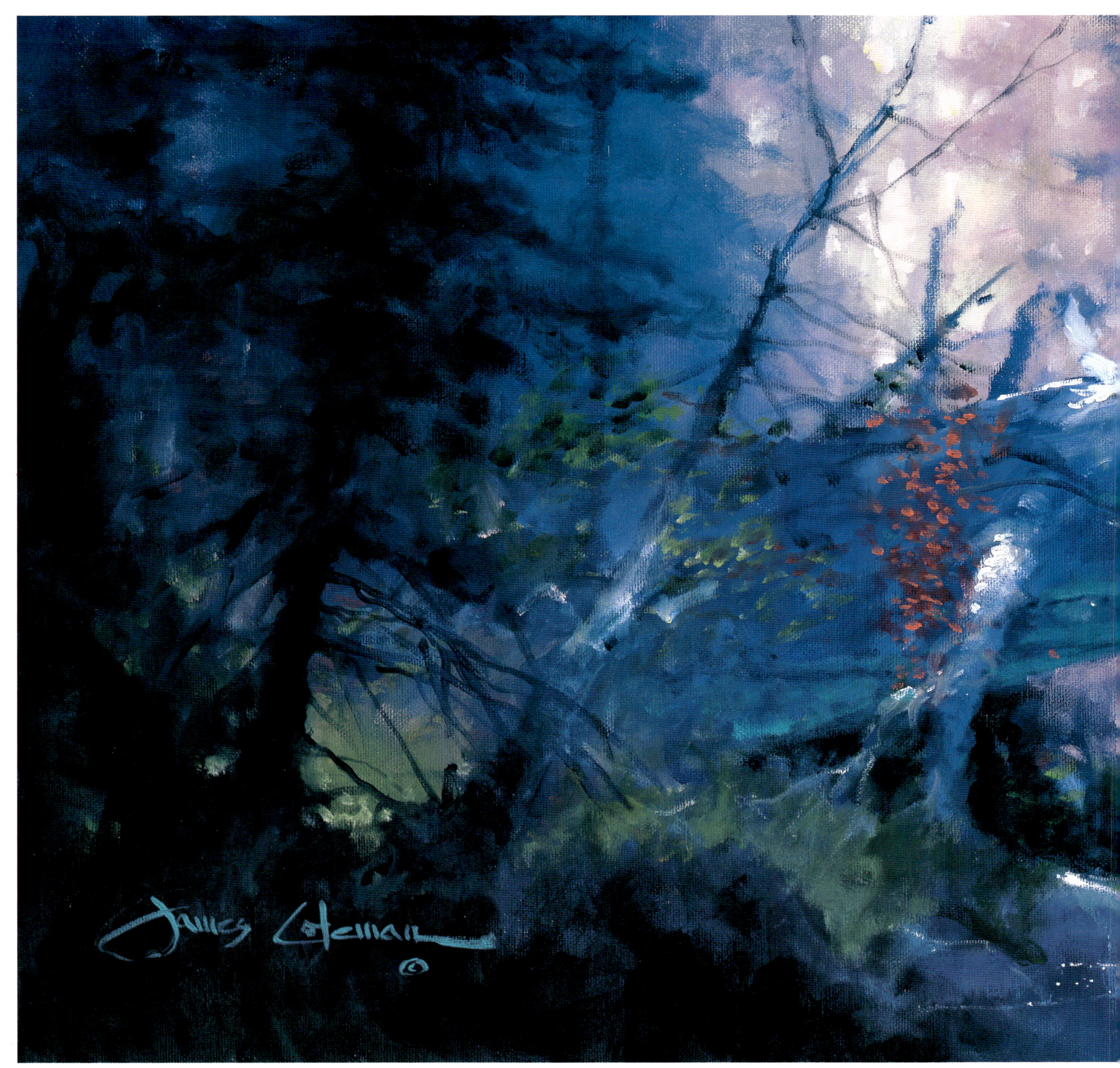

Yesterday and Today – Oil, 15 x 30 inches

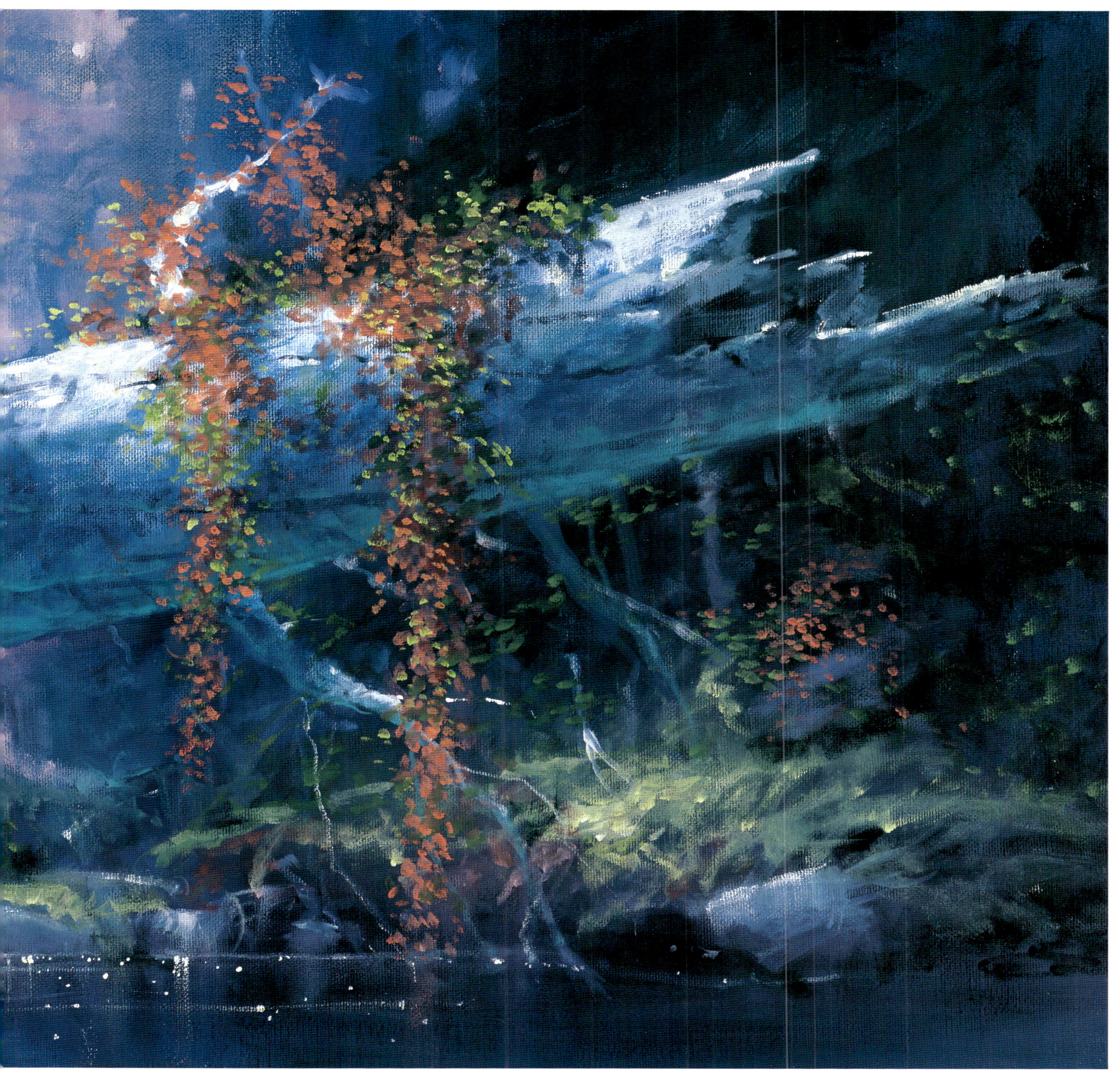

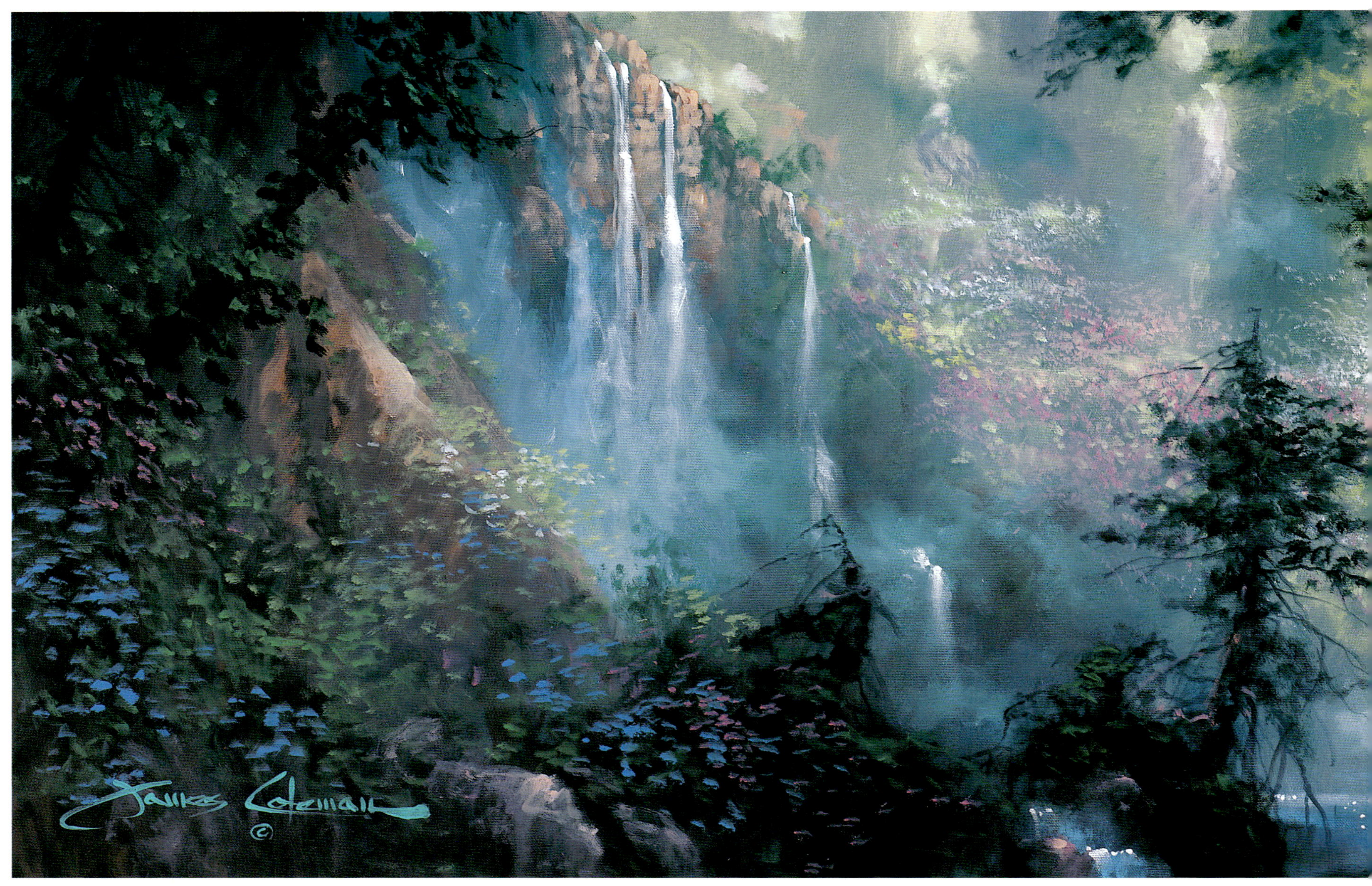

Wooded Sanctuary – Oil, 16 x 48 inches

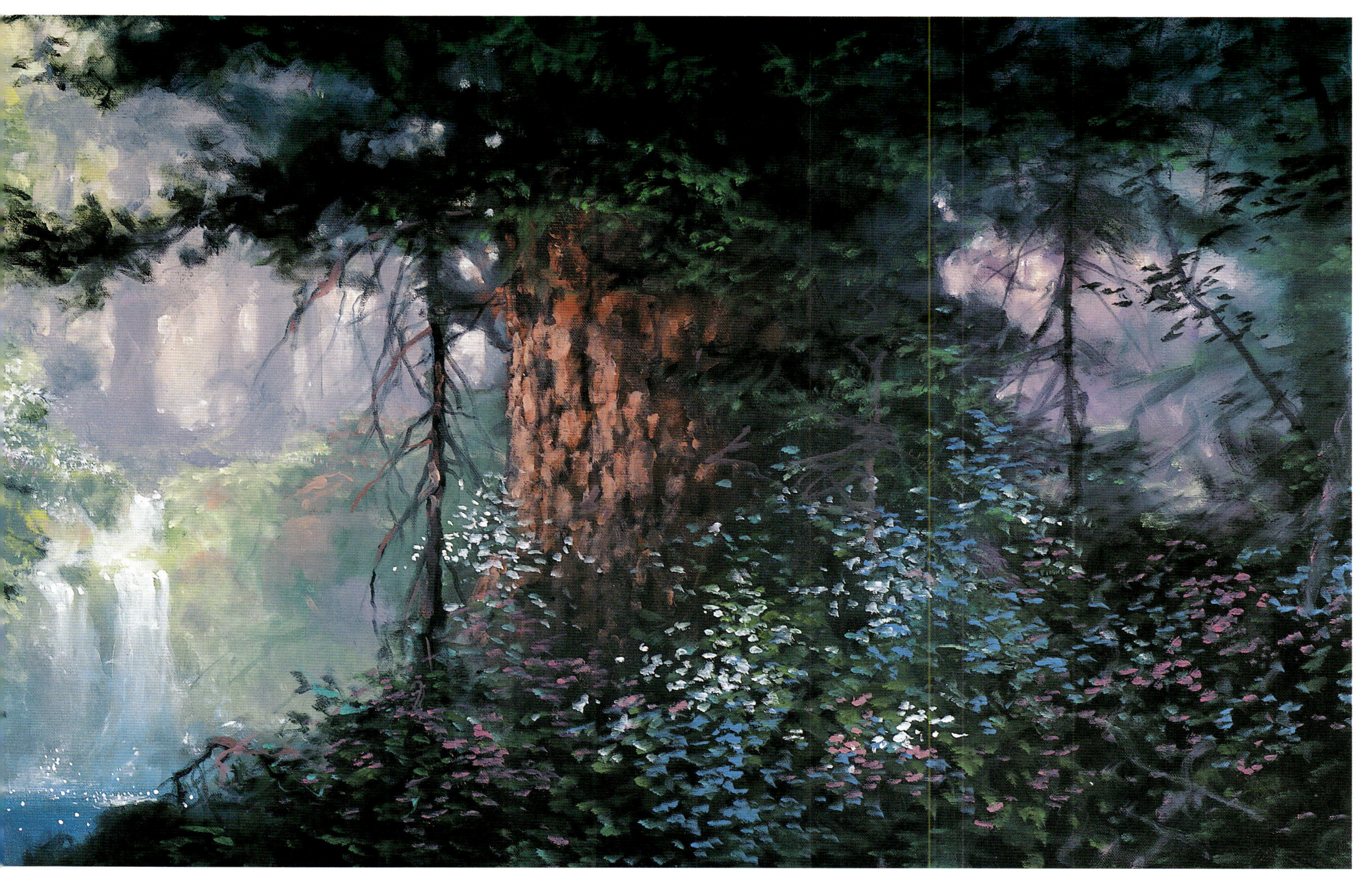

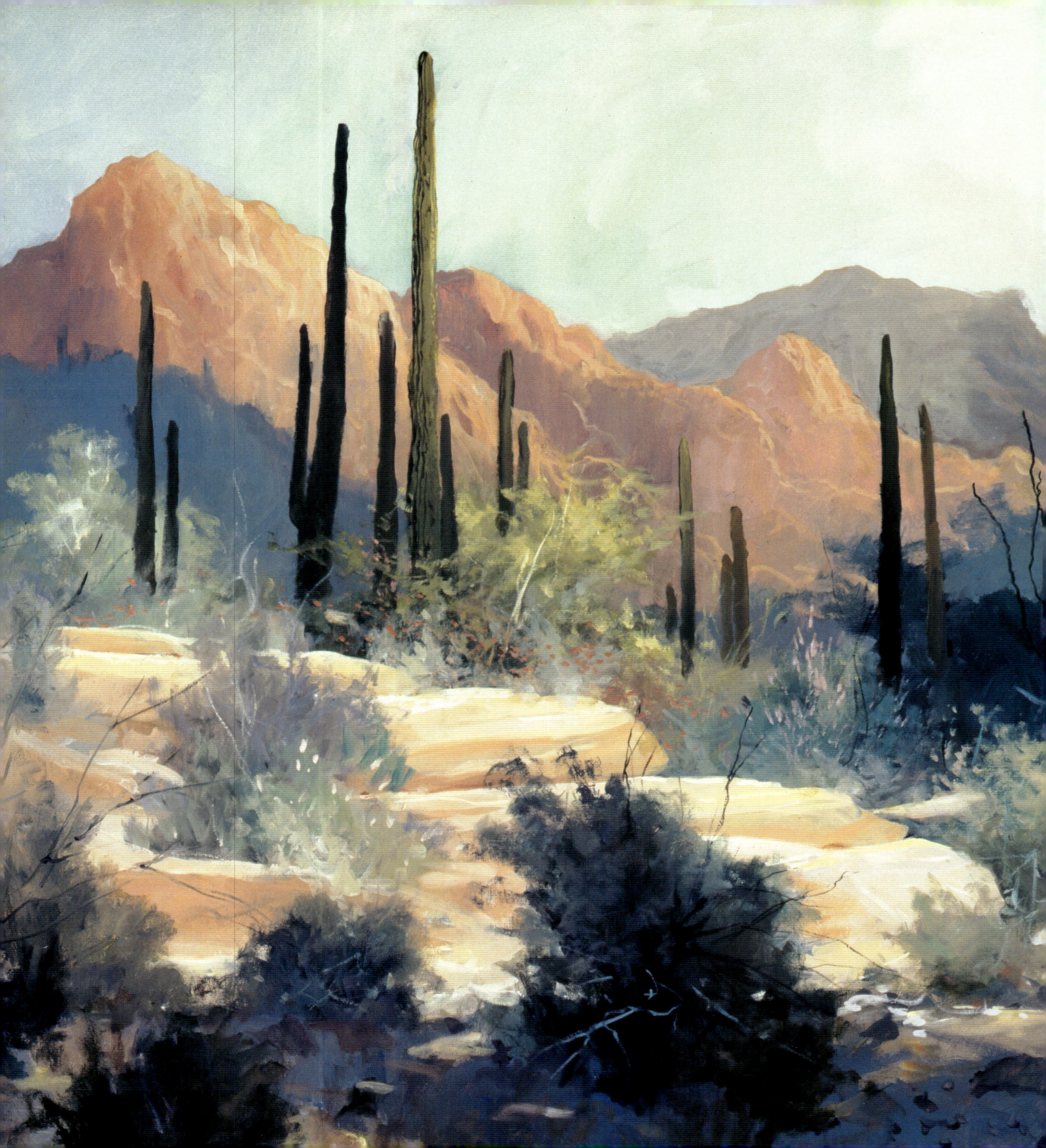

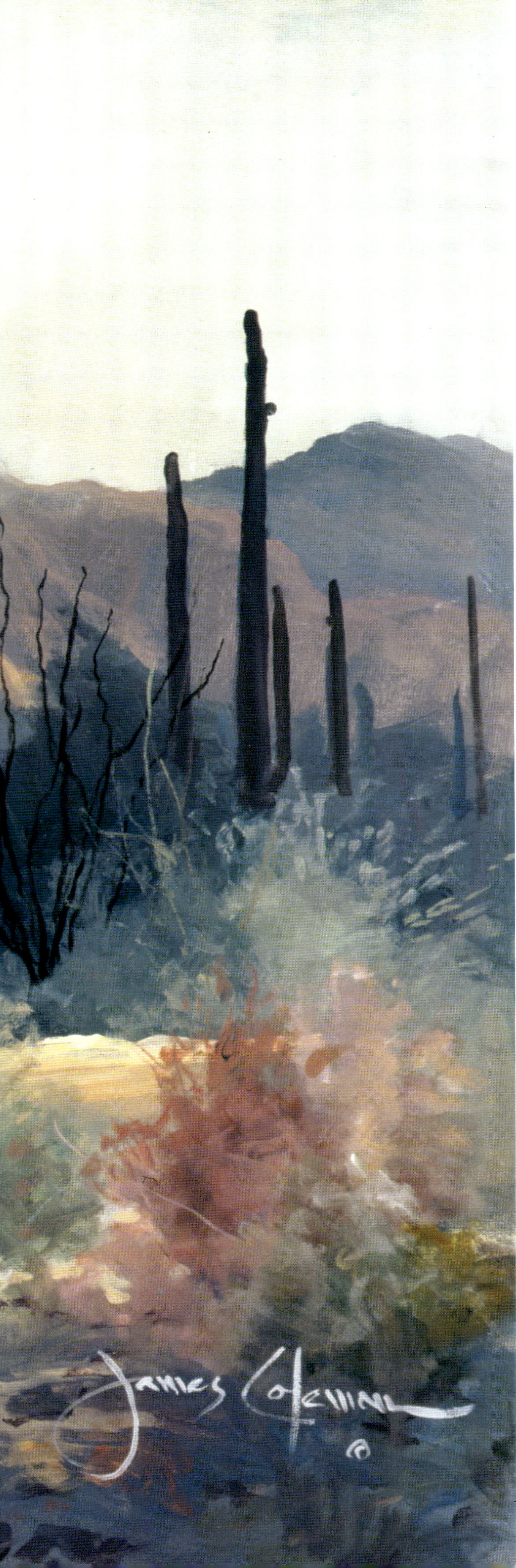

7

Hidden Life

The saguaro cactus looming nearby was almost 20 feet tall, shooting straight up out of the dry ground like a green tapered telephone pole. One of its two arms curved upward, stretching another 7 feet in the air. Another cactus, almost identical, stood proudly to the left, a dozen yards away, flanked by a smaller one, and then another and another. The entire arroyo was spotted with the lanky green protrusions, stretching all the way to the mammoth rock formations half a mile away.

Coleman got out of his rental car and sat on a flat, sandy-colored rock. It was the end of the day, and the orange sun was ready to melt behind the horizon like butter on a hot tortilla.

The air had already begun to cool before he left the gallery in Tucson, and he couldn't wait to get out of the car so he could breathe it in. The art show had been successful, but he wanted to get to the desert, away from people, away from handshaking and cocktails, away from the whole business of selling his work.

He'd always hated the desert, having grown up near it in the San Fernando Valley. It was barren, dead, uninteresting. But right now, what he wanted more than anything was to sit a spell and clear his mind. Saguaro National Monument, near town, seemed like the perfect place.

"I sat there for several hours just trying to experience the feeling of the place," he says. "It was very quiet; all you could hear were insects and a light breeze. I watched the sun go down and, as it grew darker and darker, I gained a sense of what I wanted to do with my paintings.

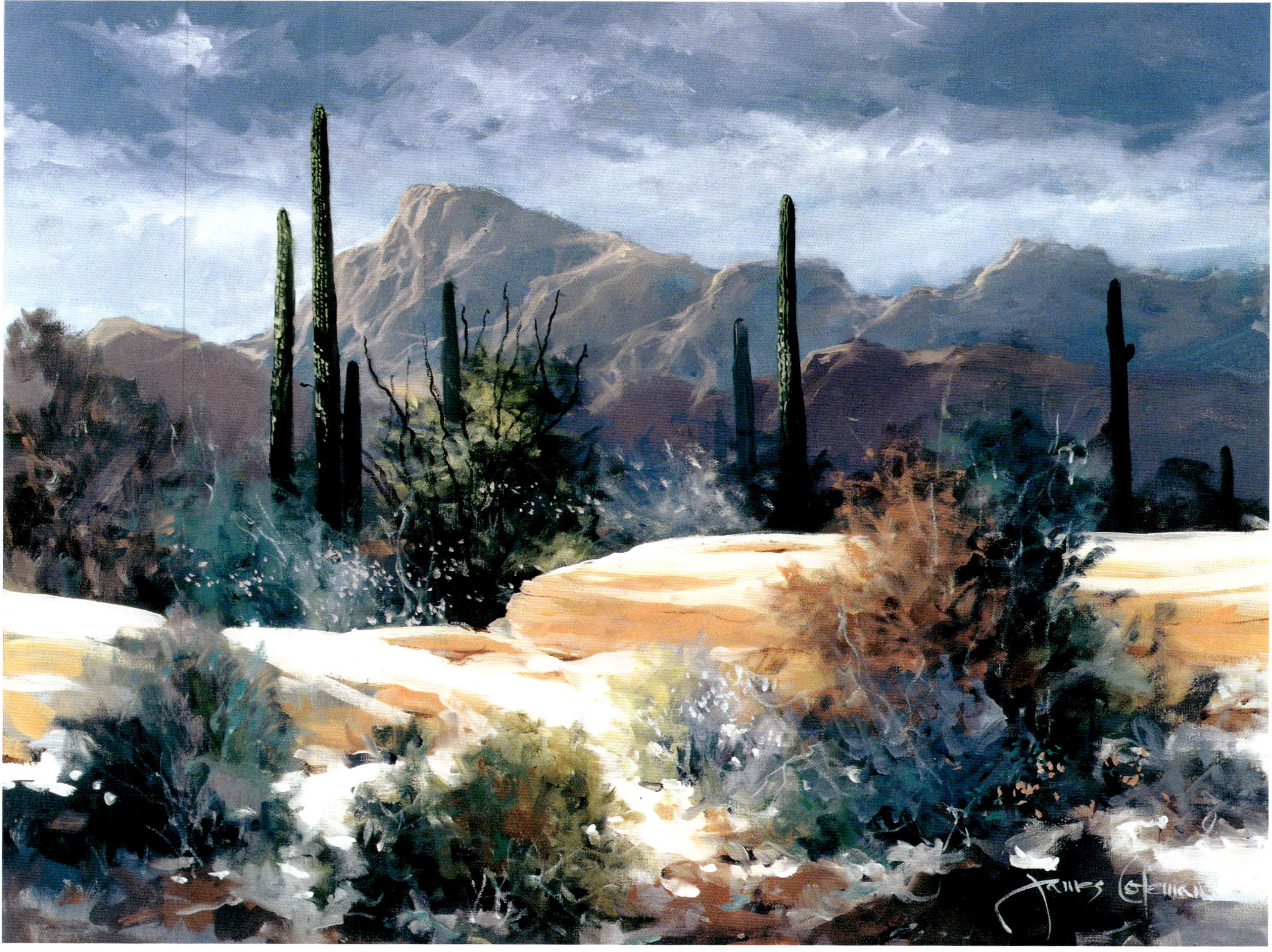

Warm Sand and Saguaro – Oil, 24 x 30 inches

Sun and Saguaro ▶
Oil, 30 x 20 inches

"I couldn't put my finger on it, but I returned to my studio to put what I'd absorbed on canvas. And when I did—I think I painted a couple of paintings—they came out pretty good."

Coleman sent the paintings to the gallery in Tucson, and the art consultants raved about how he had really captured the feeling of the area. He then decided he needed to do more of these scenes and set out to spend more time in the desert.

"I started backpacking in Joshua Tree National Park and camping out all night," he says. "After seeing and feeling the desert under a full moon at night, it changed everything about the way I felt."

He has since enjoyed the desert, particularly mountainous regions like Saguaro National Monument, the inspiration for most of his desert scenes. *One Still Moment* and *Desert Light* both portray the area, but at different times of day.

"The desert is a hard place to paint," he reveals. "It's much harder than, say, the mountains or the tropics, because there's just not much out there in the way of form and structure."

Previously, Coleman had begun to concentrate his work on the Southwest, focusing on panoramic cloud and skyscapes. "I was painting a lot of really empty deserts," he says, chuckling. "There wasn't much in them, no focal points.

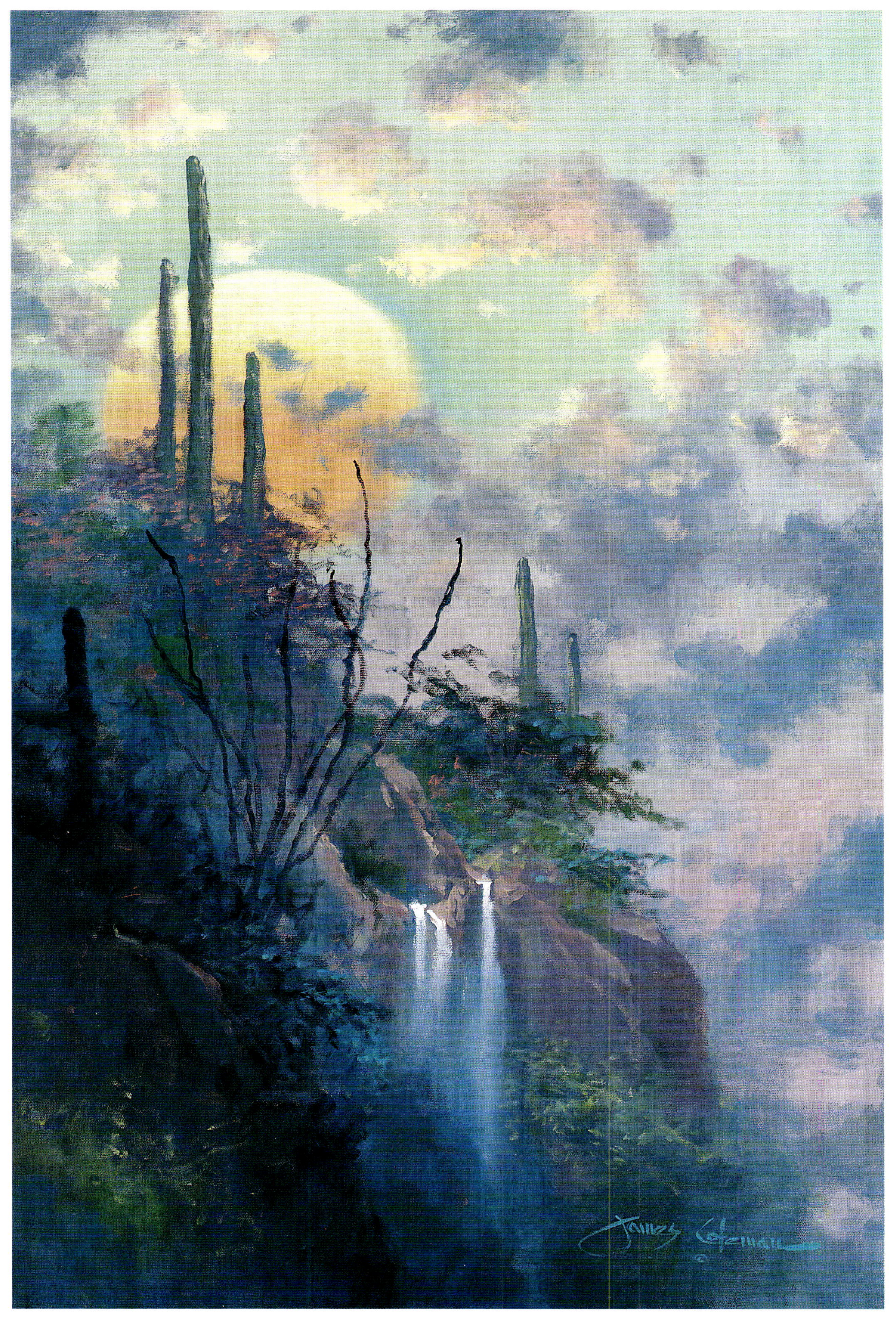

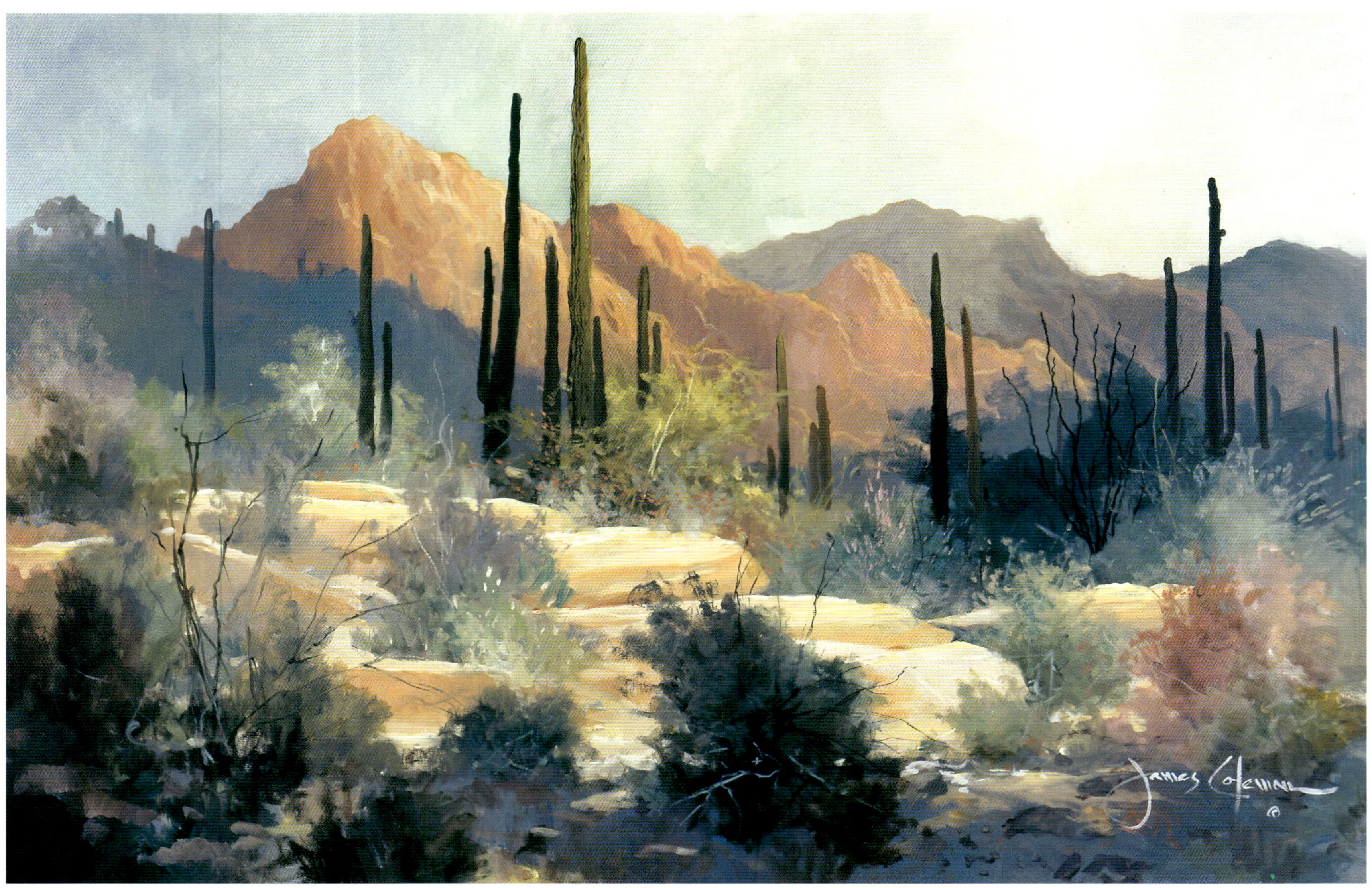

One Still Moment – Oil, 30 x 40 inches

Even though people liked them, I could tell the paintings left them kind of empty. And they left me empty, too."

After his evening among the saguaros, he started seeing much more to work with in the desert. "I started noticing all the color and the light, the way it ran across the landscape, especially in the afternoon," he says. "I noticed how dry the air is; there's not a lot of atmosphere, and the air is really clear and crisp. I just saw it all in a completely different light.

"It was like knowing a person on a surface level, and then one day sitting down and talking with him for a couple of hours. He suddenly becomes a completely different person than you had imagined. And that's what all of my paintings are like, for me. They're like friends, and we have this relationship with nature."

That relationship, he adds, can sometimes be overwhelming. On one hand, he feels like he's connected with the landscape; on the other, it's so awesome and so much larger than he is that it's beyond his comprehension.

"That's why I don't worry about coming up with images to paint," he says. "I have an intimacy with nature itself so there's a million ideas and concepts I haven't even gotten close to putting down."

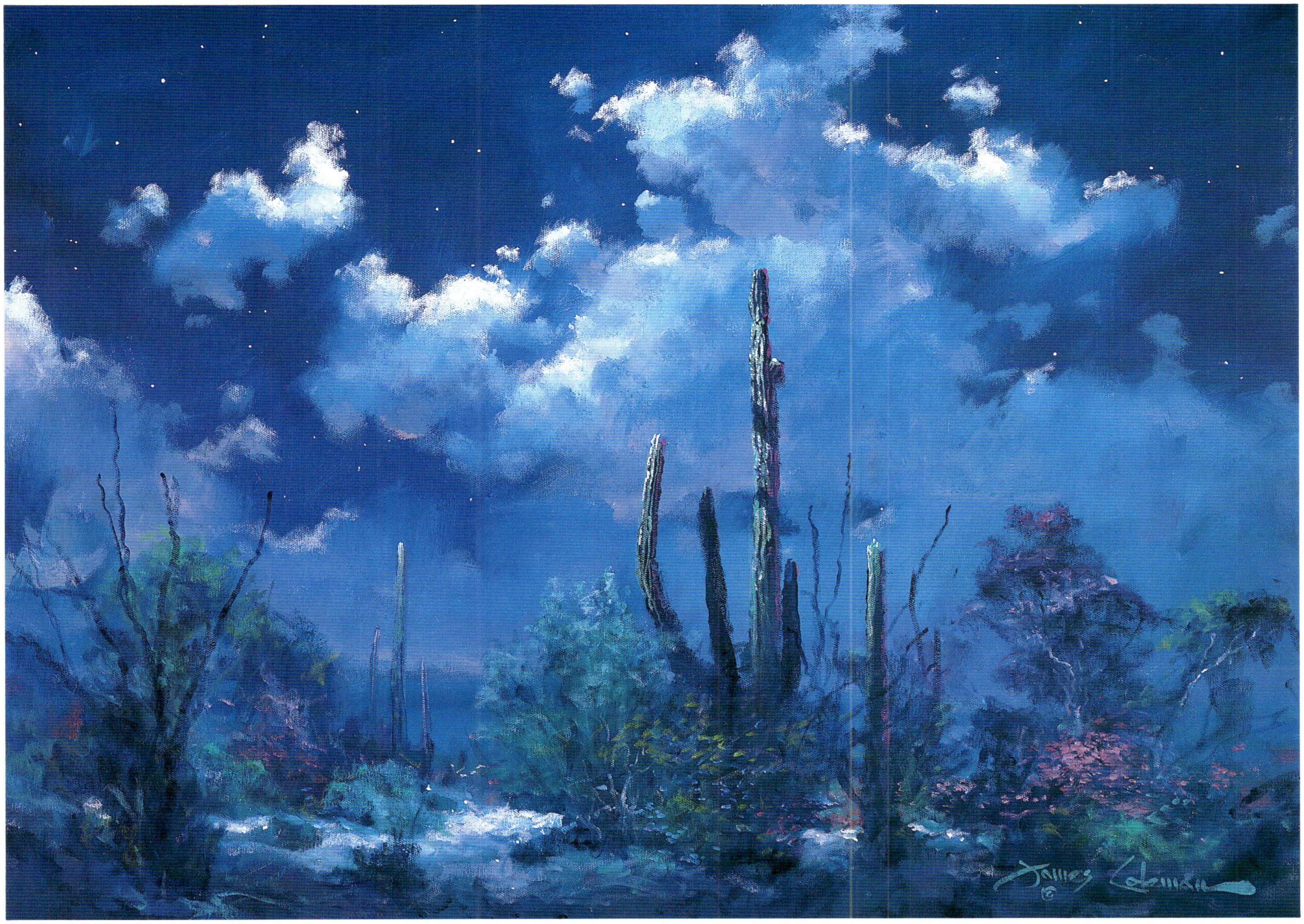

Midnight Solitude – Oil, 24 x 32 inches

It's been said that the desert is an arid place, yet Coleman's vision breathes life into the dry land. "Most people dismiss the desert, like I used to, as lifeless and boring," he agrees. "But some of the rock formations are so spectacular that they defy the imagination. It's hard to believe that someone didn't build them. It's as if they're from another world. I could look at them all day.

"To me, the rocks are organic, living elements, and so are the clouds. They're so large and beautiful. What I try to do is paint them so that they're interesting to other people as well."

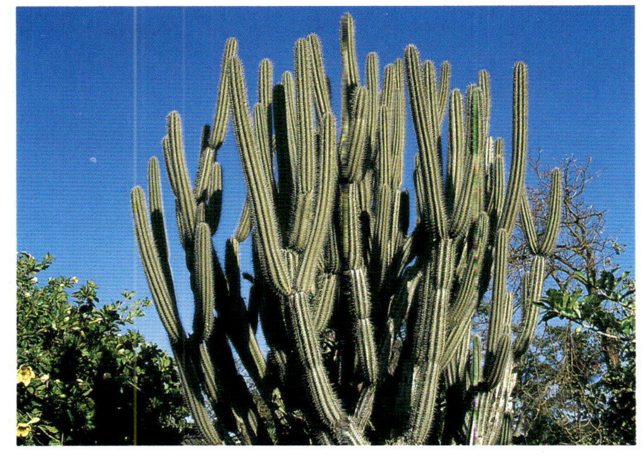

Another element he uses to its fullest potential is light. In the

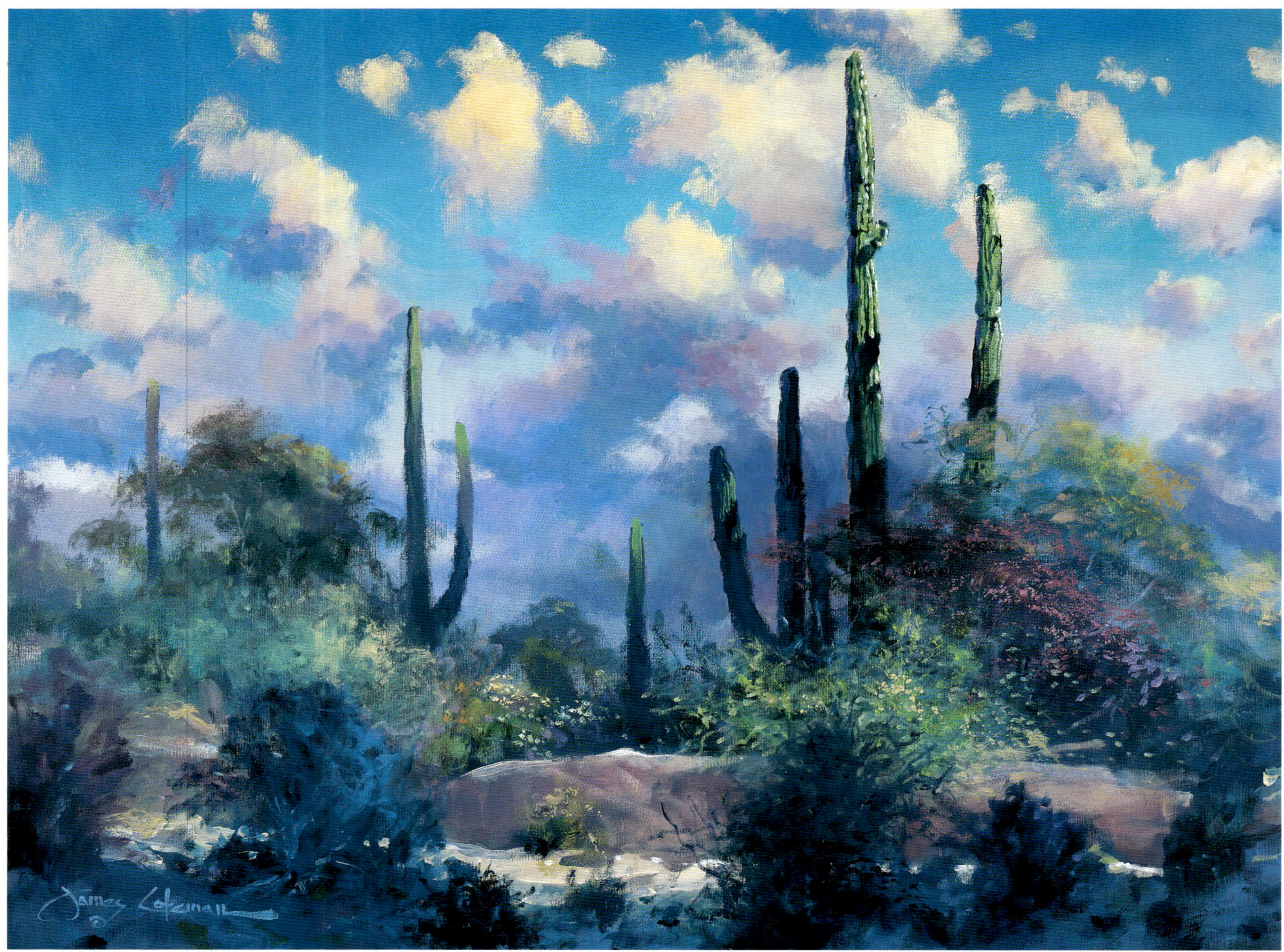

Desert Light – Oil, 24 x 30 inches

desert, he explains, the air is so clean that it doesn't diffuse the light, which gives everything a much sharper contrast. For instance, a mountain or rock formation that may be miles in the distance appears much closer because one can see detail in them from far away. Using this almost limitless depth of vision, Coleman is able to effect fascinating ranges of color and light.

"Sometimes, I find that there still needs to be more," he allows. "If the painting isn't interesting me as I paint it, then I'll enhance the color a bit, or add an element or two. If it doesn't grab me, it won't grab other people. It's just another pretty picture. And that's not good enough.

"I want something that touches the senses, and the heart. I believe that if I can do that with most of my work, then I've accomplished what I set out to do."

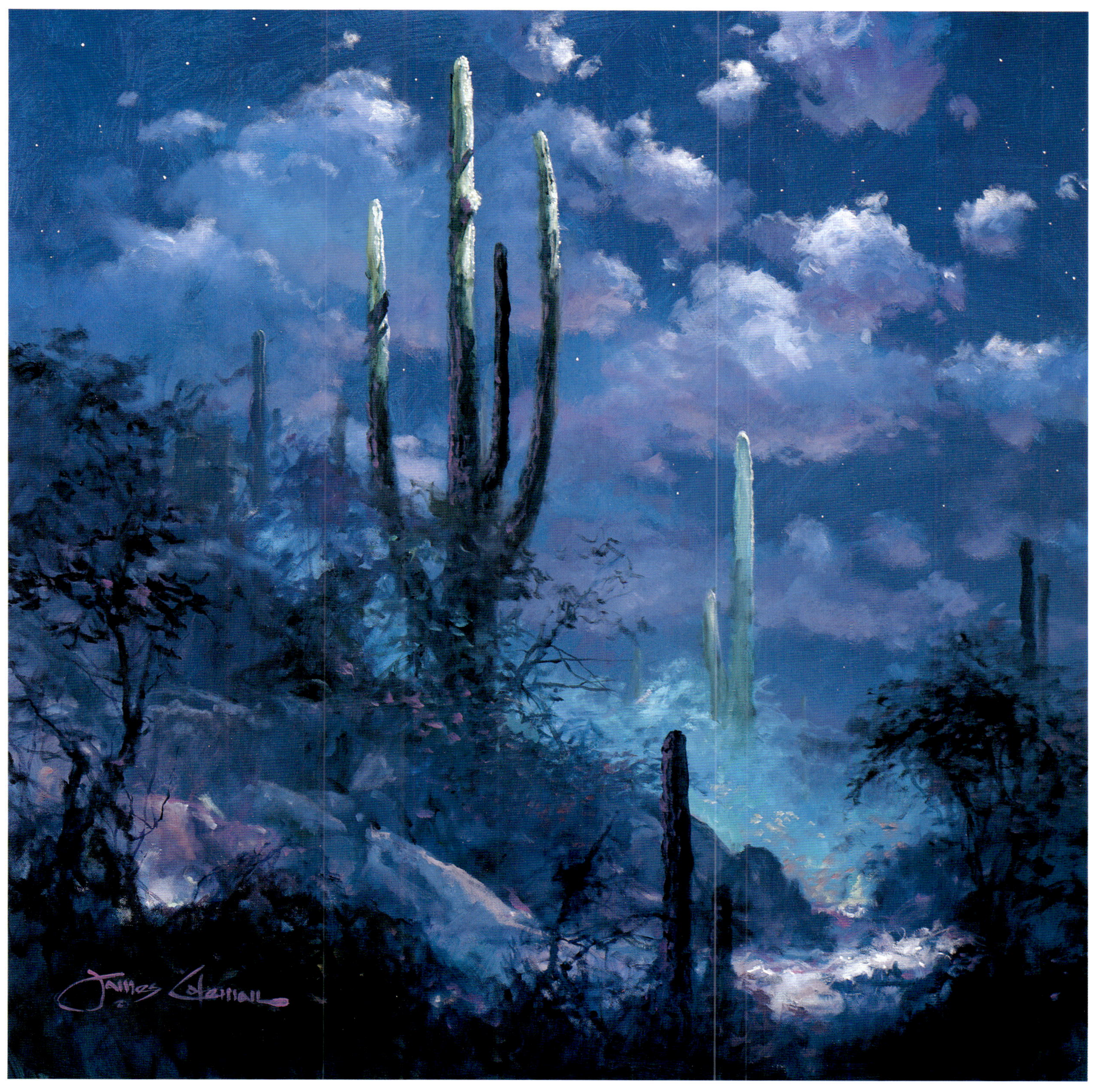

Night Peace **–** Oil, 24 x 24 inches

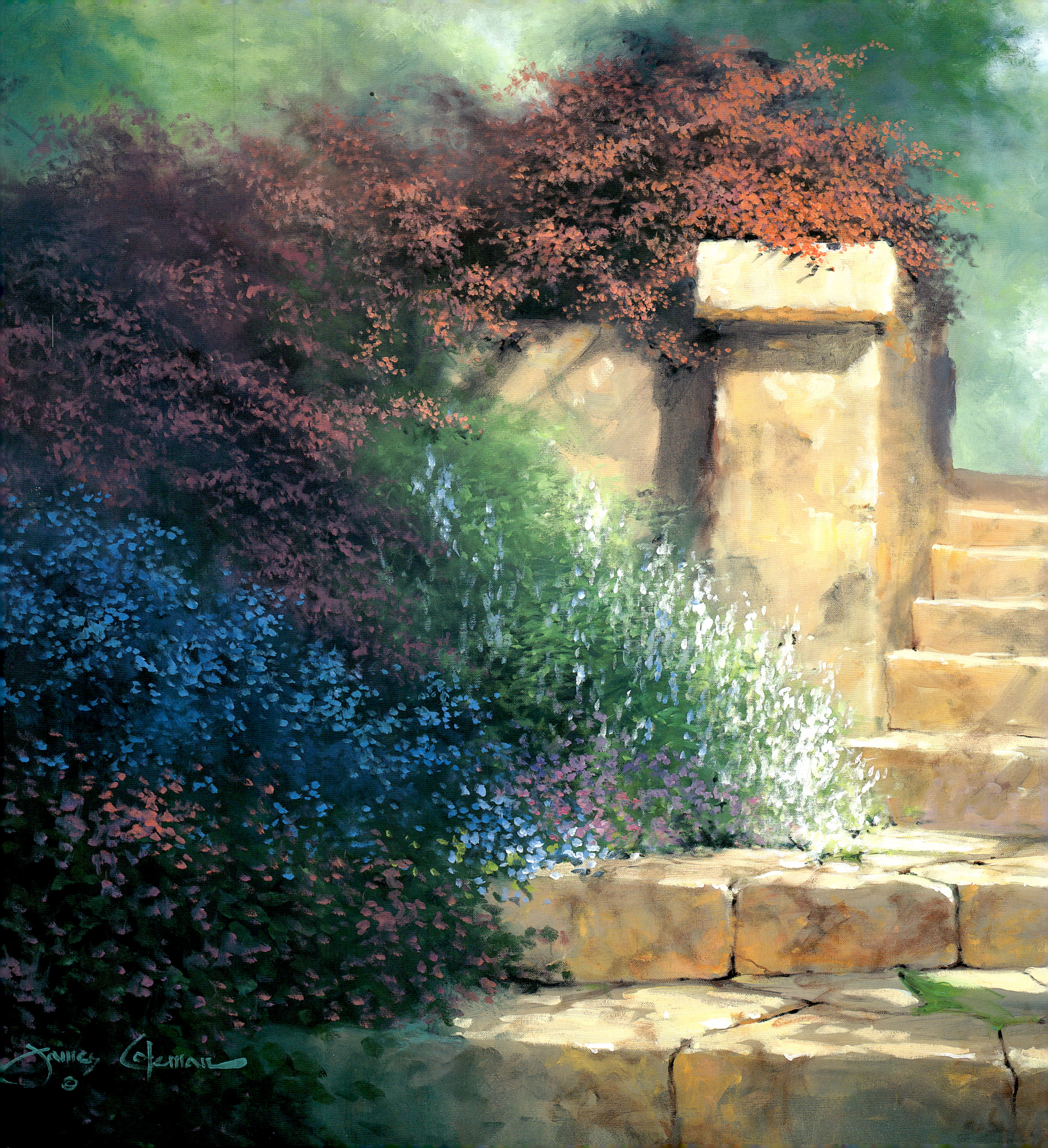
James Coleman

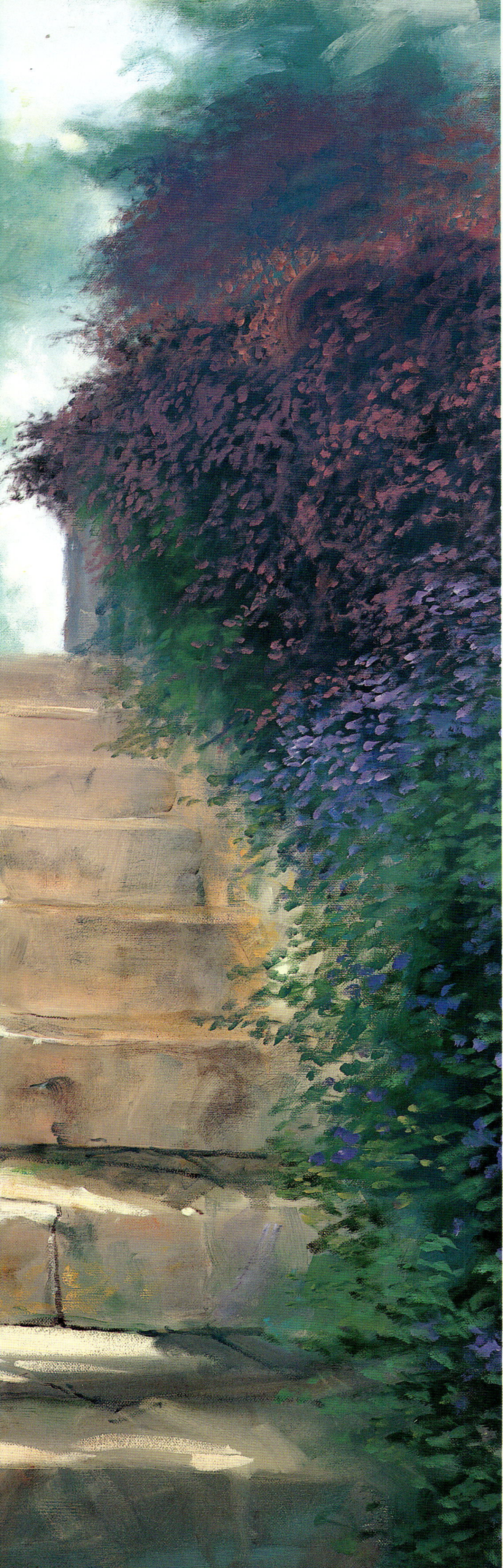

8

Garden Light

Canada was absolutely beautiful that summer. There had been majestic mountains, blanketed with pine trees and capped with snow; thick forests where bears, wolves and God only knows what else were fishing and hunting; and wide waterways winding through the pristine city of Vancouver and around colorful Victoria Island, off whose misty coast swam orca whales and other marine life.

For 12-year-old James Coleman, it had been a wonderful vacation so far. But now, his mom and dad were dragging him to a garden. He didn't care about any gardens. Who cared about a bunch of flowers? There wouldn't be anywhere to play. It would just be an hour or two of walking around until his parents were ready to leave.

When they entered Victoria's famous Bouchard Gardens, however, everything was completely different than he had expected. It wasn't merely a well-cut lawn with overmanicured sections of flowers and little brass plates nearby to identify them. This place was really "cool."

"It was huge rock quarry that had been turned into a garden," he recalls. "It was just enormous. Part of it was organic, and part was manicured. I remember these huge cascades of flowers, much like the bougainvillas I'm doing now, pouring over big rocks and walls and water fountains. And there were large expanses of green grass stretching over to the flowers, and huge trees covering the whole thing."

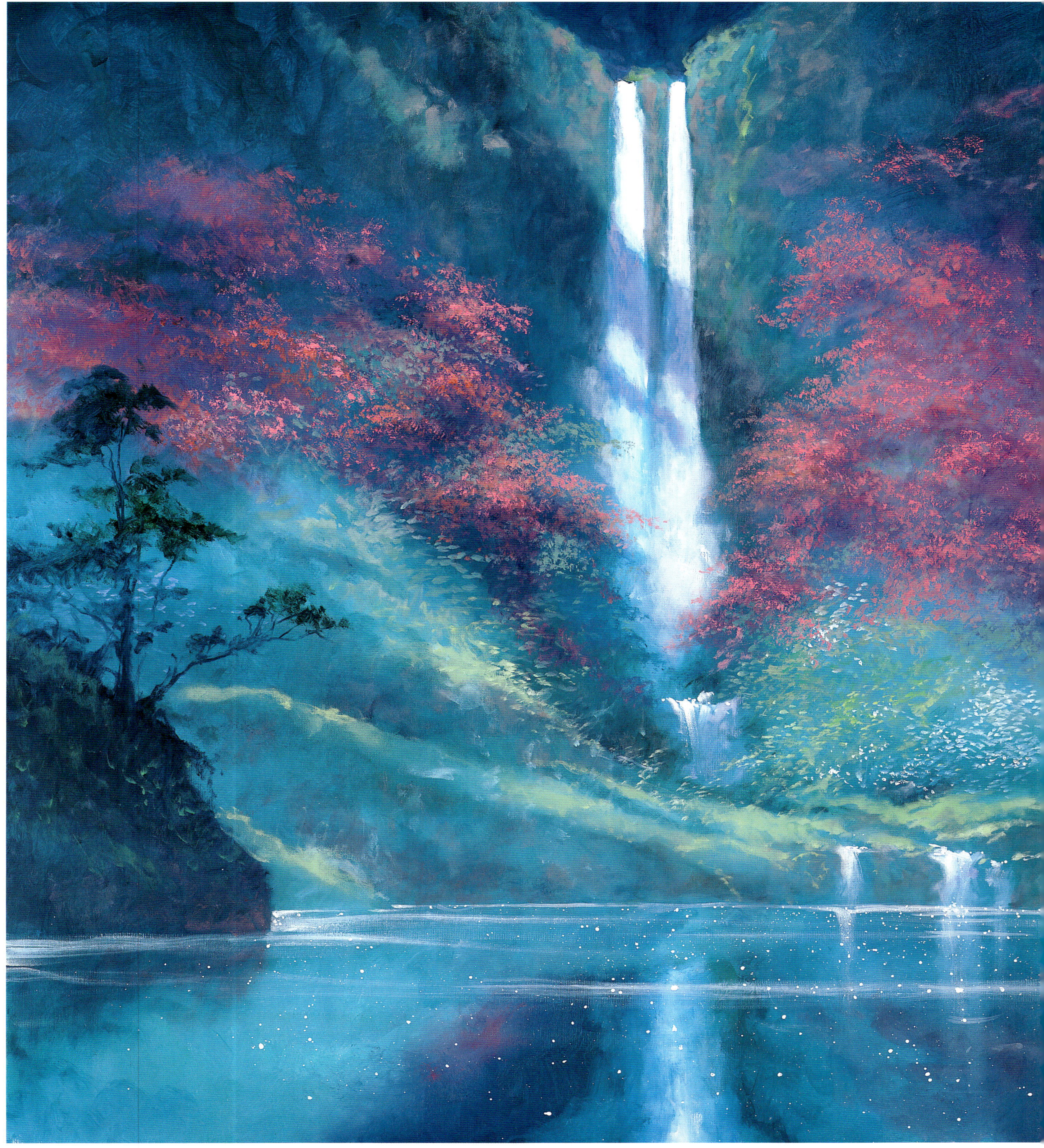

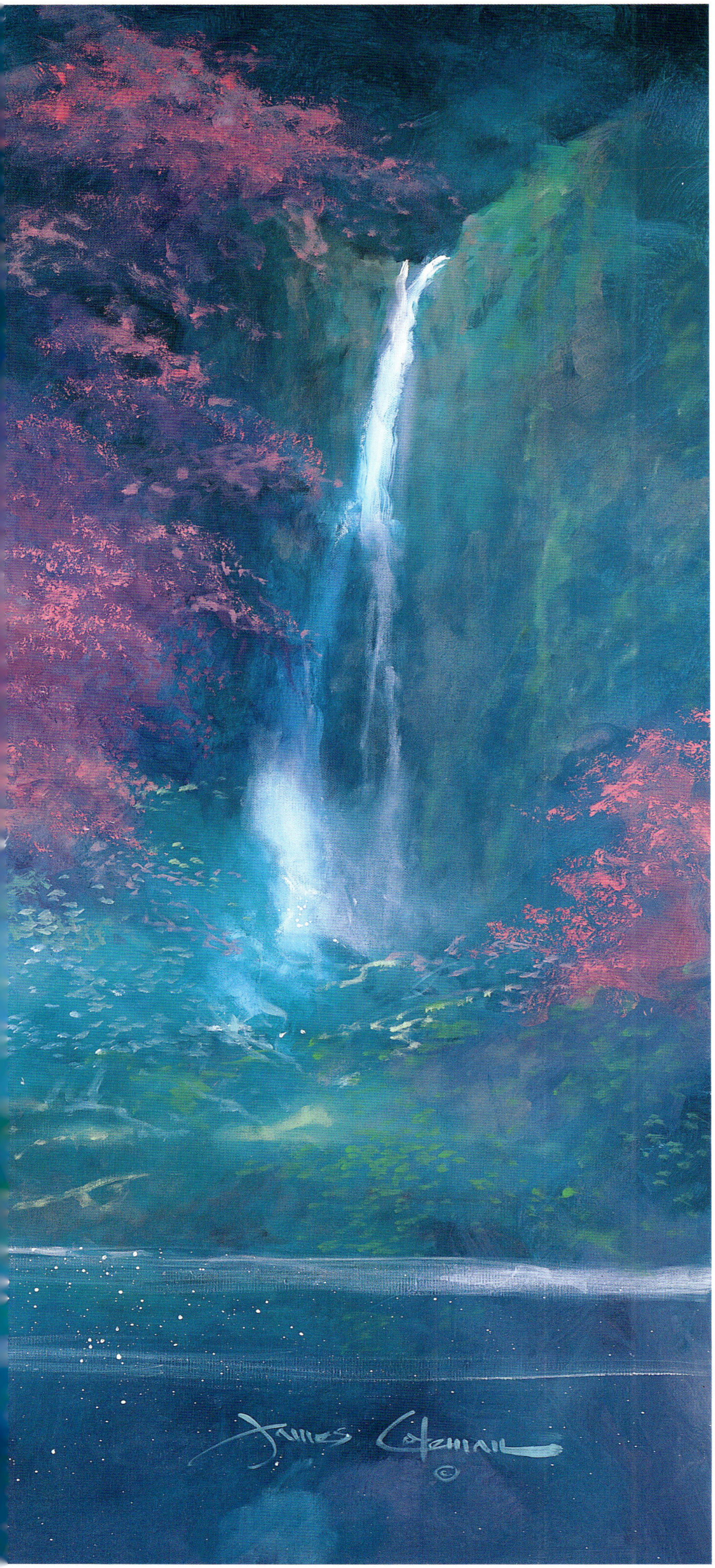

Misty Surrender
Oil, 30 x 40 inches

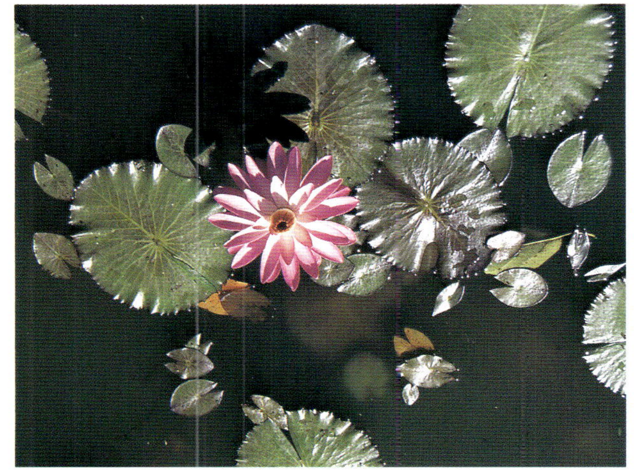

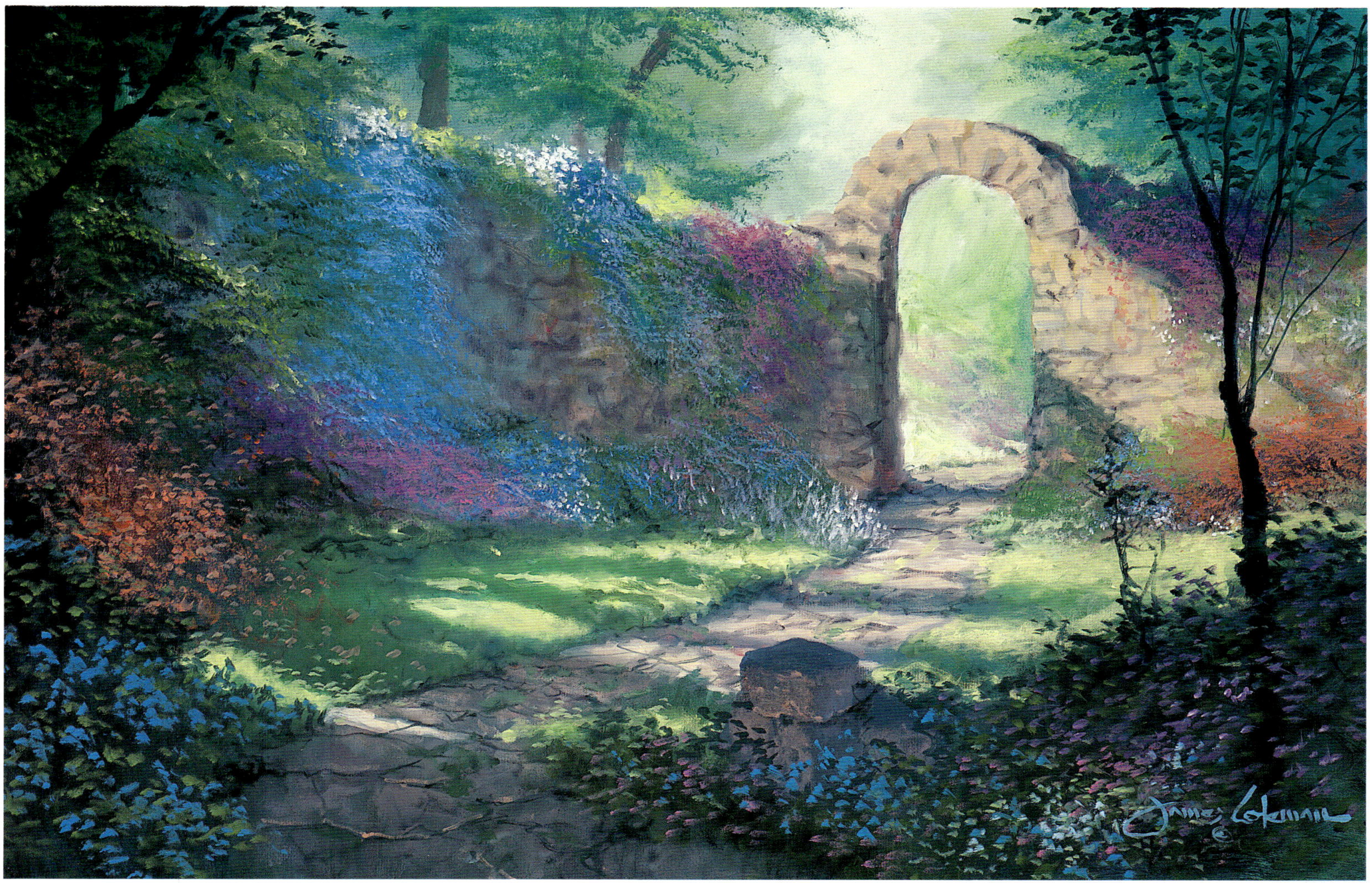

Morning Light – Oil, 20 x 30 inches

Coleman didn't know what kinds of flowers they were, but he remembers being stunned at both their quantity and beauty. They were everywhere, as if growing wild.

"Before that, I never gave any thought to flowers or gardens," he says. "I'd never been exposed to anything like that. I suppose the closest thing to it I'd ever seen was a cemetery. Now that I'm older, I try to visit gardens whenever I can, and I try to expose my children to them if possible."

Though armed with a new appreciation for gardens and floral scenery, Coleman didn't include them in his work until recently. Just as they had with so many of the masters of both early and post-impressionism, the simple but powerful images found in a garden setting began to hold a special appeal for him. For example, he saw a garden a few years ago near a mansion in Washington state that contained a large pond.

"I was taking some photos of my kids in front of the pond when I couldn't help from noticing these huge lily pads. The pond had some statues and sculpture reflecting in it, much like Monet's painting of the lily pads. It was just a knockout! I remember saying to myself: 'No wonder he was so mesmerized by that idea and painted them so large.' His painting was so powerful, yet such a simple idea."

Coleman says he really became interested in painting gardens after visiting numerous galleries and museums and seeing what other artists had done with them.

"Of course, I'd read tons of books on famous artists," he says. "But Monet probably had the biggest influence on me in this area. I'd see his work, and the work of other present-day artists, and think: 'What a way to look at this!' I was astounded at the way they had taken a pond with lilies and made it exciting and given it life.

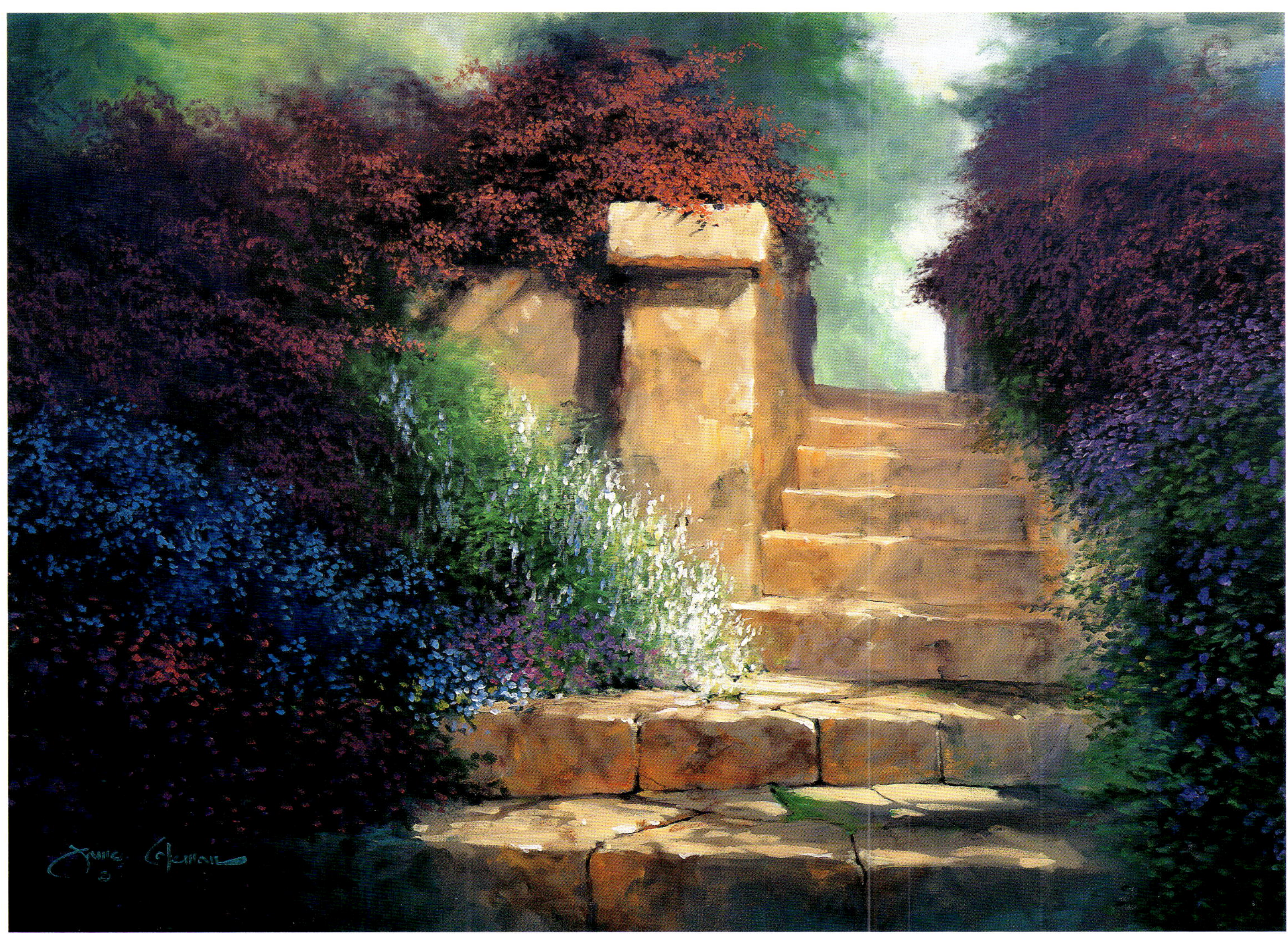

Garden Light – Oil, 36 x 48 inches

"And that's what I decided I wanted to do. I wanted to put light into these types of subjects and give them mood and passion."

Whether backyard rose bushes or large public attractions, gardens are generally grown and maintained by man. Coleman likes to look at garden books, which he says have given him an appetite to travel so he can visit some of the places he has read about.

"Most of the gardens I've painted have been more on the organic side, rather than architectural," he says. "They're not particularly formal or manicured. They have man's influence on them, but they're not something he has total control over.

"If any garden is let go for a while, it'll just go its own way and revert right back into nature. In most of my gardens, like in *Garden Light*, nature is starting to creep back over the structure. It's the same way in my tropical paintings, where flowers are growing over the top of a house."

"Nature always seems to win out over man's attempts to control it. It's God's creation, so it doesn't matter what men think they can do to alter it. Ultimately, it's going to prevail."

That's not to say Coleman doesn't appreciate man-made gardens. On the contrary, he considers them to be tributes to nature's beauty. "To me, the most beautiful gardens are the ones that have organic features built into them," he says. "It has much more impact if a garden has a formal structure that allows nature to sort of have its way. It gives the entire garden more passion."

The world is full of incredible gardens, he adds. And he'd like to paint more of them. "It's a bit like opening Pandora's Box," he muses. "Once you start appreciating them, you can't stop. The colors and textures are just too dazzling. Each time I see a beautiful garden, I find myself saying, 'Wow! Look at this! Wow! Look at that!'"

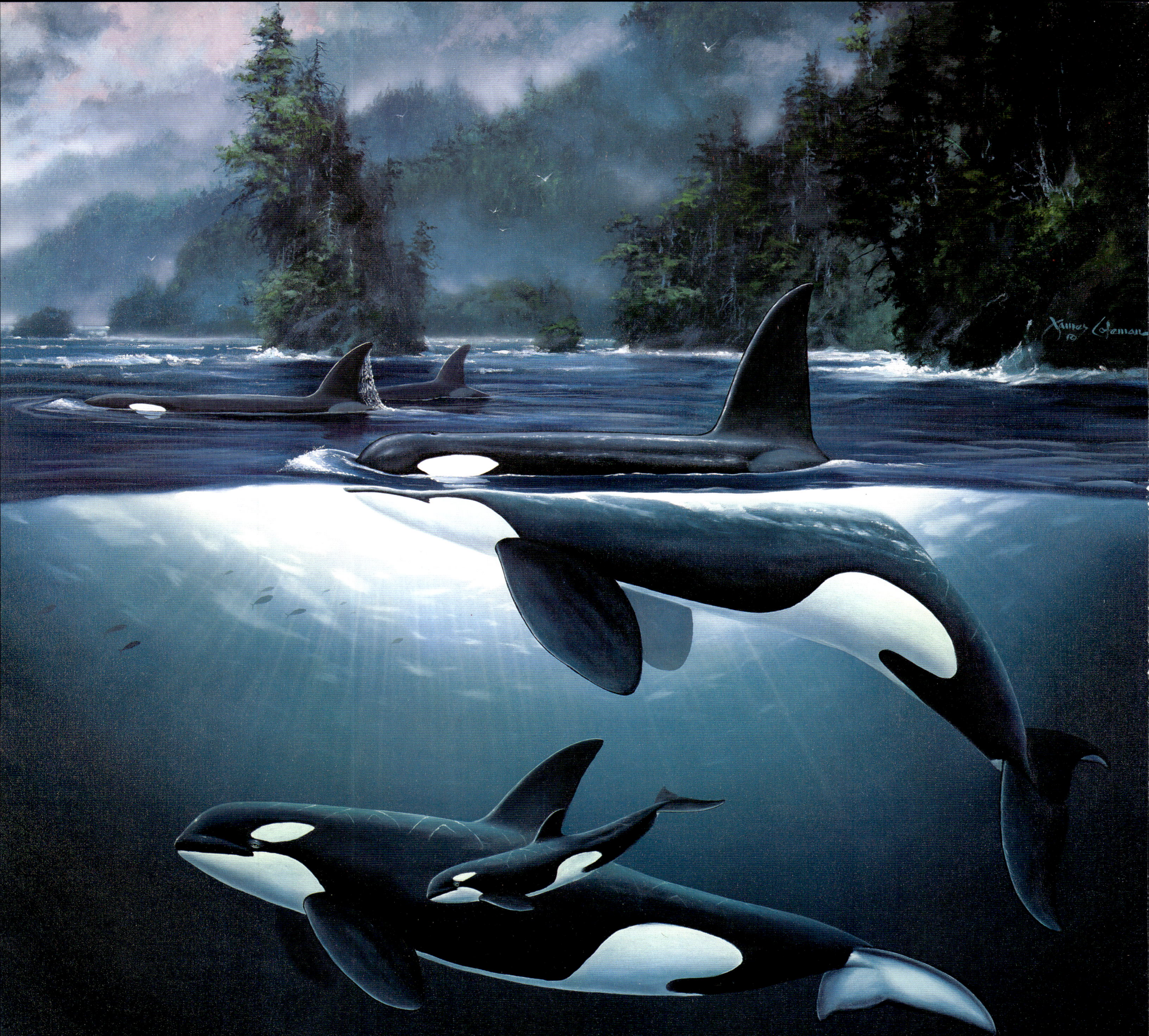
James Coleman

9

Collaborations

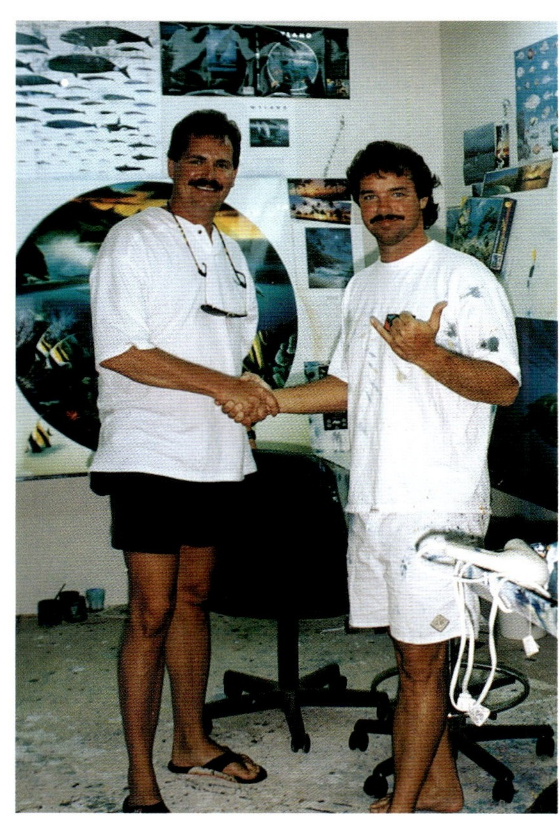

Wyland and James Coleman at Wyland's studio

◀*Northern Waters* – Oil, 4 x 5 feet

Acclaimed wildlife artist Robert Bateman gazed up at the bald eagle Wyland had just painted on the side of a building in Victoria, British Columbia, and said jokingly into the microphone, "Hey Wyland, I thought we had an agreement. You would paint below the ocean, and I was going to paint above."

Bateman made the good-natured remark during his dedication speech for the renowned marine artist's 13th Whaling Wall, a giant mural depicting a pod of 13 orca whales.

The comment sparked an idea for Wyland, whose reputation for making big ideas come to fruition is becoming legendary among his friends and collectors. Why not do a painting in which two artists lent their specialties to the work? Wyland would paint the scene below the surface, and another artist, who specializes in above-the-water subjects, would paint above it.

Interesting concept, but it wasn't quite big enough for Wyland. He decided to paint a series of collaborative paintings with 12 well known artists and call it *Above and Below. . . the Best of Two Worlds*. One of those artists was James Coleman. Wyland approached him with the idea in 1992, after having already begun his first collaboration with seascape artist Roy Gonzales Tabora.

"It was a novel idea," Coleman says, having completed four of the collaborations with Wyland. "Most artists' egos won't allow them to share a canvas with another artist. But, for me, this was a chance of a lifetime because I really respected Wyland's work.

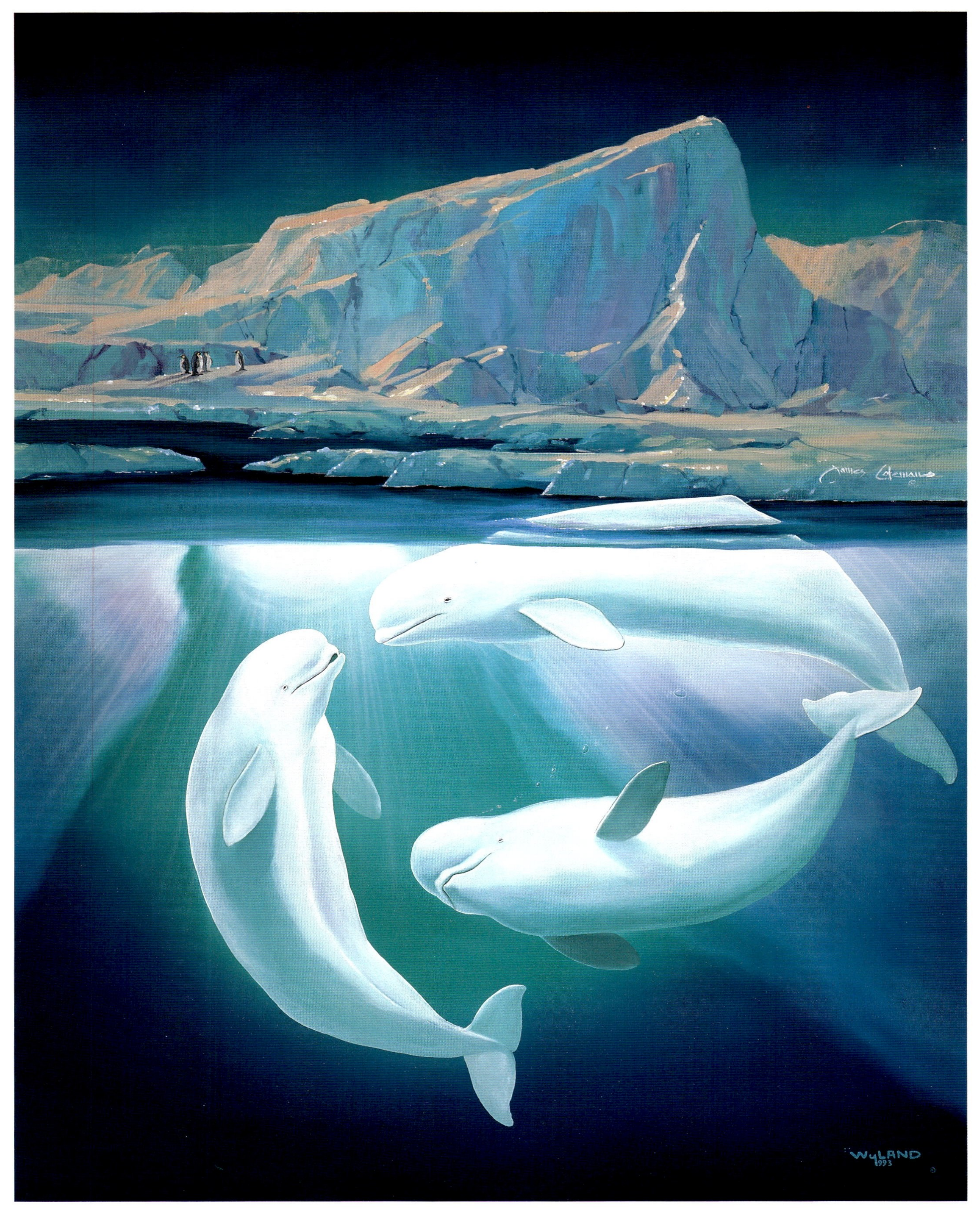

Belugas – Oil, 4 x 5 feet

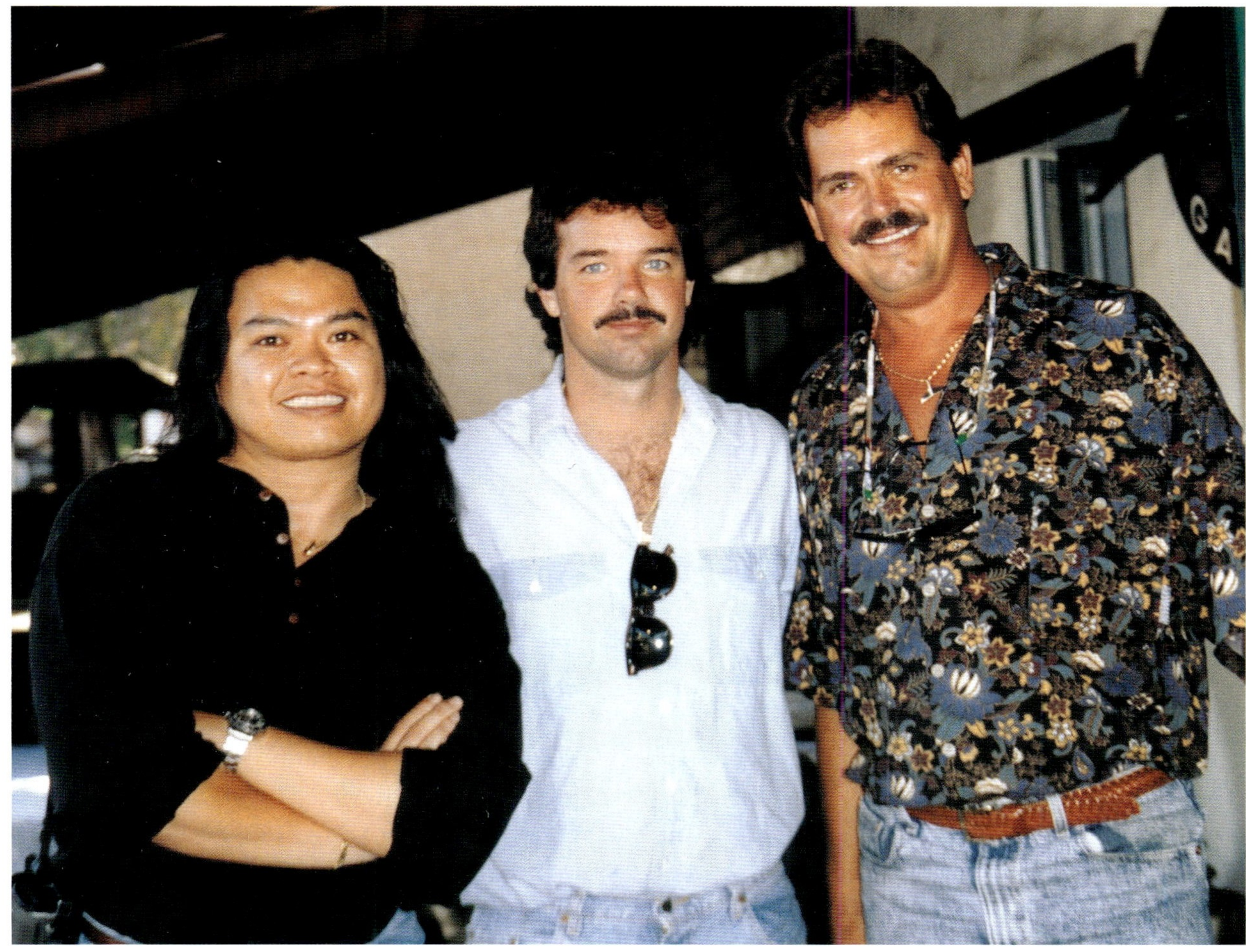

Pioneers of the collaboration series Roy Gonzalez Tabora, Wyland and James Coleman

And to be able to work with this guy was a great opportunity."

Only a few years before, Coleman had seen Wyland's picture in a magazine and thought, "This guy's got it made." He never dreamed, he says, that he would soon become one of the marquis artists in Wyland's 22 art galleries, much less work with him on a painting.

"Wyland took all of us, the artists who showed in his galleries, on a cruise in the Caribbean," he remembers. "I had just put my art in his galleries, and it was an exciting time for me. When he came up to me on the boat and asked me if I'd be interested in doing a collaboration with him, I nonchalantly said 'Sure, I'd like to try something like that.'

"But inside, I was saying, 'Yes! As soon as I get back from this cruise, I'm going to hit the easel and give him some dynamite paintings.' I had all kinds of ideas.'"

Wyland was equally excited about working with Coleman. "James Coleman is a living legend who captures in light what few artists in history have been able to achieve," Wyland remarks. "With each canvas, he invites us into a world that's uniquely his own. I consider him one of the greatest living artists today, and it's a privilege to be able to add to that world with my own art."

When he returned to California, Coleman started immediately on his half of *Paradise*, their first collaboration together. Wyland prefers to talk initially with the other artists about concepts and let them do their portion first. He then paints a scene below the surface to coincide with their halves of the paintings.

Coleman finished his part in a month and presented Wyland with a 60-inch by 48-inch canvas. Wyland called him within days and told him he really liked it and would start on the underwater section. Meanwhile, Coleman had already begun another collaboration called *Northern Waters*.

"*Northern Waters* was going to be a coastal scene of the Pacific Northwest," he says. "I figured Wyland was going to put orcas in it when I sent it to him, and he did."

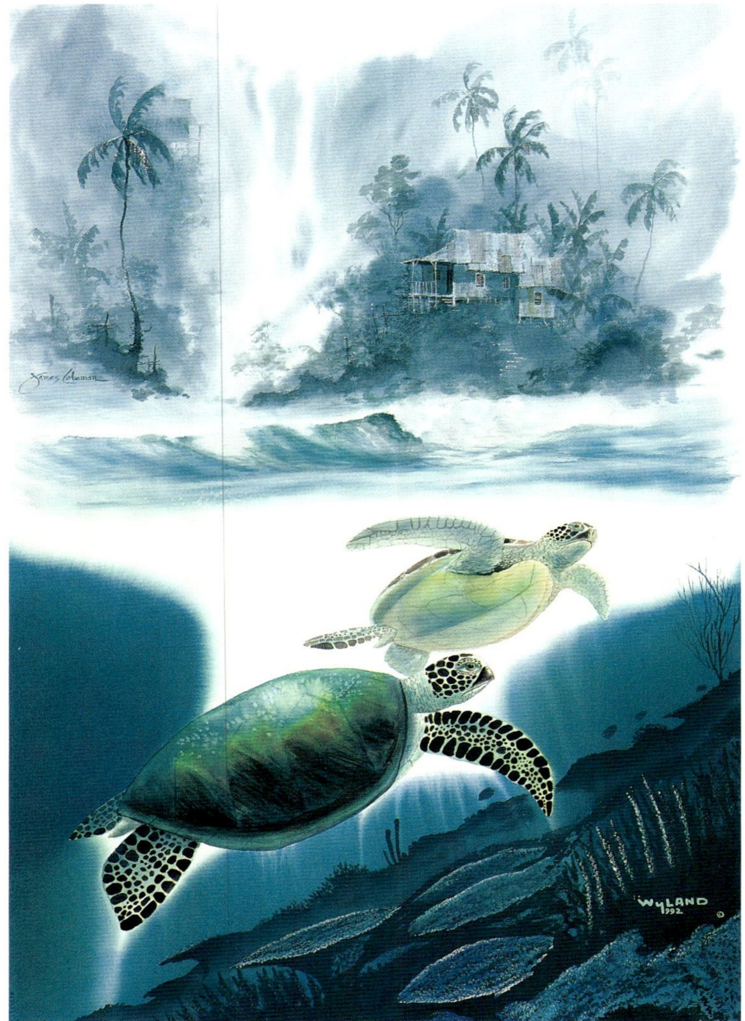

Turtle Waters – Watercolor, 30 x 40 inches

While Wyland was working on the orcas, his gallery in San Diego held an all-artists show where Coleman saw a watercolor collaboration by Wyland and Tabora. He decided he'd like to paint a watercolor with the marine artist as well. When Wyland agreed, Coleman returned home and painted two watercolors for him to choose from.

After *Northern Waters* was unveiled and drew great reviews, Coleman started a third piece on his own, a depiction of ice flows and glaciers in the arctic. "Wyland had just finished his part of the watercolor, called *Turtle Waters*," he says. "I sent him the ice floes, and he kept it about a year because he was so busy. I had put it out of my mind because I hadn't heard from him. Then, all of a sudden, this painting showed up with beluga whales circling under the ice. And he'd put some penguins above the surface on top of the iceberg.

"We called it *Belugas*, and everyone was very excited because it was so different. You just don't see belugas very often, either in real life or in a painting."

A short time later, at dinner after a show in Laguna, Wyland asked Coleman if he could keep the painting. "I told him, 'Sure,' which I think blew his mind," Coleman says. "He couldn't believe I'd just give it to him. He kept it at his house for a while and later put it in one of the galleries, which means he kind of gave my half back to me."

Unlike most artists, Coleman actually was used to collaborative efforts with his art, having worked at Walt Disney Studios for so long. "In my view, art *is* a collaboration," he states. "There isn't an artist who actually owns a piece of art, or owns an idea, or an image. We all draw from the same pool. We're using ideas and techniques people have used long before us.

"Creating collaborations is very special because we as artists can bring the best of both worlds to the piece. In the case of collectors who like Wyland's work and mine, they can now have both in one painting."

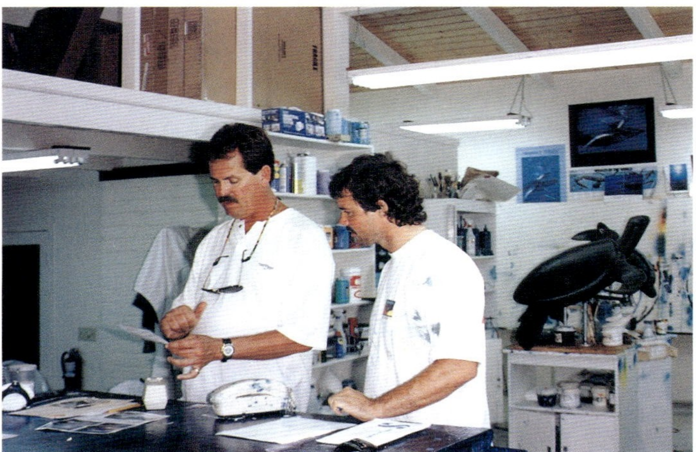

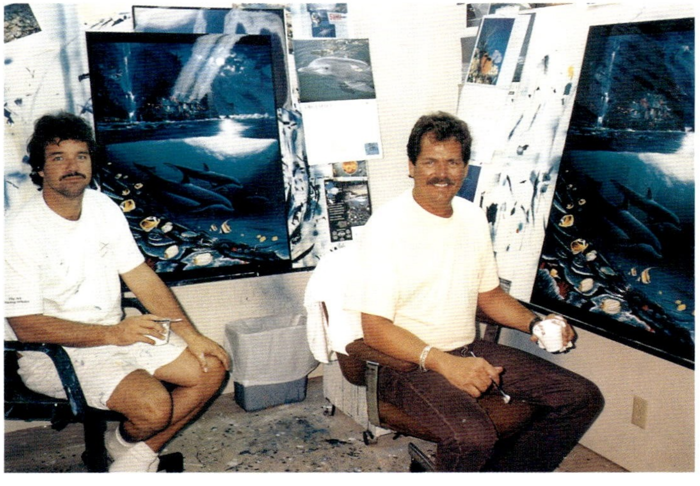

Wyland and Jim working on a collaboration at Wyland's Studio in Hawaii

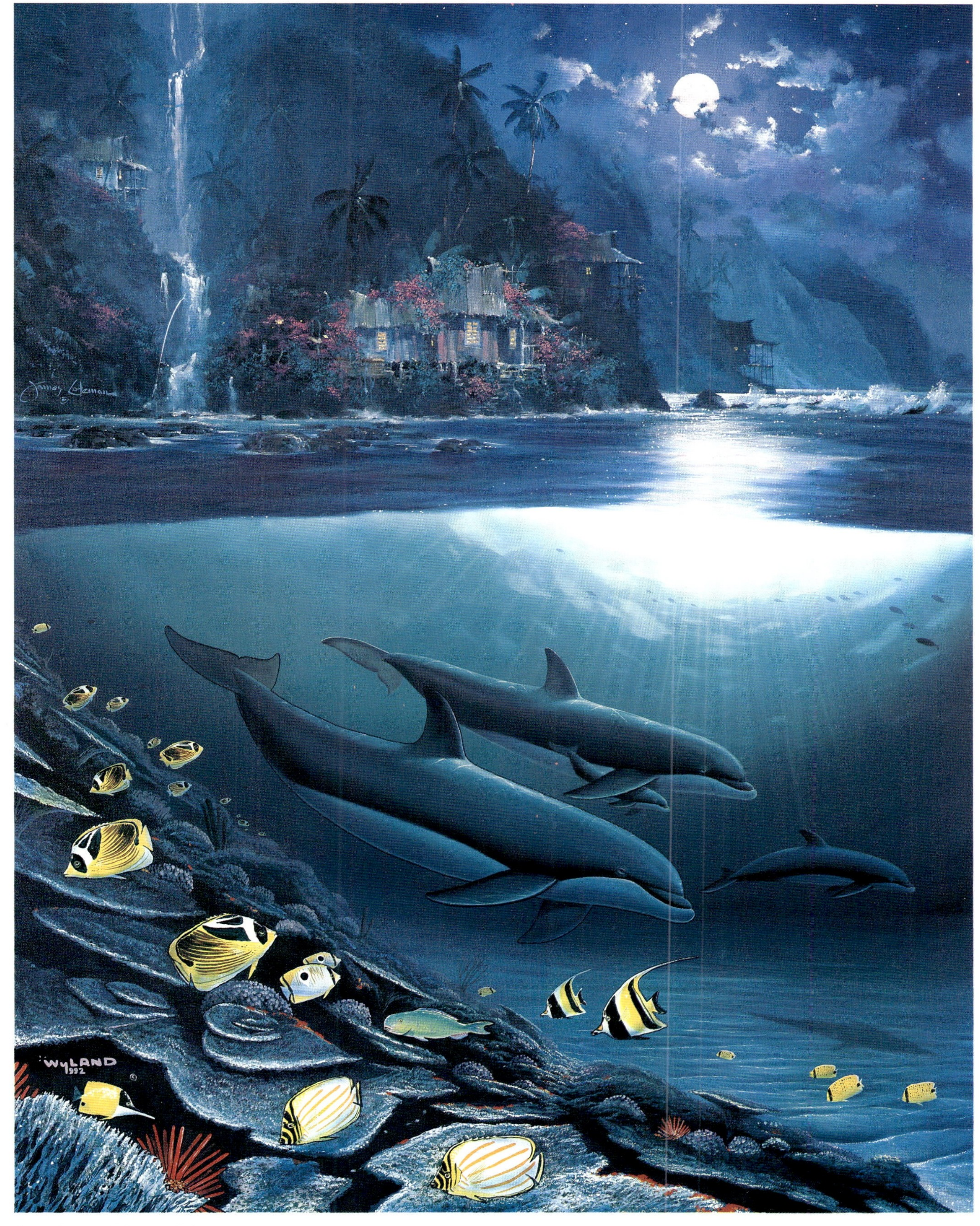

Paradise – Oil, 4 x 5 feet

Limited Editions

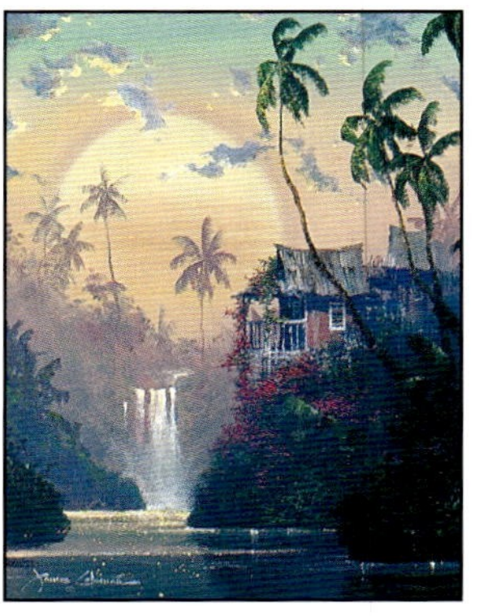

AFTERNOON SPLENDOR
Cibachrome, 30 x 24 inches
Edition 250 + Proofs

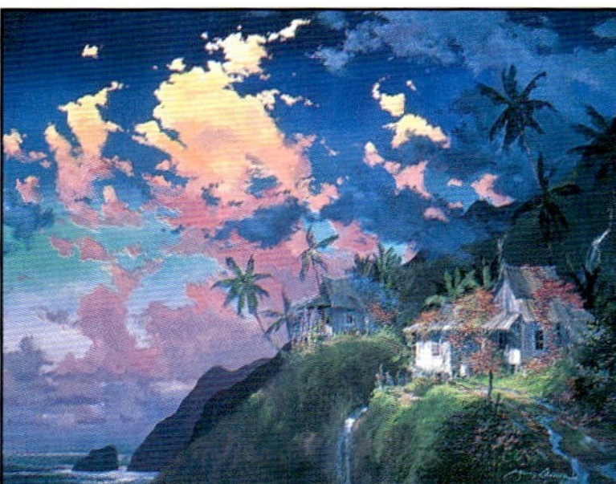

ESCAPE TO PARADISE
Cibachrome, 30 x 40 inches
Edition 250 + Proofs

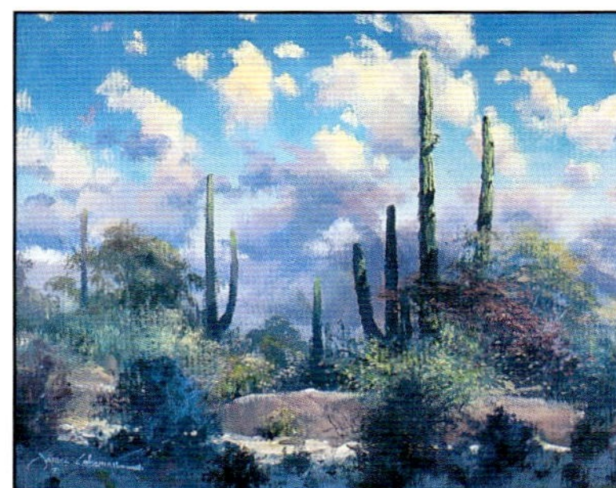

DESERT LIGHT
Cibachrome, 24 x 30 inches
Edition 250 + Proofs

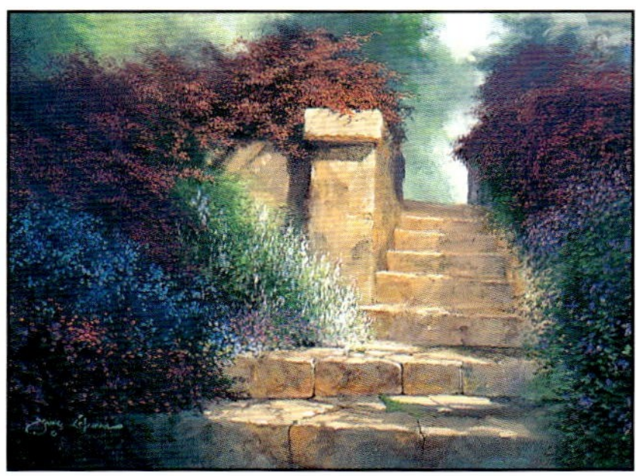

GARDEN LIGHT
Cibachrome, 24 x 30 inches
Edition 250 + Proofs

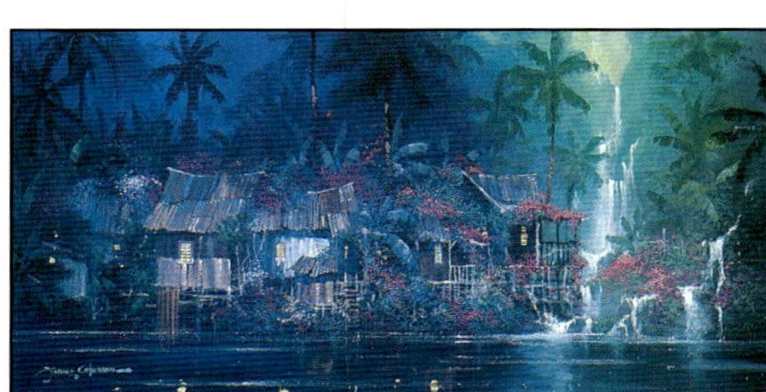

EVENING SERENITY
Cibachrome, 24 x 48 inches
Edition 250 + Proofs

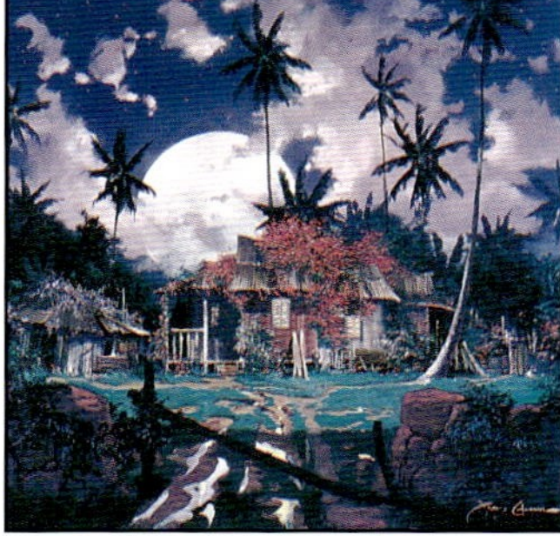

FULL MOON RISING
Cibachrome, 30 x 40 inches
Edition 75 + Proofs

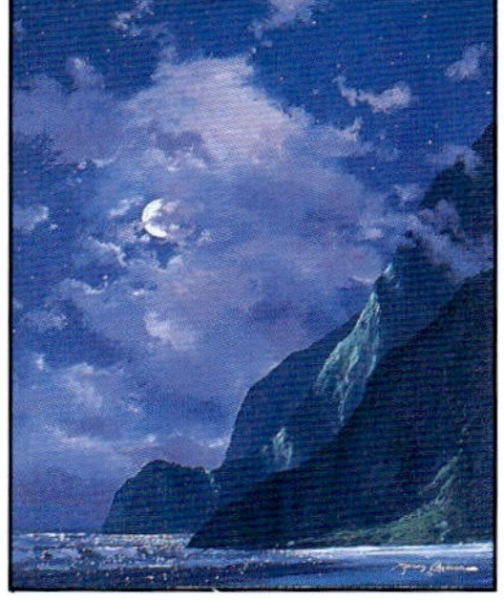

MOON SHADOWS
Cibachrome, 30 x 24 inches
Edition 250 + Proofs

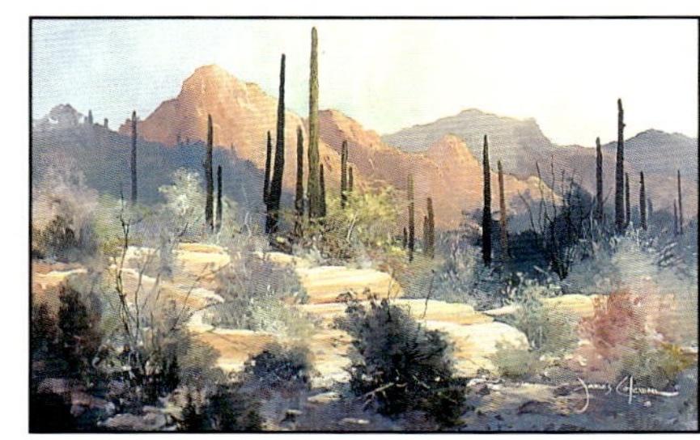

ONE STILL MOMENT
Cibachrome, 26 x 40 inches
Edition 250 + Proofs

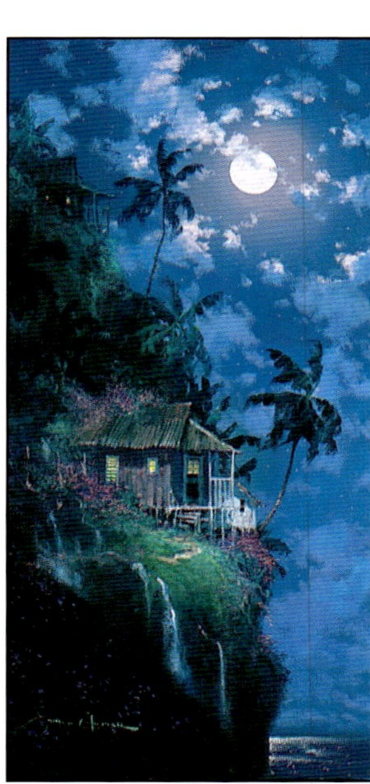

MIDNIGHT PEACE
Cibachrome, 30 x 15 inches
Edition 250 + Proofs

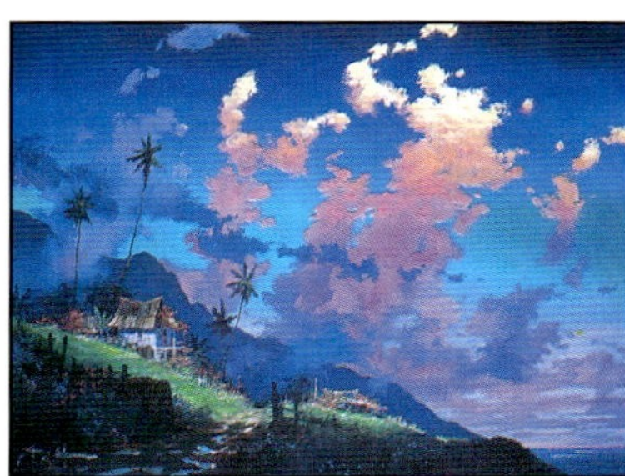

IMPRESSIONS OF PARADISE
Cibachrome, 24 x 36 inches
Edition 350 + Proofs

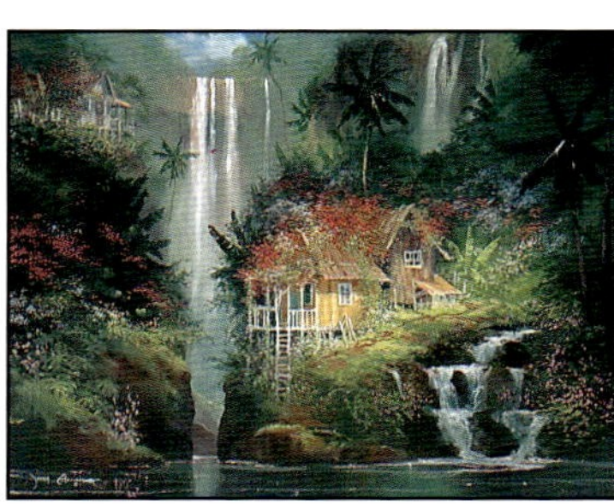

LIVING ALOHA
Repligraph, 30 x 40 inches
Edition 250 + Proofs

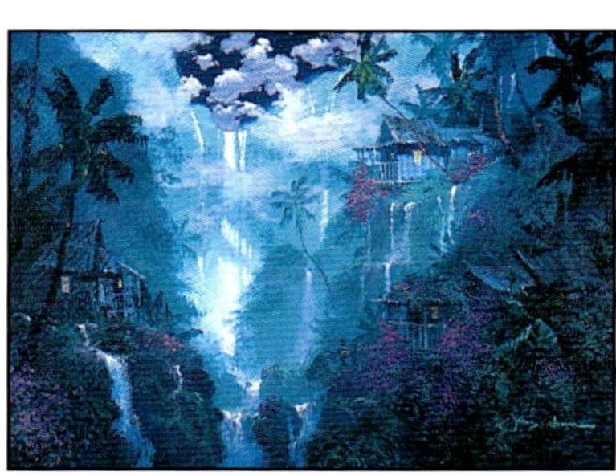

MAJESTIC FALLS
Cibachrome, 30 x 40 inches
Edition 250 + Proofs

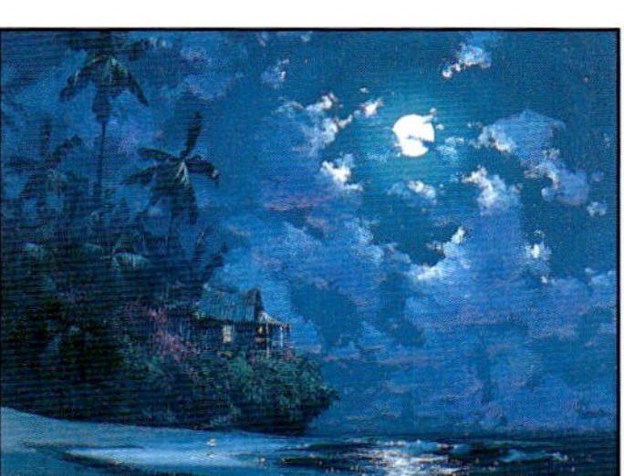

MIDNIGHT SURF
Cibachrome, 22 x 28 inches
Edition 250 + Proofs

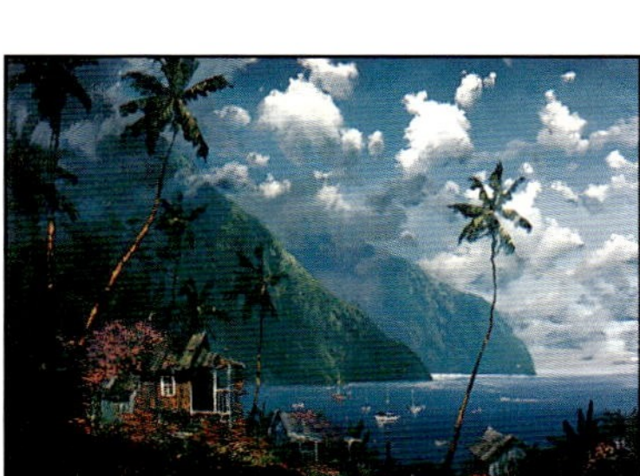

MEMORIES OF PARADISE
Cibachrome, 30 x 40 inches
Edition 250 + Proofs

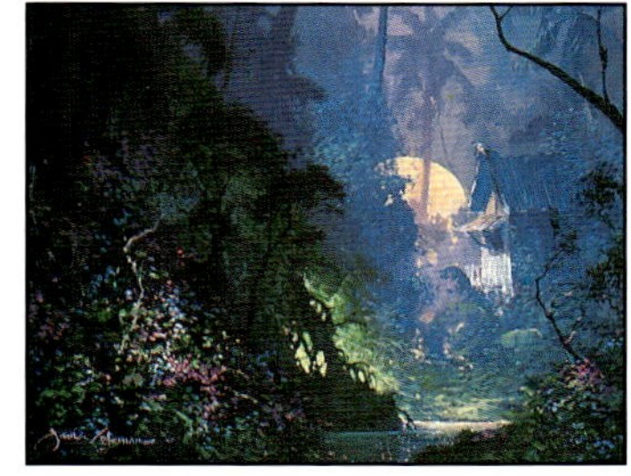

MISTY ENCHANTMENT
Cibachrome, 12 x 17 inches
Edition 475 + Proofs

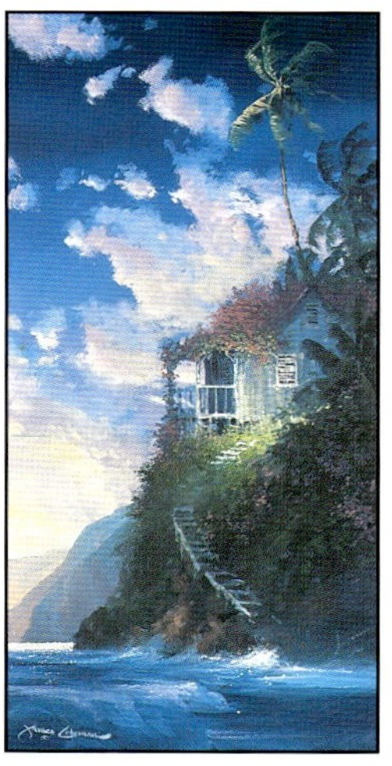

AFTERNOON BREEZES
Cibachrome, 20 x 10 inches
Edition 475 + Proofs

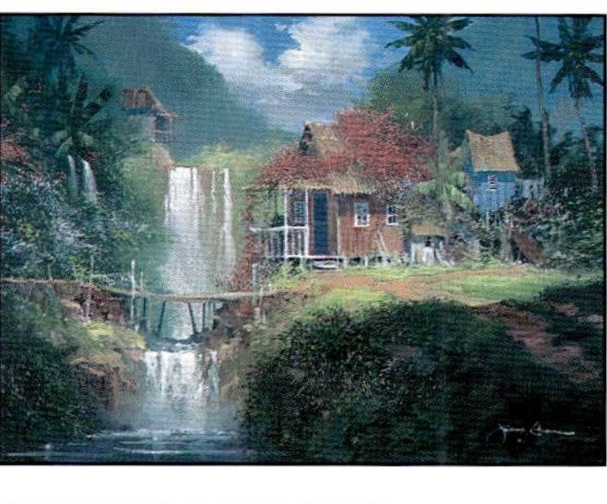

HOUSE OF FLOWERS
Cibachrome, 30 x 40 inches
Edition 75 + Proofs

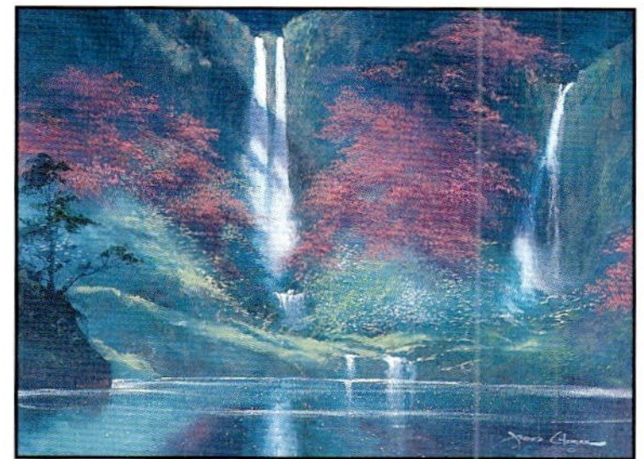

MISTY SURRENDER
Cibachrome, 22 x 30 inches
Edition 350 + Proofs

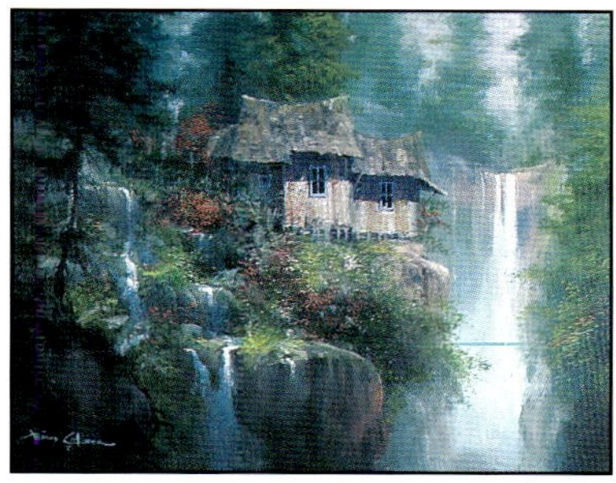

MOUNTAIN HIDEAWAY
Cibachrome, 24 x 30 inches
Edition 250 + Proofs

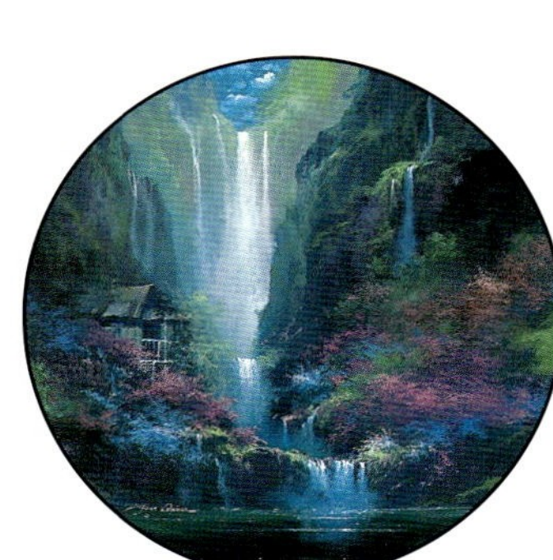

ENCHANTED HIDEAWAY
Cibachrome, 36 inches round
Edition 250 + Proofs

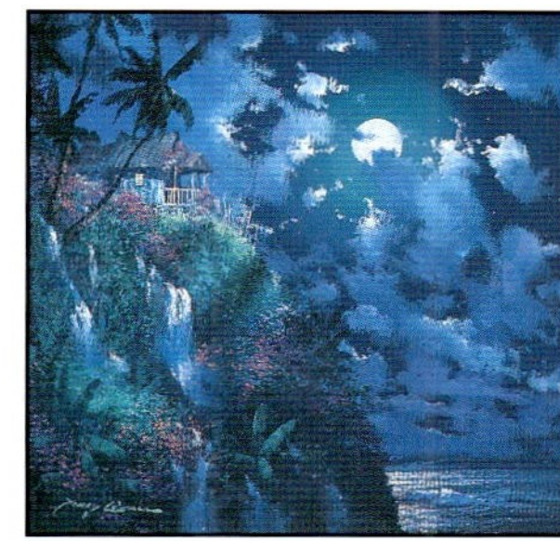

MOON MAGIC
Cibachrome, 30 x 30 inch
Edition 250 + Proofs

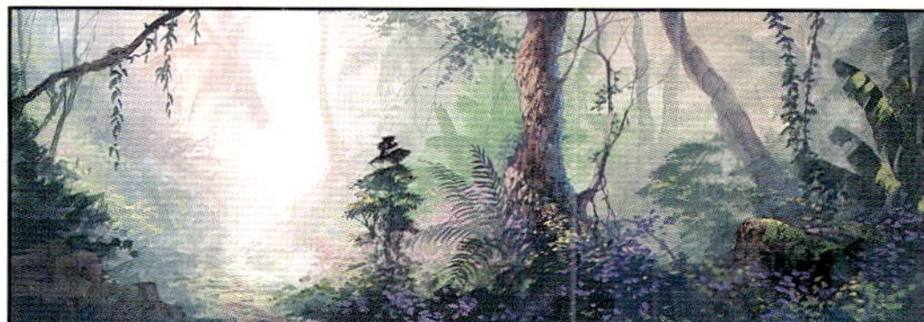

MYSTICAL PATH
Gouache, 11 x 30 inches
Edition 350 + Proofs

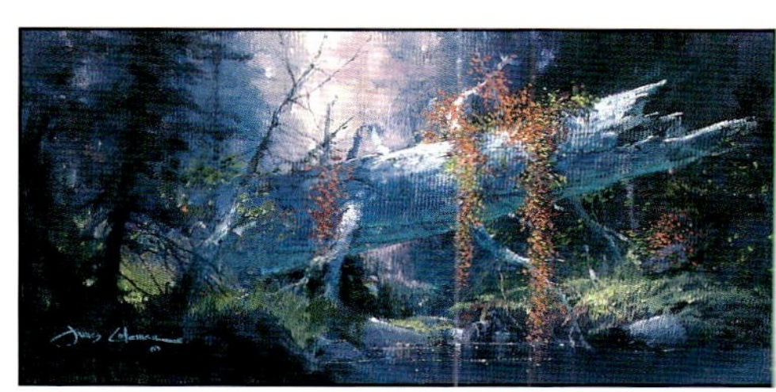

YESTERDAY & TODAY
Cibachrome, 15 x 30 inches
Edition 250 + Proofs

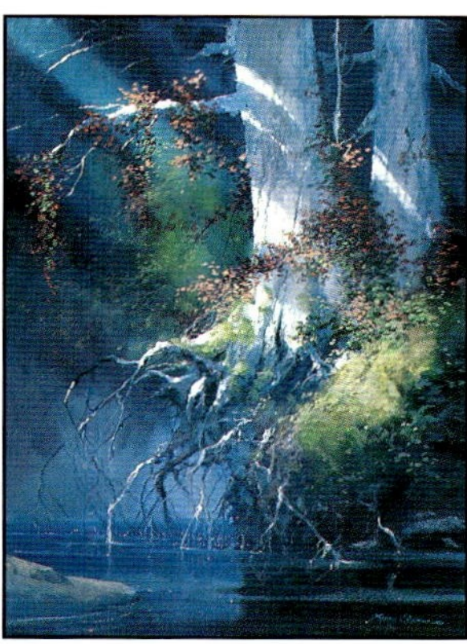

TRANQUIL DREAM
Cibachrome, 30 x 24 inches
Edition 250 + Proofs

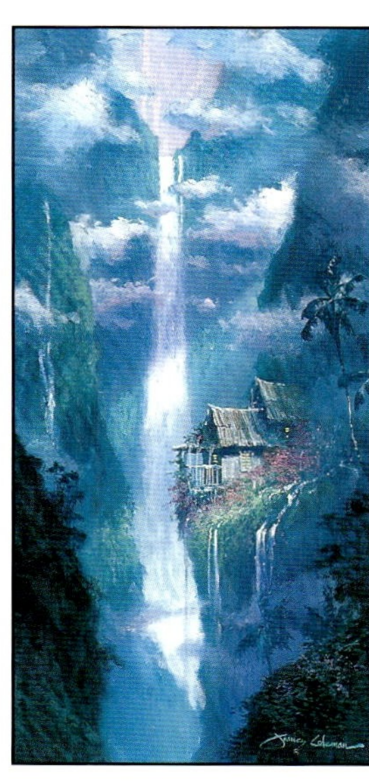

NEVER ENDING SPIRIT
Cibachrome, 36 x 18 inches
Edition 350 + Proofs

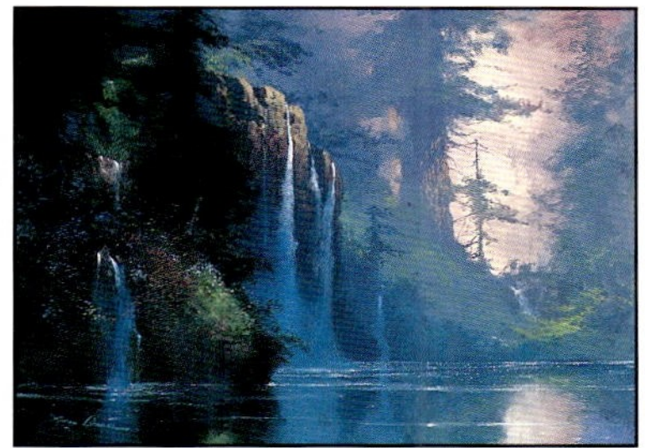

NATURES SYMPHONY
Cibachrome, 24 x 32 inches
Edition 250 + Proofs

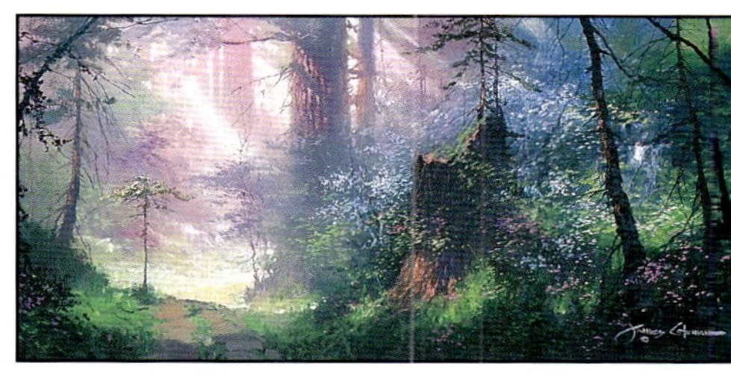

MISTY MORNING
Cibachrome, 20 x 40 inches
Edition 250 + Proofs

PARADISE MOON
Cibachrome, 12 x 16 inches
Edition 475 + Proofs

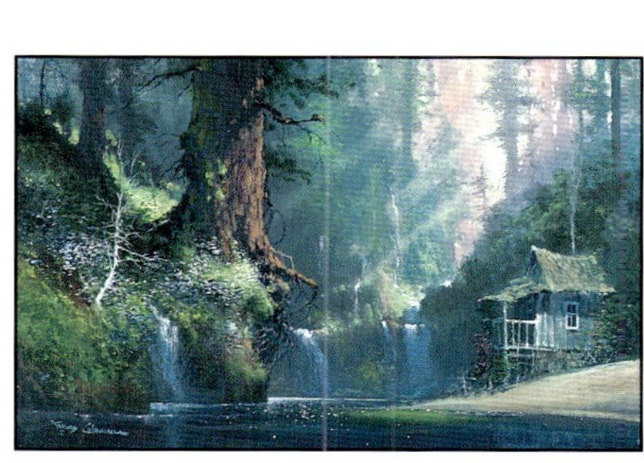

PEACEFUL SOLITUDE
Cibachrome, 24 x 36 inches
Edition 250 + Proofs

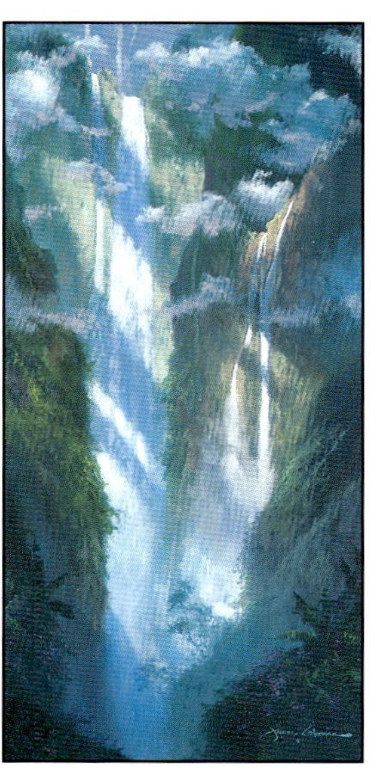

RADIANT WATERS
Cibachrome, 36 x 18 inches
Edition 350 + Proofs

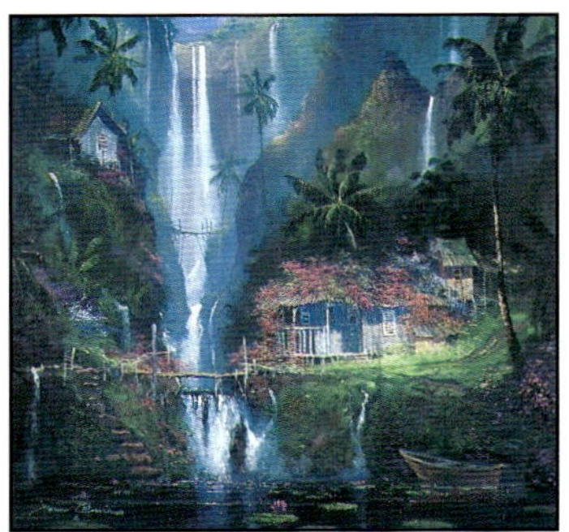

PEACEFUL RHYTHMS
Cibachrome, 36 x 36 inches
Edition 350 + Proofs

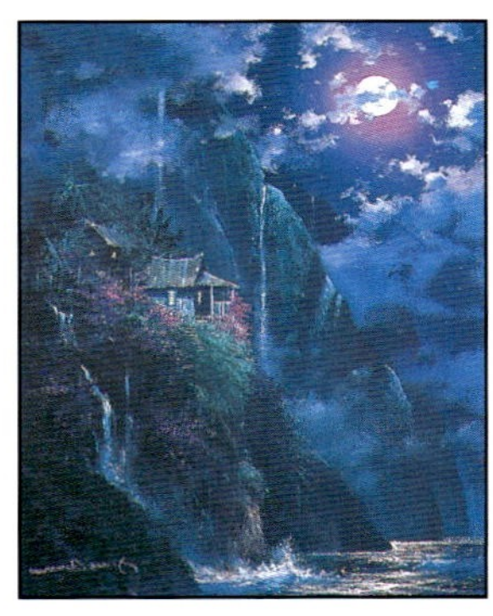

RHYTHMS IN BLUE
Cibachrome, 30 x 24 inches
Edition 250 + Proofs

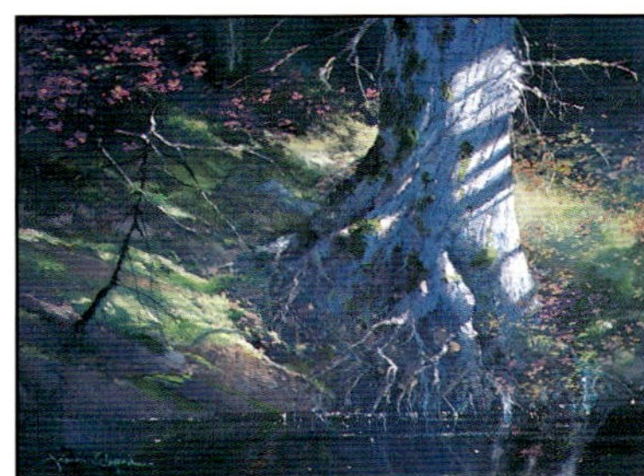

QUIET LIGHT
Cibachrome, 40 x 30 inches
Edition 250 + Proofs

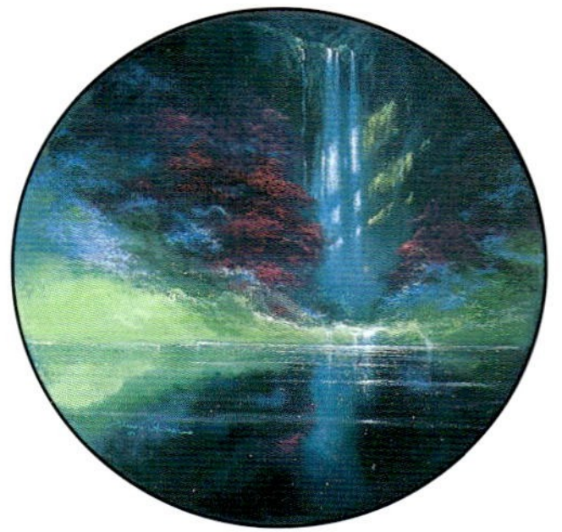

REFLECTIONS
Cibachrome, 36 inches round
Edition 250 + Proofs

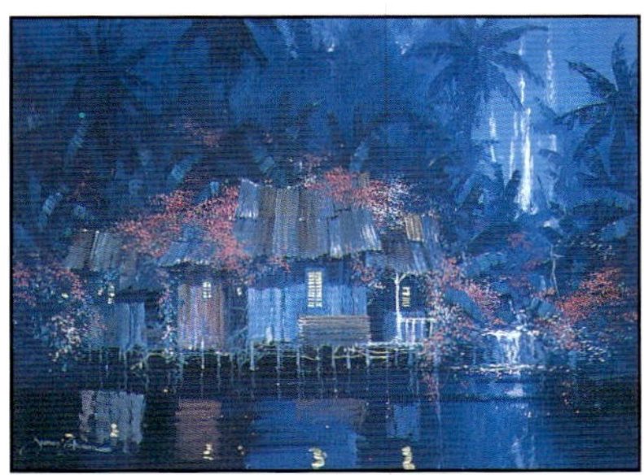

RIVER MAGIC
Cibachrome, 22 x 30 inches
Edition 75 + Proofs

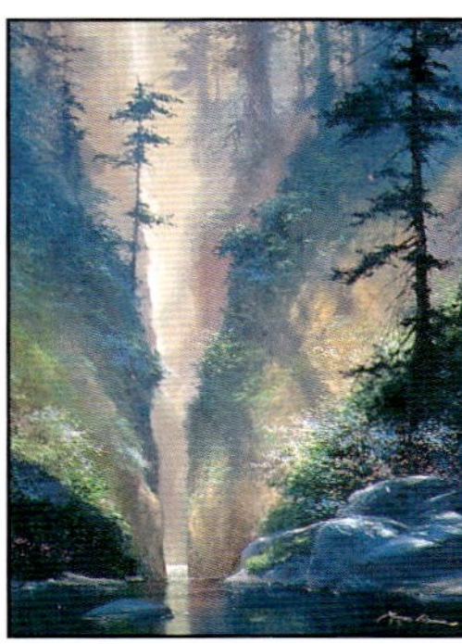

SERENITY
Cibachrome, 40 x 30 inches
Edition 250 + Proofs

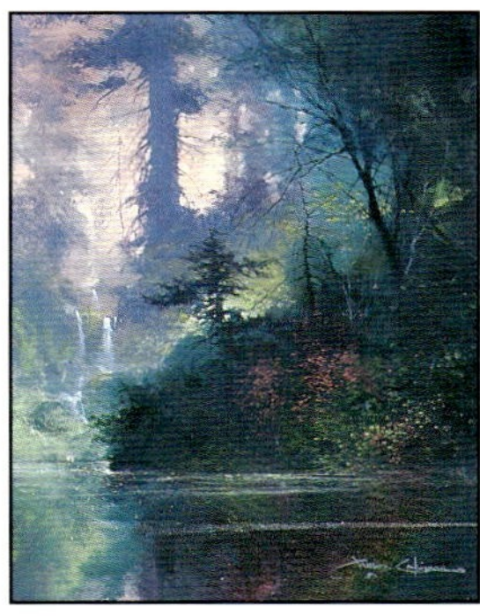

SILENT MOOD
Cibachrome, 20 x 24 inches
Edition 250 + Proofs

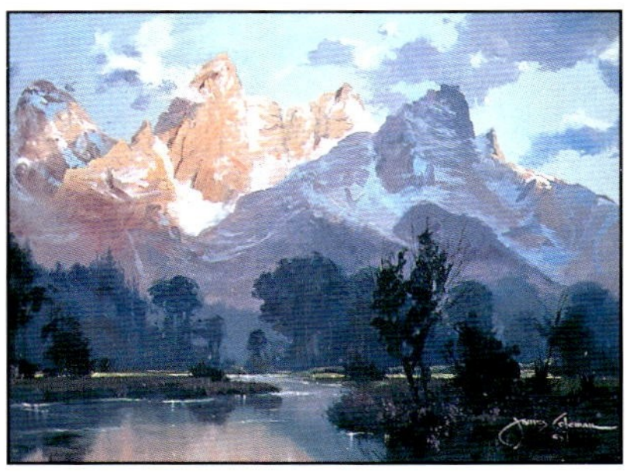

TETON MORNING
Cibachrome, 30 x 24 inches
Edition 250 + Proofs

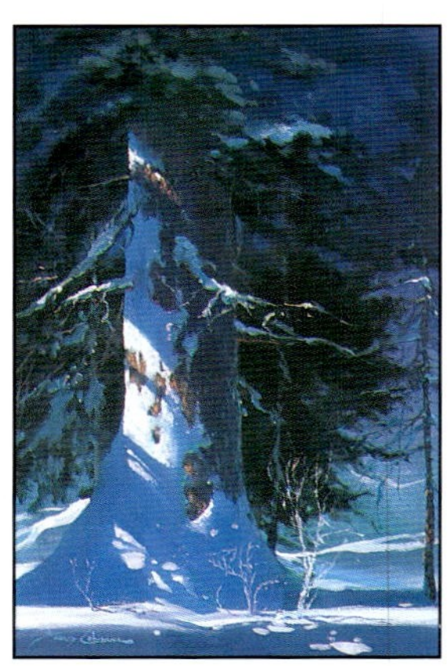

SILENT SURRENDER
Cibachrome, 36 x 24 inches
Edition 250 + Proofs

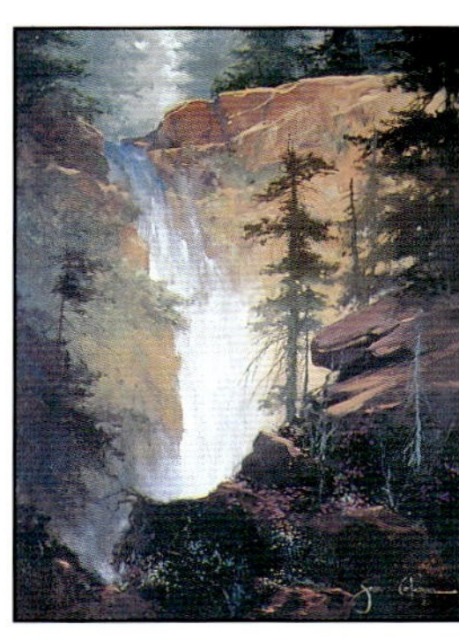

THUNDERING FALLS
Cibachrome, 30 x 24 inches
Edition 250 + Proofs

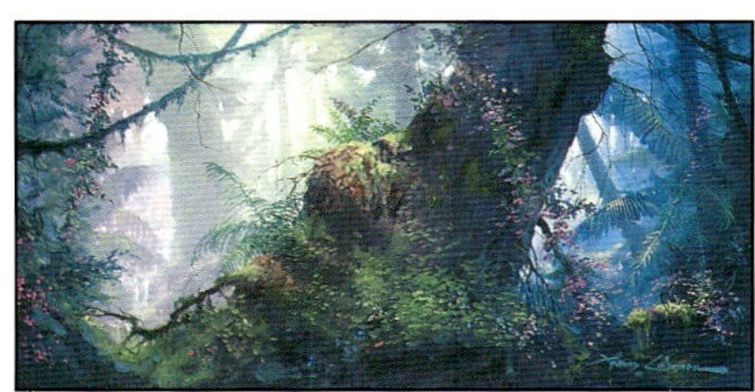

TIMELESS ILLUMINATION
Cibachrome, 20 x 40 inches
Edition 350 + Proofs

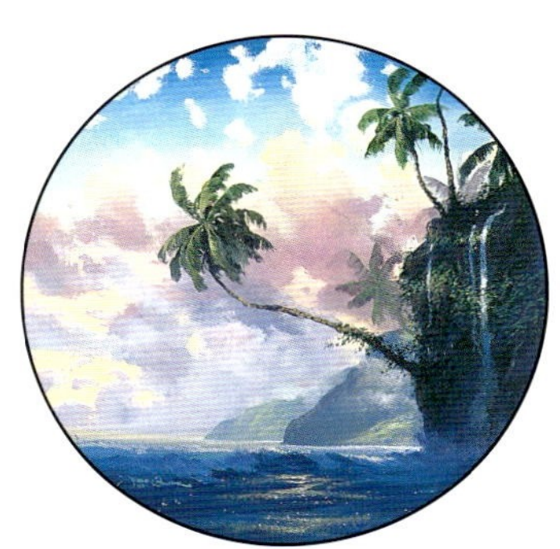

TRADEWINDS
Cibachrome, 22 inches round
Edition 250 + Proofs

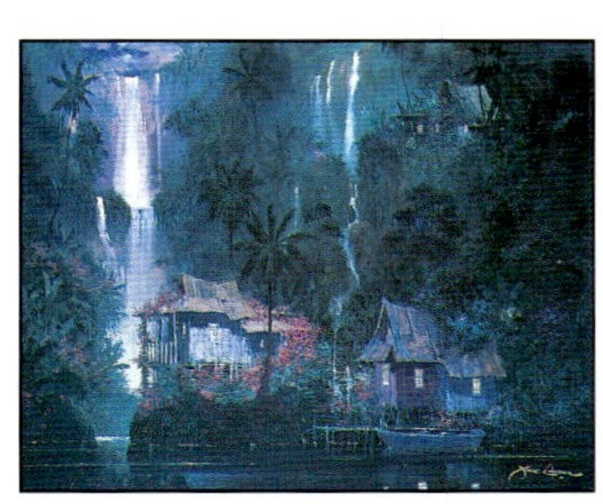

TROPICAL DREAMSCAPE
Cibachrome, 30 x 40 inches
Edition 250 + Proofs

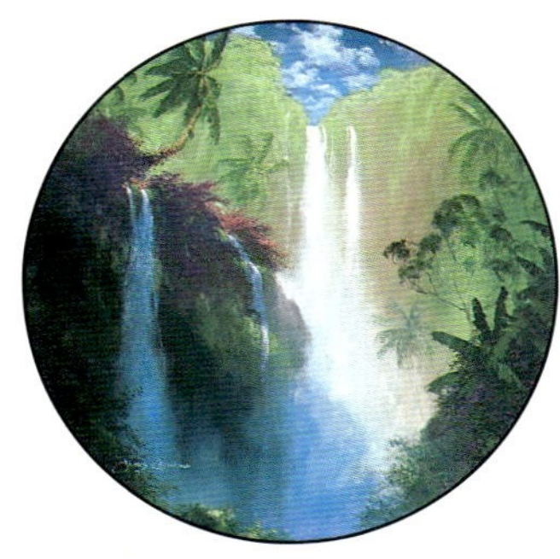

WATERS OF LIFE
Cibachrome, 30 inches round
Edition 250 + Proofs

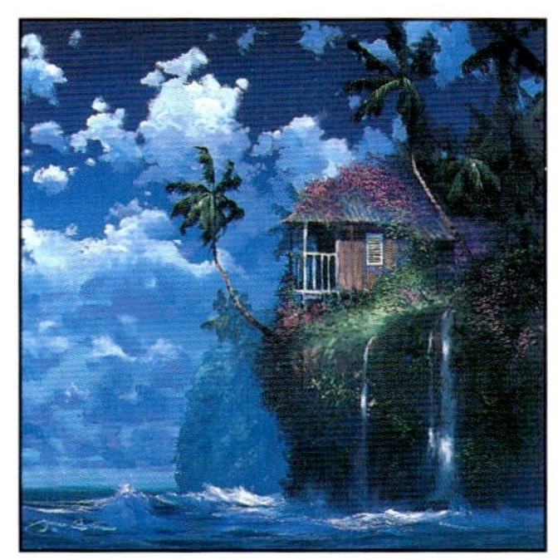

TROPICAL HIDEAWAY
Cibachrome, 24 x 24 inches
Edition 250 + Proofs

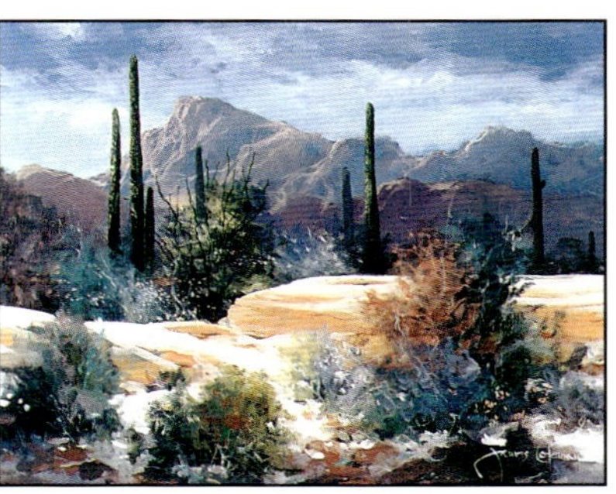

WARM SAND & SAGAURO
Cibachrome, 18 x 23 inches
Edition 250 + Proofs

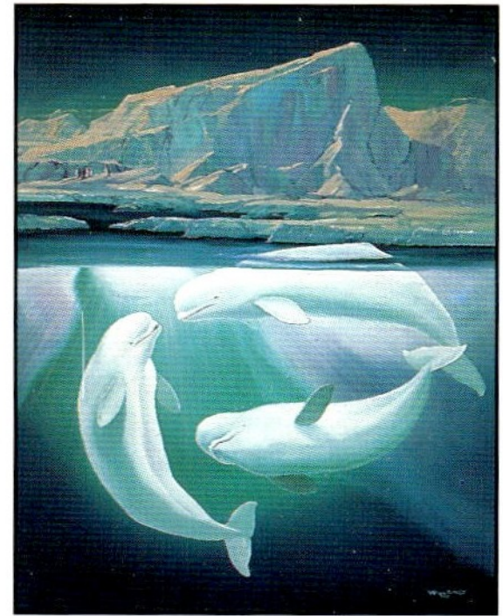
BELUGAS
Cibachrome, 24 x 30 inches
Edition 295 + Proofs
Lithograph, 20 x 26 inches
Edition 950 + Proofs

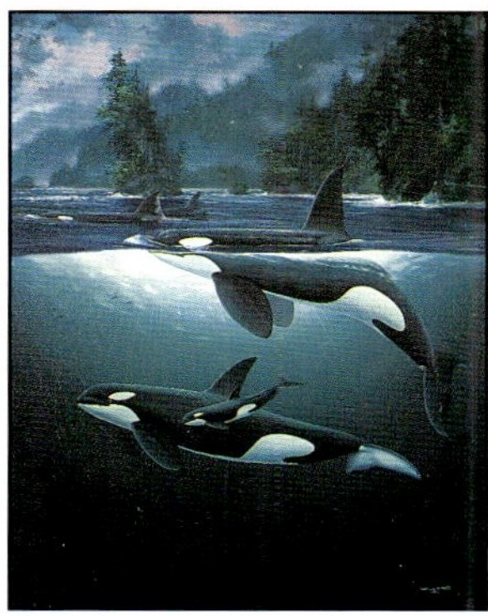
NORTHERN WATERS
Super Gloss, 30 x 40 inches
Edition 295 + Proofs
Lithograph, 17 x 25 1/2 inches
Edition 950 + Proofs

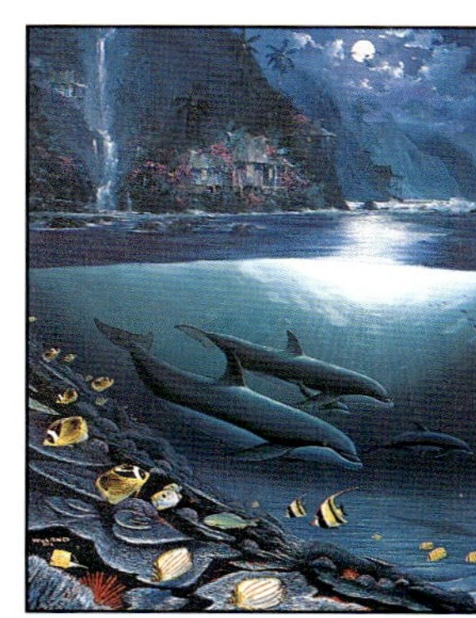
PARADISE
Super Gloss, 30 x 40 inches
Edition 295 + Proofs
Lithograph, 17 x 25 1/2 inches
Edition 950 + Proofs

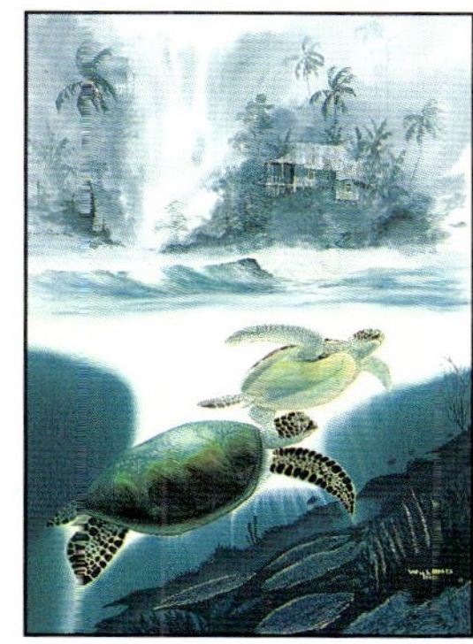
TURTLE WATERS
Super Gloss, 24 x 30 inches
Edition 295 + Proofs
Lithograph, 17 x 25 1/2 inches
Edition 950 + Proofs

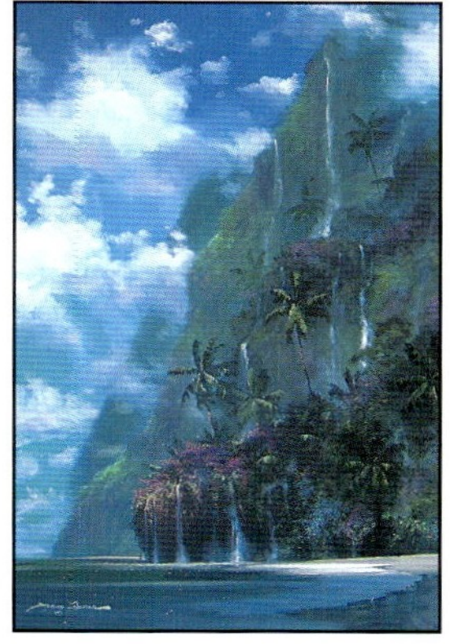
BESIDE STILL WATERS
Limited Edition Prints

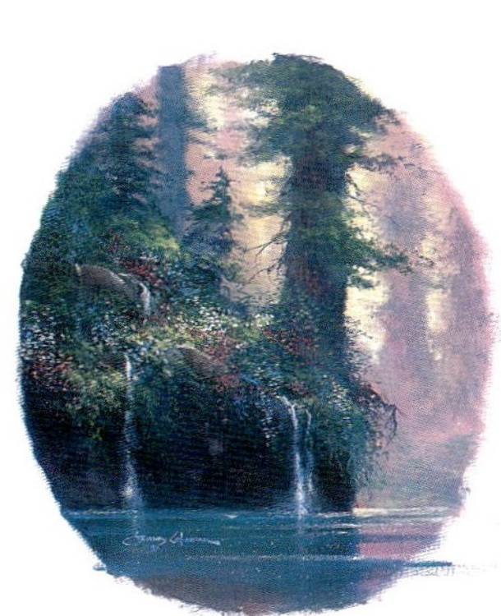
FOREST SONG
Limited Edition Prints

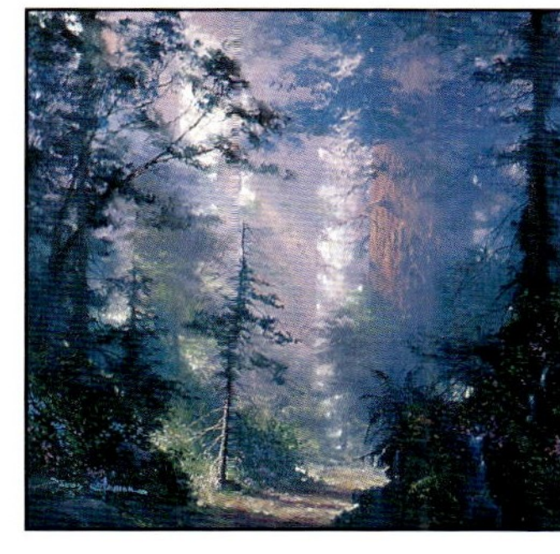
MOMENT OF PEACE
Canvas Transfer, 24 x 24 inches
Edition 450 + Proofs

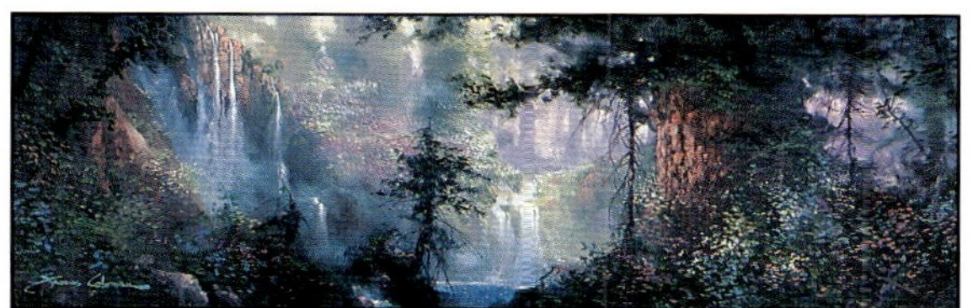
WOODED SANCTUARY
Canvas Transfer, 11 x 34 inches
Edition 450 + Proofs

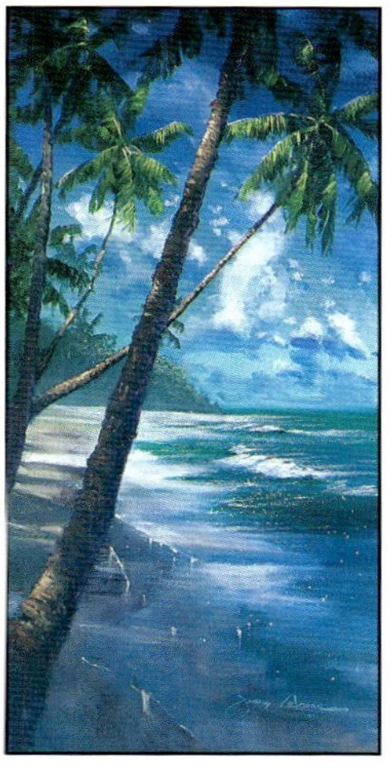
RADIANT SURF
Limited Edition Prints

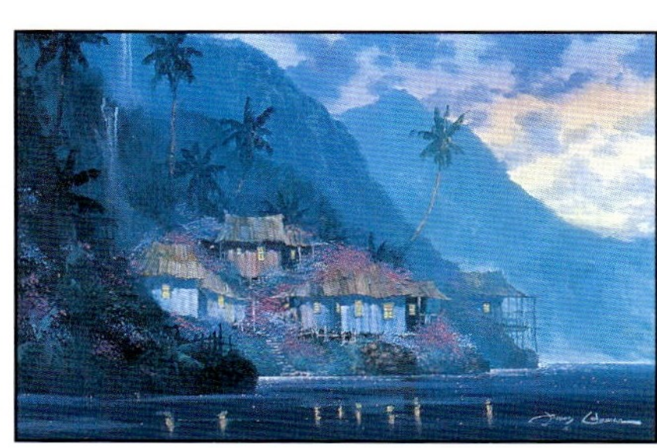
ISLAND PARADISE
Limited Edition Prints

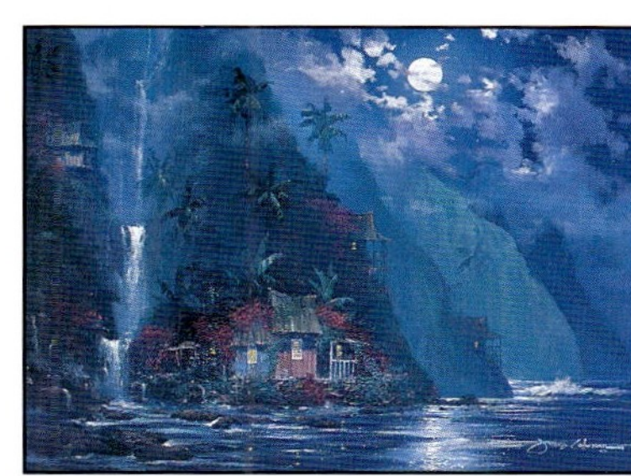
NIGHT PARADISE
Canvas Transfer, 18 x 24 inches
Edition 450 + Proofs

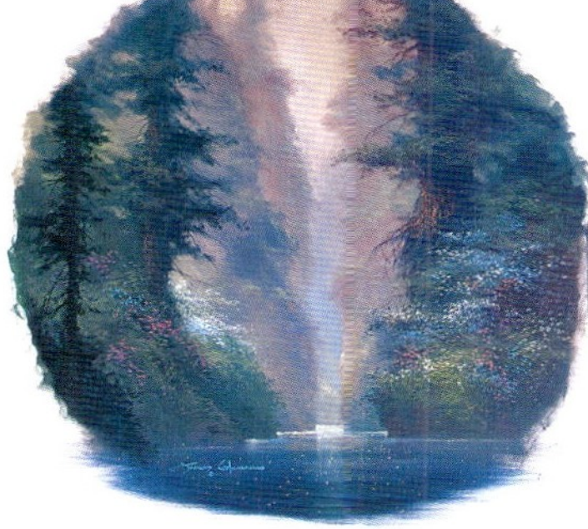
MISTY QUIET
Limited Edition Prints

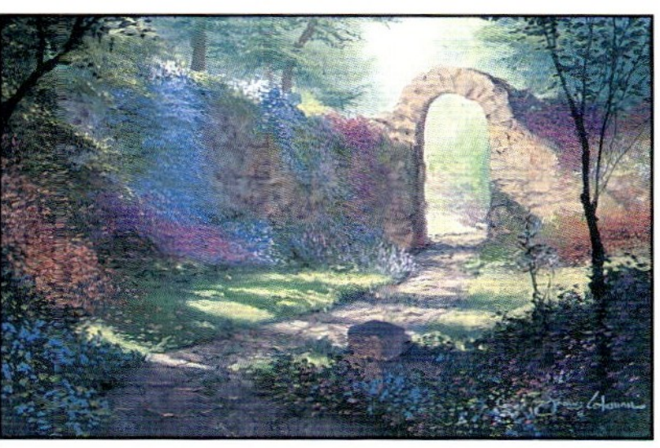
MORNING LIGHT
Limited Edition Prints

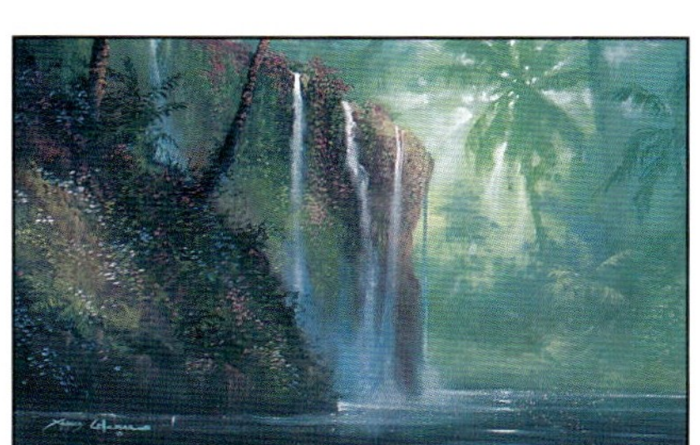
MISTY MELODIES
Limited Edition Prints

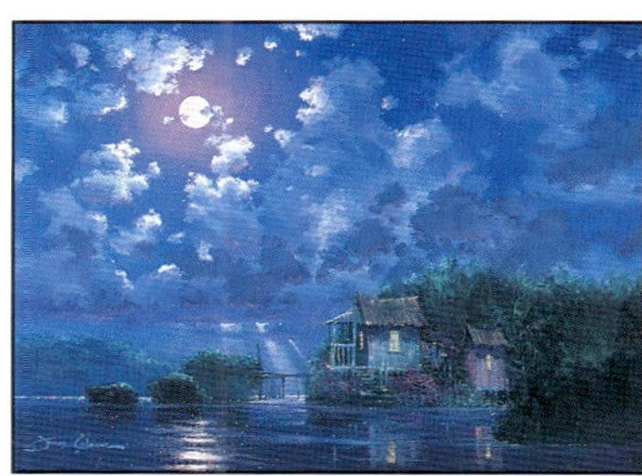
MOONLIT KEYS
Limited Edition Prints

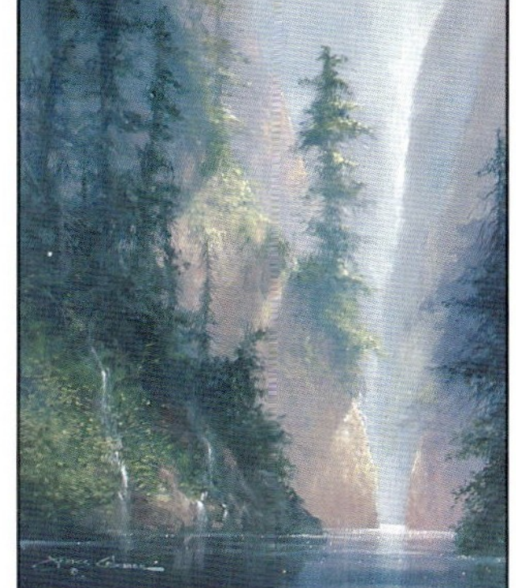
MOUNTAIN SANCTUARY
Limited Edition Prints

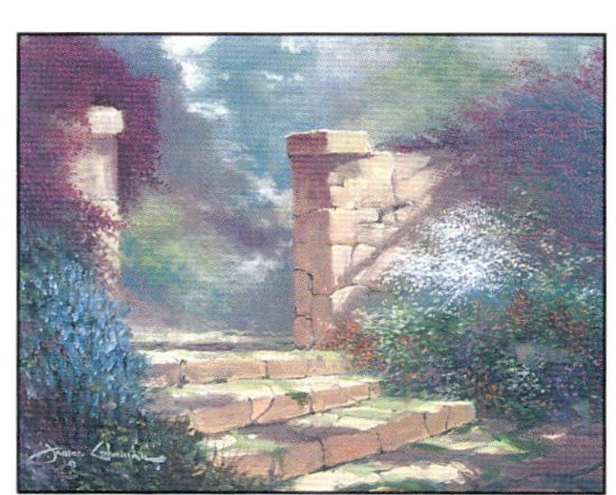
QUIET GARDEN
Limited Edition Prints

Galleries

WYLAND GALLERIES
2171 Laguna Canyon Rd
Laguna Beach, CA 92651
(714) 497-4081
(800) 777-0039
Fax (714) 497-7852

WYLAND GALLERIES
218 Forest Ave.
Laguna Beach, CA 92651
(714) 497-9494
(800) 995-6509
Fax (714) 497-2298

WYLAND GALLERIES
502 S.Coast Hwy.
Laguna Beach, CA 92651
(714) 497-4554
Fax (714) 497-0481

WYLAND GALLERIES
Seaport Village
855 W. Harbor Dr. Suite A
San Diewo, CA, 92101
(619) 544-9995
(800) 995-2635
Fax (619) 544-0945

WYLAND GALLERIES
Pier 39 - Suite M - 209
San Francisco, CA 94133
(415) 398-1922
(800) 889-9526
Fax (415) 398-4105

WYLAND GALLERIES
719 Duval St.
Key West, FL 33040
(305) 292-9711
Fax (305) 292-9669

WYLAND GALLERIES
711 SW 10th Ave.
Portland, OR 97205
(503) 223-7692
(800) 578-7316
Fax (503) 223-7692

WYLAND GALLERIES
66-150 Kamehameha Hwy.
Haleiwa, HI 96712
(808) 637-7498
Fax (808) 637-5469

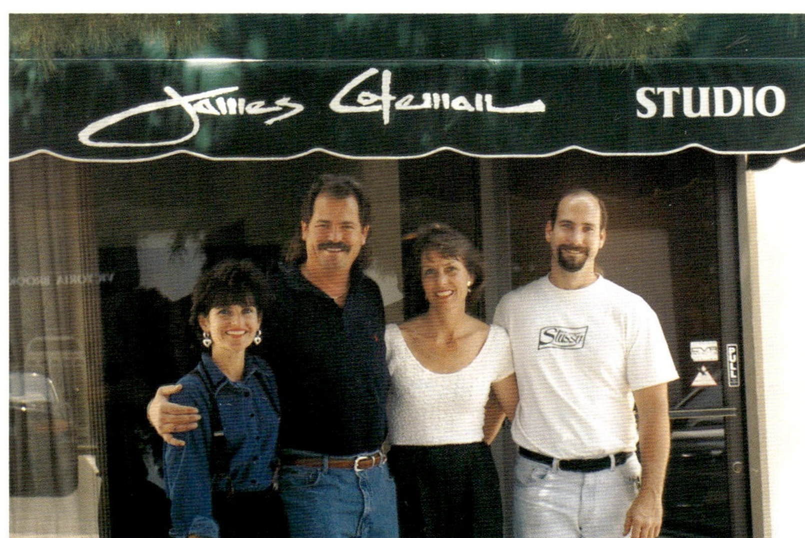

Susan Speidel, James Coleman, Conni McCarthy and Sean Clark at James Coleman Studios

JAMES COLEMAN STUDIO
31133 Via Colinas Suite # 108, Westlake Village, CA 91362
(818) 889-1949 • (800) 341-3004 • Fax (818) 889-2113

WYLAND GALLERIES
Hyatt Regency Waikiki
2424 Kalakaua Ave.
Honolulu, HI 96815
(808) 924-3133
Fax (808) 924-3622

WYLAND GALLERIES
Wyland Kalakaua Ctr Waikiki
2155 Kalakaua Ave.
Suite 104
Honolulu, HI 96815
(808) 924-1322
Fax (808) 924-3518

WYLAND GALLERIES
Aloha Tower Marketplace
1 Aloha Tower Drive
Suite 191, Unit 78
Honolulu, HI 96813
(808) 536-8973
Fax (808) 536-8981

WYLAND GALLERIES
Anchor Cove
3416 Rice St.
Lihue, HI 96766
(808) 246-0702
Fax (808) 246-0703

WYLAND GALLERIES
Poipu Shopping Village
2360 Kiahuna Plantation Dr.
Koloa, HI 96756
(808) 742-6030
Fax (808) 742-4739

WYLAND GALLERIES
Hilton Waikoloa Village
Waikoloa Beach Resort
Waikoloa, HI 96743
(808) 885-5258
Fax (808) 885-5384

WYLAND GALLERIES
Waterfront Row
75-5770 Alii Drive
Kailua-Kona, HI 96740
(808) 334-0037
Fax (808) 329-5398

WYLAND GALLERIES
Kings' Shops Waikoloa
Waikoloa Beach Dr.
Waikoloa, HI 96738
(808) 885-8882
Fax (808) 885-7219

WYLAND GALLERIES
136 Dickenson St.
Lahaina, HI 96761
(808) 661-0590
Fax (808) 661-4467

WYLAND GALLERIES
711Front St.
Lahaina, HI 96761
(808) 667-2285
Fax (808) 661-4511

WYLAND GALLERIES
697 Front St.
Lahaina, HI 96761
(808) 661-7099
Fax (808) 661-4750

WYLAND GALLERIES
Whaler's Village
Building K-1
2435 Kaanapali Pkwy.
Lahaina, HI 96761
(808) 661-8255
Fax (808) 661-3957

WYLAND GALLERIES
Kauai Village
4-831 Kuhio Highway
Kapaa, HI 96746
(808) 822-9855
Fax (808) 822-4156

GALLERY OF THE SEA
The Borgatta Suite #603
6166 N. Scottsdale Rd.
Scottsdale, AZ 85253
(602) 998-8444
Fax (602) 998-1136

ART LOVERS PRODUCTS
625 S. Missouri
Clearwater, FL 34616
(800) 866-6051
Fax (813) 445-9716

RICHARDSON GALLERY
3670 S. Virginia St.
Reno, NV 89502
(702) 828-0888
Fax (702) 828-4329

ENDANGERED ARTS LIMITED
100 Plantation Center
Hilton Head, SC 29928
(803) 785-5075
Fax (803) 785-7205

JAMES BOND GALLERY
122 N. Santa Cruz
Los Gatos, CA 95030
(408) 395-1415

FINE ARTS LIMITED
2400 Crestmoor Rd.
Nashville, TN 37215
(615) 386-7111
800) 229-4322
Fax (615) 297-6005

GALLERIE LASSEN
747 Beach St.
San Francisco, CA 94109
(415) 292-1900
(800) 938-7333
Fax (415) 292-1906

GALLERIE LASSEN
3500 Las Vegas Blvd.
Suite #D1
Las Vegas, NV 89109
(702) 731-6900
800) 275-2787
Fax (702) 731-6901